ST/ESA/STAT/SER.F/93

Department of Economic and Social Affairs
Statistics Division

Guide to Producing Statistics on Time Use:
Measuring Paid and Unpaid Work

United Nations
New York, 2005

The Department of Economic and Social Affairs of the United Nations Secretariat is a vital interface between global policies in the economic, social and environmental spheres and national action. The Department works in three main interlinked areas: (i) it compiles, generates and analyses a wide range of economic, social and environmental data and information on which Member States of the United Nations draw to review common problems and to take stock of policy options; (ii) it facilitates the negotiations of Member States in many intergovernmental bodies on joint courses of action to address ongoing or emerging global challenges; and (iii) it advises interested Governments on the ways and means of translating policy frameworks developed in United Nations conferences and summits into programmes at the country level and, through technical assistance, helps build national capacities.

NOTE

ST/ESA/STAT/SER.F/93

UNITED NATIONS PUBLICATION
Sales No. E.04.XVII.7

ISBN 92-1-161471-6

PREFACE

At its thirty-second session, held in 2001, the Statistical Commission endorsed the preparation of a guide for producing statistics on measuring paid and unpaid work. On that occasion, the value of time-use statistics was noted, "not only for issues related to gender but also more broadly for quality-of-life concerns, social accounting, care of the elderly, estimates of the workforce and total work accounts".[1] The present *Guide* is intended as a response to the interest expressed by many countries in the development of methods and concepts in the rapidly evolving field of time-use statistics.

As this is an emerging area of social enquiry, many of the unique challenges of time-use surveys have yet to be fully addressed. At the same time, great progress has been made. By offering a wide panorama of national practices and international initiatives in the field of time-use statistics, the present publication seeks to provide further impetus to the development of time-use statistics and assist countries interested in undertaking time-use surveys.

The purpose of the *Guide* is threefold. First, it is conceived as a reference tool for countries interested in conducting time-use surveys. Second, it is aimed at facilitating the harmonization of methods and practices in collecting, processing and disseminating time-use statistics. Finally it is meant to solicit comments and suggestions on the trial International Classification of Activities for Time-Use Statistics (ICATUS) which will subsequently be revised and ultimately presented for adoption as an international standard classification.

Several agencies and national institutions have contributed to this publication. The United Nations Development Programme (UNDP)[2] and the International Development Research Centre/Canada supported this work through the project "Gender Issues and the Measurement of Paid and Unpaid Work". Time-use experts, national statistics offices and international organizations such as the International Labour Organization (ILO) provided substantive input in the review of the initial draft of the trial ICATUS and the preparation of the technical papers that formed the basis of this *Guide*. This *Guide* was drafted by Ms. Margarita Guerrero, a consultant to the United Nations Statistics Division. Chapters VI and IX were drafted by Mr. Graham Kalton and Mr. Mike Brick.

The United Nations Statistics Division invites comments on the useful ways to improve this *Guide*. For this purpose, the Statistics Division is developing a web site to facilitate and promote further discussion and improvements of time-use statistics and the draft ICATUS. The address for this web site is the following:

http://unstats.un.org/unsd/demographic/sconcerns/tuse/tu1.aspx

Comments and additional material may also be sent to:

The Director
Attn: Demographic and Social Statistics Branch
Statistics Division
Department of Economic and Social Affairs
United Nations
New York, NY 10017, USA
e-mail: socialstat@un.org
Fax. + 1-212-963-1940

Notes:
[1] See *Official Records of the Economic and Social Council, 2001, Supplement No.4* (E/2001/24), para. 11 (b).
[2] Gender Development Programme and Human Development Report Office of UNDP.

CONTENTS

TABLES

FIGURES

BOXES

INTRODUCTION

1. The present publication is the first in a series of reports to be issued by the United Nations with the objective of furthering the development of concepts and methods in the rapidly evolving field of time-use statistics. The main rationale for producing this *Guide* has been to present an overview of the different approaches that have been adopted in the design of time-use surveys and in the collection and dissemination of time-use data. The *Guide* responds to the emergent interest among policy makers, researchers and advocates in furthering the understanding of time-use allocation among different societies and population groups,[1] and the concomitant increase in the number of countries that have indicated an interest in promoting the development of guidelines and methods for national time-use surveys.[2]

2. The growing interest in time-use survey techniques stems not only from the central and strategic importance of time-use statistics for both policy and research purposes, but also from the versatility and wide range of applications of time-use statistics in numerous areas of policy concern (such as transportation, leisure and recreation, pension plans and health-care programmes etc.). In addition to their early applications in areas such as the study of social change, division of labour, allocation of time for household obligations etc., time-use studies are more recently featured in the estimation of the value of household production. Time-use statistics have been identified as (a) crucial

non-monetary data for the "analysis of productive household and leisure activities ... and for some instrumental household activities, such as commuting" and (b) a common source using a common unit of measure for fundamental descriptive data not otherwise obtainable on human activities in various fields of social, demographic and related economic statistics (United Nations, 1978). More recently time-use methodologies have been recognized as a tool for improving statistics on unremunerated work, for assessing the total amount of work carried out by different population groups and for valuing the work of such groups within households. The variety of national practices illustrated in this *Guide* is a resource for countries that are conducting or are considering carrying out time-use surveys for the first time.

3. The *Guide* reviews methods and practices in collecting, processing and disseminating time-use statistics through a compilation of country experiences. Although the time-use methods presented and reviewed in this *Guide* are applicable to the diverse objectives of time-use statistics, the main focus of the publication is on the methodological design and classification issues pertinent to the measurement of paid and unpaid work. It is mainly concerned with collecting time-use data on how an individual allocates time over an exhaustive or comprehensive range of activities (that is to say taking account of all the activities that a person engages in during the course of a specified continuum or block of time, for example, over a 12- or 24-hour period) (Harvey and Taylor, 2000, p. 235, para.2).

4. This *Guide* is organized in five parts. The first four outline the different issues, modalities and initiatives that need to be considered by national statistical offices in

---

[1] See Beijing Platform for Action (United Nations, 1996) para. 206 (g).
[2] See Official Records of the Economic and Social Council, 1995, Supplement No. 8 (E/1995/28), para. 58 (e); ibid., 2000, Supplement No.4 (E/2000/24), para. 22; and ibid., 2001, Supplement No.4 (E/2001/24), para. 11.

planning, designing and conducting time-use surveys. Part one explores the multiple applications of time-use for research and policy purposes and provides insight into some of the steps that have to be undertaken by a national statistical office in planning and organizing time-use data collections. Part two addresses some key issues relevant to the design of time-use surveys including the scope and coverage of time-use data and specifications for survey instruments and frameworks as well as other issues relevant to the sample design of time-use surveys. Part three focuses on the collection and processing of time-use data with particular emphasis on the enumeration procedures relevant to time-use surveys, the processing of time-use survey data and the preparation of survey outputs. Part four examines the necessary steps for the revision and dissemination of time-use data. Finally, part five reviews the trail International Classification of Activities for Time Use taking into account alternative approaches. A wealth of country practices are reported in the annexes to this *Guide*.

Part One

Planning and organizing for producing statistics on time use

I. RATIONALE FOR PRODUCING TIME-USE STATISTICS

A. What are time-use statistics?

5.   Time-use statistics are quantitative summaries of how individuals "spend" or allocate their time over a specified period—typically over the 24 hours of a day or over the 7 days of a week. Time-use statistics shed light on:

-       What individuals in the reference population do or the *activities* they engage in.
-       How much *time* is spent doing each of these activities.

Examples of time-use statistics are:

-       Average number of hours in a day spent travelling.
-       Total number of hours in a week spent working in a paid job.
-       Average number of hours in a day working in unpaid domestic work.

These statistics pertain to a *reference population* (for example, persons 10 years of age or over, persons between the ages of 15 and 65 etc.) and are usually disaggregated by sex, age group, rural/urban, and other subgroups of interest to those analysing the statistics.

6.   In terms of coverage of activities, time-use data can be either:

-       *Exhaustive*: all activities that a person engages in during the course of a specified continuum or block of time (for example, a 12-hour period, a 24-hour day, or 7-day week) are recorded.
-       *Selective*: time spent is recorded only for a selected activity or for sets of activities within a specified

period (Harvey and Taylor, 2000, p. 235, para. 2).

7.   Activities recorded in time-use surveys constitute the whole range of activities that a person may spend time on during the course of a day, including, for example, eating, travelling, engaging in unpaid childcare, working in a formal sector job (whether as employee or employer, in the public or the private sector), doing unpaid economic work, driving a vehicle, waiting for a ride, smoking and "doing nothing".

8.   An activity may be the only one that is carried out over a particular interval of time, that is to say a *single activity*. Or, as is sometimes the case, an activity may be carried out in parallel with one or more other activities over an interval of time, the whole set being referred to as *simultaneous activities*. For example, a woman taking care of her children while listening to the radio is said to be engaged in two simultaneous activities; or a man eating dinner while carrying on a conversation with the family and watching the evening news on television is said to be engaged in three *simultaneous activities*. Thus, time-use statistics may pertain to (a) the *main or primary activities,* (b) *secondary activities* or (c) *simultaneous activities*.

An activity may be characterized by:

-       The context in which it occurs.
-       Its duration.
-       The frequency with which it takes place.

The *contexts* in which an activity takes place include:

(a) The *location* (*where* the activity occurred).

(b) The *presence of other people* when the activity occurred ("*with whom*").

(c) The *beneficiary* (person or institution) of the activity, in other words *for whom* the activity was carried out.

(d) The *motivation* (whether any remuneration was received for doing the activity, in other words, whether the work was *paid or unpaid*).

9.   One or more episodes of an activity may be recorded over the course of the reference period: *an episode* refers to one occurrence of an activity, without a change in any of the contexts (on which information is being collected). The *number of episodes* or *frequency* refers to the frequency of occurrence of an activity. The *duration* of an activity over a specified period of time refers to the total length of time the activity is engaged in. The concept of time spent on an activity has two basic aspects: the *duration* and *number of episodes* of the activity. For example, a person may engage in three episodes of eating in a day, breakfast, lunch and dinner, whose durations may differ, as exemplified by a hurried breakfast of 10 minutes, a business lunch lasting 55 minutes and a family dinner lasting 25 minutes.

10.   The temporal location and sequence of the activity are two other features that are also relevant for some types of analysis of time-use data. *Temporal location* is the time of the day, week, month or year an activity is undertaken, *sequence* represents the relationship of the activity to the activity that precedes and the activity that follows it (Harvey and Taylor, 2000, p. 235, para. 4).

11.   Basic statistics on time use are usually in the form of estimates of time spent on activities in an "average day" or an "average week". To arrive at that average or representative day or week, time-use data need to be comprehensive not only in relation to covering the whole range of possible activities but also in relation to accounting for differences between weekends and weekdays, effects of special holidays, and variations in activities across seasons in a year and across areas or regions in a country.

B. Why produce time-use statistics?

1. Origins of time-use data

12.   Studies based on time-use data (or time-budget research or time-use studies) were first developed in the early 1900s in social surveys reporting on the living conditions of working class families. The long working hours characteristic of early industrial development and organized labour's advocacy for the shortening of the working day made knowledge about the proportions of work and leisure in the daily life of labourers a concern in countries where industrialization was in progress (Szalai, ed., 1972).

13.   Many studies were undertaken beginning in the 1920s in Great Britain, the centrally planned economies and the United States of America. These include the work of two Soviet economists: Stanislav Strumilin, who used data on time use for purposes of government and community planning in 1924 and G. A. Prudensky, who replicated the study for purposes of historical comparison in 1934. Likewise, the Bureau of Home Economics of the United States Department of Agriculture conducted a survey on the effect of new technology on the time use of farm homemakers. Other historical examples of work in this area include *Time Budgets of Human Behaviour* by P. A. Sorokin and C. Q. Berger (1939) which provided new insights into psychological and social motivations; and K. Liepmann's *The Journey to Work* (1944), a monograph on the problem of commuting and the length of commuting time (Szalai, ed., 1972, p.7, para.2).

Box 1.   Analytical aims and applications of the 1964 Multinational Comparative Time-Budget Research Project

Analytical aims

1. To study and to compare in different societies variations in the nature and temporal distribution of the daily activities of urban and suburban populations subjected in varying degrees to the influences and consequences of urbanization and industrialization

2. To establish a body of multinational survey data on characteristics of everyday life in urban surroundings under different socio-economic and cultural conditions that could serve as the basis for testing various methods and hypotheses of cross national comparative social research[a]

Applications of time-use data

– Impact of television on mass media usage.

– Use of free time by type of activity (for example, reading, watching television, socializing).

– Social differentiation in leisure activity choices.

– International differences in the types and frequencies of social contacts.

– Time spent in childcare in relation to sex, employment status, number of children, age of children, daily rhythm of interaction, adult leisure.

– Problems arising from commuting between residence and workplace.

– Urban research and planning.

– Characterizing marital cohesion through correlating divorce rates with time spent on various activities such as leisure at home, leisure away from home, leisure time with or without family, conversations with family and spouse etc.

– Influence of educational status on time allocation.

– Relating changes in time allocation to changes in technological progress including: time spent at work, trip to work, time spent in housework, free time, meeting physiologic needs.

Source: Szalai, ed. (1972).
[a] United Nations (1990), p. 10, paras. 2 and 4.

Subsequent studies considered:

–   The share of paid work, housework, personal care, family tasks, sleep and recreation in the daily, weekly or yearly time use of the population.

–   Time-allocation patterns of subpopulations (for example, industrial workers, farm homemakers, college students, unemployed men) in respect of specific types of everyday activities.

–   Use made of "free time", especially leisure (Szalai, ed., 1972, p. 6, paras. 5-7).

14.   The Multinational Comparative Time-Budget Research Project involving 12 countries from both market and centrally planned economies was launched in 1964 with both analytical and methodological objectives. The analytical aims and diverse applications of time-use data collected through of this project are presented in box 1.

15. Studies based on time-use data of the general population have since evolved into a research tool utilized in various areas of application. In a report on the status of work on time-use statistics presented to the United Nations Statistical Commission at its 20th session in 1979, time-use statistics were identified as "a common source using a common unit of measure for fundamental descriptive data not otherwise obtainable on human activities in the various fields of social, demographic and related economic statistics" (United Nations, 1978, para.3).

16. In the 1970s, developing countries also started conducting time-use studies for development planning purposes. These studies were stimulated by the field of "new household economics" which recognized the productive elements of unpaid household activities. The distinction between labour in the marketplace and household production was important in this approach (Asia Society, 1978, p.2, para.2).

17. Most of the time-use studies that have been conducted in developing countries have investigated two main interrelated sets of concerns: the utilization of human resources in the household, particularly by women and children (with the new home-economics as framework of analysis), and the improvement in the measurement of employment, unemployment and underemployment (United Nations, 1990, p.56, para. 2).

18. Work on the development of welfare-oriented measures to supplement the national accounts and balances and a framework for the integration of social and demographic statistics at the national and international levels in the 1970s brought attention to the need for data that were both national in scope and internationally harmonized and comparable (United Nations, 1977, para. 211). Time-use data were identified for this work "as crucial non-monetary data for analysis of productive household and leisure activities ... and for some instrumental household activities, such as commuting" (United Nations, 1978, para.3).

2. Uses of time-use data

19. Time-use data can reveal the details of an individual's "daily life with a combination of specificity and comprehensiveness" not achieved in any other type of survey data (United Nations, 1997a). Statistics produced from such an exhaustive coverage of how individuals spend their time can paint an integrated picture of how various activities—paid and unpaid work, volunteer work, domestic work, leisure and personal activities—are interrelated in the lives of the general population and its various subsectors. With time-use data it is possible to determine what, how, why and how long activities are carried out. When properly collected and analysed, time-use data can allow for relating time-allocation patterns to the demographic and socio-economic status of the individual. It is for these reasons that time-use data have been collected on an increasingly larger scale.

20. A review of the literature[3] shows that many of the analytical objectives for collecting data on time use have revolved around the following major themes:

(a) Measurement and analysis of quality of life or general well-being.
(b) Measurement and valuation of unpaid work (domestic and volunteer work) and development of household production accounts.
(c) Improving estimates of paid and unpaid work.
(d) Analysis of policy implications of development planning issues.

---

[3] See, for example, Fleming and Spellerberg (1999); and Harvey and Taylor (2000).

A brief discussion of some of the studies and policy applications are presented below.

(a) Time use as indicator of well-being

21.   Time-use patterns of individuals have been analysed and interpreted in assessing quality of life.   These studies of living standards have emphasized the importance of leisure time as an aspect of well-being. In developed countries, time spent on leisure and indicators of "time crunch" are important measures of the general welfare of the population. In developing countries, "shortage of leisure" can be an indicator of poverty.

22.   Gershuny and others (1986) describe two issues of leisure in developed industrialized societies—one, that "we must face up to a continuing and perhaps increasing level of involuntary leisure in the form of unemployment", and second, that the "dominant characteristic of a developed society is its attempt to fit too many consumption activities into too little time". An analysis of British time-use data over two decades concludes that British society is a dual society where the "harried havers" are without sufficient leisure time to enjoy the leisure services available to them, while the "have nots" have time, but not the resources for leisure consumption (Fleming and Spellerberg, 1999).

23.   "Time crunch" is "the condition of those who feel as if they do not have enough time to do the things they need and want to do" (Ver Ploeg and others, eds., 2000). Understanding trends in how people feel about their use of time or lack of time for leisure activities can give a more complete picture of the quality of life and changes in it.

24.   The way time is allocated provides clues to the causes and consequences of poverty.   Time is one of the few resources available to poor households that have limited access to other resources such as capital and land. Thus, poor households make use of the time of all of their members to provide for the basic needs of the household (see, for example, Ilahi, 2000, p. 1, para.1). Furthermore, "many of the extremely poor are also often overworked" (Acharya, 1982, p.2, para. 3). A review of the empirical literature on the gender dimensions of time use and allocation of tasks in developing countries also shows that "households that rank poor on a consumption metric are also those where women have high work burdens" and that "these work burdens fall as household income increases provided market for labour exists" (Ilahi, 2000, p. 40, para.2).

25.   Findings from various case-studies done in the 1970s in Bangladesh, Botswana, India, Indonesia, Malaysia, Nepal, and the Philippines show that time-use data are "necessary in measuring the real work burden and leisure of different groups of population, for providing more accurate measures of employment and unemployment in developing countries, and for studying the shift of activities from non-market to the market sector in the development process."   Thus, in measurement of living standards time-use statistics are important for "developing more realistic and meaningful indicators of welfare and poverty and for providing deeper understanding of the dynamics of poverty and development" (Acharya, 1982).

(b) Measurement and valuation of unpaid work

26.   "Time-use accounts and household production accounts are two approaches that allow the detail needed for better income and production estimates to be made on an individual basis. They also have the advantage of being easily linked to national accounts through the measurement and distribution of

labour inputs and outputs of goods and services" (United Nations, 1995, p.107, para.8). The main goals for collecting time-use data for these accounts are providing a more accurate description of a national economy by including household production in traditional measures of economic status or progress—particularly measure of gross domestic product (GDP)—and improving the status of women by making their economic contribution visible and valued.

27.   In addition to household production, a large amount of unpaid work is also carried out in the community, resulting in a range of important goods and services. People run sports clubs, administer schools, care for older people and persons with disabilities, and transport those who are unable to transport themselves. In rural areas, people produce food for their own subsistence and assist each other with farm labour on a communal basis. This work too is part of the national production that is not included in traditional measures of the economy. Work of this kind may shift between the paid and unpaid sectors. Participation in voluntary work of various kinds and the connections between voluntary and market services are also investigated through time-use data.

(c) Time-use data for a more comprehensive measurement of all forms of work

28.   The uses of time-use data in the 1990s have been influenced by the international debate on including unpaid production in national economic accounts. One of the main recommendations of all four United Nations conferences on women concerned the improved measurement of both the remunerated and unremunerated work of women. In particular, the Beijing Platform for Action adopted by the Fourth World Conference on Women grew out of, and further contributed to, interest in the collection of time-use data in both developed and developing countries. The Platform for Action underscored the need to develop a more comprehensive knowledge of all forms of work and employment. A list of some of the main objectives is provided in box 2.

Box 2.   Selected objectives of the Beijing Platform for Action

---

– Improving data collection on the unremunerated work that is already included in the System of National Accounts[a], such as in agriculture, particularly subsistence agriculture, and other types of non-market production activities (para. 206 (f) (i)).
– Improving measurements that at present underestimate women's unemployment and underemployment in the labour market (p
– ara. 206 (f) (ii)).
– Developing methods quantifying the value of unremunerated work that is outside national accounts, such as caring for dependants and preparing food, for possible reflection in satellite accounts that may be produced separately from, but are consistent with, core national accounts (para. 206 (f) (iii)).

Source: United Nations (1996), chap. I, resolution 1, annex II.
[a] Commission of the European Communities, International Monetary Fund, Organisation for Economic Co-operation and Development, United Nations and World Bank (1993).

---

29.   Two lines of research that have developed involve methodologies for measuring and valuing unpaid work. Another outcome has been the use of time-use data to examine the distribution of paid and unpaid work between men and women. Time-use data has also been found useful in providing more accurate statistics on actual time spent in paid employment, holding of multiple jobs, and unusual patterns of paid employment (Fleming and Spellerberg, 1999).

Box 3.   Measuring the impact of policies on intra-household allocation of time

Intra-household allocation of time deals with how tasks and resources are allocated within a household.   Time-use data can help analysts study the nature and extent of intra-household inequality and the impact of that inequality. Having information about the way time is allocated among the various members of a household helps policy makers understand which household members will be most directly affected by a policy modification (for example, one that changes the amount of time required to fetch water or to travel to work).

Because public policies are usually based on market productivity alone, they may overlook some of the impact of an individual's influence on decisions made by the household.   For example, Berio as cited in Harvey and Taylor (2000) describes how a public policy that aimed to increase agricultural yields by encouraging the use of fertilizer on cash crops also increased the growth of weeds and thus the amount of time that farmers had to spend weeding. Since the cultivation and weeding of the cash crop was mainly carried out by women, households' balance of time allocation was altered in ways detrimental to food production and the care of children.

In analysing determinants of intra-household allocation of time use, Ilahi (2000) looks at the following questions: Do economic incentives (wages, non-wage income) matter? Do changes in access to basic services alter time-use patterns? Do idiosyncratic shocks (sickness, local unemployment) alter time use? Does agricultural modernization/technical change alter time use?

Sources: Harvey and Taylor (2000) and Ilahi (2000).

30.   Since 1995, at least 24 developing countries have initiated work on or undertaken data collection on time use in almost all regions of the world. Although geographically,

economically and culturally diverse, many of these countries have come to consider national time-use surveys as an important statistical tool for improving measurement and valuation of paid and unpaid work and for increasing the visibility of women's work both at home and in the labour market.   Advocates of the importance of nationally representative time-use information have argued that it enhances data provided by traditional labour-force surveys by recording actual time spent on labour-market activities and recording the relationship between paid and unpaid work. This information is crucial for a better understanding of the economic participation of women in the labour force (Fleming and Spellerberg, 1999) and in the informal sector (United Nations, 1990).

31.   Data from these surveys have been utilized to test these theories. Time-use data from the 1999 Time Use Survey of India, for example, was expected to provide the basis for improved estimates of the workforce in the informal sector and of work performed by women, relative to those data generated by standard household surveys and censuses. Two reasons time-use data were seen to have this advantage over other types of data in the Indian context are:

–   Sociocultural values confer a lower status on employed women and a high status on women engaged in unpaid housework. Thus, women tend not to report or underreport economic work when asked directly about it, as they are in standard labour-force surveys. Reporting such activities within the time-use survey framework is less direct and thus yields more accurate reports.

–   Even if women report economic work to survey interviewers, interviewers tend to interpret this work as non-economic and record it as such. This is partly because in many cases, it is difficult to differentiate between unpaid housework (for example, cooking for the household) and informal sector work (for example, cooking food mainly to be sold but with household meals factored in). Similarly, fetching water and collecting firewood are traditionally seen as unpaid housework even though the SNA has identified these as economic work (see Hirway, 1999).[4]

32. Initial results from the Indian survey showed that many more persons actually participate in economic activities identified by the SNA as compared with the numbers estimated by the traditional labour-force statistics (Hirway, 1999).

(d) Development planning issues

33. Data on time use can be employed to inform policy makers about the utilization and impact of public services such as public transportation, schools and electricity. For example, when policy makers are estimating the impact of providing piped water, they should have information on the amount of time that this will save for households as well as the likely health improvements that will result.

34. Furthermore, the price of using public services is often subsidized for low-income households to ensure that they have access to these services. However, the subsidized service may not actually benefit the intended household if it is located far away, as this presents a substantial cost to the household in terms of time. Thus having information on travel and waiting times may indicate to policy makers the extent to which a price subsidy may be eroded by such opportunity costs.

---

[4] These same observations have been discussed in relation to earlier studies see, for example, United Nations (1990).

Similarly, if policy makers understand how households organize their day, they can better determine what hours of the day public services should be open in order to ensure maximum access for the intended target households.

Box 4. Policy relevance of time-use data: Finland

Niemi and Paakkonen have demonstrated the policy relevance of time-use data in a study on changes in time use in Finland over a 10-year period (Fleming and Spellerberg, 1999). The analysis explored the Finnish experience in a number of areas, including the impact of new regulations on hours of paid work, a possible reduction in housework with the introduction of new technologies, changes in the division of domestic work between men and women, and leisure activities.

One significant finding from the time-use data was that the hours spent in paid employment by both men and women had increased. This change had taken place despite the regulatory change that reduced time in paid work by extending compulsory holidays and limiting work shifts.

Source: Fleming and Spellerberg (1999).

---

35. Time-use statistics have also been utilized as an indicator of human capital investment decisions. Human capital investments include education and health care. Time spent in school and time spent on homework are important measures of the investment that an individual and a household are making in education. Time-use data on children and youth are, therefore, of policy concern because children's non-school activities, such as paid work or chores, may prevent them from benefiting fully from the time that they spend in school. For example, if adults are required to spend more time on market activities, children may have to undertake the adults' household tasks, which in turn could reduce the amount of time that

they devote to their schooling. Absence of information on how much time children spend on housework could lead to unsatisfactory approaches to child labour eradication and schooling projects (Ilahi, 2000, p.42, para. 2).

36. Time costs can be an important component of the cost of using education and health services. Therefore, in order to analyse household decisions regarding schooling and health care, it is important to have a measure of these costs. Having a measure of travel time is useful even if the analyst already knows the distance to the facility in question, because not all households use the same mode of transportation. In the case of a client's availing him or herself of health-care facilities, time spent waiting to be served may be considered (conceptually) a cost to that client.

37. A relevant policy question is how much household time—such as time spent helping a child with homework—should be classified and measured as "investment", and how that factors into national accounting (see Ver Ploeg, and others, eds., 2000).

3. Objectives for collecting time-use data

38. About 50 countries have undertaken national data collection on time use since 1995. Annex 1 presents an illustrative listing of the objectives of some of these country surveys. Interest in producing nationally representative time-use statistics in both developing and developed countries is now generally motivated by two general objectives:

(a) To provide indicators of the quality of life or well-being of the nation in terms of time-use patterns of people.

(b) To improve estimates of the value of goods and services with particular emphasis on increasing visibility of women's work through better statistics on their contribution to the economy.

II. PLANNING DATA COLLECTION ON TIME USE

A. Overview of data-collection methods on time use

1. Development of national survey programmes on time use

39. Time-use studies were initially undertaken primarily by academics and research institutes (Harvey, 1999). The post-Second World War period saw a tremendous growth, however, in the scope, number and scale of time-budget studies in developed countries where time-use research integrated many of the new developments in survey sampling as well as interviewing, recording and coding techniques, and electronic data processing. One of the first applications of the new methods was in the field of radio and television audience research such as the time-budget survey (1960-1961) of the Japanese Radio and Television Culture Research Institute based on 170,000 interviews. This survey covered the daily activities of all strata of the Japanese population, in all parts of the country, in metropolitan, urban and rural settings, during all the four seasons, on weekdays, Sundays and special holidays (Szalai, ed., 1972, p. 7, paras. 2-3 ; p. 8, para. 1).

40. In developed countries, several national statistical offices began to undertake time-use surveys during the 1960s and many more began these surveys during the 1970s. At least one official national time-use survey has been conducted in Australia, Canada, Japan and New Zealand and in virtually all Eastern and Western European countries (Harvey, 1999, pp. 128-130).

41. Until recently, only a few of the national statistical offices in the less developed countries had undertaken time-use surveys.

Time-use studies in these countries were mainly case studies of a single or a few localities undertaken by academic researchers. The limited scope and methods of these studies were attributed to difficulties in measuring time in a population neither accustomed to being regulated by "clock time" nor experienced with filling in a questionnaire. Recent time-use surveys undertaken by less developed countries, however, show that national time-use data may be successfully collected in countries with a well-established national survey programme. The development and strengthening of national survey capability over the past 25 years in some less developed countries have been a critical factor in enabling these countries to undertake time-use surveys.

Figure 1. Basic components in the design of a time-use survey

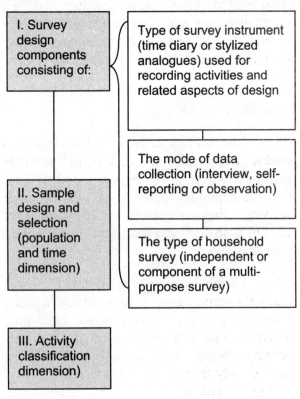

I. Survey design components consisting of:

Type of survey instrument (time diary or stylized analogues) used for recording activities and related aspects of design

The mode of data collection (interview, self-reporting or observation)

The type of household survey (independent or component of a multi-purpose survey)

II. Sample design and selection (population and time dimension)

III. Activity classification dimension)

2. Basic survey design components of national time-use surveys

42.   Data on time use are collected on a national scale through a household survey. The basic components in the design of a time-use survey are described in figure 1.

43.   Different combinations of these design component options translate into a wide variety of methods.

44.   An overview of issues related to the survey design components is presented in the present section; a more detailed discussion is covered in chapters IV and V. Sample design and selection issues are briefly discussed further on in this chapter and more fully discussed in chapter VI. Classification of activities for time-use statistics are also introduced in the present chapter.

(a) Survey instruments

45.   Types of survey instruments that have been used to obtain data on activities and their duration over a specified period of time may be classified into two general groups: *24-hour time diaries* and *stylized analogues of these diaries*.

Time diary

46.   The basic objective of a *time diary* is to enable respondents to report all activities undertaken over a prescribed period of time and the beginning and ending time for each activity. There are two basic types of diaries: the full time diary and the "light" or simplified time diary.

47.   In the basic format of the full time diary, the respondents report what activity they were doing when they began the day, what activity came next and at what time this activity began and ended, and so on successively through the 24 hours of the day. The interval of time within which an activity is reported may be fixed. In this case the 24 hours in a day are subdivided into intervals of, for example, 10, 15 or 30 minutes. Alternatively, the interval of time may be left open with the respondent reporting the beginning and ending times of each activity.

48.   With the light time diary, on the other hand, respondents report the time at which each activity occurs based on an exhaustive list, in other words the 24 hours of the day are accounted for in terms of the identified activity categories. The list of activity categories may consist of a small number of broad activity groups (such as paid employment, education, personal needs, domestic work, maintenance, and leisure) or it may contain a longer list of more detailed activity tasks (such as meal preparation, cooking, washing dishes, laundry, ironing, cleaning, sewing, shopping etc).

49.   In using the time diary, decisions have to be made on a number of specific methodological issues. These include: mode of data collection, number of days the diary should cover, which days of the week should be covered and their relative distribution, whether the diary will use an open interval or a fixed interval of time within which to report activities, the number of activities to be recorded, and which context variables will be included in the description of the activity.

Stylized analogues of time diaries

50.   In *stylized versions of diaries*, respondents are asked to recall the amount of time they allocate, or have allocated, to a certain activity over a specified period such as a day, week or year. It is different than a diary because the respondent does not report the specific time of the day the activity is performed. Stylized questions are typically of the form: "Yesterday (or last week), how much time did you spend on *activity x*?" Or: "How many hours per day (or per week) do you spend usually on *activity x*?

51. Using questions such as these, the stylized analogue collects information on the frequency and duration of time spent on a pre-specified set of activities during the previous 24 hours (or the past week). Respondents are asked whether or not they participated in a particular activity in the previous day (or on the day before that or the previous week). If the answer is yes, respondents are asked how many hours they have spent on that activity during that day. It is important that the listed activities be as comprehensive as possible in order to capture all of the activities that the respondent performs during a given day.

(b) Mode of data collection

52. Time-use data can be collected by *participant observation*, by *self-reporting*, or by *interview*. All these modes of data collection have their advantages and disadvantages relative to reliability of data obtained, effect on response rate and cost. These are discussed in detail in chapter V.

Direct observation

53. In the *direct observation* method, the time use of the respondent is observed and recorded by the survey enumerator. Observation can be carried out on a continuous basis or on a random spot basis. For continuous observation, the enumerator observes the respondent throughout the recording period. In observation on a random spot basis, on the other hand, the enumerator observes the respondent only at randomly chosen points in time during the recording period.

Self-reporting

54. Respondents may report their own time use by recording their activities in an appropriately designed time diary. One way of doing this is by asking the respondent to record the activity as or just after it occurs

(*tomorrow* or *current* or *"left-behind"* diary approach). Another way of doing this is by asking the respondent to recall and record activities performed over a specified recall period—usually the previous day or over the past week (*"yesterday"* or *retrospective diary* approach). Although not as common, a third approach is the *"experience sampling method"* (ESM) or "beeper" studies approach in which respondents are prompted by a beeper to record specified objective information, and possibly subjective information as well, on what they were doing at the time the beeper sounded.

Interview

55. Finally, time-use surveys often use the *interview* as the mode of data collection. The *personal* or *face-to-face* interview is most commonly used. The *computer-aided telephone interview* (CATI), on the other hand, though increasingly used in household surveys on a variety of topics, has so far only been applied in Canada in collecting time-use data.

56. The interview method may be used with both retrospective time diaries and their stylized analogues.

(c) Type of household survey

57. Most of the household surveys designed to collect data on time use may be classified into two basic types: (a) *independent* or *"stand-alone"* time-use surveys; and (b) *multi-purpose* or *multi-subject* household surveys with a time-use component.

Independent time-use survey

58. An *independent* time-use survey is a household survey concerned with the single subject of time use. With this type of survey, survey scope and coverage, questionnaires, sample design and selection, training plans, field operational procedures, and data-

processing systems are configured for this one purpose. Being able to plan for, design and implement a single subject survey is often a good solution for a subject as complex as time use. Thus, countries conducting a time-use survey for the first time have usually opted for an independent survey.

Time-use component in a multi-purpose survey

59. *Multi-purpose household* surveys, on the other hand, are amenable to either of two approaches: (a) a *modular approach*, where the time-use component is a separate module; or (b) an *integrated approach*, where the time-use component is included with all other components in a single module.

60. The common form of the modular approach involving a time-use component is one where there is a core module (such as a labour-force survey or an income and expenditure survey) and one or more additional or "rider" modules. A time-use module is included as a rider module. In this modular approach, population coverage, sample design and selection of households and major aspects of survey operations such as operational schedules, listing procedures, and enumerator workload are primarily guided by the requirements of the core module. Usually, the enumerator first completes the data collection on the core topic before introducing the time-use or other modules.

61. In this approach, the time-use module would utilize a separate set of survey instruments. This can be in the form of a time diary or a stylized analogue plus a background questionnaire. The time-use component is fielded at the same time as the core survey and uses the same set of interviewers. Some degree of flexibility in terms of selection of respondents for the time-use module and scheduling of callbacks is possible and the modular approach, to the extent that it

exercises such flexibility, can almost be considered an independent survey.

62. In the integrated approach, a single questionnaire is used to cover all topics and specific questionnaire items on time use are incorporated in the questionnaire. Typically, the questions are in the form of stylized questions on time use.

3. Classification of activities for time-use statistics

63. The nomenclature and classification of activities form an important part of the planning, collection and analysis of time-use data. A statistical classification provides "a set of discrete values which can be assigned to specific variables which are to be measured in a statistical survey ... which will be used as basis for the production of statistics" (Hoffmann, 1997).

64. Time-use data is about people's activities; thus, a detailed, comprehensive, systematic listing of activities needs to be available to serve as the basis for assessing completeness of coverage of activities. This listing is used as a guide in the design of survey instruments and selection of methods. It is also the interviewer's guide for eliciting from the respondent the level of detail required by the survey objectives and is the basis for developing coding rules and indexes.

65. Furthermore, an activity classification for time-use statistics defines the framework for analysis of the time-use survey data; the classification serves as the basis for defining analytical and tabulation categories of activities. Thus, the underlying principles of a classification should be consistent with the objectives of the survey.

66. Existing activity classifications are hierarchical in nature and their structures are

determined by the number of detailed descriptions of activities and the number of broad groups and subgroups into which, and on the bases of which, activities are categorized. Codes, usually numerical, are assigned at a one- or two-digit level to major divisions and at a two- or three-digit level to the first level of subgroups within a major division; the most detailed description of activities have the highest-digit level codes. The one- or two-digit levels are typically used as analytical and tabulation categories in surveys that use the full time diary.

67. Pre-listed activities in simplified time diaries often constitute the activity classification for the survey. The specified activities are typically also the analytical and tabulation categories, although it is possible that broader groups are defined for the purpose.

68. Consistent with the prevailing analytical themes in many time-use studies conducted so far, the activity classifications have focused on detailed lists of non-economic activities such as housework, caregiving, socialization, recreation, learning, mass media. The activity classification developed by the Multinational Comparative Time-Budget Research Project, for example, with its full 99-activity code or summary 37-activity code, set the initial standard for most of the national classifications of more developed countries.

69. In recent years, some countries have developed new activity classifications that encompass the expanded uses of time-use data. Examples of areas where this has occurred are the assessment of national labour inputs into production of all goods and all types of services, and the compilation of household satellite accounts consistent with the System of National Accounts. Time-use activities classifications have thus included details for economic activities and started developing means for differentiating activities relative to

the production boundary of the SNA (such as non-market work from other non-market activities, providing care for others and self-care, and intra-household transfers from inter-household transfers) (Bittman, 2000, p. 8, para. 3).

70. In addition, analyses that measure changes in time use and provide cross-national comparisons require that an activity classification be closely linked with the activity classifications used in other time-use studies within a country, among similar groups of countries and globally. The harmonized time-use project of the Statistical Office of the European Communities (Eurostat) developed a time-use classification that is intended to serve as a standard for the region. The draft United Nations International Classification of Activities for Time-Use Statistics[5] (discussed in part five) is being developed as a standard classification at the global level. A unique component of this classification is a comprehensive categorization of activities associated with household production of goods for own final use and informal sector activities.

B. Overview of issues in planning and conducting time-use surveys

71. As in any household survey, at the planning stage of a time-use survey, decisions need to be made on issues related to the following aspects:

1. Objectives and uses
2. Survey methods
3. Sample design
4. Field operational considerations

---

[5] This is a draft classification for trial use. The classification will be placed on the web site of the United Nations Statistical Division for further discussion.

5. Data-processing considerations
6. Resource rationalization

72. However, there are issues and problems that arise specifically because of the features of time-use data and the way they are analysed and utilized. The present chapter provides an overview of the major issues that need to be addressed at the planning stage of a time-use survey. In subsequent chapters of the *Guide*, these issues will be discussed in greater detail.

1. Decisions related to objectives and uses

73. The development of plans for any large-scale survey should include, at an early stage, the preparation of a set of strategic aims and objectives. The starting point for developing these objectives should be an understanding of the user requirements for data.

74. For example, to influence policy-making in areas of gender equality and women's economic empowerment, nationally representative data on time use could be analysed and used to: (a) describe differences in time-use allocation for all activities and specifically for paid and unpaid work, by sex, area and age group; and (b) construct satellite accounts on household production that incorporate the valuation of paid and unpaid work. Some of the requirements for these survey objectives are:

– Data on all activities and their duration over a 24-hour period so as to be able to describe time-use patterns of the population and subgroups of the population.
– Data for measuring and valuing unpaid domestic and volunteer work and developing household production accounts to augment standard national accounts.

– Data for analysing policy implications of development planning issues in relation to an ongoing programme or to assess current policies.
– Data for improving estimates of standard labour-force statistics including time spent on informal sector activities and unpaid productive activities.

In general, translating data requirements into time-use survey specifications requires decisions on *survey content*, *population coverage* and *time coverage*.

(a) Survey content

75. In determining the scope of a time-use survey, the following issues need to be considered:

– *Level of detail in which activities will be recorded and coded and groupings for analysis and tabulation.* The level of detail at which activities are recorded is determined by the analytical objectives of the survey as well as concerns about coding and respondent burden, among others, and is related to the selection of survey instruments. Activities may be recorded in as much detail as a full time diary allows or may be delimited by the pre-listed activities in a simplified time diary. Depending on the level of detail decided on, an appropriate activity list or classification will need to be developed for coding purposes. This detailed list would then need to be condensed to provide suitable analytical and tabulation categories.
– *Recording of simultaneous activities.* Recording simultaneous activities is important in identifying specific types of activities. For example, caregiving

activities are often performed in parallel with other activities like housework but respondents will often report the caregiving activity as a secondary activity. Thus, much of the time spent in childcare may not appear in survey estimates if only primary activities are covered. The ability to collect data on simultaneous activities depends on the survey method (for example, it is difficult to do so through a telephone interview) and the design of the survey instrument (for example, length of the time interval used in the survey instrument needs to be considered). A decision also needs to be made whether the activities are to be prioritized into primary, secondary etc. and, if so, whether the prioritization should be done by the respondent or by an analyst.

- *Inclusion of contextual information* (Where, with whom, for whom, whether paid or unpaid) and level of detail. The context in which an activity takes place is closely related to the analytical objectives of the data collection. To be able to distinguish paid from unpaid activities, for example, would require a context variable. A "for whom" context variable, for example, would be needed to identify volunteer work, unpaid work within the household, and unpaid work outside of the household.

- *Inclusion of "background" variables.* A minimum list of variables includes sex, age, marital status, work situation of the individual, and household composition (United Nations, 2000, para. 15). Depending on the analytical objectives, additional variables may have to be included. For example, information on household durables is needed for explaining time-use patterns of activities that are related to their

presence or absence in the household. Whether to collect information about wage rates and/or household income or expenditure or simply about indicators of wealth and circumstances also depends on the objectives of the survey (United Nations, 2000).

- *Recording of information on temporal location and/or activity sequence.* Information on temporal location of an activity or the time of day, week, month or year an activity is undertaken is useful in understanding the time constraints within which time allocation decisions are made. Activity sequence or the relationship of an activity to the activity that precedes and the activity that follows it, provides information on how individuals organize their day. Both require data on the beginning and ending times of activities and a chronological reporting of activities; this would thus preclude the use of stylized questions or stylized activity lists.

(b) Population coverage

76. In addition to the standard issues on population coverage that are addressed in household surveys (for example, institutional population, population in special situations and de jure versus de facto approaches) (United Nations, 1984), time-use surveys require additional decisions concerning the reference population. These are listed below:

- *Geographical coverage.* Will the analysis require comparisons of urban and rural lifestyles? Or differences in the time allocation patterns among regions within the country? For example, for purposes of developing satellite accounts, national-level data without the geographical disaggregations may suffice. However, some users may be interested in making regional comparisons but these would generally require a larger sample size compared with only national data and, hence, increase costs.

- *Age limits.* What should be the age cut-off for the survey? Studies on paid and unpaid work invariably need information on children's activities both as performers of work activities and as recipients of unpaid work. From what age should the survey cover children, given the possible difficulty in collecting time-use information from them? A related question is: Should the survey exclude those older than the maximum working age limit?

- *Individuals or households.* Do the analytical objectives require data exclusively from individuals or are data on couples, families within households or households also needed? From a conceptual standpoint, one argument for collecting time-use information from multiple persons in a household is to provide a basis for understanding intra-household resource and time allocation. For example, with data only on individuals it is possible to determine the effects of marriage or an additional child on the individual's *personal* use of time but it will not be possible to determine their effects on the *household as an economic unit* (Bittman, 2000, p. 3, para.4).

(c) Coverage of time

77. The duration and frequency of time spent on an activity may vary depending on the time of day, the day of the week, or the season of the year. Personal care activities such as eating and sleeping and housework are typically carried out every day; on the other hand, some activities like house repair or buying a refrigerator are undertaken much less

frequently. Some people have regular working hours or are in school from Monday to Friday, have weekends off and take summer vacations during the same months each year. Many informal sector work activities do not have the same regularity in working hours. Planting and harvesting of crops are seasonal as are home-based crafts-making for which raw materials are available on a seasonal basis. Other activities such as worship are often organized on a weekly basis and would predominantly occur on a particular day. Based on survey objectives, decisions will have to be made on the following:

- *Unit of time to be observed.* Should time intervals of minutes or hours within a day or a time interval defined in terms of a whole week be chosen?
- *Days of the week.* Should all days of the week be covered? If so, should coverage include each day or is it sufficient to distinguish between weekdays and weekends only?
- *Seasons.* Should time-use data take into account seasonal variations in activities?

(d) Planning outputs and dissemination of data

78. The planning process should also include the development of analytical and data dissemination plans for the survey. The analytical plan documents the research or policy issues being studied and relates these to the statistical tables that will be generated from the data. The data dissemination plan identifies target audiences and the appropriate strategy and products for each target group. Both plans should be consistent with the survey objectives.

79. Basic issues for which decisions need to be made are related to specifications of the *tabulation plan, strategy for producing tables* and *dissemination strategy and products.*

Tabulation plan

80.   Developing the tabulation plan serves to: (a) confirm that the survey content specifications meet the analytical requirements, (b) ensure that the level of detail of the cross-classification variables in statistical tables required for the research analyses are specified correctly and (c) provide a guide to ensure that, in the determination of sample size, reliable estimates can be provided for the basic cross-tabulation cells in the tables.

81.   Thus, the tabulation plan should specify the main *cross-classification variables*. For most survey objectives, the variable sex is a standard cross-classification variable. In addition to this, decisions will need to be made on the following:

–   Should cross-classification variables include rural/urban?
–   What age groupings are relevant?
–   What levels of activity groupings are needed?

82.   Another important issue has to do with the analysis of *simultaneous activities*. If simultaneous activities are covered in the survey:

–   How should time spent on simultaneous activities be counted?
–   How will the data on simultaneous activities be presented in a table?

Strategy for producing tables

83.   The number of tables that can be produced from time-use data can become quite voluminous and decisions will need to be made on which set of tables will comprise the basic tabulations and which tables will be produced and disseminated first. A phased *production schedule* may be helpful in prioritizing outputs to ensure timeliness of the release of the results.

Dissemination strategy and products

84.   If time-use data is to be used to inform policy, it will need to be presented and made available in forms that are understood by as wide an audience as possible, yet targeted and focused enough to serve as advocacy tools. Specific people and organizations may need to be identified and included in the consultative process concerning what modes of dissemination and what types of products are most appropriate.

85.   Time-use statistics may eventually be used for purposes other than those that were originally envisaged. For example, additional analytical issues may emerge after the initial results have been studied. The tabulation plan for the survey will not necessarily meet the requirements for these. Decisions therefore need to be made at the planning stage to meet specialized or emerging data needs including whether to release microdata and, if so decided, in what form. If not, what kind of system will enable the statistical office and main sponsors of the survey to respond in a timely basis to special data requests?

(e) Role of consultative process involving producers, users and sponsors

86.   Users of time-use data include policy makers (legislators and ministries), international aid and development agencies, academic researchers, and market/business researchers. Some users are sponsors and contribute funding.

87.   Identifying and formulating objectives and uses for producing time-use statistics involves a *consultative process* with potential users and sponsors of the statistics. This process should be initiated in the early stage of

planning. This collaboration should continue through all stages of the survey to keep users and sponsors informed. This consultative process is especially important in publicizing the survey and mobilizing respondent support and at the data dissemination stage.

88. The consultative process at the planning stage helps in identifying and prioritizing the topics and issues to be addressed and in formulating the survey objectives that are consistent with these. The consultative process also facilitates the identification of potential survey sponsors and strategic partners who can advocate for the importance of the time-use survey.

89. One of the decisions that needs to be taken in the planning stage is how to deal with possibly competing demands and conflicting opinions of producers, users and sponsors on how the survey should be designed and implemented. The consultative process provides a forum where everyone concerned becomes aware of the various demands and opinions and the constraints within which these need to be prioritized.

90. The desired result of the consultative process is agreement upon a practical strategy based on realistic expectations about the data that can be collected and the analyses that can be carried out. Statistical offices will need to balance the interests of sponsors and users with considerations of quality and overall usefulness of the survey data.

91. The consultative process may take various forms ranging from informal discussion groups, workshops or meetings organized by producers to the formation of a formal consultative committee of producers, users and sponsors that oversees the whole process of the survey. The discussion groups, workshops or meetings may be organized for different purposes—educating decision makers on the use and importance of time-use surveys,

reviewing past time-use studies, getting feedback on a proposed design for the survey or discussing a proposed activity classification for time-use statistics.

92. For example, the Government of India appointed a technical consultative committee to advise on the 1999 Indian Time Use Survey. The committee, whose members included government statisticians and national accountants, social scientists and economists in academia, and ministries for women, children and health, was tasked to "advise the government on designing, planning and related matters leading to conducting a time-use survey; suggest appropriate definitions and concepts, a schedule of inquiry and a suitable reference period for the purpose of data collection through a survey; suggest an appropriate methodology for building up the annual estimates of time disposition based on the survey data; and advise on any other matter referred to the committee by the Department of Statistics in respect of time-use survey" (Central Statistical Organisation, 2000, p.6). The committee was an integral part of the entire survey process.

2. Decisions on survey methods

93. Although the final design specifications for the time-use survey may be reached only after an iterative process involving testing and assessment by analysts, questionnaire designers, survey operations experts, and data-processing experts, initial decisions on the survey methods need to be made at the planning stage.

94. Deciding on survey methods for data collection involves decisions on the type of survey—in combination with decisions on the *mode of data collection* and *survey instruments*—that would best fit the survey conditions. As described in chapter II, there are different ways in which these three aspects may be combined. Two factors that need to be

considered in deciding which combination will work best are the literacy level of the survey population and its capability of measuring time "with a clock".

(a) Literacy level of the survey population

95. Literacy levels in the population influence the choice of mode of data collection and survey instruments. For example, if the literacy rate of the survey population is low, a recall interview is generally a better option than a "leave-behind" self-completed diary. If the literacy rates vary among population subgroups (for example, ethnic groups) or areas, it is possible to have a combination of self-reporting for the literate respondents and recall interview or even direct observation for the illiterate respondents.

(b) Measuring time "without a clock"

96. Some societies may not relate their activities to "clock time" or to hours as they appear on a clock face. For example, sense of time may be related to fluctuations of nature, religion, geographical conditions, productive activities, and tradition. In order to collect time-use data in such societies, survey designers need to give special attention to translating the local perception of time into a standard 24-hour timetable. Survey design must take into account and reflect the mores and traditions of the group to be surveyed. In this case, it is necessary to understand how the community identifies the hours of the day and how its members calculate the amount of time it takes them to perform an activity (Harvey and Taylor, 2000).

3. Decisions on sample design and selection

97. For time-use surveys, there are three types of units of analysis: the *household*, *household members* and *time* (hours, days, seasons). Generally, considerations in sampling the *household* do not differ from those of typical household surveys. Considerations in sampling *household members* and design of the time sample however, are unique features of time-use surveys.

(a) Sampling household members

98. An important sample design decision is whether or not to include all household members belonging to the reference population. As discussed above, the decision whether there is a need to include more than one household member in the sample depends on the analytical objectives. If the analytical objective calls for more than one household member, a decision has to be made on how many should be considered; one option is to include all household members. If sampling household members is decided on, how should they be selected?

(b) Time sample

99. Should the survey cover all days of the year or all four seasons of the year? If so, how should the sample be designed? One basic option is to conduct the survey on a periodic or continuous basis over the entire year and to spread the total sample of households over each survey period. If resources are not available to do this, are there alternatives that can be explored in combination with a single-period survey? Another option would be simply to conduct a single-period survey and acknowledge the analytical limitations of such an approach.

100. If the unit of time is the day (rather than the week), two decisions that would need to be made are:

– How many diary days should be sampled per household member?

–   Are all days of the week to be represented in the sample? If so, will this be done according to an equal or non-equal representation? How will the diary days per household member be selected to achieve the desired representation?

101.   One technique is to ensure that there is an equal representation of days of the week. To illustrate some of the issues that arise: if, 7,000 people have each completed two diary days, this gives an effective sample of 7,000 times 2 equals 14,000 diary days. With equal representation of days of the week, this translates into a sample of 2,000 Sundays, 2,000 Mondays, 2,000 Tuesdays, 2,000 Wednesdays, 2,000 Thursdays, 2,000 Fridays and 2,000 Saturdays. If an activity that typically occurs on a particular day of the week—such as paid work on Sunday—is of analytical interest, the effective sample is 2,000 diary days. Breaking the data down, by industry or broad occupational groupings, for each sex or ethnicity or educational attainment grouping of those working on Sunday, as needed by the analysis, rapidly runs up against the limits imposed by small cell size. Thus, survey designers should consider what is the minimum number of representations of a particular day of the week that will produce tolerable standard errors given specific analytical objectives (Bittman, 2000).

4.   Decisions on field operations

102.   For a specific survey method, that is to say, the combination of type of survey, survey instrument and mode of data collection, field procedures will have to be designed appropriately. The main decisions to be made with respect to field operational procedures are discussed below.

(a)   Procedures for some aspects of design

Sequence of questionnaires

103.   Time diaries or stylized analogues and a "background" questionnaire generally constitute the survey instruments for time-use surveys. As discussed earlier, the content of the questionnaire is often as critical to the interpretation and analysis of time use as the diary itself. The survey procedure should define the *sequence* in which these instruments are to be administered to the respondent, particularly for surveys using the interview method.

104.   The field procedures may become more complicated if the time-use survey is a module of a larger survey; in this case, there are additional questionnaires to coordinate and sequence.

Assigning diary days

105.   Another important decision concerns the assignment of diary days. What procedure should be used in allocating diary days to respondents? Should enumerators select the days? Or should respondents? Or should these be predetermined at the sample selection stage, that is to say, should designated diary days be assigned to each household or respondent?

106.   Ideally, diary days should be randomly selected and designated days assigned to respondents. Experience shows, however, that this is generally not strictly achievable but may be approximated by following procedures on postponing or rescheduling designated days. At the minimum, operational procedures should ensure that the selection of diary days is not left to the discretion of either the interviewer or the respondent.

(b) Quality control techniques

107. Quality control techniques aim to minimize non-sampling errors. A particular concern in time-use surveys is to minimize non-response. One way in which this concern has been addressed is through the provision of some form of incentive to respondents (for example, cash or small tokens). Some statistical offices are concerned, however, that such a practice may have a negative effect on the response rate for other regular surveys in their programmes that do not provide incentives.

108. Depending on the survey method adopted for the survey, there are concerns about interviewer and respondent effects on response quality. What techniques specific to collecting data on time use should interviewers/enumerators learn and use to minimize such effects?

5. Decisions on data-processing procedures

109. Time-use data has been described as "unwieldy" with respect to analysis because of its multidimensional character. As discussed earlier, they include time data for individuals and households in terms of type of activities, frequency, duration, location, intensity, sequence etc. that can be aggregated by activity, household, sex or age of individuals etc. Asia Society (1978). In addition, these are typically correlated to household as well as individual characteristics. Thus, although data collection may be completed within the time schedule of a survey operation, data processing and analysis may become a bottleneck in generating the survey results. The path from thousands of individual diaries to useful summaries and statistical tables needs to be carefully mapped out. Some of the main issues that need to be considered are described below.

(a) Editing

110. There is a consensus among time-use experts that primary activities must add up to 1,440 minutes per day (and the consistent arithmetic for week and year should follow). This increases the accuracy and completeness of reporting very significantly, because it provides a check as to whether the estimates of the duration of each activity were accurate or whether some activities were omitted.

111. In general, standard edit specifications and quality indicators for evaluating diary data need to be specified. Issues to be addressed in relation to this and related edits are:

– Which edits are to be done manually and to what extent should these manual edits be done?
– At what stage of the survey should editing be done? At the interview stage? For self-completed diaries, when the diaries are collected?

(b) Coding

112. Coding is one of the most expensive and time consuming tasks in time-use surveys. Data-processing experts need to work with subject-matter analysts in the formulation of coding rules and the construction of coding indexes and fit these into the processing procedures and system.

113. Coding rules are especially needed when processing the information on time-use activities in diaries (Australian Bureau of Statistics, 1992, p. 34, paras. 5-7; p.35, paras. 1-2) in order to deal with:

– Overriding activities. Descriptions of activities reported by respondents may actually be not a single activity but several activities. Examples of such activities are travelling, socializing or entertainment that involves going to a venue, visiting or receiving visitors for more than a few hours.

– Pervasive activities. Certain activities, particularly passive care of children or adults requiring monitoring may not be consistently reported.

– Omitted activities. Examples of such activities are constant background activities such as passive childcare, travel, eating and sleeping. Sometimes, no activity appears for intervals of time.

– Simultaneous activities. When simultaneous activities are recorded, it may be necessary to prioritize these as main, secondary etc.

114. The coding of diaries may be performed either in the field by interviewers or at a central site by coders; the optimal choice will depend on having appropriate coding tools and procedures. The development of a coding index for activities and for contextual information that have been included in the time-use diary is one such tool and provisions for doing so in the survey timetable would need to be made.

(c) Preparation of outputs

115. Defining data entry and computer edit specifications are standard processes for any survey but defining file structures from time diaries and identifying derived variables that can facilitate the production of tables and the presentation of results from the survey are especially critical for time-use surveys. Decisions will need to be made on which data entry and editing software to use in developing the computer programmes for these; unlike some specialized household surveys that have benefited from statistical packages that can be readily adopted, there is no standard package for time-use diaries.

116. Implementing the estimation procedure for the survey—including weighting and non-response adjustments—and generating the tables prescribed in the tabulation plan require preparation and review of computer programmes and table formats. What software to use and what the review process is to entail are decisions that would need to be made at the planning stage.

117. In addition, decisions need to be made on developing a database and the data dissemination products, as discussed above.

6. Decisions related to resource rationalization

118. The desired end-result of a survey project is that for a pre-identified set of objectives the overall statistical design of the survey optimises the use of available resources and that the survey methodology adopted and implemented yields reliable (accurate, precise and timely) statistics that meet the pre-defined uses of the survey results.

(a) Resources

119. Money, people and their time, and infrastructure constitute resources. In practice, most survey designs are fitted within known cost constraints; that is to say, the amount of money allocated for the survey is fixed and all activities related to the survey must cost less than or equal to this fixed amount. More often than not, setting the ceiling for the survey is not based on survey design options and issues: the budget is set based on other priority-funding considerations which in many cases include political ones. This has often been the case for time-use surveys. For instance, while some political backing has been given to time-use surveys in response to the Beijing Platform for Action (United Nations, 1996, chap. I, resolution 1, annex II) it has generally been in the form of funding for a single ad hoc survey.

In less developed countries, more often than not, an international or bilateral aid or development agency provided the funds and the time-use survey was conducted as part of an ongoing development programme. Hence, institutionalization of time-use surveys in the national statistical systems had not been a primary consideration.

120. In evaluating resources available for a time-use survey, countries need to impute the cost of utilizing existing staff and the infrastructure and facilities of the organizations involved in the survey (mostly, the statistical office staff and facilities). In preparing the budget for a survey, only "additional" costs are accounted for; for example, wages paid to interviewers and data encoders hired to augment the regular workforce; travel costs for training and supervising (if the time-use survey is not a rider to a regular survey); communication costs etc. For a more realistic basis for planning and organizing the time-use survey, total survey cost should include both types of costs.

121. In addition, especially for first-time time-use surveys or ad hoc surveys that are not part of the regular household survey programme, countries should assess the impact of undertaking this additional workload on the regular workload of the organizations involved. Mounting a time-use survey, especially for the first time, may have an effect on the operations of the regular surveys of the statistical office. Consequently, the impact of fitting the survey into or around them would need to be considered. For regular staff, even with the addition of new interviewers or data encoders, the increased workload may mean having to prioritize their time and attention and lesser priority may lead to sacrifices in quality. For the survey respondents, especially those who may end up answering multiple surveys, willingness to cooperate and quality of responses may decrease.

(b) Relating objectives, design and resources

122. The discussions in this chapter illustrate that arriving at an appropriate design for producing statistics on time use requires the balancing of objectives and resources. The task of striking a balance could be a complex process partly because there are no definite answers to some of the issues of survey design. Planners need to consider the following:

– Given objectives and planned overall survey design, how much will the survey cost? Are the needed resources available?
– If not, what reasonable compromises can be made, given a gap between available resources and resources needed to achieve the desired end result of the survey?

123. For example, each additional objective may require, inter alia, more survey content or an expansion of the sample to ensure that a special population group or geographical area is sufficiently represented. This in turn may require more resources such as for increased wages because of longer interview times or increased workload due to larger sample sizes. Thus, data requirements may need to be prioritized and trimmed down.

124. It may also be the case that the cost of the sample size dictated by statistical and analytical requirements may be much higher than what is available for the survey. A decision would then have to be made on a reasonable compromise between statistical and analytical requirements in respect of reducing the sample size. For example, the number of sampled individuals can be reduced by decreasing the number of study domains required, such as specific age groups or similar subpopulations. Alternatively, a reduction in the precisions requirements needed for cells in

cross-tabulations can produce the same effect. The basic principle here is that the more detailed the level of disaggregations required, the larger the sample size required.

125. Low non-response rates may be viewed as a measure of efficient use of resources. Achieving low non-response rates is one of the most difficult objectives in the design of time-use surveys, as some of the solutions, such as provision of incentives to respondents or more follow-up visits by enumerators, are relatively costly. On the other hand, cost-effective solutions such as using a light diary (or pre-coding of activities) as opposed to a full diary (or after-coding of activities) or computer-assisted telephone interviewing as opposed to a face-to-face interview may place some limitations on the scope and coverage of the survey.

126. Integrating time-use surveys into the regular programme of household surveys of a country is an efficient approach to developing a framework for a sound, continuing database and time series for time-use data. Since start-up costs are usually large, unrelated ad hoc surveys tend to be costly. With irregular operations, it is difficult to accumulate and absorb the knowledge and experience necessary to achieve efficient and reliable survey results; for example, this would limit the opportunity to develop an adequate technical and field staff well trained in time-use methods.

127. One model for a regular programme of time-use surveys as proposed by Haraldsen (2000) would involve collecting data on time use "by a combination of a few comprehensive surveys and some more frequent surveys that cover a restricted number of activities that adds up to a complete set of activity registrations after some years. For this purpose a simpler diary design is suggested. If these smaller diary surveys are linked to omnibuses or other regular surveys the external information, the composition of the household and the individual resources will normally be covered and paid for by the 'mother survey' " (Haraldsen, 2000, p.15, para.6).

Part Two

Key design specifications for time-use surveys

III. SCOPE AND COVERAGE OF TIME-USE DATA

128. As indicated in the earlier chapters of this *Guide*, the range of possible objectives and applications in respect of collecting data on time use is very wide. Furthermore, particular goals require particular data items and affect the choice of the population to be covered. It is clearly not possible to simultaneously satisfy all objectives in a single survey. The approach taken by this *Guide* is to discuss the key design specifications for the most general objective of a national time-use survey—that of measuring the daily activity patterns of the general population, women and men, children, youth and the elderly—and after that, to indicate additional requirements that may arise for some of the specific objectives.

129. Decisions on what is to constitute the scope and coverage of time-use data collection relate to the survey content and survey population. The basic content of a time-use survey are the *activities* of individuals and the *amount of time* they engage in the various activities. Context gives meaning to activities and groups of activities; thus, these dimensions also need to be included in the data to be collected to the extent that they are essential to the survey objectives. As mentioned in part one, time-use surveys must take into account the fact that individuals may engage in many activities simultaneously. Furthermore, while in a conventional household survey the population covered is typically defined in terms of sociodemographic characteristics of the human population and spatial or geographical coverage, in time-use data collection the temporal dimension also needs to be specified. The present chapter will address the above-mentioned issues in the following order:

– Describe the basic content of a time-use survey: *activities* and *time*.

– Illustrate some of the challenges introduced by recording *secondary* and *simultaneous* activities.
– Elaborate on the importance of *contextual information*.
– Elaborate on the importance of *background information*.
– Illustrate the specific aspects that have to be considered in a time-use *survey population*.

A. Activity and time

1. Describing activities

130. Time-use data seek to capture human behaviour in terms of what is being done (activity) and when, during a specified period of time. The key focus in each time period is "what were you doing?" The response to this question is typically deemed the primary activity, although some responses may describe activities that are carried out simultaneously.

131. Time-use data encompasses people's activities; thus, a detailed, comprehensive, systematic listing of activities needs to be available to serve as the basis for assessing completeness of coverage of activities. This listing is used as a guide in the design of survey instruments and selection of methods; it is also the interviewer's guide for eliciting from the respondent the level of detail required by the survey objectives and is the basis for developing coding rules and indexes. Furthermore, an activity classification for time-use statistics defines the framework for analysis of the time-use survey data; the classification serves as basis for defining analytical and tabulation categories of activities. Thus, the underlying principles of a classification should be consistent with the objectives of the survey.

132.   The nomenclature and classification of activities form an important part of the planning, collection and analysis of time-use data.   Such a classification should be constructed and tested well in advance of field operations.   The activity list tells the enumerator, the coder and the analyst how much detail is needed and how the information is to be categorized.

133.   The level of detail at which descriptions of activities are to be recorded is determined by, inter alia, the analytical objectives of the survey as well as concerns about coding and respondent burden and is related to the selection of survey instruments. Activities may be recorded in as much detail as a full time diary allows or may be delimited by the pre-listed activities in a light time diary. Too much detail may make the resulting database unmanageable or lead to increased costs in terms of coding, processing and analysing the data.   Insufficient detail, on the other hand, limits the usefulness of the survey. Depending on the level of detail decided on, an appropriate activity list or classification will need to be developed for coding purposes. This detailed list would then need to be condensed to provide suitable analytical and tabulation categories.

134.   Not only must the classification of activities conform to analytical requirements, it also needs to take account of the manner in which respondents actually categorize their time use. Thus, *pre-testing* is necessary and data obtained from pre-tests should be reconciled with the a priori classifications developed by the statistical office. The pre-test may also be used to develop written definitions of time-use categories which may guide respondents, enumerators and coders in placing activities into their proper classifications.

135.   It is suggested that countries embarking on their first national time-use

survey start with the trial International Classification of Activities for Time-Use Statistics (ICATUS) described in part five of this *Guide*. Guidance on how to adapt it to local conditions are discussed in chapter XIII of the *Guide*.

136.   Activities may be recorded verbatim or may be recorded by selecting from a pre-specified list of activities.   The method in which activity descriptions are recorded depends on the type of survey instrument (see chap. IV).

2.   Recording time

137.   Recording *time* is another aspect that has to be considered in time-use surveys. Time has several dimensions relevant to activity (Harvey and Wilson, 1998): *position* or the point in time at which actions occur (for example, weekday or weekend, morning or evening, between 9 a.m. and 10 a.m.); *duration* or the period during which actions occur (for example, 45 minutes, 3 hours); and *sequence* (before or after, past, present or future).

138.   A record of beginning and ending times provides the information needed to describe these dimensions of time. In 24-hour diaries, the options are *open recording* or the use of *fixed intervals*. The ability to provide the dimensions of position and sequence is a major strength of the 24-hour diary format. Unfortunately, these dimensions are lost by collecting time-use data through stylized questions that are able to record only the duration of the activity. These issues are further discussed in chapter IV.

B.   Secondary/simultaneous activities

139.   Humans regularly engage in more than one activity at the same time. These parallel activities that accompany a *main* or "*primary*"

activity are called *"secondary"* or *simultaneous* activities. These simultaneous activities can consist of simple combinations (such as watching television while smoking a cigarette) or more complicated combinations (such as ironing and listening to the radio and keeping an eye on children). If respondents experience their activities as simultaneous occurrences, then including the opportunity to report and record secondary activities in collecting time-use data enhances accuracy of resulting data. Requiring respondents to record a single primary activity constrains them into distorting their experience when they report. Consequently, the diary becomes more difficult for them to complete.

140. If estimates of time-use are based only on primary activities, many activities are clearly underestimated. These "missing" activities would typically be reported as secondary or simultaneous activities. Recording these activities usually changes estimates of how much time couples spend in conversation, the audience for radio programmes and, most significantly, the time demands imposed by many non-market tasks such as housework[6] and childcare[7]. The basic

reason why collecting data only for the main activity leads to underestimates of some types of activities is that respondents tend to record as the "primary" or main activity those activities that require their greatest attention. However, the respondent may be undertaking this foreground activity (for example, ironing) because of his or her responsibility for a background activity (for example, childcare[8]).

1. Recording simultaneous activities

141. Because many types of daily activities will be missed if simultaneous activities are not recorded, it is recommended that the design of a time-use survey allow for the recording of at least one secondary activity (the number of simultaneous activities captured in national surveys has ranged from two to four). This gain in accuracy achieved by recording secondary activities will, however, have to be weighed against the added length of time and the difficulty involved in collecting the data, increased complexity in editing and coding activities, and the objectives of the survey.

142. Based on country practices, the only viable survey instrument for recording simultaneous activities is the 24-hour time diary—specifically the full diary. The diary would ideally include two separate columns

---

[6] A peculiar characteristic of market work is that respondents often report that they undertake no other activities at the same time. In contrast, many non-market tasks are often performed simultaneously. Floro (1995) has argued that this form of intensification is even more prevalent in the context of the developing world.

[7] For example, the average time spent in conversation by Australians in 1992 as a primary activity was barely over a quarter-hour per day; but when conversation that accompanied another activity was included, these same "taciturn" Australians spent almost three hours per day in conversation. Suddenly husbands and wives could be seen as conversing. Similar effects occur with listening to the radio or recorded music. Australians spent five minutes per day on this primary activity in 1992. On the basis of primary activities, for every minute spent consuming audio-only media there were more than 20 minutes spent consuming televisual media. However, when primary and secondary activities were taken into

account, this ratio fell to 1 minute of audio-only media consumption to 1.18 minutes of televisual media. In other words, it becomes plain that television is mostly a foreground activity and that listening to radio and listening to recorded music are typically background activities.

[8] For example, in the Australian surveys of 1992 and 1997, for every hour recorded as a primary childcare activity, there were three more hours recorded of childcare as a secondary activity. Roughly half of this "secondary" childcare accompanied a leisure activity or an activity associated with personal care. Recording only main activities produces the illusion of voluntary leisure and time for oneself and does not reflect the constraints imposed by caring for small children.

for recording the main activity and the secondary activity. Another recording option is for all activities to be recorded in one column, differentiating main and secondary activities at the coding stage. It is clear, however, that recording, coding and editing of time diaries becomes more complicated. A more detailed discussion of recording options for simultaneous activities (including whether, for example, to use an *open-* or *closed-interval* diary; and issues related to length of interval) is presented in chapter IV; implications of editing and coding (for example, differentiating *main* from *secondary* and *simultaneous* from *sequential activities*) are discussed in chapter VIII.

2. Measuring time spent in simultaneous activities

143. Inclusion of simultaneous activities in the coverage of a time-use survey requires a decision on how to measure time spent in these activities. There is currently no theoretically and practical satisfactory approach and further research is needed on this issue. The present section describes some of the alternatives that may be considered.[9]

144. One method for measuring time spent in simultaneous activities is to allocate the *same amount of time* to the activities. For example, jointly folding laundry and watching television for an hour would be measured as an hour of folding laundry and an hour of watching television. The method is easily implemented but has major weaknesses. It does not satisfy the constraint that a day has 24 hours. More detailed descriptions of activities lead to increased number of hours of activities. The method also presumes that the "output" of an activity performed jointly is the same as when the activity is performed solely. This

---

[9] The present discussion is based on Ver Ploeg and others eds. (2000), pp. 23-25.

property becomes a problem when the data are used in valuation of housework.

145. A second approach is to count *only one* of the simultaneous activities; that is to say, in accounting for time spent in a day, only the time spent in the primary activity is counted while the sum of secondary activities may be counted and tabulated separately. This involves a determination of which activity is the primary activity.

146. This second approach has been the one most commonly used in time-use surveys usually because it simplifies estimation and tabulation. As discussed above, however, counting only primary activities in producing statistics on daily totals of time use in different activities would not count many meaningful activities that are likely to be reported as secondary activities (see note 7 on conversation above). In addition, because the method relies greatly on an accurate determination of which is the primary and which the secondary activity, analysis will, correctly or incorrectly, focus on those activities designated as primary even when the secondary activity may also be of interest.

147. A third approach is to create compound activities, that is to say, to define a joint activity as a distinct activity by itself. For example, visiting with the family while eating dinner would be a distinct activity category; similarly, cooking while supervising children would be a distinct activity. The approach is conceptually appealing. However, it may lead to an enormous number of activity categories in the activity classification scheme, although the application may be limited to a selected number of compound activities relevant to the survey objectives.

148. A fourth approach allocates time spent on joint activities on the basis of the *proportion of the time that a group spends on*

the solo activities. This method computes the total amount of time a demographically defined group of people spend on a given activity, on average, and assigns an hour of time spent by an individual jointly performing the activity on the basis for the proportion of the population totals. For example, if teenage girls spend 10 hours a week talking on the phone (as a sole activity) and 20 hours a week watching television (also as a sole activity), giving a ratio of 1:2, then 9 hours jointly spent talking on the telephone while watching television would be allocated as 3 hours on the phone and 6 hours watching television. The advantages of this approach are that the 24-hours-in-a-day constraint is satisfied and that it is a statistical imputation procedure. Critics see no justification, however, for the assumption that simultaneous activities can be divided into distinct activities. Another disadvantage is that this approach also assumes the equality of the "output" from joint activities and that from sole activities.

149.   A fifth approach (*value theoretic measure of time use*) divides time spent in joint activities by the *value* of the outputs produced by the time. For example, if a person is jointly cooking and babysitting and the value of babysitting is $5 per hour and the value of cooking is $15 per hour, then an hour of simultaneously babysitting and cooking would be allocated as 15 minutes of babysitting and 45 minutes of cooking. This approach would satisfy the 24-hours-in-a-day constraint and does not have the weakness of assuming equal outputs for joint and sole activities. It may be a useful framework for allocating simultaneous time use, particularly in valuation exercises for integrating unpaid work into national accounts. However, it poses serious practical obstacles because of the need to measure outputs or values of alternative time uses.

C.   Contextual information[10]

150.   *Activity context* refers to the physical, psychological, social, and temporal features of the environment in which a specific activity takes place.

1.   Importance of studying context

151.   Any activity occurs in time and space and under a set of circumstances that constitute its context. To understand the significance of any activity, one needs to understand the context in which the activity took place.

152.   First, context gives meaning to activities and groups of activities. For an individual, the same activity may be regarded as work or as leisure depending on the context. Likewise, an activity may be viewed one way by the individual and another by the researcher. For example, an individual may see baking as a leisure activity while the researcher may view it as a productive work activity. Eating in a restaurant alone is just that; eating in a restaurant with someone else may be seen as socializing or as a work activity (for example, a lunch meeting) based on the context variables.

153.   Second, in itself, context is meaningful. Scheuch (1972) proposed a more formalized definition of the term "activity". While the notion of activity appears clear enough for common usage, Scheuch recommended the inclusion of additional dimensions, inter alia, whether an activity was primary or secondary; its location; the instruments involved; and the interaction partner. If any of these aspects were to change, Scheuch recommended that a new activity should be recorded. Consider the following example. A person is talking on a

---

[10] The present discussion is primarily based on Harvey and Royal (2000).

cellular phone in the house before leaving for work, then the person maintains the conversation while driving to work in the car, and finally the conversation is continued at the work site. According to Scheuch, these would be considered three separate activities or *episodes*.[11]

154. Third, context facilitates data acquisition by aiding recall. Considering where they are or who they were with helps people put what they were doing into perspective.

2. Defining context variables

155. There are at least two ways of thinking about context variables. First, there are *objective* and *subjective* dimensions. Objective dimensions refer to quantitative factors that have physical or temporal aspects, while subjective ones refer to qualitative factors that measure psychological well-being, for example, tension and enjoyment. Secondly, there are *situationally-determined* context variables and *activity-determined* context variables. The former—for example, location and social contact—are relevant to every activity. The latter—for example, technology used, whether an activity is paid or non-paid, as well as type of shopping, and reading material or television programme viewed—depend on the activity itself. The distinction is important since the collection method will generally depend on whether the variables are situationally internal contextual variables. Externally determined context variables can be captured in columns that offer the same options for each and every activity. Activity-determined context variables differ across activities and hence must be captured as part of the activity or in a column allowing varied response depending on the activity.

---

[11] This theory is the basis for procedures used in delineating activity episodes as discussed in chap. VII.

(a) Objective dimensions

Location and means of transportation

156. *Location* is an important objective situationally-determined contextual variable. There have been various specifications of location ranging from generic variants (for example, home, work, other places, and mode of travel) to more elaborate ones (for example, rooms in the home). Typically, location of activity is recorded by asking respondents where each activity took place. An alternative approach has been to ask where the respondent started and ended the diary day and to code location based on changes of place stated or implied in the diary. As a general rule, if respondents are not travelling, location is given as a generic description of where they are (home, work, school etc.). If they are travelling, location is defined in terms of how they are travelling (car, walking, bus). Trip purpose is typically defined by the destination if one is going to any place other than one's home and by the origin if one is returning home. Hence, when one goes from home or work to a store, the trip purpose is shopping. If one comes home from shopping, the trip purpose is shopping. Likewise, if one comes home from work, the trip purpose is work.

157. The identification of work locations is particularly important for coding activities with respect to paid work. While traditionally paid work time has been adequately captured in a paid work code, what is captured may nevertheless be problematic. First of all, there is no one definition of paid work time (Hoffmann and others, 2000; Drago and others, 1999). One definition of paid work time states that it consists of all time spent at the workplace. Drago and others (1999), however, describe how teachers' work often invades their home and family life, thereby showing the importance of being able to capture paid work at home. Given the increase in telecommuting, it may be more problematic

38

to capture certain activities as paid work if they are not being performed at the workplace. Consider, for example, using a cellular phone to call a business contact: If the activity is performed in the car while travelling from home to school in order to drop off the children, it may be missed as paid work unless provision is made for capturing it—for example, as a secondary activity and with the designation of the recipient or the nature of the call. Examples of codes for location used in various country surveys are included in annex 3.

With whom (social contact)

158. Social interactions are a part of people's lives; hence, most studies include social contact as a source of contextual information. Social contact has been shown to impact on travel behaviour (Harvey and Taylor, 1999). If people work at home, that contact is lost and hence travel is generated to replace it (Harvey and Taylor, 1999). When and where people get together are important dimensions of daily activity and can both impact on activity content and be impacted by it. However, there has been relatively little reporting or analysis of social contact.

159. The nature of social contact and the respondent's interpretation of it have made it difficult for researchers to collect information for this variable. One could spend time with friends, family relatives or spouse. Yet, one could also spend time with friends, family relatives and spouse—all of these interactions occurring concurrently. Problems with the use of the "with whom" coding suggest that certain issues must be clarified. Blanke (1993) observed the need to evaluate these questions:

– Which objectives do we have concerning the use of the "with whom" coding?
– Do people understand the meaning of our text in the same way?

– What kind of available data can we get?

160. Harvey (1993) indicated that reporting of this variable varies from person to person. It may be regarded as "simple presence" or as "carrying out an activity together". Given these differing understandings of the "with whom" coding, it can be difficult to interpret data and make cross-national comparisons.

161. Blanke (1993) suggested the extent of the problems associated with interpreting what is being asked. Respondents were asked to report how they interpret the question, with whom did you spend your time? Twenty-one per cent of the interviewers observed that the respondents understood the question as pure presence in the building, house etc. Another 50 per cent declared that the respondents interpreted it as presence in the same room. These results suggest the ambiguity of the variable. Other problems noted included the distinction among relationships, especially the relationship between work colleagues and the relationship between friends. The same person could be regarded as a co-worker and a friend, depending on the social situation in which he or she is involved at the moment.

162. Stinson (1997) showed how respondents might use multiple interpretations of the "with whom" question if no direction or definitions were given. They generally focused on those persons: (a) with whom they were communicating (for example, performing the same activity at the same time while talking and interacting), (b) with whom they had an intentional or deliberate relationship or (c) who were in the same physical location (for example, in the same area or in the same house). Some reasons given for why someone might be "present" but not "with them" were: they did not know the person; each person was engaged in his or her own activity; one left to go somewhere alone and others just happened to be using the same mode of transportation to

go to their own destinations. This suggests that the question "Who was with you" comprises two separate questions: "Who was present, but not participating?" and "Who was participating?" Thus, it is important to clarify the meaning of the question being asked. No standard codes are available at present for the "with whom" context variable. Examples from country surveys are given in annex 4.

For whom

163. A typical difficulty encountered in classifying activities is producing descriptions of activities that correspond to the boundaries that make sense to analysts—for example, the "general production boundary" that separates non-market work from other non-market activities or the "SNA production boundary" that separates SNA work and non-SNA work.[12] For example, the activity '*care for others*' might be considered a form of non-cash transfer. To study the significance of these transfers, separating "*care for others*" from *self-care*, and distinguishing intra- from inter-household transfers are important first steps. The context variable "for whom" has been found useful in providing information for clarifying these situations. When this variable[13] was first introduced in a national time-use survey, respondents used a four-category variable to indicate for whom their primary activity was performed. These included: (a) for their own household, (b) for another household, (c) for their own household and for another one at the same time and (d) as voluntary work. The study showed that this type of variable contributed to identifying voluntary work activities. While respondents generally found no difficulties in identifying "for own household" activities, there were

difficulties in coding "for whom" when the activities involved moral support and information-sharing. These included such acts as providing consolation, being ready to engage in communication, making suggestions and offering advice.

164. "For whom" or "helping" has emerged as the most important variable for identifying purpose (motivation) of activity for economic accounting. Any time-use survey where key objectives involve the measurement of unpaid work would benefit from the inclusion of "for whom" information. This clarifies whether the work is being done for someone inside or outside the respondent's own household and assists in data coding. It also helps to differentiate work and non-work activities particularly since work is increasingly undertaken in non-traditional places.

165. Surveys that have since implemented a "for whom" variable used categories ranging from 4 to 19 values (see annex 5). The limited country experiences available indicate that one can accurately capture helping activity only by means of situationally determined contextual variables such as helping or "for whom", a diary column that applies to all activities.[14]

(b) Subjective dimensions

166. The *objective approaches* to the assessment of context provide greater analytic power but offer little or no understanding of how respondents perceive their behaviour

---

[12] Production boundaries are further discussed in part five.

[13] This refers to the 1991 German Time Use Study (Federal Statistical Office of Germany, 1995).

[14] The Australian Bureau of Statistics adopted the extra column for the 1997 Time Use Survey. This extra column more accurately identified time spent in supporting adults in other households. The Eurostat experience suggests that a well-designed questionnaire module is better able to capture inter-household transfers. For the 1998-1999 survey, New Zealand used a model where interviewers sought details on "for whom" in a personal interview when the diary had been completed.

(Michelson, 1993). Adding *subjective dimensions* to the typical objective ones for each episode of activity may help to tap into the emotional and psychological side of behaviour. Such dimensions are often less essential to survey objectives of a general-purpose national time-use data collection but may be important in specific applications, especially quality-of-life issues. For example, two aspects that are often studied include how tense people are when performing an activity (*tension*) and how people enjoy what they are doing (*enjoyment*). To establish data for a functional analysis, activities need to be linked with the feelings about them. Glorieux and Elchardus (1999) developed a typology of seven meanings that can be regarded either as a motivation for doing something or as a way of evaluating activities. These seven typologies consist of time spent:

- For the satisfaction of physiological needs.
- For personal gratification.
- As an obligation.
- Instrumentally.
- As a matter of affect or out of solidarity.
- To do one's duty.
- To kill time.

167. It is suggested that subjective dimensions of activities be included in time-use data collections only when the analytical objectives explicitly require such information, as question formulation is complex and the inclusion of the subjective dimension results in an increase in the length of the background questionnaire. Figure 2 provides an illustration of questions capturing the seven meanings of the activities described above.

Figure 2. Questions about different kinds of subjective experiences

In the list below we ask some questions about how you experienced the activities you have described in your diary.

Please indicate if you recognize any of the experiences we ask about. And if so, also indicate with a letter in the diary to which activities this applies.

A. Have you reported any activities that you would not have done had you not been obliged or forced to?

    YES → Indicate with the letter A in the diary
    NO ↓ which activities this applies to

B. Have you reported any activities that you would rather not have done had it not been necessary in order to fulfill daily tasks?

    YES → Indicate with the letter B in the diary
    NO ↓ which activities this applies to

C. Have you reported any activities that you could not skip without a feeling of bad conscience?

    YES → Indicate with the letter C in the diary
    NO ↓ which activities this applies to

D. Have you reported any activities that you just did because there was nothing else to do?

    YES → Indicate with the letter D in the diary
    NO ↓ which activities this applies to

E. Did any of the activities you have reported lead to new social contacts or to better contact with people you already know?

    YES → Indicate with the letter E in the diary
    NO ↓ which activities this applies to

F. Did any of the activities you have reported improve your health or sense of well-being?

    YES → Indicate with the letter F in the diary
    NO ↓ which activities this applies to

G. Did any of the activities you have reported leave you with a feeling of personal growth?

    YES → Indicate with the letter G in the diary
    NO ↓ which activities this applies to

Source: Haraldsen (2000).

(c) Activity-determined context

168. Another important distinction is between *situationally determined* context variables and *activity-determined* context variables. As mentioned above, the former—for example, location and social contact—are relevant to every activity. The latter depend on the activity itself, for example, technology used and paid versus non-paid activities.

Paid versus non-paid

169. A growing interest in determining the extent to which people allocate time to paid and unpaid work activities has been motivated by interest in the use of time-use data for valuating and integrating unpaid work in national accounts. Traditionally, paid work has been associated with activities performed at the workplace. Respondents were simply asked to report the starting and ending time of paid work. However, there is increasing evidence that certain paid work activities are virtually missed unless more details are sought (Harvey, 2000). For example, asking participants to report paid work would help to identify all paid work activities of the self-employed, work that people do outside the workplace and may look like personal activities (for example, reading, using a computer) and any informal activities that are remunerated (Stinson, 1997). The reporting of all paid work activities can provide greater insights into the interaction between work and family life. In addition, reporting work-related activities may help to distinguish non-paid activities that are performed for work—for example, self-employed persons may carry out various activities that are important for their business but are not formally remunerated, such as socializing.

170. Harvey and Spinney (2000a) found, using responses to a "for whom" dimension, that a wide range of activities coded elsewhere were actually related to paid work—for example, coaching, travel by car as a driver and participation in meetings. This suggests that instead of directly asking whether an activity is paid or unpaid (as has been traditionally done), an appropriate formulation of "for whom" categories may be used to capture this information.

Technology used

171. Another variable of emerging interest is the use of technology in performing various activities. The data can be used to assess the impact of new technologies on people's lives—as reflected, for example, in work activities carried out through teleworking or when away from the workplace; use of cellular phones, electronic mail and the World Wide Web. In contrast to the situationally determined context variables discussed above, technology used is an activity-determined context variable, as it varies by type of activity. Typically, the areas where types of technology have been examined in national surveys have been limited to mode of travel (for example, car, bus, train etc), some media activities (foe example, radio and TV) and communication.[15]

3. Data-collection issues related to context variables

172. Key data-collection content issues include the choice of contextual variables to be included and the level of detail for each variable. As seen in the previous section, the first context-related decision that must be made concerns what contextual data to collect (for example, objective and/or subjective dimensions). Optimal collection approaches for contextual variables need to consider the mode of data collection and the features of

---

[15] The 1997 Time Use Survey of Australia captured information on technologies employed in activities pertaining to communication and computer usage.

survey instruments. For classification purposes, it is suggested that the main *situationally determined* and *objective* context variables should be used. These include, as mentioned above, location, "with whom", and "for whom". For the collection of subjective contextual data, the stakeholders should clearly state their needs. Statistical agencies may not be interested in pursuing such information but other stakeholders (for example, time-use researchers, policy makers and private organizations) may be interested.

173. Likewise, users should specify the levels of detail desired. The nature of the questions being asked and the amount of information sought are likely to influence the degree of respondent cooperation, costs, processability (ease of manipulation, handling, coding etc.) usability (relevance to the survey objectives) and flexibility (ability of the data to be used for a wide variety of purposes or in a variety of contexts).

174. The amount of contextual data that can be collected is limited by the capacity and willingness of respondents to provide quality information (Robinson, 1999). Asking more than two or three questions per activity might result in burdensome reporting tasks, and affect the quality of respondent reporting. Asking respondents to report the details of each episode is a demanding task and the reporting of contextual information may have an adverse impact on the level of detail reported (Lingsom, 1979). However, there is currently no definitive answer to the question "how much is too much".

175. Likewise, special difficulties may be associated with the nature of the questions being asked. Asking participants to report time and location of activities may generate certain reactions, such as fear, concern for privacy, memory problems, activity overload etc. Respondents may be less willing to

cooperate and the response rate is likely to suffer (Stinson, 1997).

176. Increasing interviewing time and complex tasks may also lower the survey response rate. Adding questions to each episode may make the reporting task difficult and tedious. Thus, respondents may be less willing to participate in the interview. If, however, it is reasonable to consider the information sought as part of the activity experience, however, this decision may in fact facilitate response.

177. The amount of contextual information collected will definitely impact the study cost in many ways. Quality data can be expensive. However, detailed studies provide so much valuable information that the cost may be justified. The study cost could increase owing to: additional interviewer training; increased interviewing time; increased coding time and complexity; and increased time spent analysing data.

178. However, if activity and contextual codes are clearly defined and captured, there is, in fact, a strong possibility that coding and analysis costs can be reduced by increased reliance on machine coding. It is possible to reduce the number of human coding decisions while increasing the flexibility of coding and analysis. For example, the coder does not need to decide where eating took place and assign an appropriate code, as this can be determined from location.

179. Most national surveys collect contextual data using pre-coded options in 24-hour diaries. Open-ended entries allow more flexibility but may make reporting more burdensome for the respondent, give rise to coding problems, and thus affect the quality of the data. Since contextual data is collected for each activity reported, the issue of whether to use open time intervals or fixed time intervals

is also relevant to context variables. A more detailed discussion of the issues related to data collection is presented in chapter IV.

4. Coding issues

180. The number of coding categories employed will affect the usability and flexibility of the data collected. For instance, it is easier to aggregate data into broad categories than to try to do the opposite. Consider the following example: respondent A reported that her husband, her two children and her father (currently living in the household) were present while eating dinner, while respondent B reported that four household members were present at dinner time. For analysis purposes, it will be possible to identify how much time respondent A spent with the spouse, children or other household members. This detail is lost for respondent B.

181. Cross-national comparisons are simplified when working with *disaggregated data* because data can be aggregated into many comparable activities more easily if there is minimal grouping already existing at the national level.

182. It is thus suggested that the data collected on context variables should be relatively disaggregated.

(a) Coding meaning

183. It is not sufficient to specify a large number of coding categories; in addition, the *meaning* of each category must be specifically defined. Context variables have been coded in various ways, with the number of categories ranging from 2 to 19. Accordingly, the meaning associated with some of the coding terms may also differ. For example, the individuals making up in the "other" category for the "with whom" coding will differ according to the nature of the other available options. "Other" could imply only non-household members or, more broadly, anyone who is not a household member, relative, friend, neighbour, or colleague.

184. Not only do the coding categories need to be clearly defined, the instructions to interviewers and respondents need to be sufficiently clear so that the intended meaning is achieved. A prime example is the need to clarify the meaning of "with whom" in terms of either presence or participation, as discussed above.

(b) Multivariate outliers

185. The addition of several context variables may occasionally lead to ambiguous interpretations. The incidence of multivariate outliers in the data (or odd or unlikely relationships among the study variables) is likely to increase as the number of context variables increases. Taken individually, the options are possible (for example, being in church and swimming) but taken together, they are very unlikely combinations within the normal population. However, care must be taken in evaluating such outliers. For example, an instance of 7 hours sleep at the workplace may be considered a mistake before turning out to be on-call work on a ship. While the data should be checked for consistency with regard to such cases, care must be exercised in "cleaning" the data. Outliers may often be just that. These issues can best be addressed through appropriate interviewer and coder training.

D. Background (covariate) information

186. Survey designers need to carefully consider which covariates—that is to say, the supplementary information about respondents and their behaviour—are to be collected and how they are to be collected in a time-use survey.

1. Analytical framework for background questions[16]

187. From an analytical point of view, people's actions are the crossroad where environmental conditions and personal sentiments meet. Our actions reveal how we adapt to our living conditions. At the same time, they are a manifestation of personal values, attitudes and feelings. On the other hand, what we learn from our actions also affects what we value, believe and like. Likewise, what we do has an impact on our living conditions and environment. This four-way relationship among our actions and our surroundings and personality is illustrated in figure 3. Such information may potentially be captured in time-use surveys.

Figure 3. The social and personal meanings of people's activities

Source: Haraldsen (2000).

(a) The social and geographical environment

188. What people can do is affected both by their resources and by the *social and geographical context* within which they act.

---

[16] The present discussion is primarily based on Haraldsen (2000).

The time they need to buy food is affected by the distance to the nearest grocery store and the transportation available. If they have their own car and plenty of money so that they do not need to look for the cheapest offer, this will probably also have an impact on their shopping activities.

189. In order to understand how people utilize their resources within the environment they live in, we obviously need background information about the resources they have at hand and the environment within which they act. This information is usually collected in a background questionnaire.

190. Questions about the respondents' social and geographical environment can often be answered without asking the respondents themselves, but rather by collecting information from maps and local authorities. When several respondents from the same area are interviewed, for example, it may be preferable for the interviewer to measure the distance from different local facilities to the homes of the different respondents selected, rather than ask each respondent to measure the distance from his other home to the local facilities. The response burden will decrease and measurement will probably be more accurate because of the standardized procedures.

(b) Personal, material and social resources

191. The term "personal resources" refers to non-material skills and qualities like education and health. Material resources include concrete assets like money, cars, houses and household facilities. One's family, friends and workmates are all part of one's social resources (Allardt, 1975).

192. The relationships between personal resources and environmental variables on the

one hand and the activity patterns on the other are not always easy to establish. Even if the resources and the environment of the respondent are mapped and measured in the background questionnaire, we need to know what resources are at hand and what type of environment the respondents are in. This helps us understand what activity options they have in specific situations. Phrased in methodological terms, we often need some *mediating variables*. Location codes or codes indicating different modes of transport should be regarded as specifying such mediating variables. For example, it is only when a person is at home that he or she can use the household facilities that are in the house. Thus, it is also only at home that these facilities can affect the time spent on household activities. If it is known that the respondent has travelled to a friend's house by bus and from there is going somewhere else, the respondent could not possibly have used a car even if he or she owns one. In this last example the options cannot be read directly from the diary, but are inferred from the sequence of travelling. It is possible that the location and travel codes used in time-use surveys should be improved in such a way as to make it even easier to use them as mediating variables (this also illustrates the importance of contextual information in clarifying the nature of reported activities).

193. Health and education are resources intrinsic to the respondent and consequently necessarily impact on his/her activities. Material resources, on the other hand, may have a more complex impact. For example, one cannot necessarily deduce the amount of money at the disposal of a respondent on the basis of what he or she earns. For this and some other material resources, it may be a good idea to ask how much was available on the days covered by activity reports.

194. As discussed in relation to collection of contextual information, the presence of social resources can be measured in the separate social context column "with whom". Hence, the number of family members, the presence of some of these during the day and the social activities recorded all constitute the respondent's social life. If one looks at the social context column from a resource perspective it becomes clear how important it is to record the presence of family members, friends and workmates in time-use surveys.

195. Another even more difficult problem with respect to the relationships among resources, context and activities is to show how different activities affect individual resources and the respondent's environment.

(c) **Values, attitudes and personal feelings**

196. *Values, attitudes* and *personal feelings* are relevant in understanding why people engage in certain activities. There are two main ways this can be conceptualized. In the first approach, known as the causal model, values and attitudes are believed to influence the way in which people behave. In the case of household work, for example, attitudes towards gender roles may have an impact on the actual division of activities within the household.

197. The second approach, referred to as the functional model, asserts that personal feeling may also intervene. In the later approach, activity patterns are established because people derive more pleasure from certain activities than others.[17] This approach has been illustrated in the earlier discussion of subjective dimensions of contextual information.

---

[17] This kind of reasoning illustrates what Robert Merton called causal feedback (Merton, 1967).

198. One important problem within the time-use tradition that can be addressed with the help of this kind of subjective questions is that of the difference between activities and events. The activity records reported in time-use surveys tend to imply that it is what one does that is important and, hence, that doing little signifies an impoverished life. However, even if respondents do not report much activity, they may be taking part in highly meaningful events. One and the same activity may also have totally different meanings depending on where and within which social context it takes place. Thus, questions about the meanings add colour and taste to the neutral reports of activities.

2. Types of background (covariate) questions

199. *Background* (covariate) questions are typically organized into: (a) a personal or individual questionnaire, and (b) household questionnaire.[18] Basic personal characteristics provide the basis for analysing differences in activity patterns by sex, age, marital status, presence of children, education, and labour-force-status. Household composition and size and household income constitute the basic information captured in the household questionnaire.

200. Users' needs should guide which additional covariates are collected. For example, if the key motive for collecting time-use information is to study non-market production, then it is very useful to know something about household stocks of capital (domestic appliances etc.) and about the consumption of market services that substitute for the labour of household members (maids, childcare centres, nursing care etc.). In studying the provision of informal care, it is

important to gather information about the circumstances of this care. Useful information might result, for example, from identifying the informal carers of the frail, aged and people with disability, the disabling conditions of care recipients, the type of assistance required by those patients and the persons providing that assistance. To understand household labour-force participation decisions, it is important to have data on wages, past work experience, and income of household members.

201. It is unlikely that any single survey is going to be able to collect all the covariates that researchers will want or need. Therefore, a time-use survey may need to be linked to other data sets with a wider range of covariates. Another solution might be to add modules to a pre-existing survey or to collect the time-use data as part of a multi-purpose survey.

E. Survey population

202. The survey population of a time-use survey consists of two dimensions—the *persons* or '*population of interest*' and the *time dimension*. The combination of these two dimensions may be envisioned as a grid of points that represent the population of inference of the time-use survey. The first step in any sample design is to carefully specify the units of analysis and the target population of these units for which estimates are required.

Population of interest

203. The definition of the population of interest requires a careful specification of the persons to be represented in the survey. In most regards, the definitional issues are the same as in other population-based household surveys. The geographical area needs to be delineated, decisions need to be made about the inclusion or exclusion of temporary visitors and foreigners staying for longer

---

[18] More detailed discussion and illustrations of background questionnaires appear in chap. IV.

periods etc. Ideally, the *target population* would include persons living in institutions (prisons, hospitals, military bases etc.), the homeless and nomads, but such persons are generally excluded because of the great difficulty of covering them in surveys. Thus, time-use surveys, like most population surveys, are generally restricted to persons living at domestic addresses. However, in countries where the proportion of the population not living at domestic addresses is high, such as countries with large nomadic populations, consideration should be given to extending the survey coverage beyond those living at domestic addresses.

204. Time-use surveys employ a minimum age requirement. This minimum cut-off is primarily determined by the analytical objectives of the survey. Country practices show minimum age ranges from 6 to 15 years. In general, the lower the age-limit that can be employed, the more complete the picture that can be obtained about the time use of the population. From a global perspective, determining a lower age-limit is an issue of some consequence. In many areas of the world, children make a crucial contribution to their family's economic welfare. In many regions, child soldiers are an important military resource. Even in the most wealthy regions of the world, there is a deep interest in the likely outcomes (low educational attainment, low earnings, high rates of poverty, high crime rates) for adults who were deprived as children. However, the feasibility of data collection and the quality of time-use data collected from young people need to be taken into account in deciding on the minimum age-limit.

Time dimension

205. The *time dimension* can be categorized in various ways, for instance in terms of hours, days or weeks. A 24-hour day is widely used as the basic unit of measurement for time-use surveys. It provides a natural cycle of activities and is clearly understood by respondents. In addition, for recall surveys it has the following attraction: respondents are able to remember their activities during the previous day with reasonable reliability.

206. The definition of a day for a time-use survey may be the standard day from midnight to midnight. However, an alternative 24-hour period may be preferred because respondents can more accurately delineate their activities at the dividing points between these periods. Thus, for instance, the day may be defined as the 24 hours from 3 a.m. to the following 3 a.m., if it is assumed that most people will readily recall that they were sleeping at 3 a.m.

207. Defining the population of inference requires specifying the period of time to be represented by the survey. Given the likely cyclical pattern of activities over a year, the time period for a time-use survey is ideally taken to be 12 months. The 12-month period may be a calendar year, or it may be any other 12-month period (for example, from June 1 of one year to May 31 of the following year). While the target population of days for a time-use survey may include all the days in the year, some days may be excluded from the population of days that are sampled for the survey. These exclusions may be decided upon because of practical difficulties in obtaining time-use data from survey respondents for those days and/or because activities on these days are extremely atypical. For example, in some countries, Christmas Day and New Year's Day may be excluded from the survey population. In large-scale time-use surveys, such exclusions should be avoided if possible.

IV. SURVEY INSTRUMENTS FOR COLLECTING TIME-USE DATA

208. Basic time-use data consist of information on *activities*, the *time of the day* they occur (and their *duration*) and *contextual dimensions* of activities relevant to the analytical objectives. These basic data are typically collected and recorded through a time diary or some stylized analogue thereof. Covariates, such as household and personal characteristics, which are also frequently required for time-use analysis, are collected and recorded through household and individual questionnaires.

209. The time diary is the main survey instrument for time-use data collection. In conjunction with determining the content of the diary, a decision has to be made on the type of diary to be used, that is to say, a *24-hour diary* which records the time at which an activity occurs over a 24-hour day or a *stylized version* which typically records only the duration of the activity over a specified period of time, not necessarily a 24-hour day.

210. These decisions are also related to the *mode of data collection* (for example, recall interview or leave-behind) to be used in the survey. Table 1 summarizes the salient design features of 19 national surveys conducted from 1995 to 2001 and illustrates how survey instruments have been combined with the modes of data collection (discussed in chap. V).

A. Survey instruments based on a 24-hour diary

211. A *24-hour diary* provides the means for a chronological and exhaustive recording of all activities of a respondent over a 24-hour day. The 24-hour period may be the standard 12 midnight to 12 midnight day or may start and end at a time considered close to the typical waking time, for example, 4 a.m. The diary allows for recording of activity descriptions (including simultaneous activities if part of the design), their starting and ending times, and the attendant contextual dimensions of the activities. Total time spent on an activity during the day is derived by adding up the duration of each occurrence of the activity over the 24-hour period.

212. Main issues in the design of a 24-hour time diary are the following:

(a) *Activity description*: whether activities are to be recorded verbatim in the diary ("full" time diary) or by selecting from a pre-coded list of activities pre-printed in the diary ("light" time diary).

(b) *Recording of time*: whether the time of day over which an activity occurs is to be indicated by recording actual starting and ending times (open recording or open interval method) or by using fixed intervals of time pre-printed in the diary. When using the fixed-interval method, a further decision concerns the length of the interval.

(c) *Recording of contextual information*: whether context variables are to be recorded as part of the activity description or separately.

1. Describing activities: "full" versus "light" diaries

213. National surveys on time use have employed two types of 24-hour diaries—a full diary and a light diary. The basic difference between the two is the manner in which activity descriptions are recorded. The full

Table 1. Design components of recent national time-use surveys of selected countries

Country	Survey	Type of survey	Survey instrument	Mode of data collection
Australia	1997 Time Use Survey	Independent	Full diary; 5-minute intervals	Leave-behind; 2 diary days
Benin	1998 Time Use Survey	Module of survey on labour, income and social indicators and education	Simplified diary; 62 activities; 15-minute intervals	Face-to-face recall interview; 1 diary day
Canada	1998 General Social Survey Cycle 12 Time Use Survey	Independent	Full diary; open interval	Computer-assisted telephone recall interview; 1 diary day
Dominican Republic	1995 National Time Use Survey	Independent	Full diary; 15-minute intervals	Face-to-face recall interview and observation; 1 diary day
Finland	1999/2000 Time Use Survey	Independent	Full diary; 10-minute intervals	Computer-assisted face-to-face recall interview; 2 diary days
Guatemala	Guatemala 2000 National Survey of Living Conditions	Module of survey on living conditions	Stylized diary; 22 activities	Face-to-face recall interview; 1 diary day
India	1998 Time Use Survey	Independent	Full diary; 60-minute intervals	Face-to-face recall interview; 3 diary days
Lao PDR[a]	1998 Expenditure and Consumption Survey: Time Use Module	Module of expenditure and consumption survey	Simplified diary; 21 activities; 30-minute time interval	Face-to-face recall interview; 1 diary day
Mexico	1998 Survey on Time Use	Independent	Full diary; open interval	Face-to-face recall interview; 1 diary day
Mongolia	Time Use Survey, 2000	Independent	Full diary; 10-minute intervals	Leave-behind and face-to-face recall interview; 2-3 diary days
Morocco	1997/98 National Survey on Women's Time Budget	Independent	Full diary; open interval	Face-to-face recall interview; 1 diary day
Nepal	1998/99 Labour-Force Survey	Module of labour-force survey	Stylized questions for selected activities within labour-force questionnaire	Face-to-face recall interview; total hours spent on specified activities in last 7 days
New Zealand	1998/99 Time Use Survey	Independent	Full diary; 5-minute intervals	Leave-behind; 2 diary days
Nicaragua	1998 Living Standards Measurement Study Survey (LSMS)	Module of LSMS	Stylized diary; 22 activities	Face-to-face recall interview; 1 diary day
Oman	Overall Monitoring of Annual National Indicators Survey, 1999	Module of household expenditure and income survey	Simplified diary; 23 activities; 15-minute intervals	Face-to-face recall interview and self-reporting; 1 diary day
Palestine	Time Use Survey, 1999-2000	Independent	Full diary; 30-minute intervals	Leave-behind; 1 diary day
Republic of Korea	1999 Time Use Survey in the Republic of Korea	Independent	Full diary; 10-minute intervals	Leave-behind and recall interview; 2 diary days
South Africa	Time Use Survey, 2000	Independent	Full diary; 30-minute intervals	Face-to-face recall interview; 1 diary day
Sweden	Swedish Time Use Survey, 2000	Independent	Full diary; 10-minute intervals	Leave-behind; 2 diary days

[a] Lao People's Democratic Republic.

diary is designed for writing verbatim descriptions of activities that are coded later on (or *"after-coded"*) to an activity classification. The light diary, on the other hand, restricts activity descriptions to a comprehensive but necessarily limited categorization of "pre-coded" activities.

"Full" 24-hour time diary

214. The basic format of a *full 24-hour time diary* consists of a column for recording the starting and ending time of an activity and a column for describing the main activity. Depending on decisions on survey content, the diary will include additional columns for recording secondary or simultaneous activities and context variables. Table 2 illustrates these diary elements.

215. When administered in a recall interview (referred to as a *"retrospective"* diary), the interviewer starts by asking "What were you doing at one minute past midnight (or whatever the starting point of the diary is) on (designated diary day)? What time did this

start? What time did this end?" The interviewer then writes the verbatim response and the reported starting and ending times in the diary. Where simultaneous activities are also to be captured, this is followed by asking "Were you doing anything else during that time? What time did this start? What time did this end?" and the response is written in the corresponding columns. To make the distinction between *sequential* and *simultaneous activities*, an additional question may be asked, such as "Did you stop (main/initial activity reported) to do (secondary/additional activity reported)?" The contextual information for the main activity is elicited by asking "Where were you?", "Who was with you?" etc. The remainder of the diary is completed by a similar sequence of questions initiated by the question "What did you do next?"

216. When administered as a leave-behind or "tomorrow" diary, respondents are given instructions to write down their activities and complete the columns in the diary as they go about their day.

Table 2. Time diary with open time intervals

Starting time	Ending time	(1) What was your main activity? (Please record all activities, even if they only lasted a few minutes)	(2) Whom did you do this for?	(3) What else were you doing at the same time?	(4) Where were you?	(5) Who was with you at home, or with you away from home?

Table 3. Illustration of fixed-interval diary format with contextual information

	(1) What was your main activity? (Please record all activities, even if they only lasted a few minutes)	(2) Whom did you do this for?	(3) What else were you doing at the same time?	(4) Where were you?	(5) Who was with you at home, or with you away from home?
0.00					
0.05					
0.10					
0.15					
0.20					
0.25					
0.30					
0.35					
0.40					
0.45					
0.50					
0.55					
1.00					

217.   In the format shown in table 2, starting and ending times are written down. Another option is the use of fixed time intervals that break up the 24-hours into time segments in the diary format as illustrated in table 3 (*open-* and *fixed-interval diaries* are further discussed below). In this case, the diary is divided into rows—with each row corresponding to a time interval and the activity description is written to the right of the figure that approximates the starting time. If the activity lasts longer than one time interval, a procedure to indicate this is devised—such as drawing an arrow down to the approximate ending time.

Light 24-hour time diary

218.   Figure 4 provides an illustration of a light time diary with 22 pre-coded activity categories constituting the sub items (row entries) and 15-minute time intervals constituting the column headings. For this particular example, the 24-hour day starts at 4.00 a.m. The recording of activities is done by marking the time intervals (for example, by drawing a horizontal line) corresponding to the

row of the relevant activity category. In the figure, the activities marked indicate that the respondent was sleeping and resting from 4.00 a.m. to 5.45 a.m., engaged in personal care activities from 5.45 to 6.15 and ate from 6.15 to 6.30.

219.   The main decision point in the design of a light diary has to do with the descriptions and number of categories to include in the list. Experiences indicate that about 30 activities might constitute a practical upper level. Aside from making the diary less manageable and time-consuming, "too many activities may negatively influence the respondent's view over the alternatives and, hence, reduce the chance that all activities will be selected with the same probability, given they are the most adequate" (Rydenstam, 2000).

Full versus light time diary

220.   The choice between a *full* and *light diary* depends on the *analytical objectives* of the survey, available *resources*, *literacy concerns* and international *comparability*.

Figure 4. Illustration of a light diary

Activity categories		04.00-05.00	05.00-06.00	06.00-07.00	07.00-08.00	08.00-09.00	09.00-10.00
Sleeping and resting	1						
Eating	2						
Personal care	3						
School (also homework)	4						
Work as employed	5						
Own business work	6						
Farming	7						
Animal rearing	8						
Fishing	9						
Shopping/getting services	10						
Weaving, sewing, other textile care	11						
Cooking	12						
Domestic work (washing, cleaning)	13						
Care for children/adults/elderly	14						
Commuting	15						
Travelling	16						
Watching TV	17						
Reading	18						
Sitting with family	19						
Exercising	20						
Social visits	21						
Practising hobbies	22						
Other, specify	23						

Objectives

221. Responses resulting from verbatim reporting of activities provide data that can be used for a wide range of analyses within different subject areas. Thus, a relatively broad range of survey objectives may be met. Time diaries with predefined activities cannot serve the same wide range of objectives. An obvious reason is that in this case a substantially more limited set of activities are studied. Further, if the analytical objectives require the collection of data on simultaneous activities and the contextual dimensions of the activities, the full diary is the necessary choice over the light one. Because of the layout of a light time diary, it is not possible to collect these data.

222. If the aim is to focus on specific categories of activities, the predefined activity diary might be advantageous. For example,

this kind of diary has been applied in surveys that focus on specific activities of subgroups of the population, for example, teachers' work activities (Harvey and Spinney, 2000b and Statistics Sweden, 1971). The usefulness of a light diary is also envisioned within the framework of a continuing time-use survey programme consisting of infrequent but comprehensive surveys conducted, say, every 5 or 10 years, and more frequent but less costly and less detailed surveys in between. While the more comprehensive surveys will utilize the full diary, the more frequent surveys, which will be designed to minimize respondent burden, may then use a light diary.

Cost

223. Compared with the open diary approach, the predefined activity diary approach offers a much less expensive way of gathering time-use data. The diary could be

simple and under some conditions, more or less self-instructing. No coding of activities after diary collection is required.

Literacy concerns

224. Moreover, the predefined activity diary might not require the same high degree of literacy in the surveyed population, because it does not require the respondent to write down his/her activities. The literacy problem could be overcome to some extent with the assistance of enumerators/interviewers. In the predefined activity diary, it is sufficient to mark lines in a grid to record the activities, that is to say, the respondent must be able to read if the instrument is self-administered,[19] but he or she is not necessarily required to write.

International comparability[20]

225. As already mentioned, in the open diary approach, respondents describe their activities in their own words. These words and sentences are coded by trained staff to an activity code system. Carefully worked out guidelines support this process. In the pre-coded activity diary approach, the respondents (in recall interview, with the aid of interviewers) mark an adequate predefined activity. Consequently, the respondents must code and classify the activities themselves. The researcher has no insight into this process. Moreover; the fewer activity categories there are in the diary, the more abstract they become, and the greater is the risk that different respondents would classify one and the same activity within different categories.[21]

The risk for this kind of misclassification is presumably smaller when the coding is carried out by trained, cooperating personnel, applying the same activity code system and instructions. With respect to achieving international comparability, the coding process is crucial. Unless there is a common activity classification as well as common definitions, concepts and rules, it is unlikely that the same activity will be classified and coded similarly with a reasonable degree of reliability. It will be difficult for people in different cultures, with different languages, to have a sufficiently uniform perception of a common list of predefined activities without there being a clear explanation of which specific activities constitute a category in the short aggregated list. This problem will be greater for some activities than for others.

2. Recording of time

Fixed versus open interval

226. To record the period of time in the day during which an activity is performed, survey designers have to make one of two choices. The choice is between that of using: (a) *fixed intervals* of time where non-overlapping time segments of uniform length[22], covering the 24-hours of a day are pre-printed in the diary or (b) *open recording* (or *open intervals*) where respondents report start and finish times of each activity. If the choice is to use fixed intervals of time, a decision has then to be

---

[19] If activities could be defined by means of pictures rather than verbal expressions, the required degree of literacy would decrease further.

[20] The present discussion is based on Rydenstam (2000).

[21] The following could serve as an example. Suppose that two of the activity classes in a predefined activity diary are *housework* and *hobbies*. One respondent regards his weekend cooking as an enjoyable hobby: it is leisure for him, hence he classifies the cooking as a hobby. Another respondent regards cooking as housework, and classifies it as such. Thus, the same activity is classified differently. In an open diary, both respondents probably would have described it as cooking, and the coder staff would have coded it as such.

[22] Time intervals are typically taken to be uniform throughout the 24-hour period, although some diaries have been designed with longer intervals for night-time activities.

made on the length of the time interval to adopt. Table 2 provides an illustration of an open interval diary. A fixed interval version of such a diary utilizing 5-minute intervals is illustrated in table 3.

227. Tests comparing fixed interval diaries against open interval diaries have indicated that the open method yields large variations in the quality of data obtained and that data editing and processing are more complicated with the open method. On the other hand, fixed time intervals measure time less precisely than the open method and they are not as well suited to measuring activities of very short duration (for example, interrupting a task to engage in a couple of minutes of conversation; child assistance episodes). If these short-duration activities last less than the time interval specified in a fixed-interval diary, they may end up unreported, as indicated by results that show fixed interval diaries recording a smaller number of activities than open interval diaries.[23]

228. The effect of the type of time interval used on the length of interview time may also be a consideration. For example, it might be expected that fixed interval recording allows for a more systematic way of reporting activities sequentially and thus decreases interview time. Available information, however, indicates that there is no substantial difference in this regard between fixed interval and open recording methods.[24]

229. Choice of an open or fixed interval diary also has implications for the basic unit of analysis provided by the diary (International

Research and Training Institute for the Advancement of Women (INSTRAW), 1995). If an open diary format is used, the activity episode is the unit of analysis. However, if fixed intervals are used, the unit of analysis becomes the time slot. Each can be converted to the other, although it is easier to go from activity episode to time slot analysis. As with any aspect of methodology, the choice of time interval will be determined by the survey objectives and, in particular, by the ways in which the data will be used.

230. Perhaps because the fixed interval method simplifies editing (for example, by minimizing errors related to recording of starting and stopping times) and processing (since record units, for example, are based on fixed time slots) and ensures that the 24-hour-a-day constraint is not exceeded, most time-use surveys that utilize time diaries have implemented the fixed interval method (see table 3, for example). This is true regardless of the mode of data collection, although some studies suggest that the open recording method may be more appropriate for recall interviews, while the fixed interval method may be more appropriate for leave-behind diaries[25]. For a telephone-based interview, however, the preference has been for the open interval method.[26]

Length of fixed time interval

231. If the decision to use fixed time intervals is made, the *length of the interval* becomes critical. Country practices in this regard include 5-, 10-, 15-, 30- and 60-minute intervals with most time diaries utilizing shorter rather than longer intervals.

232. One advantage of short time-intervals is that they conduce to the reporting of short-

---

[23] These results of pilot tests for Finnish, Norwegian, Canadian and American time-use survey methodologies are as reported in Fleming and Spellerberg (1999) and International Research and Training Institute for the Advancement of Women (INSTRAW) (1995).
[24] Results of a pilot study in relation to telephone interviews for a 1986 Canadian time-use survey.

[25] As reported in Harvey and Taylor (2000), p. 265.
[26] This is true for the Canadian surveys and the planned national 2002 American survey.

duration activities to a greater degree than longer intervals do. Since fixed intervals can only approximate starting and ending times of activities (and hence their duration), shorter intervals provide better approximations. With fixed intervals, in general, one or more main activities may be reported as having occurred during the interval; the longer the interval, the greater number of main activities. When this occurs, editing and processing of diaries become more complicated. One complication arises from the need to differentiate between sequential and simultaneous activities. Another arises from the need to allocate non-overlapping starting and ending times to the multiple activities that actually occurred sequentially and not simultaneously.

3. Contextual information

233.   In addition to recording each activity undertaken and the length of time spent thereon, time diaries often record contextual information as well. As discussed in previous chapters, context information can include the place in which the activity was undertaken, who was with the respondent at the time, how the respondent travelled if travel was involved, the person(s) or institutions for whom a particular activity was being carried out, and whether the respondent was being paid for the particular activity. These items of information are included in time diaries not only for their analytical uses but also as an aid to memory recall (for example, questions on location of activity and persons present during the activity are known to aid respondents in recalling activities undertaken) and to assist in the task of activity coding (discussed further in part five).

234.   Issues related to the selection of context variables to be included in a time-use survey were discussed in chapter III. Once the variables have been selected, decisions on how the information is to be recorded need to be

made. There are two basic ways in which this may be achieved. The first method is to include *columns for contextual variables* side by side with the columns on activity descriptions in the time diary. The second method is to obtain the information less directly—for example, as part of the *activity description*. These alternatives are illustrated below for survey instruments applicable to interview and leave-behind modes of data collection.

235.   Table 3 shows a diary layout using the first approach. In this format, the contextual variable questions (columns 2, 4 and 5) are asked and recorded for each main activity. Responses need to be as specific as possible to facilitate accurate coding outside the interview process. This format is straightforward and simplifies recording and coding.

236.   The first format is suitable for collecting contextual information for all main activities—no exclusions. On the other hand, some types of information may be required only for specific types of activities—for example, technology or communication codes pertain only to activities involving communication or computer use; or the "for whom" information may be required only for volunteer- or care-related activities. In this case, the information may be obtained as part of the activity description.[27] For this method, clear instructions need to be given to respondents indicating that such information should be included in their report of activities. In recall interviews, enumerators would need to probe respondents to elicit the needed detail. Compared with the first method, this method

---

[27] Some country surveys have obtained information on all contextual information including location and "with whom" also as part of the activity description. This approach allows for obtaining all such information for both main and simultaneous activities, although this is not the case for the diary illustrated in table 3.

may lead to incomplete or vague responses and to more difficulties in coding the contextual information. One way in which this problem may be minimized is by systematizing the probing questions by including them in the diary. One such format is shown in annex 6 where a series of questions regarding caregiving activities and unpaid activities are fielded after completion of a leave-behind diary.

B. Survey instruments based on stylized questions

237. *Stylized questions* have been widely used to obtain data on time allocated to specific activities. The questions require the respondents to recall the amount of time they allocate, or have allocated, to specified activities of a specified period such as a day, week or year. Variations of the stylized questions are illustrated below:

– Yesterday, how much time did you spend preparing meals?

– How much time do you spend each day preparing meals?

– During the past week, how much time have you spent preparing meals?

– Last week, did you spend any time doing housework including cooking, cleaning, grocery shopping and laundry for your household? If yes, for how many hours?

238. There are two approaches to collecting data on time use using stylized questions. The first approach is typically used in surveys that *target specific activities* and are not concerned with a comprehensive and exhaustive coverage of activities over the specified period of time. For example, a multi-subject survey covering various topics such as paid work, health and education may include a stylized question on

the use of time covering activities related to each of these topics.[28] Or, to improve coverage of unpaid activities, a labour-force survey may include stylized questions on time allocated to a list of these activities.[29] As mentioned earlier, this *Guide* does not deal with the design of such surveys. However, the advantages and limitations of data collected using stylized questions which will be discussed later also pertain to the outcomes of these surveys.

239. The second approach is the use of a *stylized analogue of a time diary*. In this approach, respondents provide information on their time use by assigning their activities to a short list of categories. This listing of activity categories is designed to be as comprehensive and exhaustive as possible (similar to the pre-coded lists of activities in light diaries). Instead of starting and ending times, however, total time spent on each category of activities during the period of observation (for example, a day or week) is recorded. In this approach, total time spent on all activities is constrained to the 24 hours in a day, 168 hours in a week etc. Annex 7 shows a sample page of a stylized diary. As this page illustrates, the stylized analogue of a diary is able to provide information on main activities and duration but generally not on simultaneous activities, the chronological order of activities, number of episodes per activity, or contextual information.

---

[28] This approach has been used in the World Bank LSMS surveys. Living conditions surveys or living standards measurement study surveys (LSMS) have been implemented in many countries using the methodology developed by the World Bank. The LSMS was established in 1980 to explore ways of improving the type and quality of household data collected by statistical offices in developing countries with the goal of increasing use of household data as a basis for policy decision-making (World Bank, 1996).

[29] The 1999 Nepal Labour-force Survey used this approach.

C. Stylized analogues versus 24-hour diaries[30]

240.   As discussed above, a 24-hour diary can be designed and administered in different ways. Regardless of these differences, all 24-hour diaries will produce records of how days or parts of days are spent. The basic data will consist of sequenced sets of activities and provide bases for obtaining measures of durations of the same types of activities in units of minutes and hours covering a day; the diary thus also enables the study of how activities are sequenced. With inclusion of context variables, the 24-hour diary places activities in their spatial, temporal and social contexts.

241.   *Stylized questions* have the advantage of being the least expensive way to measure how people use their time. They can also be used effectively to measure incidence of certain activities, especially those activities that occur infrequently, inter alia, how much time is spent on vacations or home repairs and how many days were spent in the hospital over the previous year. Stylized questions may be preferable for a specific and short time period (with regard, for example, to whether the respondent performed a particular activity yesterday) than questions about usual activities over a day or week (concerning, for example, whether the respondent usually does a particular activity on a weekly or daily basis). Stylized questions have been used to supplement 24-hour diaries to gather information about activities that the diary may not capture (for example, time spent being "on call" for childcare); or information about activities that respondents are unwilling to

report in a diary (for example, drug use); or information for a longer reference period, when the activities in question may be unlikely to occur on a specified day.

242.   However, studies have shown that the answers that respondents give to stylized questions have a high degree of error, that is to say, respondents *underreport* or *overreport* time spent in different activities. There are several reasons for this. First, people may overreport activities that are perceived as socially "good" or acceptable. For example, after comparing stylized analogues with time diaries, Hofferth (2000) concluded that parents, when asked stylized questions, exaggerated the amount of time they spend reading to children and seriously underestimated the amount of time that their children watched television (watching television may be perceived as a "bad" activity).

243.   Another reason why stylized questions may provide inaccurate data is that respondents may have a difficult time recalling what they did over the time period that the question references, especially if the question asks how much time the respondent spent performing a certain activity over the past week (or day, month or year). Respondents may also have difficulty recalling and conceptualizing what a "typical" or "average" week is like in responding to such questions about time-use activity over the week. For activities that take place on a daily basis, such as time spent commuting to work, the respondent may be able to make a much better estimate of the average time spent in the activity over the week. However, for activities that take place on a more variable basis, such as talking on the telephone, respondents may have a more difficult time recalling the total amount of time spent in the activity.

244.   Third, stylized measures of time use do not take into account activities that occur

---

[30] The present discussion is based on papers presented by Juster (2000), Hofferth (2000) and Robinson (2000) in the Workshop on Time-Use Measurement and Research, May 2000, Washington, D. C., as discussed in the report of the workshop.

simultaneously. As a result, these activities may be underreported or overreported depending on whether the respondent thinks the activity simultaneously performed is worth reporting. This may be an important consideration in measuring passive activities like watching television.

245. Although stylized methods typically overestimate time uses, there are some notable exceptions. For example, stylized estimates of time spent on home repairs and alterations "during the past 12 months" may be only about half as large as the cumulative total of home repair and alteration time obtained from four time diaries covering the same 12 months. Hospital stays also appear to be seriously underreported relative to administrative record data for a recall period of six months or more. These underreports from stylized questions are almost certainly due to the length of the retrospective time-horizon (for example, such comparisons are typically relative to one week at the most and not six months or a year). Moreover, most of the activities collected with stylized methods are typically ones that are engaged in regularly, not rare activities, such as home repairs and hospital stays. Also, over a recall period as long as a year, certain activities will not be recalled by respondents.

246. Another disadvantage with stylized questions is that the questions must be worded so that the respondent understands the types of activities for which he/she is asked to report on time use. This means that in stylized questions the activities need to be defined and classified within the question (similar to the requirement in pre-coded light diaries); this entails an extra step, that is not needed for after-coded time diaries.

D. Background questionnaires

247. Time diaries or their analogues are the main instruments of time-use surveys. As discussed in chapter III, however, additional pieces of information are often needed that are as critical to the interpretation and analysis of time use as those already contained in the diary. This supplementary information might include characteristics of either the household or individual household members, as well as information (other than contextual) about specific types of activities. Time-use surveys therefore typically often require administering a household questionnaire and a personal or individual questionnaire in addition to the time diary.

248. The main issue in the design of these questionnaires is the selection of topics and specific data items to be included (see chap. III). Once the content of both types of questionnaires is determined, questionnaire design considerations relating to question formulation, sequence and layout are revealed to be similar to those of a general household survey questionnaire. Design principles used should include considerations of whether the questionnaires are to be *self-completed* or administered through an *interview*. These aspects of design are not discussed in this *Guide*. For illustrative purposes, the background questionnaires used in Australia and New Zealand surveys are included in annex to the *Guide*.

249. The order in which the time diary and *background questionnaires* are administered is an important operational consideration. A main concern is ensuring that the quality of the time-use data is not affected by possible *respondent fatigue* or interviewer effects arising from the efforts expended in providing and recording responses to background questions. Such efforts may occur, for example, if the household and individual questionnaires were completed prior to the recording of diary data. In general, the number of questions asked prior to completing the time diary should be kept to a minimum. Another related operational concern is minimizing the number of visits per

respondent needed to complete all survey instruments.

250.   A possible approach to the issue of sequencing background questions and the order in which survey instruments are administered in an interview-based survey that takes these two concerns into account is described below (Haraldsen, 2000):

−   Respondents should not be burdened with questions related to the social and geographical environment of the household. The enumerator should be charged with collecting this external information prior to the first visit to the sample household.
−   Household roster questions need to be administered at the start of the first visit and before the introduction of the time diary. This information is needed to identify persons selected for the survey. It is also necessary for defining the "for whom" or "with whom" context columns of the diary.
−   Completion of the time diary should immediately follow the household questionnaire. In a recall interview, memory aids such as recording spontaneously remembered events and activities in an activity list, and then filling in the diary on the basis of the activity list and context-based probing may be useful.
−   Hindsight questions about personal feelings, payments and unpaid services might be asked after completion of the time diary (see annex 8 for an illustration of how these types of questions may be included in the time diary).
−   The individual questionnaire is to be completed last. Questions on income, if included, should be last in the sequence.

251.   The approach assumes the inclusion of topics as summarized in table 4 and adopts the principle that, to the extent possible, more questions should be linked to the activities reported and fewer questions should be asked in the separate background questionnaires.

Table 4. List of information and sources of information in time-use surveys

Kind of information	Source of information			
	Externally collected information	Background questionnaire	Time diary	Questions linked to the activity records
Social environment	X			
Geographical environment	X			
Personal resources		X		
Material resources		X		
Social resources		X		
Main activities			X	
Simultaneous activities			X	
Personal values and attitudes		X		
Personal feelings				X
Payments				X
Unpaid services				X
Quality of life			X	X

Source: Haraldsen (2000).

V. SURVEY FRAMEWORK FOR COLLECTING TIME-USE DATA

252. In addition to the survey content and the corresponding survey instruments, the other major components in the design of a time-use survey are *type* of household survey (for example, "stand-alone" or multi-purpose), *mode of data collection* (for example, recall interview, self-reporting, or observation) and *sample design*. The survey framework for time-use data collection is therefore a result of a combination of type of survey, mode of data collection and type of survey instrument. For example, a 24-hour full time diary may be used to collect data through a recall interview in a stand-alone household survey. Replacing the recall interview with a leave-behind diary approach is another option. A survey framework using a multi-purpose survey often involves a light time diary administered through a recall interview (see table 1 for examples of country practices).

253. Decisions on the type of survey framework to be implemented for collecting national-level data on time use depend on technical and operational considerations. Whether or not a continuing household survey programme is in place also affects these decisions. In addition, decisions on the survey framework to be adopted are also intertwined with decisions on the sample design (discussed in chap. VI).

254. The types of household surveys and modes of data collection that may be considered in the design of time-use data collections are described in the present chapter. Advantages and limitations of the various options are discussed to provide some guidance. Countries, depending on their own specific needs and situations, may adopt extremely different yet highly appropriate survey frameworks. Particular emphasis is

given throughout this chapter to the pros and cons of each approach.

A. Type of household survey

255. National data collection on time use has primarily been carried out through either: (a) a *specialized independent* or *stand-alone* household survey; or (b) a *multi-purpose* or *multi-subject* household survey with a time-use component. For either type of survey, data collection has been carried out: (a) on an ad-hoc basis or (b) as part of a continuing survey programme, although in the latter case the survey may not necessarily have been repeated as planned (for example, owing to resource constraints, the survey may not have been conducted or the implementation might have been delayed). On the other hand, countries implementing time-use surveys for the first time usually have done so on an ad hoc basis but with the intention of assessing the feasibility of including one in the regular survey programme.

1. Independent versus multi-purpose surveys

(a) Independent or "stand-alone" time-use surveys

256. Independent (stand-alone) or specialized surveys are those concerned with a single subject or issue. Stand-alone time-use surveys have been implemented historically to deal with such special issues as leisure, housework and valuation of unpaid work in national accounts.

257. The survey instruments have typically used background questionnaires to collect household and individual characteristics and a

time diary to collect time-use information. Specialized surveys collecting time-use information on specific activities (for example, volunteer work, recreational activities, childcare) have also been carried out at the national level. This type of survey, however, is not discussed further in this *Guide* as its planning and design issues are similar to those of general household surveys.

Advantages

258. The fact that specialized surveys permit concentration on a single subject in the course of data collection is important in cases where a great deal of detail is needed or where the subject matter is highly complex or covers new and unfamiliar ground, such as time allocation. Decisions on survey instruments, field operations and data-processing requirements are focused on the specific data quality and analytical requirements of time-use data. Respondents are less likely to become confused and exposed to "respondent fatigue" in a specialized survey with a highly trained interviewer than in an operation where the questioning deals with a wide range of subjects. An independent time-use survey also permits the optimization of sample designs (see chap. VI) from the standpoint of a single subject, unlike multi-subject surveys.

Limitations

259. The relatively high costs of an independent time-use survey is often cited as its main limitation. In recent years, developed countries have increasingly found it difficult to obtain resources for a stand-alone time-use survey. Resources are often mustered by involving different government ministries and stakeholders, leading to a wide range of analytical needs. As a result, one trend has been to implement time-use data collection as a module in an existing continuing survey (a basic variant of a multi-purpose survey) that

expands the database for analysis and spreads the costs over the two data collections.

(b) Multi-purpose survey with a time-use component

260. Time-use data may be collected as part of a *multi-purpose* or *multi-subject survey*. There are two basic ways in which this can be done. The most common format uses a *modular approach*, that is to say, each subject-matter area has its own survey instruments and specific procedures but the operations are integrated and the different surveys share a core sample. A second type of format—the integrated approach—involves the use of an integrated questionnaire for all areas of subject matter.

261. In surveys that have implemented the modular approach, all three types of diaries have been used; the most common, however, has been the *light* time diary. The number of modules has ranged from two to four—typically, the time-use module is combined with either a labour-force survey or an income and expenditure survey where the latter survey is the core or main module and time use constitutes a "rider" module. In this case, the overall survey design is based on the requirements of the core module. Integration of operations usually involves utilizing the same set of interviewers and fielding the various questionnaires for a sample area over the same period (see chap. VII for further discussion.) Coding and processing activities are also closely coordinated. As further discussed in chapter VI, all surveys may share the same sample but there are other sample design options.

262. Most of the recent time-use data collection using the integrated approach has been implemented as part of a "living conditions survey" which covers a wide range of social, economic and demographic topics

(see footnote 28). Typically, individual stylized questions on time spent in activities related to various topics (for example, education, labour force and health) are integrated in the corresponding section of the questionnaire. A simpler version of the integrated approach consists of a single topic survey, such as a labour-force or a health survey, in which stylized questions about time spent on related activities are asked.

Advantages

263. Combining data collection on time use in a multi-purpose survey can produce efficiencies in data collection and substantially reduce costs. This is especially true when this approach is viewed in comparison with conducting a series of independent surveys covering the same range of subjects. More efficient use is made of survey samples and field and processing staff. Travel time and costs are also much lower.

264. Also, the combination or integration of topics provides the means for jointly analysing the time-use data with the other data—possibly at the individual and household level or at least at the area level or for comparable demographic or socio-economic groups. This opportunity to cross-classify the different variables measured in the integrated surveys for the same households and individuals may be achieved more efficiently relative to increasing the number of data items in the background questionnaires of a stand-alone survey. This is especially true for analysis variables such as personal and household income and expenditures and labour-force characteristics for which data-collection vehicles have been developed.

Limitations

265. A principal limitation of multi-subject surveys is the potential length and complexity of the survey operations as well as potential

delays in data processing which have cost and quality implications. A key issue is that of response burden. Each data-collection undertaken individually places demands on the time and energy of sampled members of households and in combination these demands may become too great. There is a significant risk that increased burden will result in higher levels of non-response and lower data quality from those who do respond. This issue is of particular salience for time-use surveys since, of themselves, these surveys place heavy demands on respondents: the time-use data needed for analysis are extensive and not simple for respondents to report. Respondents must make considerable efforts if they are to report time-use data accurately. Response burden is therefore a major factor to be addressed when considering combining a time-use survey with another survey. For example, more training and supervision of enumerators are necessary to minimize non-sampling errors and to conduct relatively lengthy interviews efficiently.

266. Issues of compatibility may also arise and the compatibility of the different areas of subject matter need to be carefully assessed; and to the extent that the different areas of subject-matter have different requirements, compromises need to be made. These issues include, among others:

–   *Operational feasibility of combined data-collection procedures in the modular approach.* The flow and sequence in which each area of subject matter is addressed during interview procedures affect data quality. In addition, varying reference periods and designated days need to be synchronized. Callback schedules and supervision also need to be coordinated.

–   *Consistency of populations surveyed.* It is possible that the core survey and the time-use module may have different survey populations. For example, a labour-force survey may cover only the working age population (for example, aged 15 years or over), while a time-use survey may need to cover time use of children.

— *Suitability of a common sample design.* Certain types of designs may be more efficient than others for certain kinds of subject matter. When different subjects are combined, some compromises will generally be needed which may not be optimal for any one subject (see chap. VI for further discussion).

267. Limitations of the integrated approach are those related to the use of stylized questions. When the survey covers only specific types of activities and does not account for the 24 hours in a day, the range of analysis possible is restricted and so this approach will not be applicable for all types of survey objectives.

2. Continuing versus ad hoc surveys

268. Both independent and multi-purpose surveys on time use may be planned and/or conducted either as ad hoc surveys or as part of a continuing survey programme.

269. If the statistical office is implementing a continuing household surveys programme then decisions regarding the frequency with which time-use data are to be collected, the scheduling or timing of the enumeration and even the sample design for the survey should consider the features of the existing programme. This would be especially critical when available resources and skills for statistical work are limited. For example, where the survey programme calls for a considerable variety of data, the multi-subject approach may be more appealing compared with a specialized survey. On the other hand,

an ad hoc specialized survey approach may be preferred in the case of a complex subject like time-use surveys of which are not readily integrated with other surveys when the survey is being conducted for the first time. This approach simplifies planning and operational considerations and facilitates processing and timely release of results.

270. While ad hoc surveys, in general, have a role in meeting immediate specific statistical needs, the varied and encompassing uses of time-use data call for the establishment of a continuing database and time series on the subject. Ideally, this continuing programme should be integrated with the overall household surveys programme of the national statistical system[31]. Or, at the very least, the survey framework design should have features of a continuing data-collection programme rather than an ad hoc perspective. There are different ways in which this may be achieved; one suggestion is to collect time-use data using a combination of a few comprehensive surveys spaced over long intervals of time (for example, 5- or 10-year intervals) and some more frequent surveys in between these intervals that cover a restricted number of activities that add up to complete activity coverage over the years (Haraldsen, 2000).

271. A continuing time-use survey programme may also be in the form of a longitudinal or panel study. This would entail successive surveys of the same units over time. Aside from providing measures of change that are not available from cross-section data, there is some evidence that longitudinal time-use data are of higher quality than cross-sectional data. Juster (1985) reports, for example, that respondents who provide data during the initial wave of the panel survey and drop out in the

---

[31] The time-use surveys of Canada and Australia illustrate how time-use data collection can be integrated with the ongoing household surveys programme.

next appear to have lower-quality responses than those who remain. Also, there appears to be panel learning in the sense that the later interview waves appear to have higher quality than earlier ones. On the downside, the attrition rate in a panel survey may become high enough to affect the representativeness of the sample; and respondents who are persuaded to stay on may reluctantly do so but provide less accurate reports.

B.   Mode of data collection

272.   Collecting the data on time use from survey respondents, has traditionally been achieved through three main modes: (a) recall interview, (b) self-reporting and (c) direct observation.

273.   In the self-reporting approach, the respondent personally records the time-use information on the survey instruments while in both the recall interview and direct observation approach, recording is done by someone other than the respondent. In the recall interview, the respondent is asked to report about time use in the recent past—usually the past day, past two days or past week. In the direct observation approach, the time-use information pertains to the current or ongoing period of observation. Depending on the reference period specified in the survey design, the self-reporting approach can provide information for either a past or an ongoing period of time.

1.   Recall interview

274.   One way of administering time-use diaries—whether 24-hour full diaries, light or stylized diaries—is by interviewing respondents and asking them about their time use during a previous period (yesterday, the last seven days etc). Respondents and interviewers may be face-to-face or the interview may be conducted over the telephone.

275.   The main issue for recall data is that of memory recall errors—in other words, respondents may not be able to recall accurately what they did and when they did it. Three validity studies (Robinson, 1985) point to a strong correspondence between what people in the aggregate report in a recall interview using the 24-hour diary (retrospective diaries) and the apparent distribution of their behaviour using methods with greater presumed validity but higher implementation costs. These studies indicate that retrospective diaries may underestimate telephone conversations and may overestimate both time spent shopping for groceries and other necessities and time spent visiting with friends. They further indicate that, in general, systematic sources of bias (that is to say, over- or underreporting of an activity) do not exist in the 24-hour diaries employed to measure time use. Nevertheless, two possible sources of such bias were said to warrant more information—overreporting or underreporting of activities on the basis of their social desirability and underreporting activities that involve only fleeting amounts of time or attention.

276.   Respondents may tend to project socially desirable images of themselves when they answer survey questions (*normative editing*); in time-use surveys, this tendency may account for the overreporting of participation in socially desirable activities and for the underreporting of those that are deemed undesirable. However, this type of possible bias generally shows up to a very minimal degree and for limited types of activities (for example, activities related to biological functions; intimacy; illegal or illicit activities) in 24-hour diaries, possibly because of the neutral way in which respondents are asked to report activities as well as the internal consistency check imposed by the 24-hour constraint on the total time devoted to all activities in a diary (Robinson, 1985).

277. Examples of activities that may be underreported in diaries include those that occur very quickly such as combing one's hair, opening doors, looking for something, and answering a short phone call. While such bias might arise when using 24-hour diaries, it is less compared with that of "beeper" estimates and random-hour diary entries.

278. The measurement problem presented by recall error also relates to sampling time and, particularly, to the use of designated days. A question of interest, for example, is what length of recall period is possible without significant deterioration of quality. This issue is discussed in chapter VII. Below, two approaches to recall interviews, the *face-to-face* and *computer-assisted telephone* recall interview, are described, as well as the pros and cons of each approach.

(a) Face-to-face recall interview

279. In the recall interview approach, respondents are interviewed about their activities over a previous time period. A typical procedure when using a time diary is to visit the sample household one day after the designated day or days (see chap. VII for the discussion on field operation procedures) and administer the background questionnaires as well as the time diary.

Advantages

280. Data collection through face-to-face interviews with survey respondents still represents the most common technique in time-use surveys and often the most viable approach in countries with low literacy rates and in the absence of communication facilities that would allow for telephone interviewing. The face-to-face interview usually achieves higher cooperation and response rates. In highly complex fields or involved multi-

subject undertakings, this may be the most feasible alternative even where literacy is high.

281. Because of the opportunities for detailed probing during the interview process, the face-to-face approach provides more reliable data relative to self-reporting through leave-behind diaries on simultaneous activities and context variables. The 24-hours-per-day constraint in the reporting of activities is also readily validated.

Limitations

282. In general, face-to-face interviews are relatively more costly owing to the need for more manpower, extensive training and close supervision of data collection. Face-to-face recall interviews are prone to recall error, as discussed above.

(b) Computer-assisted telephone recall interview

283. Computer-assisted telephone interviews are the second main approach to recall interviews. So far only two countries, Denmark and Canada,[32] have used this approach to collect time-use data in a national survey. In a computer assisted telephone interview (CATI), respondents are asked to recall their activities over a past 24-hour period; interviewers follow on-screen prompts to ask the questions in a retrospective time diary. The CATI software allows validation of answers (activities, codes for contextual information) while an interview is ongoing so that the interviewer is notified when a value given by the respondent falls out of a valid range of answers.

---

[32] CATI interviews were conducted in Denmark in 1997 and in Canada in 1992 and 1998. This discussion is primarily based on the experience of Canada in computer-assisted telephone interviews.

Advantages

284.   Experience from the Canadian General Social Survey and its module on time use shows that CATI is a mode of data collection that generally has a reasonable cost per interview, a high response rate relative to self-completed mail-back questionnaires and is suitable even for multi-purpose surveys.

285.   Cost is the single biggest advantage of telephone interviewing over other modes of data collection. Telephone interviewing costs less than personal interviewing as neither travelling time nor travel expenses have to be paid; and because interviewers take less time to complete an interview over the phone, a smaller field force is required for the same achieved sample size. Control and monitoring of interviews are considerably easier than in a field operation.   Collection costs are thus considerably lower than those incurred through having interviewers visit dwellings. Another source of cost reduction is the random digit dialling (RDD) sampling technique which reduces the sample design costs.[33]

286.   The immediate feedback mechanism for validating data provided by the CATI software improves data quality.   Automated coding of activities, which also takes place during the interview, speeds up the processing cycle.

Limitations

287.   Telephone interview as a mode of data collection is clearly not practical for areas where many households do not have telephones. Even if these percentages are low,

households without phones are likely to be concentrated in certain population groups (for example, low-income groups, isolated rural populations, and people with disabilities) so that excluding them from the survey may impact on the representativeness of the results. Depending on the objectives of the survey, alternative means of contact may need to be found for these groups of people.

288.   Recording of secondary or simultaneous activities in a time-diary format has not been successfully implemented through telephone interviews.   In addition, collecting data for more than one day per person or for more than one person per household has yielded low response rates (Statistics Canada, 2000b).

289.   Lists of telephone numbers as sampling frames and use of RDD limit the types of sampling design that may be implemented. For example, if the time-use survey objectives call for oversampling certain ethnic groups in the population, then the technique cannot easily provide for this type of selection.[34]

290.   A potential problem in using CATI for time diaries stems from the fact that interviewers may be permitted to exercise considerable discretion with respect to classifying activities while the interview is in progress which may give rise to large variations in the classification of similar activities by different interviewers.

291.   Response rates for telephone interviews tend to be lower than for face-to-face interviewing. Two possible reasons are that respondents seem to find it easier to refuse to participate over the phone; and that new technologies, such as answering machines,

[33] There are, of course, the additional resources expended owing to the development of the computer-assisted interviewing software but within the context of a continuing household survey programme such as the General Social Survey of Canada these costs are eventually "recouped".

[34] The 1998/99 Time Use Survey of New Zealand called for over-sampling Maori to obtain robust estimates of the time use of Maori people.

which enable people to screen their incoming calls, allow them to avoid answering surveys.

292. Telephone interviews also rely on respondent recall of activities and would therefore have the same limitations in this regard as face-to-face recall interviews.

2. Self-reporting by respondents

293. The usual way in which respondents are asked to provide self-reports of their time use is by asking them to complete a *"current"* or *"tomorrow"* diary—that is to say, to fill out a diary over the course of the day. A variant of this is one where respondents are asked to *self-accomplish retrospective* or *"yesterday" diaries*—that is to say, in place of a recall interview, diaries are given to respondents to be completed. Another type of self-reporting is the *experience sampling method* (ESM). Although ESM has not yet been used in national time-use surveys, it is included in the present discussion to highlight its strengths and potential in obtaining information on time use for some types of analysis and as a method for evaluating results of the other modes of data collection.

(a) "Leave-behind" current diaries

294. In the *leave-behind* or *tomorrow* diary approach to data collection, the time diary is given to respondents to complete on an assigned day (or days) as the assigned diary day progresses. The diary is then either collected and reviewed by the enumerator or mailed back to the statistical office. Prior to leaving the diary with the respondent, the enumerator typically interviews the respondent to administer the survey background questionnaires and to orient the respondent to the survey and the diary.

Advantages

295. The leave-behind diary approach is suitable for populations with high literacy rates and may be considered less intrusive by respondents. It also provides a fairly straightforward procedure to be followed by people who run their day by clock time.

296. Leave-behind diary data are of somewhat higher quality than data from recall interviews, but the difference is something in the order of 10 per cent (when measured by number of activities reported). Thus, survey users and designers need to decide whether this justifies a cost difference which may be of the order of 3 or 4 to 1.[35]

Limitations

297. The leave-behind diary approach is not feasible for populations with low literacy. For this reason, some surveys have adapted a combined recall interview and leave-behind diary approach.[36]

298. The data-collection costs may become greater relative to recall interviews because an orientation interview for the study must usually be given to the respondent prior to leaving the diary and a follow-up interview may also be needed after each diary day is completed so as to clarify the answers or fill in missing information. In a recall interview, a single interview would be needed to achieve both purposes.

---

[35] However, better interviewing techniques (for example, interviewer "feedback" techniques which give respondents positive reinforcement when they report activities with the appropriate level of detail and context, and negative reinforcement when activities are reported without an appropriate level of detail; and probing for further information about activities) may produce, better-quality data than leave-behind diaries (Juster, 1985).

[36] In the 1998 Survey on Time Use of the Republic of Korea, this combined approach was also used after pilot tests showed that the elderly population preferred the recall interview (Schon, 1999).

299. Data quality may be affected if respondents are asked to complete more than one diary day: the consistency in recording activities may diminish in time or because they become aware of the nature of their activities, they may change their daily routines (Harvey and Taylor, 2000).

(b) Experience sampling method (ESM)

300. In the *experience sampling method* (ESM)[37] for collecting time-use data, survey respondents are given a pager, beeper or programmable wrist watch that is either pre-programmed or randomly activated to produce a "beep" or "vibration" several times a day. When respondents are beeped, they are asked to fill out a self-report concerning what they were doing at the time and the various aspects of the activity (for example, who they were with; how they felt during the activity; what they were thinking about at the time of the beep). A sample self-report form is shown in annex 9.

301. The study may be designed so that the respondent is contacted several times during the day and may cover a day, a week or longer. The number of beeps per day and the length of the observed period are determined by research objectives, subject to the limitations of privacy, interference in daily life, and the respondent's attention capacity.

302. ESM studies have typically been conducted to understand experiential, cognitive and motivational aspects of activities. Much of the original research was psychological in orientation and focused on analysis of the qualitative aspects of the daily life of varied populations (for example, workers, adolescents, retired adults) as evidenced, for example, by leisure, freedom, loneliness, anxiety etc. Current interest in the

method arises from its use for studying organizational behaviour in the workplace—including relationships among perceived progress towards goals, skills, task enjoyment etc.—and for studying relationships among the use of time, time pressure, chronic stress, and mental and physical health.

303. Although these studies have also been used to estimate time spent in different activities, the ESM approach typically does not have the goal of *completely* accounting for an individual's time use over the 24 hours of a day.

Advantages

304. The strength of the experience sampling method is that it provides contextually specific information about daily activities (for example, motivational, cognitive and emotional aspects of human behaviour; behavioural and experiential dynamics of interpersonal relations etc.) that cannot be captured in a comparable manner through recall interviews or retrospective diaries and current diaries. ESM could be thus used to cross-validate data produced from time diaries and stylized questions.

305. A methodological advantage, relative to recall interviews, is that since activities are recorded soon after the beeper signal is sent, recall error is not a concern. Responses may also be less susceptible to normative editing (that is to say, overreporting of activities deemed to be socially desirable or of interest to the research) because respondents are asked to immediately record what they were doing and hence have less time to construct an "acceptable" response. Furthermore, because the random beep method is more free-form and respondents are often encouraged to express how they feel during the activity, respondents may feel less pressure to record only normatively sanctioned responses and hence may give more genuine responses.

---

[37] The present discussion is based on Zuzanek (1999).

Limitations

306. ESM studies are intrusive and prone to self-selection bias since they place a severe response burden on respondents. Because of the hardware required and the contact strategy involved, experiential sampling methods for collecting time-use data are more expensive than other modes of data collection and it would, therefore, be unlikely to be the main mode for a national survey on time use.

3. Observation approach

307. In *observational studies*, an individual's daily activities are directly observed and recorded by a third person (for example, a researcher or survey enumerator). The recording of activities may be done by the enumerator in the presence of the respondent or, more discreetly, via observational rooms, cameras and other electronic devices or even by "shadowing" (Ver Ploeg and others, eds., 2000, p 45, para. 3) the respondent. Anthropological and ethnographic studies have long used this approach in studying different cultures, particularly in developing countries (International Research and Training Institute for the Advancement of Women (INSTRAW), 1995, pp. 75-78). The approach has also been applied to capture information in restricted settings such as hospitals and classrooms or for particular subgroup behaviour (for example, that of children, students) (ibid., p. 74, para. 4).

308. The period of observation in observational studies may be *continuous* or *random*. In the continuous observation approach, the enumerator observes the respondent for a fixed period of time (for example, an hour, a morning, a day or longer) and records each activity as it occurs along with any contextual information required by the study (ibid., p. 75, para. 2). An alternative to the continuous approach is the random spot approach where respondents are observed at randomly selected points in time (ibid., p. 77, para. 3).

Advantages

309. The key advantage of collecting data on time use of individuals through direct observation derives from the fact that this approach makes it possible to extract sets of rich contextual information about the activities being observed.

Limitations

310. A main limitation of direct observation is that it is intrusive and, because respondents know that they are being watched, they may change their behaviour for the benefit of the observer.

311. At the operational level, observational studies are expensive, making extensive demands on both time and financial resources. Thus, data on fewer households or on less of their total time may be collected using this method compared with an interview. In an interview approach, for example, enumerators may be able to collect information from more than one person per household and several households in a day. This would not be possible in the direct observation approach which is more time-consuming: most likely, the enumerator would be able to follow only one person over the course of a day. There are other operational constraints on observational studies. For example, for practical reasons the time period for which data can be collected may have to be less than 24 hours; typically observation studies cover only daylight or non-sleeping hours. One obvious result would be overrepresentation of activities performed during the observation period and under-representation of those performed during other hours of the day.

312. Mainly owing to the operational constraints, the observational approach has not

been used as a main mode of national data collection on time use. It has been applied and may be considered in settings and populations where recall interviews or self-reporting may yield unreliable results, for example, when respondents are illiterate or have no sense of clock time. The approach has been used in combination with recall interviews in a national sample[38] as well as in small-scale studies to supplement data from diaries. In addition, the approach may be useful for validation studies of time-use data collected through the other methods.

C. Survey frameworks: illustrative examples

313. The combinations of survey instrument and mode of data collection that have so far been demonstrated to be feasible for national-level or large sample-data collection are summarized in table 5.

314. Most national surveys conducted between 1995 and 2001 were independent surveys, utilizing the full-24 hour diary. In the less developed countries, information was mainly collected through a face-to-face interview or an interview combined with a leave-behind diary approach. The leave-behind diary approach was a common mode of data collection in more developed countries. The telephone interview has been used only in the Canadian time-use surveys and in Denmark.

---

[38] A combination recall interview and direct observation approach was used in the 1995 Dominican Republic Time Use Survey. A household was visited up to a maximum of four times a day. During each visit, the enumerator conducted a recall interview to record activities engaged in when the enumerator was not around and a one-hour direct observation study of the activities currently being undertaken by the respondents. In a pilot study, this method was found to be effective in rural areas but not in urban areas (International Research and Training Institute for the Advancement of Women (INSTRAW), 1995).

315. A few multi-purpose surveys were implemented in both developing and developed countries. In developing countries where a multi-purpose survey was used, a time-use module with a light diary using a face-to-face interview was usually the chosen method of data collection. In developed countries, the time-use components were attached to a regular household survey with the full diary as the survey instrument.

316. As discussed above, the range of options for time-use data have different implications in terms of cost, ease of management of operations, data quality and degree of detail of the data collected. Countries planning a national time-use survey thus need to assess the various options in light of available financial and human resources and the existing statistical infrastructure. While there are fixed overhead costs associated with any survey, the variable costs associated with specific survey designs can be minimized. This can be done not only through careful planning and selection of appropriate instruments and tools for the survey but also by adopting a continuing or integrated household survey programme philosophy. In this way, short-term survey expenditures become long-term investments in staff training and development, software, raising the statistical literacy of the population, infrastructure, and institutional-building.

317. Level of staff capability, the social, demographic and economic characteristics of the survey population, transportation and communication facilities and geographical factors influence the level of complexity of survey operations.

318. Data quality is partly related to cost (for example, of better training, close supervision, higher wages consequent to hiring enumerators with better qualifications, incentives for respondents to increase response rates). Different survey instruments and

modes of data collection provide different levels of data quality and the survey designer would need to determine an acceptable level of quality. For example, Juster (1985) describes choosing between the use of the recall interview and the leave-behind approach as involving a trade-off "between the higher quality per unit of leave-behind diaries (which may have to involve a personal interview and always require a follow-up interview), and the higher quality of a recall diary survey that results from the larger sample size obtainable at the same total cost".

319. In respect of choosing a method for measuring time use, the analytical purpose of the study should be the guiding principle. This applies as much to issues of acceptable levels of error as it does to the specific objectives of the survey. Thus, the choice of survey framework also relates to the level of detail and the kind of information provided by virtue of the choice of instrument and mode of data collection.

320. Advantages and limitations of the different framework components for time-use data collection are essentially known. What may be of further use is knowledge on how multiple options may be applied in a single study so as to exploit the individual strengths and marginalize weaknesses so as to better understand time use. For example, it will be useful to know which stylized questions can be used in tandem with time diaries to save survey costs. Understanding the methodological underpinnings of these methods used in tandem is an important area of research. In addition, if certain methods are known to produce biases in reporting, research could be conducted to measure the extent of the bias. If the bias can be determined, then less expensive methods of collecting data may be used despite their biases, because adjustments can be made to correct them (Ver Ploeg, and others, eds., 2000).

Table 5. Illustrations of national time-use survey frameworks

Type of household survey	Mode of data collection	Survey instrument			
		Full 24-hour diary	Light diary	Stylized diary	Stylized questions
Independent or stand-alone	**Recall interview**				
	Face-to-face	X	X	X	X
	Telephone interview	X			
	Self-reporting				
	Leave-behind or self-complete	X	X		
	Experience sampling method				
Multi-purpose	**Recall interview**				
	Face-to-face	X	X	X	X
	Telephone interview				
	Self-reporting				
	Leave-behind or self-complete	X	X		
	Experience sampling method				

VI. SAMPLE DESIGNS FOR TIME-USE SURVEYS

A. Standard considerations in sample design for time-use surveys

321. As with any survey, the sample design for a time-use survey needs to satisfy the survey objectives, to take into account the mode of data collection and the fieldwork constraints, to be efficient in terms of cost and the precision of the survey estimates, and to be readily implementable in practice.

322. The sample designs for different national household surveys within a country often have a broadly similar structure, although they differ in detail according to the specific needs of a particular survey.[39] In most countries, a *stratified multi-stage sample* design is used. For example, in developing countries, the *primary sampling units* (PSUs) are often the *enumeration areas* (EAs) used for the last census. In essence, a sample of EAs is selected, listings are made of the households in the selected EAs, and samples of households are selected from the listings (with appropriate modifications for very small and very large EAs). If the unit of study is the individual, either all individuals in selected households are included in the survey, or a sample of one or more individuals is selected; if the unit of study is the household, survey data are collected on the sampled households. A stratified multi-stage sample design of the type used for other household surveys is in general suitable for a time-use survey, although some modifications may be required for efficient data collection.

323. The issues of sample design for the purpose of selecting persons and households for a time-use survey are the standard ones for any population survey. In this regard, no precise prescriptions can be given since the choice of sample design is highly dependent on local conditions, resources, available sampling frames, and the specific objectives of the survey. The discussion in this *Guide* therefore mainly aims to raise some special issues that need to be considered in designing a sample for a time-use survey and provide some general guidance.

324. The main complexity of sample design in time-use surveys is encountered when incorporating the time dimension in the design. Most household surveys collect data that relate to a specific point or period of time or that are assumed to change little over the time period of data collection. In time-use surveys, however, the estimates of interest are not for the activities that people engage in during a particular day or week, but for a longer period of time, typically a year. Since people's activities can vary markedly by day of the week and season of the year, time-use surveys need to ensure that the sample design provides a suitable representation of the time period for which estimates are required.

325. The methods employed to satisfy this requirement must be ones whose implementation is feasible in a large-scale survey within the constraints that apply in the given country. Different methods may be

---

[39] Readers interested in the general literature on the construction of national household survey sample designs are referred to Kish (1965). Recommendations on national sample designs for developing countries for specific international survey programmes are provided by the World Fertility Survey (1975); Scott (1992) for the World Bank Social Dimensions of Adjustment Integrated Surveys; Macro International, Inc. (1996) for the Demographic and Health Surveys programme; and the United Nations Children's Fund (UNICEF) (2000) for UNICEF Multiple Indicator Surveys.

needed depending on the mode of data collection, the nature of the interviewer field force (for example, whether it consists of resident or travelling interviewers)[40] and the ease of travel (which may differ for different parts of the country). As with any survey, the sample design for a time-use survey should be developed as an integral part of the overall survey design. As a result, different sample designs will be suitable for different circumstances.

326.   The chapter amplifies on the definition of the population of inference for a time-use survey. It also describes the different units of analysis in time-use surveys (namely person/days, persons, and households) and the requirements that the sample design must be fulfilled in order to undertake analyses of these units. The chapter discusses how days should be sampled and how many days per sampled person should be selected in order to give appropriate representation of all days in the time period. With regard to the sampling of households and of individuals within households, the discussion is mainly restricted to the special considerations that apply with respect to stand-alone or independent time-use surveys. The discussion includes issues of sample size and the allocation of a multi-stage sample for a time-use survey across the stages of selection. Since time-use data are sometimes collected jointly with data on other subjects, the sampling issues involved in incorporating time-use data in a multi-purpose survey are also considered.

---

[40] One consideration in the design of field operations has to do with whether the interviews will be conducted by a team of interviewers who travel from one sample PSU to another or by interviewers who are assigned to sample PSUs and are generally local residents. The rationale for each design is discussed below.

B.   Sample design issues related to the population of inference of time-use surveys

327.   The first step in any sample design is to carefully specify the units of analysis and the target population of these units for which estimates are required. As discussed in chapter III, the population of inference for a time-use survey is defined in terms of: (a) the population of individuals relevant to the survey objectives; and (b) the period of time to be represented by the survey.

328.   Given the likely seasonal pattern of activities over a year, the time period for a time-use survey is ideally a year—either a calendar year or any other 12-month period (for example, 1 June of one year to 31 May of the following year). Taking a 24-hour day as the basic unit of measurement, the sample design should thus aim to select a sample of days that represents all the 365 days in the year (with some possible exceptions, as discussed in chap. III).

329.   The population of inference for a time-use survey covering an entire year can be viewed as a two-way grid, with persons arrayed along one axis and days of the year along the other axis, as illustrated in figure 5. The cells in the grid represent person-day combinations; for example, the top left cell designates person 1 on the first day of the survey year and the bottom right cell designates person N on the last day of the year. The collection of person-day combinations or cells may be viewed as constituting the population of inference of the survey. With unlimited resources and a cooperative population of individuals, data could theoretically be collected for all the applicable cells of the grid. In practice, however, only a sample of person-day cells is selected to represent the full population of person-days.

Figure 5.   The population of inference for a time-use survey

Person	Day						
	1	2	3	4	...	364	365
1					...		
2	X	X	X		...		
3					...	X	X
4					...		
⋮	⋮	⋮	⋮	⋮	⋮	⋮	⋮
N					...		

330.   The population of persons to be covered by a time-use survey will change to some extent over the time period of the survey owing to new entrants to or to exits from the population.   Entry into the population can occur through "birth" (that is to say, reaching the defined minimum age for the survey), through immigration, or through entering the non-institutional population by leaving an institution (for a survey confined to the non-institutional population).   A person may leave the population through death, emigration, or entry into an institution.

331.   Such changes in the population of inference are shown in figure 5 by the cells in the grid that are marked with Xs.   These represent situations where a person-day is not in the target population.   For example, the cells for days 1, 2 and 3 for person 2 are marked with Xs; this means that person 2 had not been in the target population prior to day 4 but entered on day 4.   Similarly, the cells for days 364 and 365 for person 3 are marked with Xs; this means that person 3 had been in the target population prior to day 364 but left it on day 364 and remained outside the population.   It is also possible for Xs to appear in the middle of a year, for example, when a person goes abroad or enters an institution for a period but then returns to the population at a later point in the survey year.

332.   For some sample designs and forms of analysis, the variation in the composition of the target population over time due to "births" and "deaths" may be readily accommodated.   This variation raises problems, however, for sample designs that involve repeated interviews with sample persons to collect time-use data for several days (particularly when the interviews are widely spaced across the year) and for analyses at the person level, where a person's time-use data for several days are aggregated.

C.   Analytical   and   operational   considerations in sampling for   time-use surveys

333.   Given a strictly defined population of person-days, how does one select a sample from this population?   Factors that affect decisions on sample design include: (a) the analytical objectives of the survey; and (b) operational considerations.   In addition, sample size is an important issue.

1.   Levels of sampling and analysis

334.   Different objectives may involve different units of analysis and require different sampling combinations of days and persons.   Three levels of analysis may have to be considered in relation to the various analytical objectives described in chapter I: (a) the *person-time unit level*; (b) the *person level*; and (c) the *household level*.

(a)   Person-time unit level analysis

335.   For analytic objectives that require only estimates of average levels of time use in different activity categories (and for different population subgroups), all that is needed is a probability sample of the person-time grid, with the basic unit of time being defined in any way (for example, hour, day, week) and the unit of analysis being the person-time unit (for example, person-day).   In particular, this is the case for developing estimates for

satellite accounts of household production.[41] For example, the proportion of time that a subgroup of the population spends in paid work can be estimated in this way regardless of how the basic unit of time is defined.

336.   A day is generally a convenient unit of measurement, and it can be used for this kind of analysis.   It is important to note that analyses of average levels of time use do not require time-use data for more than one day per respondent.   However, if data are collected for more than one day, these data can be readily incorporated into the analysis by constructing a person-day data file, with one record and associated weight for each sampled person-day.   Analyses of average levels can be conducted in a standard way from this file.[42]

(b) Person-level analysis

337.   For some other analytic objectives, the appropriate unit of analysis is the person rather than the person-day combination.   For example, an analysis may aim to measure the extent to which the amount of time women with children spend on childcare affects their children's intellectual growth.   Here the focus is on how the variation among women in respect of time use on an activity averaged over a period of time affects an outcome rather than the variation in average level of time use among women in different population subgroups.   A sample of a single day per person is inadequate for a study that aims to measure the effect of time use in a given activity on various outcomes because of the substantial within-person or intra-person variation in time use from day to day that applies to many activities.   Thus, multiple days

of time-use data are needed for each sampled person for this type of analysis.

338.   The design for a study of the effects of between-person variation in time use would ideally involve the collection of time-use data for a sizeable number of days per sampled person in a way that covered the major temporal patterns of time use.   Moreover, the sample of days would include at least two days of each type for each sampled person in order that intra-person variability in time use might be estimated for each type of day; these estimates of intra-person variability could then be used to compute the reliabilities of the person-level time-use measures.

339.   For example, a design that takes into account each of the seven days of the week and the four seasons of the year would result in 28 (7 days x 4 seasons) *strata* of day-of-the-week/season combinations.   In order to estimate *reliability*, at least 2 days selected at random in each stratum would be required; the resultant sample would be of at least 56 days per sampled person.   The response burden of this design is clearly excessive and some relaxation would be needed.

340.   One form of relaxation would entail dispensing with the seasonal stratification and stratifying days of the week into weekdays versus weekend days.   There would then be only two strata (Mondays to Fridays throughout the year; Saturdays and Sundays throughout the year) so that with a minimum of two days sampled per stratum, only four days would need to be sampled per sampled person.   Even that number of sampled days might still be larger than desirable in the sense that it could increase non-response and yield data of lower quality.   Dropping the requirements of measuring reliability could halve the number and, instead, a separate study of reliability could be made.   The allocation of some resources to a reliability study is well justified, since not only do the reliability data

---

[41] A brief discussion on the analysis of household production based on time-use data can be found in chap. XIII.
[42] Descriptions of data file formats for time-use survey data are presented in chap. XII.

provide an indication of intra-person variation in time use, but reliability estimates from the study can also be used to make adjustments for unreliability in some forms of analysis.[43]

341. Another consideration is that for some analyses the preferred unit of analysis may be a person/week rather than a person/day. If person/week data are needed, then a common practice is to sample both weekdays and weekends for each sampled person and to construct a "synthetic" week based on the sampled days. For example, data may be collected from each sampled person for two weekdays, a Saturday and a Sunday. The data can then be aggregated to construct a synthetic week for each respondent, weighting the weekdays by a factor of 5/2 in constructing the aggregate. To avoid a serious loss of precision in constructing synthetic weeks, the weighting factors should be kept small, which, in this case, argues for sampling two rather than one weekday per respondent.

(c) Household-level analysis

342. A further type of analysis of time-use data is performed at the *household level*. This type of analysis examines the time use of the household as a whole and the trade-offs between different household members. An example would be the ways in which a household allocates housework and childcare among its adult members. For such analyses, time-use data are required for all eligible household members and for the same days.

343. In most countries, population surveys are conducted through a sample of households, with either all eligible persons or a sample of one or more eligible persons selected per sampled household. Selecting all eligible

persons per sampled household is often cost-efficient, and is widely used except when it creates a high response burden that could reduce response rates. Given the added advantage of the potential for household-level analysis, the selection of all eligible persons per household is widely recommended for time-use surveys. However, for households with many eligible persons, the response burden could be excessive. In this case, a maximum number of persons could be specified for sampling in households with more eligible persons than the maximum (see below).

2. Sampling and operational considerations

344. As indicated above, the choice of the combination of sampled persons, households and days to employ in a time-use survey depends on the survey's analytical objectives. It also depends on operational considerations regarding data collection.

345. The most straightforward design in respect of implementation is one that collects data for a single day for each sampled person. The data collection is simple to conduct and the data are easy to analyse. The feasibility of collecting time-use data for multiple days depends on the organizational structure available for survey data collection. If, for example, there is a master sample of primary sampling units (PSUs) with resident interviewers in each sampled PSU, then it may not be too difficult to conduct repeat visits to sample persons in order to collect data for multiple days.

346. The collection of data for multiple days per respondent is more problematic in countries where survey data are collected by teams of travelling interviewers, as is the case in many developing countries. In this case, either the teams need to stay in selected PSUs

---

[43] See, for example, Fuller (1991, 1995) and Kalton (1985). A brief discussion on reliability studies is included in chap. XI.

long enough to collect data for several days for each respondent, or they need to revisit the PSUs at different times. In such cases, the complexities of operating a multiple-day design may lead to the choice of a single-day design (see below).

347. The issue of how many persons to sample in each selected household is less dependent on operational considerations. As a rule, it is relatively straightforward and cost-effective to collect data for all age-eligible persons in sampled households. Thus, in general, the selection of all household members is appropriate. However, household response burden needs to be considered.

3. Sample size considerations

348. In principle, sample size is determined by identifying key estimates to be obtained from a survey and calculating the sample size needed to produce these estimates with specified levels of precision. In estimating precision, sampling error needs to be estimated in a manner that takes account of the complex sample design that is planned. Also allowance needs to be made for non-response.

349. Not infrequently, the sample size needed to satisfy the precision levels for all key estimates is found to be larger than can be achieved with the resources available. In this case, the requirements are often cut back by dropping some members of the initial set of key estimates and/or lowering the specified precision levels.

(a) Sample size and analytical considerations

350. The standard approach to sample size determination can be applied to time-use surveys in the usual way. However, there is the possible complexity of more than one unit of analysis: for person-day analysis the sample size is the number of person/days, for person-level analysis it is the number of persons, and for household-level analysis it is the number of households. Many household surveys employ persons and households as units of analysis, but the person/day unit is rare. A distinctive feature of the person/day unit is that sample size is a product of the number of persons and the number of days per person. Thus a sample size of 10,000 person/days could be achieved by, say, sampling 10,000 persons for one day of time-use data each, 5,000 persons for two days each, or 2,500 persons for 4 days each. Of course, these alternatives will not yield estimates of the same precision. When a sampled person provides time-use data for more than one day, the person is included in an additional stage of *clustering*. The effect of this clustering on precision will vary by activity, and the homogeneity of the time spent on the activity by persons across days. The precision also depends on the sample design for selecting multiple days. In particular, if, say, one weekday and one weekend day are sampled for each respondent, the effects of the stratification by weekday/weekend day, with the differential sampling fractions for the two strata, need to be taken into account.[44]

351. Another important determinant of overall sample size is often the need for estimates for various domains. Frequently time-use estimates are needed separately for different regions of the country, for urban and rural areas, for a variety of population subgroups, and for days of different types (for example, weekdays and weekend days, days in different seasons). Population subgroups are commonly defined by age and sex, but other subgroups may be of particular interest in specific cases. For example, a survey may be designed to produce estimates for single

---

[44] See Gershuny, and others (1986) and Gershuny (1995) for a related discussion of the precision gains from multiple days per respondent.

parents, couples by number of children, and working mothers, or to produce estimates for persons aged 60-69, persons in households containing children aged 1 and 2 years, and persons with disability benefits who have children under age 18 living at home.

352. The production of domain estimates of specified precision often involves sampling smaller domains at higher sampling fractions. For geographical domains, the sampling fractions can be set separately to produce the domain estimates. In most cases, population subgroups cannot be pre-identified for sampling at higher rates. Thus, a two-phase sample design may be needed; in the first phase, a large-scale screening sample is selected to determine subgroup membership, and in the second phase, the samples in the smaller subgroups are retained whereas subsamples are selected from the larger subgroups in order to produce the desired sample sizes for each of the subgroups.

(b) Subsample size in multi-stage designs

353. In most countries, national household surveys conducted by face-to-face interviewing require the use of a multi-stage design, both for sampling purposes and for the interviews in sampled locations. An important decision to be made with a multi-stage design is how to distribute the sample across the stages. For example, a sample of $n = 5,000$ households could be produced by taking a sample of $a = 100$ PSUs with an average $b = 50$ households in each; or a sample of $a = 200$ PSUs with an average $b = 25$ households in each. In this example, the households are the secondary sampling units (SSUs). In general, for a given total sample size, the larger the value of a, and hence the smaller the value of b, the greater will be the precision of the survey estimates. However, increasing the number of sampled PSUs increases the survey costs, since it means an increased number of

household listings to be made, increased travel costs, and possible increases in other costs also, such as interviewer training. Thus, a suitable balance needs to be struck.

354. Useful guidance on a suitable allocation of the sample across stages can be obtained by employing a simple cost model for the total survey costs C as

$$C = aC_a + nc \qquad (1)$$

where C_a is the cost of including a PSU in the sample and c is the cost per sampled unit. Using a simple two-stage design as an approximation, and considering the estimation of the overall population mean of some characteristic (for example, mean minutes per person/day spent on housework), the optimum value of b is

$$b_{opt} = \sqrt{\frac{C_a}{c} \frac{(1-\rho)}{\rho}} \qquad (2)$$

where ρ is a synthetic measure of the within-stratum *homogeneity* of the characteristic involved within the PSUs —see, for example, Kish (1965). Application of this formula requires estimates of C_a, c, and ρ, and usually only rough estimates are possible. However, the effect of small departures from the optimum are relatively minor, so that rough estimates may suffice to indicate a suitable choice for b. There is, however, a more important limitation to this formula for time-use surveys in countries where travelling interviewers are used. In this case, interviewers need to be in each PSU long enough to collect data for specified days, and it is often desirable to cover at least a full week in each PSU, including a weekend (or longer if a substitute day is used when the respondent is unavailable on the sampled day). In countries where interviewers need to travel together in teams, the effective use of their time entails keeping them occupied for at least a week in each PSU. Thus the choice of b may well be best determined by such logistic considerations.

355. An effective multi-stage design for a time-use survey in a country where travelling interviewers are used must be constructed in such a way as to take into account the interviewing organization and the travel constraints. The choice of the number of PSUs and the spread of the sampled PSUs across the time-span of the survey should take these factors into account. The spread over time has also to be effected in such a way as to ensure that different geographical areas are represented across time. Achieving temporal representation by region may require the sampling of a sizeable number of PSUs.

D. Technical considerations specific to sampling for time-use surveys

356. Basic decisions specific to the sample design for a time-use survey that need to be made include the following: (a) representation of the time dimension; (b) number of days of time-use data to be collected for each sampled person; and (c) number of persons to be sampled in a household.

1. Representation of the time dimension

357. In the ideal design for a time-use survey, data are collected over a 12-month period to give representation to the time dimension throughout that period. In many countries, a fieldwork plan can be developed to satisfy this requirement, for instance, spreading the interviews evenly over the 12 months both nationally and at subnational levels. However, such a design is not always possible. When it is not, the aim should be to approximate the ideal to the extent possible.

358. When an annual survey is not possible, an alternative is to take a sample of time periods, such as weeks or months, and concentrate the data collection in those periods. In this case, the more periods can be covered, the better, and strong efforts should be made to choose a set of periods that are representative on average of the full 12 months. In practice, the number of time periods selected is generally small, say, from two to four, in which case they may best be chosen by purposive selection. Thus, for instance, the data collection may be confined to two separate months, perhaps one in the spring and one in the autumn, chosen carefully so as to be "representative". Within the chosen months, the sample can then be spread across weeks and days of the week according to the survey specifications.

359. In some circumstances, resource constraints may restrict a time-use survey to a single period of, say, one or two months. In particular, these constraints may occur when the time-use data collection is part of a multi-purpose survey. In this case, the statistical estimates made from the survey relate only to the given time period. The time period should be carefully chosen to be as typical as possible with respect to time-use patterns if the survey findings are to be interpreted as relating to a more extensive period, such as a year.

360. No matter whether the sample is spread across a full year or is concentrated in certain periods, it is important to select days for collecting time-use data by probability methods in order to avoid selection biases. If the choice of day is left to the interviewers or respondents, they will choose days that are convenient for them—for instance, days when the respondent is at home—and those choices may well lead to distorted estimates of time use. While, in theory, probability sampling of days guarantees time-use estimates that are free of selection bias, it does so only if the data

are collected for the specified sample days. Every effort should therefore be made to collect the data for the specified days. However, in practice this will not always be possible. Failure to collect data on a specified day can be viewed as non-response, with the resultant risk of non-response bias.

361. Some form of non-response compensation should be used to reduce the risk of non-response bias associated with sample persons who do not provide time-use data for their designated days. For sample persons who are total non-respondents, the standard method of compensation by non-response weighting adjustments can be applied (see chap. IX). However, a different form of compensation is appropriate for sample persons who cooperate with the survey but for whom time-use data cannot be collected for the designated day. In this case, the time-use data for a "comparable" day may be substituted for the missing data for the designated day. Given the variation of time use by day of week, the substitute day is often defined to be the same day of the week one week later. If the time-use data cannot be collected for that substitute day, then another substitute day two weeks later may be accepted. Rules for the selection of substitute days need to be carefully specified and applied so as to minimize the risk of bias. The main emphasis, however, should be on developing procedures and training interviewers in methods that eliminate the need for substitutes whenever possible.

362. A particular issue with respect to substitution occurs when all eligible persons in selected households are sampled. In this situation, there will be cases when time-use data can be collected for the designated day for some but not all of the household members. One possible substitution procedure then would be to collect the time-use data for the designated day for all the household members

for whom this is possible and to use the substitution method described above for the remainder. Another possible procedure would be to apply the above substitution procedure at the household level, collecting time-use data for all household members on the same substitute day. By collecting data for all household members for the same day, the latter procedure has the attraction of providing consistent data for analysing the trade-off of activities between household members. As such, it may generally be preferred for household-level analysis. However, this procedure involves more substitutions than the first alternative. Collecting data for the designated day for as many household members as possible is therefore preferable for person/day analyses.

2. Number of days of time-use data to be collected for each sampled person

363. The simplest design collects time-use data for a single day for each sampled person. Such a design avoids problems of tracing mobile sample members and places the least burden on respondents. If sample members are to be asked to provide data for more than one day, the burden on them needs to be considered. The number of days sampled per person is therefore generally kept small, mostly between two and four days. The selection of four days per person enables two weekdays, one Saturday and one Sunday to be chosen. From these four days, a synthetic week estimate can be constructed.

364. In some circumstances, collecting time-use data for more than one day per person may be attractive because it is economical. Sometimes, the data-collection cost for the second and subsequent days may be lower than that for the first day. Thus, for example, sampling costs are incurred in selecting persons for the initial day's reporting, but no

further sampling costs arise in returning to the same persons for time-use data on subsequent days. Also, the cost of data collection on subsequent days may be much lower, for instance, when data for the initial day are collected by personal interview and those for subsequent interviews are collected by telephone. When self-completion diaries are used to collect time-use data, the additional cost of a second and subsequent days may also be minimal.

365. For person-day analysis, the decision regarding the number of days to be sampled for each person entails determining which number produces estimates of the greatest accuracy for a given budget (or, equivalently, which number produces estimates of the specified level of accuracy for the lowest budget). The decision cannot simply be made on the basis of the number that produces the largest sample size for person/days for the given budget because of the effect of the within-person clustering that arises when time-use data are collected for more than one day per sampled person. The situation is further complicated by the fact that the effect of within-person clustering varies by type of activity being analysed. Furthermore, consideration needs to be given to the possibility of improvement or deterioration in quality of response across days and to the likely increase in non-response for later days.

366. Whether a time-use survey should collect data for multiple days per person thus depends mainly on two factors, namely on the importance of person-level analysis in the plans for the analysis of the survey; and on the feasibility of collecting data for multiple days and the cost-effectiveness of doing so. Despite the analysis-related benefits of multiple days, the simple procedure of a single day per person may be the best choice for countries where collecting data for multiple days is difficult to implement.

367. Even when the general decision is made to collect time-use data for a single day per person, consideration should be given to collecting data for two or more days for a subsample of respondents. The data for two days can be used to measure the level of intra-person variation in time use across days, which can then be used to make adjustments to person-level analysis. If possible, the subsample should be nationally representative but, if not, useful insights can still be obtained from a subsample that is confined to areas where collecting data for two days is feasible.

368. Whether the decision is made to sample only one day or to sample several days for each sampled person, the issues involved in deciding how to sample the day or days are broadly similar. Across the whole sample of persons, the sample of days should represent the population of days for the period under study (ideally 12 consecutive months). Practical considerations in data collection exert a strong influence on how the sampled days are selected for specific sample persons. A further consideration is that if household-level analysis is to be conducted, all the persons in a household should ideally be assigned the same sampled days.

3. Methods for sampling days

369. In discussing methods for sampling days, it is useful to distinguish between time-use surveys that employ interviewers who are located in the sampled PSUs for the duration of the data collection period and other surveys. These two situations are discussed in turn below.

(a) Time-use surveys with resident interviewers

370. Consider first the simplest situation where the time-use survey is to be carried out in a master sample of PSUs in each of which

there is a resident interviewer who can conduct interviews throughout the 12-month period. Suppose that 56 households are sampled in a PSU, that all household members are to report their time use for the same sampled day, and that each day is to have an equal probability of selection (in other words, the sample design does not require, say, a larger-than-proportionate sample of Saturdays and Sundays). To achieve a good balance of the sample of days, the days can be stratified by day of the week and quarter of the year. Thus, within each quarter, two Mondays, two Tuesdays etc. would be randomly sampled, and then randomly allocated to the sampled households of the PSU.

371. Further refinements of this stratification are possible. For instance, 1 of the 13 weeks in each quarter could be selected at random to be duplicated, thus creating 14 weeks. Then, the 14 weeks could be divided into two half-quarters of 7 weeks each, with each of the seven days of the week then being randomly allocated to 1 of the 7 weeks in the half-quarter. Thus, each week of the year is represented once, with one week per quarter being represented twice, and each day of the week is represented in each half-quarter. In general, schemes of this type can be fashioned to provide a sample of days of the week that are evenly spread across the weeks of the year. By this means, a better representation of the time dimension is achieved than would occur with an uncontrolled random selection of sampled days.

372. The example given above involves sampling a single day for each sample person. The approach outlined can be extended to multiple days per sample person in a natural way. However, there are additional considerations relating to how the days for a sampled person should be distributed within the 12-month period. To illustrate the extension to multiple days, suppose that the

situation is as described earlier, except that now each person is to provide data for four sample days, consisting of two weekdays, one Saturday and one Sunday. With 56 sampled households, each of the weekend days through the year would be sampled, and four Saturdays and four Sundays would be sampled twice (one of each in each quarter of the year). With 112 sampled weekdays, each weekday (Monday through Friday) would be sampled 22 or 23 times. The sample weekdays could be chosen, for example, using a systematic fractional sample with an interval of $52/22 = 2.36$ (or $52/23$) throughout the year (Kish, 1965).

373. A sampling scheme for multiple days like that described above could be applied independently for each type of day for each sample person, in which case there would be no control over the spread of each person's sample days over the 12-month period. For logistic reasons, it will often be preferable to concentrate the sample days for a given person within a shorter period, say, a month or a quarter. Among the advantages of this concentration are less need to trace mobile persons (since fewer persons will move) and fewer losses due to persons leaving the survey population (through death, emigration or entry into an institution) in the shorter period. One approach for achieving a concentration of sample days for each sample person is to select the days as described above and, in the case of four days per person, to group the sampled days into sets of four with the required specified combination of days (two weekdays, a Saturday, and a Sunday) based on closeness in time, and to then allocate a set of four days to each sample person (or household). Note, however, that in this type of scheme each sampled person's time-use data relate to a specific season. Consequently, some of the variation across persons will reflect seasonal variation which will need to be taken into account in person-level analyses.

374. When time-use data are collected for several days by means of self-completion diaries, it will often be economical to have respondents complete diaries for consecutive days. For example, in a design where 20 households are sampled in each sample EA, the 20 sampled households might be divided into five groups with 4 households in each group. Household members in group A could then be asked to complete diaries for Friday and Saturday; those in group B, for Sunday and Monday; those in group C, for Tuesday and Wednesday; those in group D, for Thursday and Friday; and those in group E, for Saturday and Sunday. In this way, Fridays, Saturdays, and Sundays would be sampled twice as often as other days.

(b) Time-use surveys with travelling interviewers

375. We now turn to the more difficult situation in which teams of travelling interviewers conduct the survey. A fieldwork organization of this type is used in many developing countries. In this set-up, each team operates by visiting a selected PSU, listing the households in the PSU and selecting a sample from the list, carrying out interviews in the selected households, and moving on to the next PSU in its allotted set. In these circumstances, the sample of days in a PSU cannot be spread across the year. However, an annual spread can be obtained by collecting data for different periods from different PSUs. Various schemes can be developed for this purpose, with the actual choice being made so as to suit the fieldwork operational constraints that apply in a particular case. Some general approaches that may be employed are illustrated below, but it should be recognized that they need to be adapted so as to fit the specific circumstances.

376. Consider, first, a time-use survey that is designed to collect data for a single day for each sample person. For simplicity's sake, suppose that a team of interviewers collects data relating to seven consecutive days in each PSU with a sample of 56 households selected per PSU. With an even distribution for the sample of days of the week, time-use data would be collected for each day of the week from the eligible persons in eight sample households, with a random allocation of days to households. The annual spread of the sample can then be achieved by assigning different PSUs to different weeks. This assignment needs to be carefully balanced across the sampled PSUs to avoid, for instance, PSUs of particular types (for example, PSUs in certain regions, rural PSUs) being represented only in certain parts of the year. As an illustration, the 52-week time period can be divided into 13 periods of 4 weeks with the sampled PSUs systematically allocated to these periods, and the PSUs for a given 4-week period systematically allocated to the weeks. The systematic allocation from ordered lists of sampled PSUs provides a balance of the characteristics used in the ordering by month and week. This general approach can also be applied when the survey is restricted to a shorter period of time.

377. Collecting time-use data for multiple days for each sample person will generally be operationally difficult when travelling teams of interviewers are used. As a result, it will for the most part be preferable to restrict the number of sample days to one or two. If required, the above designs can be modified to handle multiple days per sample person, for instance, two randomly chosen days, or one weekday and one weekend day, for each sample person.

378. Even though a survey generally uses non-resident interviewers, there will often be parts of the country where resident interviewers may be used. Resident interviewers are, for example, often to be

found in the capital and other large cities. In this case, the survey can take advantage of the resident interviewers by using a scheme that spreads the sample of days throughout the 12-month period in the strata with resident interviewers, while using the type of design described above for the rest of the country. A mixed design of this type will produce more precise person/day estimates. In particular, it will produce much better domain estimates for the strata with resident interviewers since the time period is well represented in these strata.

379.   Another version of a mixed design entails using a two-phase sample. In this case, the single design is used for a main sample and a multiple-day design is used in a subsample of the sampled PSUs.

380.   A further extension of a mixed design involves collecting data for more days per sample person in the strata with resident interviewers. For instance, two or four days may be selected for each sample person in those strata, while only one day is selected for each sample person elsewhere. Provided that the response rates for the multiple days are kept high and the quality of response remains the same for all sampled days, the person/day data can be readily aggregated from persons with data for varying numbers of days (using appropriate weights, as discussed in chap. IX). A mixed design of this type also permits the extra types of analyses described earlier for the strata where sample persons provide data for multiple days.

4. Number of persons sampled in a household

381.   To be able to carry out person-day and person levels of analysis, all that is required for the sample of persons is for those persons to be selected using a probability sample design with known selection probabilities. These forms of analyses can be performed irrespective of the number of persons selected in sampled households. Household-level analyses, however, require that time-use data be collected for all household members, or at least for the set of household members whose interrelated time-use patterns are to be analysed (for example, all adults or both parents). One reason, then, for selecting multiple persons per sampled household is to provide the data needed for household-level analyses.

382.   Another reason for selecting multiple persons per household is cost-efficiency. Most population surveys are based on household samples. It is generally less expensive to collect the survey data from a sample of persons clustered in a smaller number of households than to spread the sample over a larger number of households. From the perspective of cost-efficiency, the most efficient design is the one that minimizes the sampling errors of the survey estimates for a given budget. To determine an efficient design therefore requires an evaluation of the effects on sampling error of clustering the sample of persons within households. This evaluation involves both the effect of weighting for unequal selection probabilities and the effect of cluster homogeneity.

383.   Consider the case where households are selected with equal probabilities. If all persons are then selected in sampled households, persons are also selected with equal probabilities. However, if one person is selected from each sampled household, the persons selected have selection probabilities that are inversely proportional to the numbers of eligible persons in their households. In general, these unequal selection probabilities cause an increase in sampling error in the survey estimates. The cluster homogeneity effect will vary by type of activity. If household members have similar patterns of time use for a given activity, a sample design

that selects multiple persons per household will have larger sampling errors than would a sample design of the same size that selects only one person per household (with all sampled persons being selected with equal probability).

384. A further factor to be considered in determining the numbers of persons to be selected from sampled households is that of household response burden. If time-use data are collected for several persons in selected households, the household burden may be perceived as excessive, even though it is distributed among the sampled persons. This perception may then lead to unacceptable levels of non-response. Household response burden is particularly high with large households and when all persons are selected per household. When the sample design generally specifies the selection of all persons in selected households, it may nevertheless be advisable to subsample persons in large households in order to reduce the burden.

385. If one objective of a time-use survey is to produce the data needed for household-level analyses, then either all eligible persons or specified key persons need to be sampled in each household. When the survey does not have this objective, however, there is a great deal of flexibility in the ways persons can be selected within sampled households. As one example, the selection rules could specify that one person is to be selected at random in households with between one and three eligible persons, that two persons are to be selected in households with between four and six eligible persons, and that 3 persons are to be selected in larger households. This rule has the benefit of restricting the range of selection probabilities. As another example, the rule could specify that the householder and, if applicable, the householder's spouse are to be selected with certainty, together with one other eligible household member selected at random.

Various rules of this type can be developed to produce sample sizes that satisfy specific analytic objectives, that are cost-efficient, and that address issues of response burden. In most cases, the selection of more than one person per household will be preferred.

E. Sampling for time-use data collection in multi-purpose surveys

386. Sometimes data on time use may be collected in conjunction with data on other topics—that is to say, as part of a multi-purpose survey. As discussed in chapter IV, whenever the possibility of combining two surveys arises, many issues need to be considered—one of which is whether it is possible to create an efficient dual-purpose design in which the time dimension is properly represented. As noted earlier, ideally a time-use survey should represent a full 12-month period. Failing that, a purposive selection of a "representative" set of, say, two, three, or four individual months may be used or, if resource constraints so dictate, the data collection may be confined to a single "typical" time period. Whatever the chosen period, within that period the day or days for which each respondent reports time use should be pre-specified and chosen by a random selection procedure.

387. Few other household surveys need to spread their data collections over a 12-month period—or over any period—in a balanced way. Most surveys are carried out in the shortest time needed to complete the data collection, with the spread of data collection within that time being determined by logistic considerations. For instance, when travelling interviewers are used, the data collection may be organized to minimize the travel costs incurred in moving the interviewers between the PSUs for which they are responsible. Apart from time-use surveys, very few surveys require that data be collected for specific days.

Thus, in general, the need to represent the time dimension appropriately in a design that combines a time-use survey with another survey requires a modification in the data-collection procedures that would be used by the other survey if it were a stand-alone survey. Since the modification will almost certainly impose restrictions on the timing of interviews, it may lead to a lower response rate for the combined survey than would be achieved if the other survey was conducted alone. This factor also needs to be taken into account when a combined survey is being considered.

388. A time-use survey will most readily fit together with another survey that also involves spreading data collection over time. The other survey may itself require a similar representation of the time dimension as, for example, is often the case with a nutrition or family budget survey. The main concern here is that of response burden. The response burden in such surveys is often substantial so that, when combined with the high burden of a time-use survey, the overall burden may become excessive.

389. Another type of survey that involves data collection over time is a continuous survey that is repeated at regular intervals to chart changes in population characteristics over time. A labour-force survey is the most obvious example. If a continuous survey is conducted at short intervals, say, monthly, it may give a good representation of the time period. Even a quarterly survey may give adequate time representation. If a continuous survey is used, the issue of the selection of days for collecting time-use data within each round of the survey needs to be addressed.

390. If a time-use survey is to be combined with a single cross-sectional survey, the timing for the combined survey is an important consideration. Can the data collection for the combined survey be conducted during a period that is thought to be reasonably "typical" for a year? If it can, then issues of arranging the data collection so as to give proper representation to days and perhaps weeks for time-use data across the sample need to be resolved. Given the high response burden involved in collecting time-use data, other things being equal, a combination with another survey that has a low burden is preferable.

Part Three

Collecting and processing time-use data

VII. ENUMERATION PROCEDURES FOR TIME-USE SURVEYS

391. Basic considerations in the design and implementation of field procedures for conventional household surveys apply to time-use surveys as well. These include: pre- and pilot tests; survey publicity; field organization and recruitment of enumerators and supervisors; training and supervision of field staff; determining workload and remuneration; interview scheduling and procedures; quality control over fieldwork; control of non-response; and considerations regarding the use of incentives for respondents.

392. The present chapter further discusses some of these aspects as they relate specifically to time-use surveys.[45] Of special concern are the known difficulties in inducing respondents to accurately describe their activities and in inducing interviewers to transcribe these verbal descriptions into the format of the diary. Because time-use surveys typically involve a household questionnaire and a personal questionnaire in addition to a diary, the potential for respondent burden and refusals and their effect on the quality of diary data are also of concern.

A. Main considerations in designing and implementing field procedures

393. Field procedures are determined by the type of survey, mode of data collection, survey instruments and the sample design. Main considerations in the conduct of time-use surveys include:

– *Type of survey*: In the modular approach to collecting time-use data, a major consideration is coordination of interview schedules and re-contacts or callbacks with other modules in the survey. With multiple topics and survey forms being handled, training and supervision of interviewers become more complex.

– *Mode of data collection*: Face-to-face interviews, computer-assisted telephone interviews (CATI) and self-completed or leave-behind diaries have all proved to be feasible methods for national data collection on time use. In less developed countries, face-to-face interviews or a combination of face-to-face with leave-behind diaries still represents the most viable among these methods. The discussion in this chapter does not cover procedures for implementing CATI as well as direct observation[46] and experience sampling methods.

– *Type of survey instruments*: Collecting data on time use through diaries requires procedures for measuring time when respondents are not accustomed to clock time, and techniques for ensuring that activities are reported as accurately and in as much detail as necessary for proper coding.

– *Sample design*: Maintaining the allocation of diary days required by the time sample is a major consideration in designing the field procedures.

---

[45] For a detailed discussion on enumeration procedures for household surveys in general, see United Nations (1984).

[46] The 1995 Dominican Republic Time Use Survey used a combination of recall interview and direct observation. This is so far the only national-level survey that has utilized the direct observation approach.

394. While some of the detailed procedures may vary depending on the combination of these survey design components, the common goal would be to ensure the highest level of quality possible in the data collected. Specifically, the procedures should ensure that sample selection is implemented as called for in the design and that non-response and response errors are minimized. This chapter looks at likely causes of errors and discusses what can be done to address them at the enumeration stage of the survey.

395. Pre-testing of questionnaires and diary formats, activity classifications and field procedures are essential. Pilot testing[47] after thorough pre-testing of these separate aspects of fieldwork needs to be conducted to observe how all the survey operations, including the administration of questionnaires and diaries, work together in practice. A pilot duplicates the final survey design on a small scale from beginning to end, including data processing and analysis. The pilot provides an opportunity to fine-tune the questionnaires and diary and enumeration procedures before their use in the actual survey operations. It also provides additional grounds for validating assumptions for determination of workload of field staff and for the number of enumeration days needed to complete the survey round.

1. Field procedures

396. Main fieldwork activities in collecting time-use data through diaries for which procedures need to be set out include the following.

Informing the public about the survey

397. To elicit cooperation and interest in the survey, it is important to inform the public

about its objectives and uses, the dates when interviewer visits will occur, and what will be expected of sample respondents. This can be done as part of the general publicity campaign for the survey. Some countries have, in addition, allotted one day of the enumeration period for a pre-interview visit to sample households. This visit is intended to provide basic information about the survey and to elicit cooperation from respondents. During the enumeration period, interviewers would also need to convince sample households to participate in the interviews or in diary completion. Appropriate print and multimedia materials need to be prepared for this purpose.

Identifying respondents and scheduling interviews

398. For this activity, interviewers need to first locate the sample household. If the sample selection plan calls for it, the interviewer would then have to select the sample household members who will be asked to complete diaries. Instructions for sample selection should be clear. At the design stage, a decision on whether or not to allow substitution of sample households and/or respondents would need to be made and instructions to interviewers should be clear about this.

399. For the leave-behind approach, this would also be the time when the interviewer will explain how the diary is to be completed and when it will be collected. For the face-to-face interview approach, time for the diary interviews would also need to be set. The main consideration here is to ensure that the time sample is followed—in other words, that sample households and sample household members provide the time-use data for their assigned diary days. The use of appointment cards or reminder cards to be left with the sample households may be useful.

---

[47] A pilot duplicates the final survey design on a small scale from beginning to end, including data processing and analysis.

Re-contacting sample households and household members

400. Every effort should be made to contact all sample households. Thus, survey procedures should require interviewers to re-contact households that are not available during the first contact visit. A maximum number of *callbacks* should be set, however, so that the enumeration timetable is not delayed. In addition, too many callbacks will increase the cost of the survey. When households are not contacted as originally scheduled, it will be necessary to reassign the diary days. It is important to set a procedure for rescheduling the assigned diary days. This topic is further discussed below.

Interviewing sample respondents

401. As discussed in part two, with face-to-face interviews the sequence in which the various survey instruments are to be completed needs to be considered. To complete the household questionnaire, the interviewer will need to identify "a responsible adult". Criteria for selecting the household respondent should be clearly spelled out and explained to interviewers—this would usually be the same criteria for the regular household surveys being conducted by the statistical office. For the personal questionnaires and diaries, however, the ideal is for respondents themselves to be interviewed. The procedures should be clear about whether or not personal questionnaires and diaries can be completed by a person other than the respondent (that is to say, whether there can be *proxy reporting*). A typical arrangement that should be discouraged is the interviewing in the sample of parents or adults in place of their children. In the case of leave-behind diaries, proxy-reporting may be allowed in special cases; for example, caregivers may complete the diary of the person they provide care to or visually impaired persons or persons with other types

of disability may ask someone else to complete the diary.

402. Some of the difficulties that interviewers may face in eliciting clear and accurate reports from respondents about their daily activities are discussed later in this chapter.

Reviewing, editing and coding of questionnaires and diaries

403. After interviews are completed and/or diaries are completed, interviewers must review the diaries before leaving the respondent. A basic check on 24-hour diaries entails ensuring that activities have been reported for the full 24 hours. When editing and coding are to be done in the field, appropriate procedures would need to be designed and implemented (see chap. VIII for further discussion on this topic).

Quality control of fieldwork[48]

404. Proper training and supervision of interviewers are essential to the ensuring of data quality. In addition, it is important to put in place a quality control system for detecting and minimizing non-sampling errors.[49] Field review and editing of the questionnaires and diaries, observing interviewers, and re-interviews by supervisors are some of the approaches that are used for quality control. Field review and editing and observation of interviewers should be carried out early enough during the enumeration period to detect and correct their errors immediately. Supervisors can also re-interview a sample of households contacted by interviewers at the

---

[48] See chap. XI for a more detailed discussion of data quality evaluation.

[49] Non-sampling errors include non-response and response errors. This topic is discussed in detail in chap. XI.

early stage of enumeration to provide them with immediate feedback as part of the overall data evaluation programme.

Reporting of response status

405.   For purposes of data quality monitoring and evaluation, it is important to have a procedure and forms for reporting refusals, final non-contacts, sample loss (for example, out-of-scope units, vacant dwellings) and other response categories. The number and reasons for refusals or for non-contact should be included as part of these records. The status of completion of personal questionnaires and diaries (for example, complete, incomplete or not obtained) should also be reported. Criteria for classifying status of completion of the survey forms need to be determined. A useful set of response categories for sample households would include those as listed in table 6.

2. Field procedures: some illustrations

406.   The number and allocation of diary days and the mode of data collection are two main factors that are considered in designing field procedures for time-use surveys. These affect the length of the enumeration period, the number of visits that interviewers would have to make exclusive of *callbacks*, and the maximum number of callbacks that would be reasonable before declaring a household or respondent to be a non-contact.

407.   Generally, an increase in the number of diary days would increase the number of minimum visits required and thus would affect the length of the enumeration period. The length of the enumeration period would also be affected by the number of callbacks required to contact a sample household or person.

Table 6. Sample criteria for classifying status of completion of the survey forms[a]

FULL RESPONSE	All personal questionnaires and diaries were fully complete for all eligible sample household members.		
NON-RESPONSE	**Refusal** (sample units were contacted but refused to participate)	*Full refusal*	All sample household members refused to participate in the survey.
		Partial refusal	Questionnaires not obtained for one or more household members owing to refusal and/or diary/diaries not obtained for one or more household members with no reason given.
	Non-contact	*Full non-contact*	Household could not be contacted during the enumeration period.
		Partial non-contact	Household was contacted but even with required number of callbacks made, questionnaires and diaries were not fully completed for some household members.

---

[a] See chapter XI for a more detailed discussion of data quality evaluation and response categories.

Table 7. Illustrative interviewer work schedule for recall interview approach with one designated diary day

PRIOR TO FIRST VISIT	Contact sample household to inform them of the schedule for the first visit.
FIRST VISIT	Explain survey objectives and importance of time-use data. Explain the importance of responding in relation to being randomly selected and therefore representative of a portion of the population. Conduct interview for household questionnaire. Select sample of household members by applying coverage rules and sample selection procedure. Set appointment for interview for designated diary day for sample respondents.
SECOND VISIT (One day after designated diary day of household/sample respondents)	Conduct face-to-face interview for completion of diary. Conduct interview for completion of personal questionnaire. Arrange for new interview schedule and assign new designated diary days if postponement is necessary.
THIRD VISIT	If necessary, reschedule interviews.

408. Table 7 provides an illustration of how an interviewer's schedule would look for a survey design that collected diary information for one day—the same day for each sample household member—by recall interview. In this case, the minimum number of visits would be two.

409. Table 8 illustrates a schedule for a survey design using the leave-behind diary approach where each sample respondent completes two diary days that will be the same for all household members. In this case, the minimum number of visits is four.

3. Recruitment, organization and training of field staff

410. The role of interviewers and supervisors in ensuring high-quality data cannot be overemphasized. Field staff need to be skilled and motivated enough to carry out the sample selection as designed, to elicit cooperation from respondents, to record activity descriptions in the diaries, to re-contact and reschedule initial non-responding households, to perform field edits and coding,

and to execute the quality control procedures of the survey operations. Thus, special attention needs to be given to their selection, remuneration and training.

(a) Staffing and organization

411. It is suggested that the time-use survey staff be drawn from the pool of experienced field staff available to the statistical office—both regular staff and seasonal or temporary interviewers of other household surveys, especially those who have been involved in expenditure surveys utilizing diaries. In countries where several languages or local dialects are spoken, a key consideration in the recruitment and selection of field staff should be the ability to conduct the survey in the vernacular.

412. The field organization structure that is used for regular household surveys should be mobilized for the survey. This is especially needed with use of the modular approach where time-use data collection is only one of several forms of data collection being implemented in the particular survey.

Table 8. Illustrative interviewer work schedule for leave-behind diary approach with two designated diary days (same days for all sample household members)

PRIOR TO FIRST VISIT	Contact sample household to inform them of the schedule for the first visit.
FIRST VISIT (No later than one day before the first designated diary day. No interviews should be carried out during the diary day as this will influence the time use during that day).	Explain survey objectives and importance of time-use data. Explain the importance of responding in relation to being randomly selected and therefore representative of a portion of the population. Conduct interview for household questionnaire. Select sample of household members by applying coverage rules and sample selection procedure. Explain procedures for filling out diary, inform respondents of the days that they will need to complete the diaries and the days when the diaries will be collected. Arrange for new interview schedule and assign new designated diary days if postponement is necessary.
ONE DAY AFTER FIRST DIARY DAY	Collect first diary. Review diaries with respondents for the purpose of clarifying procedures, solving problems and field-editing the diary. Conduct personal questionnaire interview. Remind respondents of second diary day.
ONE DAY AFTER SECOND DIARY DAY	Collect second diary and review diary for completeness.

413. Appropriate workload determination—or the average expected number of interviews per day or total expected interviews over the enumeration period—is important. Pre-tests and a pilot test are crucial in setting realistic assumptions about the duration of interview times and the system of setting appointments for interviews and collection of diaries.

(b) Training of field staff

414. Interviewers and their supervisors are critical to the success of data collection and should thus have appropriate training and be provided with effective tools to complete their tasks. The amount of training to be given generally depends on their background and experience and the complexity of the survey. Detailed instructional and training materials must be developed for supervisors and interviewers. Manuals of instruction, coding tools particularly for coding activities,[50] survey instruments translated into the local dialects, home-study materials and materials for group training are the basic types of materials usually needed by the field staff.

415. Recommendations on training practices for household surveys are found in several United Nations publications[51] and therefore are not discussed at length in this *Guide*; additional guidelines are, however, provided. For example, a training technique that specifically applies to time-use surveys is the requirement that the field staff complete their own time-use diaries prior to training. They may also be asked to have household members complete diaries of their activities. These completed diaries can then be brought to the training sessions and used as a basis for discussing the difficulties and problems involved in completing a time-use diary and for coding and editing exercises.

---

[50] See chapter VIII for more detailed discussion on coding tools.

[51] See, for example, United Nations (1984).

416. It is also necessary to train field staff so that they can properly respond to questions raised by reluctant respondents. Among these questions are those related to the uses of the data on time use. In discussing the importance and uses of time-use data, various responses may need to be prepared depending on the characteristics of the respondents—for example, whether they are families with children, the elderly or young people, people from lower or higher socio-economic classes etc.

417. Interviewers should have a good understanding of how people normally report their daily activities, the difficulties in translating these *verbatim reports* into the diary format and the difficulties and errors that may arise in coding as a result of inaccurate recording of activities. Training should include intensive practice sessions for both interviewing and coding. Other difficult tasks such as sampling of respondents, and maintaining the required allocation of diary days, should also receive attention, where applicable. Practice interviews should include not only the mock interviews designed for illustrating specific situations but also actual field interviews.

418. A sample training schedule showing various activities that address the above concerns is contained in annex 10.

B. Managing fieldwork: some specific issues

1. Ordering of interview sequence

419. Time-use survey instruments consist of a household questionnaire, a personal questionnaire and a time diary. In modular or multi-purpose surveys, there are also the additional questionnaires from the other modules. In face-to-face interviews, implementing procedures for the survey would

need to specify in which order these instruments are to be administered. Typically, the later in the sequence a questionnaire or diary is administered, the higher the chances of respondent burden affecting the responses to the interview questions. In this regard, it is suggested that the interview for the diary take place as early as possible or that the number of questions asked prior to administering the diary interview be kept to a minimum. One way to do this is by conducting the personal questionnaire interview after the diary has been completed.

2. Maintaining sample design for diary days

420. As discussed in part two, it is recommended that diary days/dates be allocated to households/individuals by a controlled random procedure; that is to say, given the sample allocation plan for diary days, specific reporting dates[52] or "designated days" are initially assigned to each sample respondent. These are the dates on which the respondents will be asked to report on their activities. Ideally, these designated reporting dates should not be changed. If the interviewers visited households according to their own convenience, the resulting data would be biased. For example, if the interviewer was to take a day off, then the reporting days that would be affected would be underrepresented in the data. On the other hand, if interviewers systematically elect to conduct interviews on weekends in areas with a great deal of formal sector employment, the groups for which data are collected on those days will be over represented.

421. Country experiences have shown, however, that it may be difficult to contact some respondents on their assigned days.

---

[52] It could also be only one date, if only one diary day is to be reported.

Thus, in designing the field enumeration procedures, a decision has to be made on whether or not to allow for postponement of reporting dates. If the decision is to allow for postponement, every attempt must be made to reduce this to a minimum. Moreover, a set of rules to determine under what conditions a postponement is necessary and how to select the new reporting dates needs to be established as part of the enumeration procedures to be followed by field staff.

422. One option would be to keep the original designated day and perform the data collection at a later date. Consider, for example, a recall interview survey where respondents are scheduled to be interviewed the day immediately after their designated day. Suppose a person was scheduled to report his or her activities for Monday but could not be reached on the interview date, a Tuesday. That person would then be contacted on Wednesday to report their Monday activities. For this option, the result is a longer recall period. Thus, it would be best if the new interview was scheduled as close as possible to the reporting date, as data quality would be compromised by extending the recall period beyond one day (Horrigan and others, 1999). There is, however, a potential bias if the interviewer tries to reach the respondent on consecutive days. The bias comes about because the survey will collect data on a disproportionate number of busy days (assuming that interviewers are less likely to reach respondents on busy days) (United States Bureau of Labour Statistics, 2000a).

423. A second option is to systematically reassign reporting dates. One way of doing this is to postpone the reporting date to one week later on the same day of the week, that is to say, substitute a Monday for a Monday, a Saturday for a Saturday etc. The procedure would need to specify the maximum number of weeks that would be allowed for postponement or, equivalently, the number of callbacks or re-contact attempts before treating the respondent as a non-response. This would of course have an effect on the length of the enumeration period. The Statistical Office of the European Communities (Eurostat) recommendation on this is a maximum of two weeks (or two re-contact attempts), while Finland has allowed for up to three weeks. Regardless of the number of attempts, it would be useful to obtain information on the original reporting date, particularly on unique or special features of the original reporting date (for example, a trip taken by the respondent). This could help to determine if certain activities (such as travel) are grossly underestimated.

424. A third option is to reassign designated dates systematically, as above, but not limit the substitute day to the same day of the week. This has been suggested based on studies that show that weekdays are similar to each other with respect to the type and range of activities carried out and the time spent on these activities. Specifically, Monday-through-Thursday are substitutable; in addition, Monday-through-Friday substitution is feasible as long as the main objective is to determine the average time spent in various activities rather than how those activities were distributed across the different days of the week (United States Bureau of Labour Statistics, 2000b).

425. Assigning designated days may be done at the respondent level or at the household level, as discussed in part two. When assignment of the designated diary day(s) is done at the household level, then each sample household member has the same designated day(s). If one or more of the household members is unable to report on the designated day(s), ideally all household members should be rescheduled for the same new designated day(s). This procedure keeps

the distribution of diary days across the sample and yields diary information that can be cross-referenced across household members; this is useful in the editing and analysis of the data.

426.   However, it may be difficult to find a common date for all the household members. Thus, if the majority of the household members can provide the information for the initial designated day, it would be advisable to proceed as scheduled.   Then, only the unavailable respondent would be assigned a new designated day.

427.   Enumeration procedures should be clear about when interviewers can postpone or change designated days for reporting. Some possible reasons are: that the household cannot be contacted on the scheduled date; and that the household can be contacted but the sample respondent is not available for the interview (for a recall interview approach) or for briefing regarding the completion of the diary (for a leave-behind diary approach).

428.   The reasons for postponement should be recorded and compiled as part of the process of obtaining information for quality evaluation of the field procedures and the resulting data.

3. Understanding how people report their daily activities

429.   People have different ways of recalling their activities and thus different ways in which they report them. Some may use atypical activities as a springboard for recollecting sequences of events (for example, a person may remember the exact time she went to bed because it was much later than usual) while for others daily routines provide the time framework (for example, a person may know the exact time it takes to drive to church because "that is how much time it always took"). Some persons recall activities and estimate their duration more easily when

there was an appointment or time commitment. Other activities occurring immediately prior to or after the appointment are also more easily remembered. Some have difficulty identifying the starting and stopping times for some activities and report the duration of the activity instead; for example, checking e-mail at work took about 15 minutes; eating lunch took about 15-20 minutes; the telephone call lasted 5 minutes.

430.   Interviewers should be aware of the variety of ways in which respondents may report their activities in order to be able to translate these reports into the diary format of the survey. For example, when respondents report duration of activities instead of beginning and/or ending times, interviewers should help respondents give the beginning and ending times. In addition, it may be useful to know why respondents fail to report activities. Some types of unreported activities are:

–   Activities that have a very short duration such as short telephone calls or picking up clothes off the floor.
–   Activities that occur simultaneously with other, more dominating activities. Examples of these include balancing a chequebook while talking on the telephone, playing word games while watching television, or buying or eating snacks while working. The dominant activity (namely, talking on the telephone, watching television or working) is reported, but the simultaneous secondary activity is not. Some of the secondary activities are pervasive—that is to say, they occur over long durations "in the background" (for example, passive childcare) and so are not reported.
–   Activities that are performed quickly en route to accomplishing a more notable task. These include dropping a

load of laundry in the washing machine as the respondent heads out the door to work, stopping at the bank on the way home from work, or looking quickly through the mail while going indoors to change clothes. In these cases, as with activities that occur simultaneously with other more dominating activities, the major activity is reported, but the smaller activity is "lost" in the accomplishment of the greater activity.

– Activities that are so routine that they seem almost automatic and are not remembered. These activities include putting food away after a meal, rinsing dishes after a meal, or reading newspaper.

4. Measuring time without a clock

431. In some societies or areas of a country, people may relate their activities not to hours as they appear on a clock face but to other "markers" such as fluctuations of nature, religious activities during the day (for example, the five daily prayers of the Islamic religion) or other traditional cultural practices, productive activities, schedules of daily radio and television programmes, and routine activities included in their daily schedules. In order to collect time-use data in such societies or households, survey designers need to give special attention to translating the local perception of time into a standard 24-hour timetable. In this case, it is necessary to understand how the society identifies the hours of the day and how its members calculate the amount of time it takes them to perform an activity. This understanding of time can be integrated into the time diary, and used to develop individual questions and answer codes. Table 9 illustrates one such method employed in a time-use study in southern Ghana. In this illustration, clock time is translated into time markers used by the local households (Grosh and Glewwe, eds., 2000).

Table 9. Illustration of time terminology and corresponding "clock time"

Standard time	Time indication used by farmers (English translation)
Midnight	Deep darkness
1.00 a.m.	First cockcrow
4.30 a.m.	Third cockcrow or inability to recognize other faces
6.00 a.m.	Morning
6.30 a.m.	Farm-going period or day is on
9.00 a.m.	Sky is dry
10.30 a.m.	Sun about to be still
Noon	Sun still
1.00 p.m.	Sun turning
2.00 p.m.	Sun has turned
3.00 p.m.	Closing time
4.00 p.m.	Palm wine tapping period
5.00 p.m.	Sun about to set
6.00 p.m.	Sunset
7.00 p.m.	Sleeping agent
9.00 p.m.	Day is over
11.00 p.m.	Night is advanced, town is dead silent

Source: Grosh and Glewwe, eds. (2000).

432. As mentioned above, it will be also necessary to determine how respondents might answer questions regarding duration of an activity such as, "How much time did you spend fetching water?", and to determine how to convert certain answers into time. For example, what would it mean for a given activity to have taken "all morning" to be completed. Interviewers must have, and be briefed on, standard conversions so as to minimize subjective interpretations.

433. The need to reflect local perceptions of time in the collection of diary data may not, however, necessarily be as large a problem as some may expect. For example, at an expert meeting in Osaka in 1994, representatives of seven Asian countries all agreed that a diary was not particularly problematic with respect to time consciousness. A similar observation was made in relation to the 2000 Time Use Survey in South Africa, namely, that even if

respondents do not have a clock, those who have a busy life will pick up the time from radio or television programmes, regular events or other sources (Haraldsen, 2000).

5. Probing techniques

434.   Probing can help minimize vague responses, help recall missed activities and contextual information, and bring out unreported simultaneous activities. Probing is also important in ensuring that there are no logical gaps in the sequence of events that have been reported. For example, before a respondent goes for breakfast, he/she must have woken up and got out of bed. Or, after preparing a meal, eating is an expected activity. Or, when the respondent changes location, there must have been some kind of travel in between. By probing for these kinds of logical relationships, activities that are often omitted from diary reports will be picked up.

435.   Events stored in memory may be represented by several different retrieval codes, such as (a) location information, (b) information about other persons present or (c) links with other activities that immediately precede or follow it. Consequently, probes are especially important for the retrieval of precise and detailed time-use information. Thus, if one retrieval path fails to activate a memory record, probes about the location or about other people present may help the respondent remember previously overlooked information. This may be very important for the measurement of non-market work activities, some of which may appear to be routine (household chores) or passive (watching over children, the sick or elderly when active care is not being given) and, consequently, may be easily forgotten or unreported (United States Bureau of Labour Statistics, 1997).

436.   As part of the review process after the diary is completed, the interviewer should try

to pick up more details by checking the relationship among activities, the social context ("with whom") and the locations or modes of travel. Some examples of questions that can be asked are reported in box 5 (Haraldsen, 2000).

Box 5. Examples of questions to be asked to check the relationship among activities, social context and the locations or modes of travel

–   During the period from 9 to 10 you reported that you were alone and were preparing and eating a meal. Can you remember any other activities that you might have engaged in during this period?

–   Is it correct that the rest of the family did not turn up until after you finished the meal?

–   What was the purpose of the half-hour bus trip you made just after 12 o'clock?

–   While on the bus did you do anything else besides reading the paper?

–   Even if your son was present from 6 to 8 o'clock in the evening you have not reported that you were doing anything together. Is that correct?

–   When you socialized with your friends from 8 to 10 in the evening, were talking and eating the only activities you took part in?

Source: Haraldsen (2000).

---

437.   There are other probing techniques that have been used to bring out often underreported activities such as probing for childcare not spontaneously mentioned during the completion of the diary. Another is to list often-forgotten activities. These methods are called respectively targeted probing and checklist probing. While these kinds of probes may be helpful in aiding memory recall, they should be used with caution because asking about specific activities or presenting a selective list of activities may lead to biased results owing to overreporting of those activities.

438. A potential drawback of probing is that it may increase interview time and respondent burden while producing additional detail that may not be necessary to the goals of the survey. There would thus be a need to assess to what extent additional probing questions should be asked.

6. Giving incentives to respondents

439. Time-use surveys demand much time and effort of respondents and thus may lead to total refusals or partial non-response (for example, incomplete diaries). As part of the strategy for increasing the chances for full cooperation, some countries have provided incentives to respondents. Incentives may be in the form of money or a small gift such as phone cards and wall clocks.

440. There is as yet no known formal evaluation of the effect of incentives in increasing response, improving data quality and increasing efficiency of the interview process in time-use surveys, specifically. The more general experience is mixed. In situations where cooperation is usually poor, there may be some gain. Where compliance is ordinarily good, there may be little further advantage. Some studies have shown that incentives have a positive effect on response rates, especially among low-income families

(United Nations, 1984, para. 4.170). In other cases, however, incentives have proven to be equally effective across income groups (Statistics Canada, 2000a). For example, in a study to determine whether $10 and $20 incentives would increase both the current response rate and the response rate for subsequent interviews, the United States Bureau of the Census Survey of Income and Program Participation concluded that the $20 incentive had a positive effect on response rates at the overall level as well as for both low- and high-poverty strata. They also found both the $10 and the $20 incentives to be effective in reducing follow-up non-response both at the overall level and in high poverty. A test of incentives undertaken by Statistics Canada in the 1997 Survey of Household Spending (ibid.) indicated that incentives had differential effects on increasing response rates depending on the type (in this case, telephone cards led to slightly higher response rates compared with magazine subscriptions).

441. The cost of giving incentives must be weighed against the expected gains in data quality. It should also be noted that the practice of giving incentives may have negative implications for other surveys in that respondents may also expect the same incentives even when surveys are not as demanding of their time and effort.

VIII. PROCESSING OF TIME-USE SURVEY DATA

442. The data-processing cycle involves many interdependent activities. The major ones are: coding, data capture, quality assurance, editing, and validation leading to the production of core tabulations. The inputs into the processing cycle are the survey forms—household and personal questionnaires and time-use diaries. The basic output—the data files—serve as inputs into the data analysis and dissemination phases of the survey.

443. While data collection constitutes the most critical phase from the standpoint of the accuracy of the survey results, the ability to obtain these results within a reasonable time period rests even more on the efficiency of the data-processing system for the survey (United Nations, 1984, para. 6.1). The development of an efficient data-processing system for a new and non-standard survey can be a relatively complex task needing coordinated efforts of survey statisticians, subject-matter specialists and users of data and survey findings, and information technology staff. It may be even more complicated for time-use surveys because of the special processing issues associated with the use of time diaries.

444. Strategies for the processing phase need to be established early in survey planning. A key factor in expediting data processing is the early completion of tabulation plans. This phase is crucial for identifying the variables that would need to be edited and coded, variables that are to be derived from the survey information, and the logical relationships among these variables. This information is needed for editing and imputation specifications as well as for preparation of the table formats. Furthermore, assessing the consistency between the data specifications as they appear in the survey instruments and those required by the analytical tabulations is an important part of questionnaire design.

445. The principal aspects of the development of a data-processing strategy for time-use surveys include the following:

–   Determination of the basic processing methodology. This entails decisions on how various processing steps will be carried out. In relation to data editing and coding, decisions need to be made on whether these are to be done by clerical staff (or manual processing), by computers or through some combination of both methods. In addition, decisions need to be made on how errors detected in processing will be handled and whether and how imputations will be made for missing items.

–   Preparation of necessary instructions, manuals and other tools for coding and editing, and other clerical operations.

–   Decisions on data capture procedures or means of transferring data from questionnaires and diaries to create computer data files.

–   Decisions on technology, both hardware and software, to be utilized for processing, estimation and tabulation and for subsequent preservation and use of the data.

–   Decisions on the extent of centralization or decentralization of data-processing functions.

446. General discussions and recommendations on these matters can be found in various United Nations handbooks on

surveys and censuses.[53] As a general recommendation, decisions on the processing methodology and technology to be adopted for the time-use survey should take into account the existing data-processing system of the statistical office. This means utilization of both regular processing staff and infrastructure—both hardware and software. In the event that some aspects of the time-use data-processing system need to be introduced into the existing system, proper documentation and technology transfer should be undertaken. Processing of time-use diaries is an area in which countries have found it useful to consider application software other than that normally used in the statistical office for developing data entry systems, implementing computerized edits and generating tabulations.[54]

447. This *Guide* focuses on the processing of time-use survey questionnaires and diaries. Issues related to the processing of household and personal questionnaires of time-use surveys are essentially similar to those for typical household surveys. Many demographic and economic variables are therefore similar. Questions unique to time-use surveys are expected to be resolved following current standards such as those prescribed in the United Nations handbooks mentioned earlier.[55]

448. There is, however, much less experience in the processing of time-use diaries. The task involves classifying reported activities according to activity classification codes, editing where necessary, recording activity and context variable codes on coding forms or in the diary, and preparing for data capture.

A. Planning and organizing coding and editing operations

449. Assembling the right resources to ensure timely and efficient processing of data and managing these resources are major tasks in any survey. Decisions about resource requirements influence strategic processing decisions having implications for, inter alia, the number and location of processing staff and pay rates, development of coding tools etc. Managers who plan and supervise editing and coding need to collaborate closely with the technical staff involved in the design of the classification and coding procedures, the recruitment and training of coders/editors and data validation and analysis. In this regard, statistical offices with little experience in processing of time-use data from diaries need to be acutely aware that coding and editing could easily become a bottleneck in the survey plan. It is thus important that estimates of the rate of coding as well as of querying be generated as part of the planning through tests designed for the purpose. Likewise, it is important to make good estimates of the number of coders/editors, and first-line supervisors needed to control the coding/editing process, and the number of specially trained staff needed to resolve coding queries.

450. The success of coding and editing is a key factor that affects the quality of diary data and the usability of survey results. The relationship among editing, imputation and coding of diaries is sequential as well as iterative. Some of the coding problems are resolved by appropriate applications of editing and imputation, while results of some edits and imputations are eventually coded. Thus,

---

[53] See for example, United Nations (1984, chap. VI) and United Nations (2001b, chap. IV).
[54] For example, Blaise was used by Australia in its 1997 time-use survey; it was tested for the pilot surveys of the European Time Use Surveys (ETUS) and is being recommended for the harmonized time-use surveys.
[55] For editing and processing common demographic and economic characteristics and coding of occupation and industry, see United Nations (2001a); and Hoffmann (2001).

oftentimes in the staffing pattern set-up for processing diaries, the same set of people serve as coders, editors and data entry staff and need to be trained to do both coding and editing. Some critical activities that need to be undertaken to ensure a high degree of success in processing include:

- Selecting and training coders/editors and supervisors and organizing them into efficient work teams.
- Developing coding tools to guide the coding process.
- Designing and testing procedures for monitoring and supervising.
- Handling coding problems and queries.
- Quality assessment and control.

1. Training of coders/editors

451. Coding and editing of activities for time-use statistics require an understanding and interpretation of the textual descriptions provided in the diaries in terms of the framework of the activity classification developed for the survey. Data quality is enhanced when coded data result from a uniform interpretation of the listing of activities; thus, the training design should provide coders and supervisors with the information and tools needed to acquire the required level of understanding.

452. A training programme for coders/editors who will be working in a centralized office-coding[56] environment should include discussion on uses of the data and the organization of coding work. The background questionnaires should also be discussed with emphasis on how the information from these questionnaires provide information that may be needed for editing and

coding of activities. In discussing diary coding, the structure of the diary, the activity classification and coding index, and the codes of context variables should be explained in detail. Coding procedures need to be explained and demonstrated and trainees should be given practical exercises on the use of coding tools and the handling of different situations. To enhance understanding of the diary, they should fill out a time-use diary based on their own activities before the training begins. Annex 10 provides an illustration of a training design where training on coding and editing was integrated with interviewer training.

2. Developing tools for coding activities

453. Basic tools required by coders for the coding of activities (Hoffmann, 1995) include:

- *Coding instructions.* Instructions should cover all the operations that the coder is required to carry out: document control; which items in addition to the activity descriptions are to be edited and coded and the order in which these are to be undertaken; procedures for delimiting episodes; use of the coding index; when and how to use data from household and individual questionnaires to edit and code diaries.
- *Coding index for classifying activities.*[57] A coding index is the key coding document through which verbatim descriptions of activities in diaries are translated into the appropriate codes as defined by the activity classification adopted for the survey. The coding index guides the coder by listing information, for example, key words, that can be found

---

[56] Two main options for implementing coding operations are field-coding and office-coding. These are described below.

[57] See annex 11 for further discussion on coding indexes.

in the responses. It indicates how different responses are allocated to the detailed or more aggregate groups of the classification, depending on the nature of the information in the response and on the instructions for the coding process. Thus, a coding index for an activity classification must be a reflection of the type of responses that one will find written in the diary by the respondent, or written by the enumerator on the basis of the information received from the respondent. The coding index should reflect the type of words and expressions that the respondents will use when asked to give the information about the activities they engage in during the course of the day. Coders should not be encouraged to interpret verbatim responses in terms of their own conception of the purpose or criteria of the classification, but rather to follow in a conscientious way the instructions laid down for consulting the index. The use of the coding index, instructions and procedures need to allow for updating so as to reflect decisions made in resolving queries and problems that arose and were dealt with in the course of coding.

- *Query system.* Queries are the most useful inputs to both immediate and future work to update the coding index and the classification itself. There should be clear instructions on when and how coders should raise queries and on how to make a record of the query and its resolution.

- *Control forms.* For purposes of monitoring, supervising and documenting the coding process, various forms need to be designed and used—for example, forms for recording queries and their resolution, for controlling the flow of work and

reporting progress, for quality monitoring.

3. Monitoring and supervising

454. For the processing of time-use diaries, statistical offices adopt the same basic philosophy and system for monitoring and supervising that they implement for household surveys.

455. One special concern in coding and editing of time-use data is documenting editing and coding problems and solutions tried. The information thus obtained is essential in further developing and improving the activity classification. In addition, decisions made in resolving queries and problems that arose during coding should be reflected as updates or modifications to the coding index. It is recommended that as part of the monitoring procedures, a supervisor is given the tasks of updating the coding index and informing coders of changes on a regular basis.

4. Handling coding/editing problems and queries

456. Appropriate procedures need to be laid down in advance for reporting and recording queries and the decisions made in resolving them and for incorporating any consequent modifications in the coding documentation and procedures. No matter how carefully coding and editing instructions and the coding index have been prepared, it is to be expected that problems and queries will arise during the coding and editing operations. This happens for several reasons, for example, actual activity descriptions are more varied than anticipated; respondent has not provided enough information in the diary to allow the coding of a reported activity etc. (see section B below for a discussion on problems and difficulties related to coding activities). The roles of supervisors in processing queries and reflecting changes in the coding index need to

be defined. Particular attention needs to be given to coordinating query reporting and communicating updates in the coding index and procedures where coding is being carried out in several locations or in the field (Hoffmann, 1995, p. 33).

5. Quality control

457. The purpose of quality control at the processing stage is to measure the quality of the input process in order to improve the output. An important step in this process is the development and maintenance of quality control statistics. The basic source of this information is the type and number of "errors" made by the coders. The information about the type of error is conveyed to the individual coders to improve their performance. The information about the number of errors is used to monitor the coder's improvement over time and set the level of quality control applied to each coder. A list of quality control statistics is shown in table 10.

458. The process of generating the quality control statistics be can designed so that the data may be used to estimate average levels of coding accuracy and inter-coder consistency for the entire coding exercise. A basic design would entail obtaining a random sample of coded diaries for each coder (original coder) and having the same diaries re-coded by another (quality control coder). Discrepancies in the output of the original and quality control coders can then be analysed.

B. Coding of activities

459. As discussed in part two, one of the major decisions in the design of survey instruments for collecting time-use data concerns the choice between a pre-coded time diary and an after-coded time diary. The merits and disadvantages of each have been discussed in part two and will not be repeated

here. The discussion in the present section assumes that an after-coded time diary is used in the data collection.

Table 10. Illustration of quality control statistics

Number of episodes

1.	Number coded
2.	Number omitted or mistakenly added

Errors (number of instances)

Incorrect allocation of time to any particular episode

1. For primary activities
   - First digit of code is incorrect (activity is incorrectly coded)
   - First digit of code is correct but second digit is incorrect (activity is coded to the correct major group but to an incorrect minor group)
   - First and second digits of code are correct but third digit is incorrect (activity is incorrectly coded at the detailed level)

2. For secondary activities
   - Miscoded (coder has coded the episode incorrectly)
   - Omitted or missed

3. For each selected context variable/ background variable
   - Miscoded
   - Omitted or missed

Source: Australian Bureau of Statistics (1997c).
Note: The activity codes in this example are three-digit codes.

460. The discussion below focuses on the processing of time-use diaries, specifically the coding of activity descriptions, including:

(a) Objectives and level of coding.

(b) Given the activity classification developed for the survey, a decision on the level of detail in coding of activities recorded in diaries.

(c)   Decision on whether diary data are to be coded in the field or centralized in the office.

1. Objectives and level of coding

461.   When coding the information recorded by a respondent in the time diary on the activities he or she had engaged in, the main aim is to determine which group in the activity classification the activity belongs and record it correctly. The coding process converts textual information into standardised numeric codes which facilitate processing and tabulation consistent with the intended analytical framework for survey results. This task has to be completed within an overall processing plan, according to a timetable that is to be met, and in a manner that makes optimal use of resources.

462.   Although the major uses of the survey data would have been specified at the planning stage, it cannot be expected that all potential uses were taken into account. Since suitability for specific analysis objectives depends on the level of detail available for analyses, results of the coding should retain as much as possible of the information contained in the descriptive responses given. The coding process should therefore be designed to find and record the most detailed code supported by the activity description.

2. Level of detail in coding

463.   For other statistical classifications such as the occupational classification, some countries have opted to use less detailed levels for coding survey responses. The reasons given for this include: (a) actual responses would not support coding to more detailed levels; (b) it is not possible to publish results for the more detailed groups because of the lack of observations; and (c) it would be too costly to code to a large number of categories

both in terms of coding errors and in terms of working hours (Hoffmann, 1995).

464.   These arguments may also be made for coding at less detailed levels of activity classifications.   Country experiences have shown, however, that this may not necessarily be advantageous. Coding at a detailed level is a good strategy for ensuring that procedures for either interview or self-reporting are designed to induce respondents to report activities in more, rather than less, detail. More information decreases opportunities for coding errors as well as the time needed to find the suitable code for the activity. In addition, more detailed coding increases the usefulness of the diary data by ensuring that fewer activities are coded as "not fully defined". As mentioned in previous chapters, the decision to aggregate results to less detailed activity categories in coding, because of a small number of observations, can and should preferably be made at the tabulation stage rather than at the coding stage.

3. Field or office coding?

465.   In relation to the issue of who should do the coding, three strategies are generally considered:

–   Option 1. Respondent does the coding.
–   Option 2. Interviewer does the coding either during the interview or before the survey instrument is forwarded for further processing.
–   Option 3. Coders do the coding in a centralized processing centre.

Respondent does the coding

466.   In the case of coding activities as recorded in time-use diary data, the first option is not recommended. It would certainly be impractical for a face-to-face interview approach. It might be considered for the

"leave-behind" or self-completed diary approach but this would entail having to provide respondents with a coding list. If the coding list consists of a large number of categories, however, printing costs would be high, the interviewer would spend some time in explaining the coding procedures and the additional task would contribute to respondent burden. The alternative would be to use a list with a limited number of categories; a better option than this, however, is to use a pre-coded or light time diary instead.

Interviewer does the coding ("Field coding")

467. Field coding is feasible for face-to-face interviews provided the coding is done by the interviewer not during but after the interview. Thus, an interviewer's workload would include both interviewing and coding. For coding leave-behind diaries that are collected from the respondents in the field, the ideal set-up would be for the interviewer to do the coding as part of the review process while he or she is still in the enumeration area.

468. To ensure reliability of field coding, the interviewer would need to receive adequate training and detailed instructions; that is to say, aside from the field operations training, the interviewer would also need to be given training as a coder. Coding indexes and other coding tools including a procedure for forwarding queries to coding supervisors would have to be made available to interviewers.

469. One advantage of field coding is that an interviewer will often retain in memory more details about the respondent's description of the activities. Another advantage is that, as the interviewers gain experience with coding, they become better versed in the level of detail in the activity information that would be needed to code more efficiently and accurately. Thus, they

are able to assess the sufficiency of the description given by the respondent and prompt for more details when needed. Field coding also contributes to timeliness and cost-efficiency and simplifies processing procedures because the questionnaires and diaries can then be encoded directly: the intermediate step of office clerical processing is eliminated. This would especially hold when the reported activities are the only items that will require a major coding operation. Where a permanent field staff carries out the enumeration, it may be cost-effective in the long run for them to be trained in activity coding and to accumulate experience in this area.

470. When interviewers are geographically scattered and are trained in different training centres and supervised by differently trained people, a potential main disadvantage of field coding is the possible decrease in data reliability and consistency due to differences in coding decisions. Compared with office coding (further discussed below), field coding sacrifices the important advantages of a controlled and supervised coding environment (office coding) which can provide direct feedback on coding quality to coders. Furthermore, field supervisors may not be equipped to give high priority to quality control of coding (their priority would tend to be the enumeration process) or be in a position to resolve coding queries as they occur.

Office coding

471. Most national statistical offices will have a specialized, centrally located unit of coders for censuses and regular surveys. Coding staff may be entirely specialized in coding particular classifications or in coding in general and may thus be tapped for coding ad hoc surveys such as a first time-use survey. Another possible centralized coding set-up is one where inexperienced coding staff are

specially recruited and trained for coding. As discussed above, the advantage of this type of set-up over field coding is the better possibilities for training, supervision and immediate query resolution. The disadvantage is the increased distance from the original response or data source and the complete dependence on what the interviewer or the respondent has recorded in the diary.

472. Two basic options may be considered for office coding. One option would be to first write the codes in the diary prior to data capture (manual coding); another option is to integrate the coding into the data capture process by having the codes automatically assigned through a *computer-assisted coding* (CAC) system that is an integral part of the data capture system.[58] A CAC system also allows coders to place an activity description manually in the system should an automated search fail to assist with the coding. A well-designed CAC system simplifies, speeds up and reduces the cost of data processing. It can potentially improve reliability of activity data owing to consistency in coding and reduced chances of coding and data capture errors. However, experience with CAC for activity coding for time-use statistics is still too limited[59] to be able to provide an objective cost-benefit analysis.

473. Office coding is the recommended option over field coding primarily because of the more controlled environment which contributes to consistency in coding, quick resolutions to queries, and uniform applications of procedures and their modifications.

C. Aspects of planning and organizing coding activities

474. The verbatim descriptions of activities recorded in diaries need to be numerically coded to the corresponding activity categories of the classification used in the survey. When the survey design calls for reporting of multiple activities, both main activities and secondary activities need to be coded. In addition to coding main and secondary activities, the chronological list of activities reported in the diary needs to be delimited into episodes.

475. In the discussion that follows, it is assumed that an activity classification has been developed for the time-use survey. Without loss of generality, it is also assumed that the activity classification is hierarchic in structure and when referring to the level of detail of the activity descriptions, the first level represents the least detailed level or the broadest grouping of activities and the three-digit and higher levels are hierarchically more detailed than the preceding levels. In the case of the proposed International Classification of Activities for Time-Use Statistics (ICATUS),[60] the six-digit codes are considered as the most detailed level of classification.[61]

1. Coding rules

476. Coding rules provide a basic set of instructions on how tools for coding should be applied and what actions to take when situations arise that are not covered by these instructions.

---

[58] Computer-assisted coding systems may be used in field coding in, for example, computer-assisted telephone interviews as was done, for instance, in the 1997 Time Use Survey of Canada.
[59] Australia, Canada and New Zealand employed computer-assisted coding of activities as part of their data entry system for diaries.

---

[60] This is a draft classification for trial use. The classification will be placed on the web site of the United Nations Statistics Division for further discussion.
[61] See chapter XIII for description of the structure of the ICATUS.

Table 11.   Illustrative rules to be followed in coding activities

Rule 1.	Code up to four digits according to the activity coding index.		
Rule 2.	If an activity is described well enough to be coded to the four-digit level but no corresponding four-digit activity description is found in the coding index, use the four-digit "not elsewhere classified (n.e.c.)". If this particular activity is reported relatively often, it may warrant adding a new code in the index.		
Rule 3.	If the activity description does not have enough information so that it is not possible to select a four-digit code:	Rule 3a.	If there is sufficient information for coding at the three-digit level, then use the four-digit code ending with one "x" which corresponds to the "not fully defined (n.f.d.)" category at the group level.
		Rule 3b.	If there is insufficient information for coding even at the three-digit or division level, then use the "not fully defined (n.f.d.)" category at the division level.
		Rule 3c	If there is insufficient information for coding even to one of the tabulation categories, use code "9999".

477.   The following basic rules for coding activities using the four-digit level or group level of the proposed United Nations ICATUS classification illustrate basic instructions for coding. For the divisions that are not further broken down into specified four-digit groups, the three-digit codes need to be converted to four-digit ones by adding a zero to the three-digit code. In this set of rules, activities are to be coded to the most detailed level. Table 11 gives an outline of some of the most important rules that should be followed in coding.

478.   Additional rules for coding should cover determination of main activities, coding of secondary activities and coding of special situations. These are described below.

(a) Coding activities that are not clearly described

479.   Some respondents may use descriptions that do not provide enough information to allow coding to the most detailed level of the classification. For example, a respondent may simply write "reading" as the activity whereas the classification may require information on the type of material being read—whether a book, periodical or other specified material—to enable coding to the most detailed level. Another example concerns the reporting of "work" activities. In order to be able to code at the most detailed level of the proposed ICATUS, needed pieces of information include those that would differentiate between household and non-household production (for example, type of institution) and, for household production activities those that would allow classification into work activities by type of economic activity.[62]

480.   To take care of this situation, a "not fully defined" category at the division and group levels is defined in the ICATUS. It is suggested, however, that use of this type of coding category be minimized. To achieve this, instructions for interviewing and recording activities should ensure the

---

[62] See chapter XIII for more detailed discussion on the ICATUS.

provision of all information needed to do the detailed coding.

(b) Coding of multiple main activities

481. Each activity recorded in a diary needs to be uniquely coded. Where the diary is designed to record only one activity per time interval and more than one activity is recorded, the rules for determining the main activity to be coded have to be specified. A diary may also be designed to record multiple activities within a time interval. For this type of design, it has been suggested in chapter III that simultaneously-done activities need to be prioritized as primary, secondary etc. and, ideally, that the activities should be recorded under separate columns in the diary. Nevertheless, respondents may still report more than one activity as occurring within the same time interval without differentiating primary from secondary.

482. When multiple entries are recorded in diaries, there are two tasks that need to be carried out: (a) appropriate coding of the activities as main and secondary; and (b) editing in the time for each activity. In determining the main or primary activity, editing may be required to take care of inconsistencies in the reports or to apply prioritization rules (for example, overriding activities, multifaceted activities) as discussed in part two. Editing procedures will be discussed further below. For purposes of illustration, a set of procedures for how to determine a main activity when two activities are reported at the same time is given below.[63] The criterion for selecting the main activity from among multiple activities is dependent on whether the activities are performed simultaneously or sequentially and on

---

[63] This set of rules follows the suggested guidelines for the Eurostat Harmonised Time Use Surveys.

assumptions about the duration of the activities.

– If the activities are clearly simultaneous and one of the activities is likely to be a consequence of the other, then the activity that is a consequence is to be coded as secondary and the other as the main activity. Example: "Had supper and talked with the family." It would be reasonable to assume that the respondent was talking with family because the members of the family were having supper together and not that they were having supper because they were talking. Thus, "talking with the family" is the secondary activity and "having supper" is the main activity.

– If the activities are simultaneous, and none of the activities is likely to be a consequence of the other, then code the activity mentioned first is to be coded as the main activity and the other activity as the secondary activity is to be.

– If the activities are sequential, then the one that has the longer duration is to be coded as the main activity.

– If the activities are sequential and there is no clear difference in their durations, then the activity listed first is to be coded as the main activity.

(c) Coding of secondary activities

483. It is recommended that the same set of codes be used for coding main and secondary activities. Some studies, however, may use classification criteria that specify that certain activities are always to be coded as secondary activities unless they are reported as a sole activity. For example, the Eurostat activity classification specifies that "Lunch break, related to employment" should always be

coded as a secondary activity and that respondents should report what they did during the lunch break. In this case, the activity being conducted during lunch break is considered the main activity. Another example is that of "Visiting or receiving visitors" which is to be considered as a secondary activity; respondents should report specific activities performed while visiting (for example, helping in preparing meals, watching television etc.) as the primary activity.

484. A code of "no secondary activity undertaken" should be included in the coding index. The code for "doing nothing" should not be used to indicate that there is no secondary activity. This code should be used only if "doing nothing" is reported as a main activity.

(d) Coding when main/primary activity is not determined by the respondent

485. In some countries,[64] the decision as to which is the primary and which the secondary of two simultaneous activities is not left to the respondent. Rather, the ordering of the activity is determined by pre-specified rules which are applied at the coding stage. The set of rules applied in the 1999 New Zealand Time Use Survey is described here for illustrative purposes. In this survey, the ordering rules first prioritized the broad activity groups of the classification and then prioritized activities within the broad categories. The first-level priority ranking was based on the two-digit-level codes as shown in table 12.

486. A second-level prioritization also needs to be applied if more than one activity from the same activity grouping defined at the first level is reported in the same time slot. In this

case, primary activity is determined using a priority order of three- and four- digit codes. Table 13 shows the ordering by rank of activities within group 04, Household work.

Table 12. Illustration of priority ranking of activity categories for purposes of determining primary and secondary activities

Rank	Activity category
1st	01- Personal care
2nd	02- Labour-force activity
3rd	03- Education and training
4th	05- Caregiving for household members
5th	04- Household work
6th	06- Purchasing good and services for own household
7th	07- Unpaid work outside of the home
8th	08- Religious, cultural and civic participation
9th	09- Social entertainment
10th	10- Sports and hobbies
11th	11- Mass media and free-time activities
12th	99- Residual

Source: Statistics New Zealand (1999).

(e) Codes for special situations/activities

487. Codes may need to be assigned to handle special cases such as the activity "filled in the time diary".[65]

488. A "missing data" code should also be pre-specified for cases where the respondent fails to report any activity over a time period and no edit or imputation is made to fill in an activity.

---

[64] For example, in the 1999 New Zealand Time Use Survey and the 2000 South Africa Time Use Survey.

[65] Some countries choose to classify this activity as "performed civic duty".

Table 13. Illustration of priority ranking of activities within an activity category for purposes of determining primary and secondary activities

Activity category	
0412	Meal or snack preparation and clean-up
0411	Preserving and brewing
0422	Laundry and other care of clothes
0421	Indoor cleaning
0471	Gathering and collecting food for household consumption
0451	Household administration
0432	Tending domestic animals (excluding pets)
0433	Other grounds maintenance and pet care
0431	Tending edible plants
0441	Home repair or improvement
0442	Heating and water upkeep
0443	Vehicle maintenance
0449	Other home maintenance n.e.c.
0461	Production of household goods
0488	Travel associated with household work
0499	Other household work n.e.c.

Source: Statistics New Zealand (1999).

489. An example of an activity that may require attention in coding is travelling. An activity classification may categorize travel according to the purpose of travel. For such classifications, travel involving several activities or "journeys" may present difficulties in coding. A useful tool is that of viewing a journey as a "circle" with common starting and ending points and a turning point. The coding of a journey starts with the identification of this circle. The number of circles found in one diary depends on how the respondent travels around during the diary day. Some examples of how journeys are to be coded are described below.

– *A straightforward journey to one's place of work and back home.* The person's dwelling or house is the common starting point and ending point of the journey and the journey is "interrupted" (marks the turning point) by the time spent at the place of work. This is an example where both travel from home to work and from work to home are regarded as having the same purpose—related to work—and would thus have the same code.

– *A journey to and from work "interrupted" by an errand.* Consider the following example: a child is brought to school on the way to work in the morning and picked up in the afternoon on the way home from work. The journey, then, has two purposes, each corresponding to a separate travel activity. Travel to school in the morning is connected with childcare and the travel onward to work is related to work; the return travel may also be broken up into two travel-related activities.

– *An errand (for example, trip to store) during lunch break at work.* In this case, the travel to and from work constitutes one circle and would be coded as in the first example. The trip to the store constitutes a circle of its own with the workplace as the starting and the ending point and the store as the turning point of the circle. In some cases, it may be difficult to identify the turning point. For example, if many different errands were carried out during lunch break, then the turning point could be defined as the errand that required the longest time (or some other rule).

– *Leaving home, doing different activities/errands at different places before returning back home.* In this case, the journey is described by a single circle with the house as the starting and the ending point and the turning point being determined by a rule (for example, errand with the

114

longest duration). Travel is to be coded in relation to the specific type of activity/errand, for example, shopping, help to other household etc.

– *Leaving home to go to another locality in order to do several activities before returning home.* The starting point and the ending point of the journey are the home. The turning point is determined by arrival and departure from the location. The travel to the locality from home and travel from the locality back to home would both have the same code. Some classifications have a specific code for such travel (for example, Eurostat activity code 991, Travel related to changing locality).

2. Delimiting episodes

490.   Analysis of the time spent on an activity may be based on: (a) the total time spent on the activity in a day; and (b) the number and time spent on individual occurrences or *episodes* of the activity during the day. Consider, for example, the activity of brushing one's teeth. Time use on this activity can be described in terms of total time spent brushing one's teeth, number of times during the day a person brushes his teeth (each time he brushes his teeth is an episode) and the total time spent each time he brushes his teeth. For other activities, such as homework, the more important aspect may be the duration of the activity. For other activities, knowing the duration of each individual occurrence may be as important as knowing the total duration of the activity; for example, four hours of continuous strenuous labor might place a greater burden on an individual than two two-hour episodes.

491.   An episode of an activity is generally defined in terms of a starting and a finishing time, the contextual information describing the dimensions of the activity and the other activities that are associated with this period of

time. Where an episode ends, a new one begins; an episode is said to end when there is a change in the activity being done or in at least one of the specified context variables associated with the activity. In surveys where one or more simultaneously performed activities are recorded, a change in the secondary activity would also signal the beginning of a new episode.

492.   Consider, for example, a fixed interval diary which collects information on main and secondary activities, persons present during the main activity and the place or location where the main activity occurred. In this example, an episode of a main activity occurs for each time interval for which the secondary activity (if any), persons present and location remain unchanged. Any change in any of these three, signals the start of a new episode even if the main activity remains the same. A change in any of the main activity also signals the beginning of a new episode. Figure 6 shows a page of a fixed interval diary as described above with eight unique episodes. Episode 1 (waking up children) ends at 07.10 and changes into episode 2 (eating breakfast) because of the change in the main activity. Episode 2 lasts for 20 minutes and ends when a new main activity (clearing the table) begins. It is to be noted that episodes 6 and 7 have the same main and secondary activities but the fact that the "persons present" variable changes from "others" in episode 6 to "alone" signals the end of episode 6 and the beginning of episode 7.

Delimiting episodes

493.   Prior to data entry, episodes in the diary should be delimited. The basic output of this procedure delineates the start and the end of the unique episodes for each diary. This is done by marking the starting time of each episode (for example encircling the fixed time interval on the form or the recorded starting and ending times for open interval diaries).

Figure 6. Illustration of episodes in a diary

Episode	Time	Main activity	Secondary activity	Persons present				Location
				Alone	Children aged 0-9	Other hh member	Others	
1	07.00-07.10	Woke up the children			X			Home
2	07.10-07.20	Had breakfast	Talked with my family		X	X		
	07.20-07.30	↓	↓		X	X		
3	07.30-07.40	Cleared the table	Listened to the radio	X				
4	07.40-07.50	Helped the children dress	Talked with my children		X			
5	07.50-08.00	Went to the day-care centre, by foot	↓		X			Travel on foot
6	0.8.00-08.10	By bus to job	Read the newspaper				X	Travel by bus
7	08.10-08.20	By bus to job	↓	X				
8	08.20-08.30	Regular work		X				Work place

New episode due to change in "persons present" from "others" to "alone".

New episode due to change in main activity. Episode starts at 07.10 and ends at 07.30.

494. To facilitate data entry, all relevant information about an episode should be recorded on the first marked line for the episode (the line corresponding to the starting time.) Where the diary does not have a pre-specified column for codes (for example, contextual information), these need to be written close to the written description. It is important that there be no ambiguity about which code is connected to which activity and/or time intervals in the diary. When notes, edit corrections and codes are written in the diaries, differently colored pen or pencil marks should be used to distinguish among these.

495. An illustration of the result of coding and marking of episodes in a diary is provided in annex 12. In the diary shown, the activities are coded to a three-digit classification. Information on "location" is included as part of the activity description and thus has to be coded; the codes are written in the last two columns of the diary. An episode is marked off by encircling its starting time.

3. Coding of context variables

496. Contextual information may be collected in time-use diaries. As discussed in chapter III, this is best captured by a prudent selection of the context variables and by developing and testing the coding categories so that they provide the data needed for the planned analysis.

497. Chapter III also presents two options for collecting data on contextual information. One option is including in the diary a column for each of the context variables of interest. This column is to be completed by the

respondent using pre-coded categories. Another option is to collect the information as part of the activity description as in the following examples: mode of travel—travelled to the health centre by bus; location—sold fruits at the street corner; purpose/"for whom"—bathed and dressed wounds of sick father living with the respondent.

498. The main concern is to check that the responses to context variables are coded correctly. If the recorded response does not seem consistent with the nature of the activity or with related information or if the response is not coded, then an edit procedure to assess whether it is possible to correct or impute the response needs to be applied.

D. Editing of diaries

1. General considerations in editing

499. *Data editing* is the application of checks that identify missing, invalid or inconsistent entries in the survey instruments or that point to data records that are potentially in error. Some of these checks involve logical relationships that follow directly from the concepts and definitions. Others are more empirical in nature or are achieved as a result of the application of statistical tests or procedures (for example, outlier analysis techniques) or by external consistency checks from previous collections of the same survey or from other sources.

500. Editing tasks are performed as part of field checks at the data-collection stage[66] and prior to, during and after data capture. At the data processing stage, the tasks typically involve clerical (or manual) procedures (for example, coding, correcting entries in the diaries, marking episodes) as well as the

running of computerised edit checks which automate some of the tasks (for example, range checks, logical checks, imputation) and flag situations that need further review or action. *Further editing of data records are also undertaken as a result of data validation[67] prior to the generation of final tabulations from the survey data.*

501. The goals of editing are threefold (Granquist, 1984): to tidy up the data, to provide information about the quality of the survey data, and to provide the basis for future improvement of the survey vehicle. "Cleaning up the data" typically consists of removing invalid, inconsistent or other "fatal errors". These edits are best implemented as part of automated data processing. Query edits point to records that may potentially be in error. This form of editing results in manual procedures, respondent follow-up and, more often than not, little or no change in the data. Country experiences have shown that data editing could be the single most expensive activity of the sample survey and that query edits are generally the ones that are responsible for the high cost of editing (Fellegi and Holt, 1976). It is thus suggested that query edits be rationalized. Not only is the practice of over-editing costly in terms of resources and timeliness, but it can also lead to severe biases resulting from the fitting of data to implicit models imposed by the edits. Thus, statistical offices should find an appropriate balance between error detection and cost (ibid.).

502. Traditionally, the focus of editing has been on cleaning the data and not on the much more useful aim of providing information about the survey process, either to serve as quality measures for the current survey or to suggest improvements for future surveys. In this role, editing can be invaluable in

---

[66] The role of editing at the enumeration stage of a time-use survey is discussed in chapter VII.

[67] Data validation is discussed in chapter XI.

sharpening definitions, improving the activity classification and survey instruments, evaluating the quality of diary data, and identifying sources of non-sampling error. To accomplish this goal, statistical offices would need to monitor the process and produce audit trails, diagnostics and performance measures in order to identify best practices (ibid.).

503. The editing process for time-use diaries is an integral part of the coding process. Thus, the planning and organizing issues on training, monitoring and supervision and quality control discussed above also pertain to the editing process.

2. Edit checks for time-use diaries

504. Some of the common situations that require applying edits to diary data and illustrative country practices are described below.

(a) Basic checks

505. In a 24-hour diary, the total time for activities must cover 24 hours. A basic check is to verify that there are no gaps in the diary, in other words, no time intervals where there are no activities reported. This means that the ending time of a main activity should be the beginning time of the next main activity. When an open-interval design is used in the diary or where beginning and ending times of main activities are reported, there should be no overlaps in the beginning times of consecutive main activities.

506. Other specific checks are described below.

(b) No entries in a particular time slot

507. The options for dealing with this situation are: (a) code as missing data; or (b) impute an activity to the time slot. Imputation may be based on information in the diary (for example, information indicating that the previously reported activity is likely to continue) or on information derived from diaries of other household members covering the same time slot. An example of a common imputation is the following. When the time slot corresponds to the normally accepted sleeping period at night, "sleeping" is coded into the time slot.

508. Not all blank time slots need to be or should be imputed. For example, Australia's 1997 survey did not impute for time slots that occurred during the day unless this could be clearly derived from diaries of other household members. Canada's 1997 survey did not impute if the missing time was longer than 10 minutes. In addition, diaries with more than four hours of unreported activities during the day were considered unit (diary) non-response.

(c) Overlaps

509. Overlapping beginning times of consecutive main activities need to be edited to eliminate the overlap. In figure 7, for example, the beginning time of the activity "ate dinner" (11.40) overlaps with the reported time interval of the previous activity "watched tv" (11.00-12.00). To remove the overlap, the ending time of the previous activity is adjusted and the beginning time of the next activity is edited to coincide with this new time.

Figure 7. Illustrative rules for editing overlapping intervals

Activity	Was	Edited to
Watched TV	11.00 – 12.00	11.00 – 11.50
Ate dinner	11.40 – 12.15	11.50 – 12.15

(d) Omitted activities

510. There are some activities that should obviously have occurred but are not reflected in the diary. For example, it might reasonably be expected that everyone would have at least

one episode of sleeping, of eating or of a personal care activity each day. If a diary does not contain any report of eating and/or drinking or personal care activities (for example, bathing), information from other diaries of household members can be used for imputing these activities if available.

511. One of the most common errors in completing diaries is not reporting night sleep. An editing procedure for this situation used in the 1997 Time Use Survey of Australia is represented by the following sequence (Australian Bureau of Statistics, 1997a): Are all times accounted for?

– Yes: Do the activities in the diary seem reasonable (for example, studying all night for an exam) or is there an explanatory comment by the interviewer?
  ▪ Yes: Accept the recorded activities.
  ▪ No: Flag as missing (for resolution by supervisor).
– No: If there is any indication of going to bed, or getting up, then code a sleep episode.

(e) Essential intermediate step missing

512. Respondents may report a sequence of activities for which there may be a logical gap because of a missing activity that should have followed or preceded another. For example, the respondent reports that she prepared a meal but does not report that she ate. Or a respondent may report "reading a book" and then "took medication" with a substantial gap in time until the next entry. In this case, it may be assumed that the respondent continued to read after taking medication.

513. A more complex but common problem of this nature is when a change in location is reported without a travel episode. Here the missing pieces of information are the time used for the travel and the context variables

(for example, mode of transport) in relation to travel. A procedure to impute travel time, provided in Australia's 1997 Time Use Survey, is presented in box 6.

Box 6. Procedure for imputing travel time adopted by the Australian Bureau of Statistics

– If the return journey is shown, use the duration for the missing episode of travel.

– If the destination or departure point is "at work" or an activity with a definite start and finish time, take the journey time from the episode before or after the work period, on the assumption that people usually know their work starting and finishing times.

– If the destination is shops or another activity location with an indeterminate arrival time, take the travel time from the current activity.

– If the whole cycle of the journey is omitted, look in other diaries in the household to see if they have the information needed (for example, other members of the household may have been with the respondent while travelling). If no information is available, then impute a 10-minute travel episode unless there are strong grounds for selecting a different duration (for example, information on locations and distances in the area).

– If the activity with the missing travel episode is of too short a duration for travel to be significant, then just code the activity as recorded.

Source: Australian Bureau of Statistics (1997a).

(f) Multiple entries

514. Respondents may report two or more activities in the "main/primary activity" column. Main versions of statements of multiple activities are:

– Case 1. Activities that take place at the same time (in other words simultaneous activities).

- Case 2. Sequential activities over a number of time slots where one is momentary or almost "instantaneous" and the other has a relatively much longer duration (for example, brushed teeth and went to bed)
- Case 3. Sequential activities written in one time slot.
- Case 4. Two activities that are recorded as being simultaneous but are obviously sequential.

515. In case 1, there will be a need to determine which is the main activity and which is the secondary activity, and there may be some situations that call for editing to ensure that the prioritization rules are consistently applied in coding the activities. For sequential activities (cases 2-4), each activity is to be treated as a main activity and the time allocation should be distributed among the activities following some rule. For case 2, if the momentary activity has too short a duration, then the rule could be that it is not to be coded. In case 4, it might be possible that the two activities can actually be treated as a single one (for example, cooked and prepared lunch boxes for sale).

(g) Secondary activities

516. There are two situations for which edits may need to be made in reports of secondary activities: when more than one activity is recorded as a secondary activity; and when no secondary activity is reported. The variations in the reporting of multiple secondary activities are similar to those discussed for main activities. The procedures for editing and coding are thus similar to those discussed in the previous section.

517. In the case when multiple activities have been reported, it is important to set prioritization rules by which one or more activities can be selected. Bearing in mind that many important activities are often regarded by respondents as secondary and would thus not be reported if only main activities were collected, priority should be given to these types of activities such as unpaid domestic work, childcare, elderly care and care of the sick and disabled.

518. Following similar principles, when no secondary activity is reported, it may be necessary to review whether activities that are often underreported—usually, childcare or care of elderly, sick or disabled persons—were actually carried out. This may be done by checking against relevant contextual and background information (for example, "with whom"; family composition). When indications of underreporting are found, decisions on whether to use the information to edit in or impute or flag the record for further review need to be made.

(h) Contextual information

519. Responses to context variables may be either missing or found to be inconsistent with other entries in the diary. If missing, the coder would have to determine an appropriate code from the activity description or from other information in the diary or the background questionnaires or "corroborating" diaries of household members. Table 14, sets out a procedure that may be applied if the "location of activity" context variable for a reported activity is missing (Australian Bureau of Statistics, 1997a, p. 11).

520. In this example, the code "00" represents a pre-assigned code for handling missing data for this context variable.

521. Deciding on whether or not to edit or impute a context variable depends to a great extent on the information available and the intended analytical use of the variable. An example of how the analytical purpose determines editing and imputation specifications is provided by the specifications

for the "for whom" context variable in the 1997 Time Use Survey of Australia. One of the analytical objectives of the survey concerned volunteer work and care episodes. Thus, the editing procedure used the following guidelines (Australian Bureau of Statistics, 1997a, p.10).

Table 14.   Possible procedure to apply in the case of a missing "location of activity" context variable for a reported activity

Step 1.	Can it be validly inferred from the nature of the activity?	If Yes, then code accordingly
		If No, go to step 2
Step 2.	Can it be validly inferred from the location of the previously reported activity in the diary?	If Yes, then code accordingly
		If No, go to step 3
Step 3.	Can it be validly inferred from information in corroborating diaries?	If Yes, then code accordingly
		If No, go to step 4
Step 4.	No available information. Code as "00"	

Source: Australian Bureau of Statistics (1997a).

522.   Information provided by the respondent may be changed only if:

–   It is needed to capture the purpose of the main activity; in other words, if a voluntary work or care activity would otherwise not be identified as such.

–   Evidence in the diary is overwhelming.

–   The purpose of the activity may be interpreted differently because the "for whom" information is incorrect.

523.   The same survey devised a complex set of guidelines for editing and coding the "with whom" context variable which utilized information from other context variables (for

example, location of activity) and from diaries of other household members (ibid., pp.14-16).

(i)   Other difficult cases

524.   Editing procedures need to be developed for cases whose resolution by coders and editors is foreseen to be difficult. These cases would depend on the classification used, the analytical framework of the survey, the prioritization rules for determining primary activities, and the ways people generally report their activities.   A systematic way of identifying these situations involves a review of experiences of similarly situated countries and the conduct of methodological studies, pre-tests, pilot tests on interview procedures and coding of activities.   A listing of some possible cases is given below:

–   Uncodeable activities.

–   Conflicting information in diaries within households.

–   Coding pervasive activities.   For example, passive childcare.

–   Description of an activity not carried out by the respondent.   For example, friends arrive; wife leaves for work.

–   Coding travel activities.

–   Coding "waiting".

–   Coding activities of short duration, for example, "arrived at home".

–   Report does not include purpose for activities that have different codes depending on the purpose.   For example, swimming can be engaged in for exercise, for sport, in a competition or as part of health therapy.

3.   Checking entries against other survey information

525.   As illustrated in the earlier discussions, some editing procedures make use of the respondent's background questionnaires as well as diaries of other household members for

imputing missing data in the diaries. Conversely, personal questionnaires can be edited using information found in the diary. One important application involves checking consistency in the data on the labour-force activity of the respondent. For example, a respondent may have indicated that he or she was undertaking a labour-force activity in the diary but the personal questionnaire contained the answer "no" to labour-force participation questions. In this case, the two entries would need to be made consistent with each other.

526. Beyond the editing considerations, however, the results of this type of consistency check can be the basis for assessing the methods for collecting labour-force participation data. In fact, for some countries such an assessment is one of the objectives in conducting a time-use survey.

E. Imputation

1. General considerations

527. *Imputation*, as mentioned earlier in this chapter, is the process used to resolve problems of missing, invalid or inconsistent responses identified during editing. This is effected by changing some of the responses or missing values on the record being edited to ensure that a plausible, internally coherent record is created. Some problems of missing data are eliminated earlier in the survey process through re-contacting the respondent or through a review of the original survey forms. It is generally impossible, however, to resolve all missing data problems at these early stages owing to concerns of response burden, cost and timeliness. Imputation is then used to handle remaining edit failures at the processing stage, since it is desirable to produce a complete and consistent file containing imputed data.

528. Although imputation can improve the quality of the final data by correcting for

missing, invalid or inconsistent responses, choosing an appropriate imputation methodology is important, as some methods of imputation do not preserve the relationships between variables or can actually distort underlying distributions.

529. Imputation procedures may be automated or computerized, manual or a combination of both. Good imputation limits the bias caused by not having observed all the desired values, has an *audit trail* for evaluation purposes and ensures that imputed records are internally consistent. Good imputation processes are automated, objective, reproducible and efficient. Under the *Fellegi-Holt principles* (Statistics Canada, 1998b, p. 38) changes are made to the minimum number of fields to ensure that the completed record passes all the edits.

530. Imputation is especially effective when the sampled unit has responded to other items closely correlated with the item with missing values and those items are used in the imputation procedure. A flag should be created whenever a missing item is imputed, irrespective of how the value is imputed. This practice is essential because sometimes analyses may reveal unexpected relationships and the imputation flags can be used to verify that the relationships are not the product of a poor imputation strategy.

531. No attempt is made in the present section to summarize the large literature on imputation for household sample surveys.[68] It may be desirable for the same types of imputation strategies used in the existing household surveys in the country to be adopted for the imputation practices for time-use

---

[68] See, for example, United Nations (2001a). Kalton and Kasprzyk (1986) offer a systematic review of imputation methods and the relationship among these methods.

surveys. For this discussion, the goal is to define a few simple terms and focus attention on methods that are easy to implement and may be useful in the data analysis stage for time-use surveys.

532. Imputation methods are sometimes defined as either deterministic or stochastic. Deterministic methods specify how each missing item is to be imputed, without adding any component of random variation. A common example of a deterministic imputation method is mean imputation, where every missing observation is imputed using the mean of the respondents. Stochastic imputation methods introduce some randomness. Hot deck imputation is an example of a stochastic imputation method. In hot deck imputation, a unit that has completed the item is randomly selected and the value from that respondent is imputed for the missing value. Stochastic methods are generally preferred for time-use surveys because these methods preserve the shape of the distribution better than deterministic methods. For example, mean imputation often causes lumping at the sample mean that distorts estimates of quantiles, while this does not happen with hot deck imputation.

533. Hot deck imputation is a commonly used stochastic imputation method and there are many approaches to implementing it. The approaches described in this *Guide* use imputation classes, which are very similar to the classes used in weighting non-response adjustments (see chap. IX). Once the classes are defined, hot deck imputation operates by filling in the missing item with the reported value from a respondent in the same class. The "donor" is the record that supplies the value that is imputed to the missing record called the "recipient". A variety of methods have been devised for choosing donors, including sequential, random, and hierarchic hot deck methods. An important consideration

in selecting one of these methods for use is the ability to control the number of times a particular case can be used as a donor. Using donors many times reduces the precision of the estimates.

534. To illustrate the procedure, an example of a hot deck that is relatively simple to implement is given below. The first step is to arrange all the cases into imputation classes and randomly sort them within the classes. A pool of a small number of potential donors is stored, say, three, within each class. When a record with a missing value is encountered, the value is imputed from one of the stored values. If the record is a respondent for the item, then it replaces a previously stored value in the pool of potential donors and can be used for imputing other missing values. This method of replacing the elements of the pool limits the number of times a record is used as a donor.

535. The choice of the imputation classes is a decision that has important implications for the quality of the statistics. The general principle for determining classes specifies that the classes should be created using data that are highly correlated with the variable to be imputed. The goal is to create classes such that all the cases within the class have the same distribution. Classes formed in this way also preserve relationships between variables used in the imputation. For example, suppose analysis of time use of women with respect to childcare is an important statistic estimated from the survey and time use is missing for some sampled persons. Some variables that might be used in creating imputation classes include: sex and age of the adult, whether there are young children in the household, employment status, income level, and geography. The class variables must be determined for each item in a survey and should be specific to the conditions in the country. One way of helping to choose the class variables is to examine the tables of

statistics that are planned for the analysis of the survey. The variables used to determine the rows of the tables (these are often explanatory variables) are generally good variables to consider in developing imputation classes. Of course, the classes should also be chosen so that impossible values are not imputed. For example, if only women are asked some items, then sex is a class variable that must be included to prevent imputing an impossible value.

2. Imputation procedures for time-use surveys

536. For the purpose of discussing some specific imputation procedures that might be appropriate for situations that arise in time-use surveys, assume the time-use survey has a basic questionnaire component and a time diary component. Sampled adults first complete the basic questionnaire that contains items such as age, sex, marital status, place of birth, employment status, income, number of persons in the household, number of children in the household etc. The sampled adult is also asked to complete a time-use diary for one day.

537. For items missing from the basic questionnaire, a hot deck imputation method could be used to impute missing key variables that are expected to define the rows for tables produced from the survey. It might be decided not to impute other items in the basic questionnaire.

538. If the sampled adult does not complete the diary, then a weighting adjustment is recommended instead of imputing all the missing time-use data. If the person completes most of the data in the diary, but leaves one or two time slots missing, imputation should be considered. In this case, a hot deck imputation method might be beneficial where the classes could be created from the variables from the basic questionnaire, such as age, sex, marital

status, employment status etc. The missing data could be imputed from other sampled adults in the same imputation class who completed all the time slots in the diary. Since the missing data are time-use activities in a specific time slot, the donors should be the reported time-use activities from the same time slots. If multiple time slots are missing for a person, then all the missing time slots should be imputed from the same person.

539. In some missing data situations, the use of weighting adjustments for non-response rather than imputation is recommended. Two specific cases—where only one diary day out of two designated days is completed and some where sampled persons within a household do not respond—are discussed in chapter IX.

F. Data preparation and management

540. After data capture and edit and imputation procedures are completed, information from household and personal questionnaires and diaries are stored as a computer output file, the master file for the survey data. This data file is the basis for generating the basic outputs of the survey: planned statistical tabulations, key analytical reports and microdata files for use in specialized analysis.

541. In preparing the statistical tabulations, analysis or "derived" files are produced to systematize and simplify the production of tables. Setting up a database of the survey data facilitates the dissemination of the survey outputs and makes them available over time.

1. Preparation of analysis files

542. For purposes of generating the tabulations for analysis, countries have found it useful to organize time-use data files in specific ways. Some of these practices are described below.

(a) File formats for diary data

543. Diary data may be organized into data files using different formats and principles. Two types of formats are described here. For diaries using fixed time intervals, one alternative is to create files where each data record corresponds to one diary day. The record includes the identifier for the time interval and the data items pertaining to it such as the main activity code, the secondary and other activity codes, codes for context variables and estimation weights corresponding to the diary day. This kind of data file would have as many records as diary days.

544. The diary day record format does not provide information on episodes and thus limits the analytical uses of the survey data.

As mentioned above, number and duration of episodes of an activity constitute essential information in many types of analysis. A preferred file format would thus be one where each data record corresponds to an episode. The episode record would include the data on starting and ending times of the episode and the items that delineate an episode—the main, secondary and other activities and context variables—as well as the diary day weights. This type of data file would have as many records as there are episodes and a varying number of records for each diary day and for each respondent.

545. Table 15 shows a sample episode file record layout that may be applied to the diary shown in figure 6. The contents of the first episode in the diary for this file is shown in table 16.

Table 15. Sample episode file layout for diary shown in figure 6

Field	Format	Position	Description
Record identification	Numeral	01-05	Includes identification particulars of respondent and household
Episode weight	Numeral	06-15	Estimation weight associated with episode
Episode number	Numeral	16-17	Identification number of episode
Diary day	Numeral	18	Identifier for diary day if more than one diary day
Code for day of the week of diary day	Numeral	19	1-Sunday, 2- Monday etc.
Main activity code	Numeral	20-23	Main activity
Secondary activity code	Numeral	24-26	Secondary activity
Starting time of episode	Character	27-30	Time at which episode started
Ending time of episode	Character	31-34	Time at which episode ended
Duration of episode (in minutes)	Numeral	35-38	Derived as ending time - starting time
Alone	Numeral	39	Code 0 (person was not alone) or 1 (was alone)
Children up to 9 living in household	Numeral	40	Code 0 (person was not with children) or 1 (person was with children)
Other household members	Numeral	41	Code 0 (person was not with other household members) or 1 (person was with other household member)
Other persons	Numeral	42	Code 0 (person was not with other persons) or 1 (person was with other persons)
Location code	Numeral	43	Place where main activity occurred

Table 16.   Sample episode record for first episode in sample diary shown in figure 6

Field	Value
Record identification	10001
Episode weight	15
Episode number	01
Diary day	1 (first diary day)
Code for day of the week	2-(Tuesday)
Main activity code	Code for "Woke up the children"
Secondary activity code	Code for "No secondary activity"
Starting time of episode	07.00
Ending time of episode	07.10
Duration of episode (in minutes)	10
Alone	0
Children up to 9 living in household	1
Other household members	0
Other persons	0
Location code	Code for "Home"

(b) Analysis files

546.   Data file formats for household and personal questionnaires in time-use surveys would generally follow the standard practices of household surveys. The household-level file contains all data items from the questionnaire and the estimation weights[69] corresponding to the household level. Similarly, the person-level file contains the data items from the personal questionnaire and the estimation weights.

---

[69] Creation of sampling weights and other calibration weights and estimation procedures are discussed in chapters IX and X.

547.   The analysis file for the survey is formed by merging the diary data files with the personal data file and the household-level file. Countries have found it useful to create a hierarchic file. As an illustration, consider a survey design with three units of observation—household, persons within households, and diary days. Assume further that each sampled person completes two diary days and that the diary data are organized where each record corresponds to an episode. There would then be two diary day-level files for each person-level file. Persons are then grouped into households—the household-level file would consist of the person-level files of all sampled persons within the household.

548.   To facilitate the generation of tables, derived variables or variables obtained by recoding or manipulating initial data elements as captured from the survey forms are also included in the analysis file. For example, the person-level files can include total time spent on each activity, at various locations, and with various persons. Or, data recorded at a more detailed level of the activity classification (for example, three-digit) can be converted into various recodes representing planned tabulation categories such as "SNA production", "non-SNA production" and "non-productive activities". Another useful recode is that of coding the day of the week for which diary data were obtained for a particular respondent into "weekday" or "weekend".

549.   Another type of analysis file that can be useful is a file listing all main activities with the attendant starting and ending times and contextual information and personal and household characteristics. This type of file allows for the more complex manipulations, such as the distribution of an activity over population groups or by time of day, that are required for statistics on daily rhythm.

2. Preparation of planned tabulations

550. One of the ultimate goals of data processing is the preparation of the planned tabulations for the survey. For this purpose, careful preparation of specifications is required for each proposed table. Among other things, the specifications must spell out the codes or values that make up each analysis variable and classification variable in the table, the data file to be processed, and the location of the information in the data file. A useful tool is the "table format" or a "dummy" table that spells out the specifications.[70] As discussed above, preparation of analysis files representing different units of analyses of the survey helps simplify the programming of tabulations.

551. Countries have used various types of software in generating statistical tables from time-use surveys. Most of these are statistical software packages[71] that are different from those used for data capture but the same as those used for computerized editing and imputation.

552. The processing system should also be set up so that the statistical office is able to prepare special tabulations to meet emerging needs for data analysis.[72]

3. Construction of a database for time-use data

553. Many specific applications and research objectives of time use require specialized tabulations from the survey data file that are not part of the tabulation plan of the survey or, even if part of the tabulation plan, may be given lower priority and processed at a later time. To help ensure that the life and usability of time-use data files are maximized and accessibility to users is optimized, national statistical offices are encouraged to store the survey information in a computerized database.

554. The contents of the database would ideally consist of both macrodata and microdata. Macrodata formats include publication equivalents and tables that can be further manipulated. Microdata formats include the master data file as well as the derived analysis files. Metadata and general documentation should also be part of the database. The establishment of such databases enhances the dissemination of the survey results as these can be used for developing various products particularly microdata files for public use.[73]

555. Computerized databases, along with providing the appropriate documentation, are major tools for disseminating and preserving time-use data. These topics are discussed in greater detail in chapter XII.

---

[70] Tabulation plans and table formats are discussed in greater detail in chapter X.
[71] Developing countries have used SAS, SPSS and STATA.
[72] Special tabulations constitute one mode of disseminating survey data. Dissemination strategies are further discussed in chapter XII.

---

[73] Definitions of micro-, macro- and meta- data and related topics on dissemination strategies are discussed in chapter XII.

IX. WEIGHTING AND ESTIMATION FOR TIME-USE SURVEYS

556.   Estimation refers to the process of computing estimates of unknown population characteristics from data collected in the sample. After the survey data are collected and edited, estimation weights are attached to the records of the respondents to produce the estimates of the population. The estimation process accounts for sampling by creating weights that are the inverse of the probability of selection (base weights). These base weights are then adjusted to account for sampled units that do not respond (non-response adjusted weights) and may be further adjusted to make the estimates consistent with known population totals, such as the number of persons in the country, by age and sex. While this process is standard for general household sample surveys, accounting for sampling over time in time-use survey data introduces another dimension in the estimation procedures.

557.   Whether estimates are computed for a sample, it is also important to estimate the precision or variance of the estimates. Time-use surveys are very similar to most other national household surveys with respect to variance estimation. Since the literature on variance estimation for these types of surveys is considerable, this topic is discussed only briefly.

A. Issues in weighting and estimating of time-use statistics

558.   In the discussion that follows, it is assumed that a probability sample of households and possibly persons within those households has been selected using a multi-stage sample design with enumeration areas from the latest census as primary sampling units (PSUs). The sample of households is selected from listings of households made in the sampled PSUs. Within a household, either all eligible persons are included or a sample of household members is selected. The time use of the sampled persons is measured for a limited period of time, perhaps one day or up to a few days during the year.

559.   In many cases, a single weight for each interview is all that is needed to meet the analytic goals of the survey. For example, a person/day weight could be used to produce estimates needed for accounts of household production, the proportion of time spent on paid work, and the proportion of time spent by women on childcare. In some surveys, however, multiple weights might be needed because more than one unit of analysis might be used. For example, estimates of households as well as of persons might be produced and separate weights could be developed for these two purposes. Another example that might involve a different weight is dyad analysis, where the time use of the spouse/partner pair is the focus of the analysis. The weighting procedures discussed here are primarily aimed at producing a person/day weight, but minor modifications resulting in other types of weights are also mentioned.

560.   A major issue in the estimation scheme for a time-use survey is the treatment of the time dimension. Since every estimation procedure is heavily dependent on the sample design, the way the sample treats the time dimension should be reflected in the weighting scheme. For example, if the design calls for a sample of weekdays and a sample of weekend days, then the estimation scheme should account for this explicitly. The estimation process can even go further than the sample design with respect to controlling the estimates

by time period, for example, by day of the week or season of the year. Ways to control the estimates by time period are discussed in the present section. It is to be noted, however, that there may be problems associated with this and the procedures must be carefully evaluated for each survey.

561. Estimation weights also adjust for non-response typically, unit non-response in which a sampled unit provides no data. Item non-response, in which a sampled person might respond to most of the survey items but fail to answer a small subset of them, is more often treated by imputation of the missing items. In time-use surveys, another major issue for determining appropriate weighting adjustment and imputation methods arises when the person responds for some of the sampled time periods but not for others. The choice, in this case, is whether to impute for the missing time period or adjust the weights for the missing period accordingly. This decision is similar to the one that is required when multiple persons are sampled within a household but only some of them respond to the time-use survey.[74] Procedures for adjusting weights for unit non-response and issues related to imputing missing items are examined in the present chapter.

B. Weighting

562. In time-use and other types of surveys, the typical process is to include a weight in the record for each respondent. This weight is then used to produce estimates. These weights: (a) account for sampling, (b) compensate for unit non-response and (c) make the estimates consistent with known population counts. The procedures associated with these three stages of weighting are discussed in the present section. Variation in the weights associated

with any of these procedures may result in unstable estimates. This section also discusses methods by which to decrease the variability and increase the accuracy of the estimates.[75]

563. Weighting methods are best understood when the structure of the data file and terms, such as a respondent or a record in the file, are defined clearly. In time-use surveys in which a person is sampled for one time period, the file structure is obvious. A person who responds does so for the one sampled time period and one data record suffices for both the person and the time period. The situation is more complex when persons are sampled for more than one time period. In this case, the data record needs to be at the level of a "person/time period". A person sampled and responding for two days would thus have two records on the data file. Each of these records would have one estimation weight, but the weights might not be the same, as will become clear subsequently. Thus, the earlier statement that a single weight for each interview is all that is needed implies that an interview is at the person/time period level, not at the person level. Further, as mentioned earlier, more than one weight may be necessary if statistics for more than one unit of analysis (for example, person/days, persons, households) are computed from the survey.

564. The ability to create weights that produce approximately unbiased estimates of population characteristics requires careful coordination between the survey's operations and statistical analysis. For weighting, the probabilities of selection must be tracked for every record so that the data needed for this must be properly captured and associated with the data records. Similarly, non-response

[74] See chapter XI for additional discussion on non-response errors.

[75] Sharot (1986) gives a relatively simple introduction to weighting which might be useful to those unfamiliar with this method. A more comprehensive and technical review is provided by Brick and Kalton (1996).

adjustments require that data from the sampling frame or another source be linked to all the records. For post-stratification type of adjustments, care in the design of the data-collection instrument is essential so that the survey and the source of the data for the post-stratification are consistent. The link between the operations and the statistical methods is essential to making any survey successful.

1. Base weights

565. The standard procedure for producing base weights in a household sample survey is to constitute the weight as the inverse of the probability of selection of the unit. In multi-stage samples, the weights are created at each stage and then multiplied to produce an overall weight for a sampled unit.

566. As an example, suppose that a sample of PSUs is selected, that within the sampled PSUs a sample of households is selected, and that within the sampled households a sample of persons is selected. The overall person weight is the product of three terms, with each term being the inverse of the probability of selection at the respective stage. The weight for a sampled person is

$$w_{(hi)j} = w_h \cdot w_{hi} \cdot w_{hij} \qquad (1)$$

where w_h is the inverse of the probability of selecting PSU h, w_{hi} is the inverse of the probability of selecting household i within PSU h, and w_{hij} is the probability of selecting person j from household i in PSU h.

567. For example, if PSU h is sampled with a probability proportional to size that is equal to 0.10, then its weight is $w_h = 10$. Suppose further that within PSU h, 50 households are listed and 4 are selected. The weight for any of these sampled households in the PSU, w_{hi}, is 12.5 (= 50 divided by 4). If every eligible person in the household is sampled, then $w_{hij} = 1$. In this case, the overall weight, $w_{(hi)j} = 125$ (=10 x 12.5 x 1). If, on the other hand, only one person is sampled per household, and household i has three persons, then $w_{hij} = 3$ for sampled person j. More generally, if every eligible person in the household has the same probability of selection, then w_{hij} is the number of eligible persons in the household divided by the number of persons sampled.

568. The weight given in equation (1) is the typical household survey weight, but it does not explicitly deal with the time dimension. In a time-use survey, this weight would be sufficient if data for the sampled person were collected for the entire time period of the survey. An additional weighting factor must be introduced to account for the sampling of time periods. For example, suppose that a sampled person is asked to report on two selected days during the year. The time-dimension weighting factor for producing person/day estimates in this case would be the 365 days in the year divided by 2 days in the sample. In general, the time weighting factor, w_{hijk}, is the number of eligible time units in the period divided by the number of these units for which the person is sampled. The overall weight for estimating person/days (or any other unit of time) is

$$w_{(hij)k} = w_h \cdot w_{hi} \cdot w_{hij} \cdot w_{hijk} \qquad (2)$$

569. This formulation of the time-dimension weight allows time periods to be sampled using different selection criteria. For example, if one weekday and one weekend day are sampled for a person, then the two periods have different weights. The appropriate weight, w_{hijk}, for a weekday would be the number of weekdays in the year, while the corresponding weight for the weekend day,

w_{hijk}, would be the number of weekend days in the year. Each record on the person/day data file would have the single weight that is appropriate for that day.

570. This formulation also allows for variations in the number of sampled time periods for sampled individuals. For example, since w_{hijk} is specific to the sampled person, it accommodates designs in which some persons are sampled for one day, others for two days, and yet others for a full week.

571. The basic weight given in equation (2) is appropriate for producing person/day estimates. For household estimates, the same process could be followed, eliminating, however, the factor associated with sampling persons within a household.

572. The standard weighting procedures presented above may have some undesirable consequences. The weights may have greater-than-desired variability owing to the sampling of persons within a household or the sampling of time units within a year. The estimates may also not have the expected distribution by day of the week or season of the year. Some of these problems can and should be addressed in the sample design stage, but invariably some must be handled in the weighting procedure. Methods for dealing with problems like this are discussed later in this section.

2. Non-response adjustments

573. The weight given in equation (2) assumes that complete data are collected for every sampled unit at each stage. While this is clearly the ideal situation, unit non-response is almost always encountered in practice. For example, a sampled household is not contacted or refuses to participate in the survey and as a result no time-use data are collected for that particular household. A variety of adjustment methods exist to offset for the losses due to

non-response[76] but only weighting class adjustments are discussed here. Weighting class adjustments are relatively easy to implement and are effective for handling unit non-response.

(a) Weighting class adjustments

574. The first step in forming weighting class adjustments is forming groups or classes of sampled units that are expected to be similar with respect to their probability of responding to the survey or with respect to other key variables in the survey. To do this, the variables used to form the classes must be known for all sampled units, not just the responding ones. The second step is to divide the ratio of the sum of the weights of the sampled units by the sum of the weights of the responding units in each class. If all the units in the class have the same weight, the ratio is just the ratio of the number of sampled units to the number of responding units. The ratio is the non-response adjustment factor that is applied to all the responding units in the class. The non-responding units are either assigned a zero weight or simply dropped from the analysis file.

575. For example, suppose some households did not respond to the time-use survey and the non-response adjustment classes are regions of the country ($r = 1, 2, \ldots, R$). Equation (2) should be modified by multiplying w_{hi}, the weight of selecting household i within PSU h, by the appropriate regional non-response adjustment factor given by

---

[76] There are many articles on adjusting for non-response in sample surveys. Elliot (1991) supplies a very readable introduction to the topic. Bailar, Bailey and Corby (1978), Chapman, Bailey, and Kasprzyk (1986), and Tremblay (1986) cover practical methods of non-response adjustment with emphasis on weighting class adjustment methods.

$$NR_{hh,r} = \frac{\sum\limits_{i \in r} w_{hi}}{\sum\limits_{i \in r} w_{hi}\delta_i} \qquad (3)$$

where the sum is over all the sampled households in region r and δ_i is equal to one if the unit responds and to zero otherwise. The numerator of the adjustment factor is the sum of the weights for the records in a specific region (r). The denominator is the sum of the weights over the same set of records, but only the weights for respondents are included in the summation. The same procedure can be used at each stage of weighting to account for unit non-response at that stage. The base weight for that stage is replaced by the product of the base weight and the non-response adjustment. The result is still an overall weight like equation (2), but the weights are the non-response adjusted weights at each stage and only the records for the respondents are included in the analysis file.

(b) Issues in the development of non-response adjustments

576. In the development of non-response adjustments, several issues deserve special attention. One issue is the number of respondents in each class; the number should be large enough so that the adjustment factor is stable. A common choice is a minimum of 20 to 30 respondents in each class, although classes with more respondents are recommended. Another consideration is the size of the non-response adjustment. A useful rule of thumb is that the non-response adjustment for a class should not exceed two times the overall average adjustment. Classes may be combined or redefined to avoid these two situations. The choice of variable to be used in forming the classes is another key decision. Often, only a few variables are known for both respondents and non-respondents so the choice is very limited. For example, it may not be possible to go beyond classes that separate units into urban and rural cases. When many variables are available, more sophisticated methods such as search algorithms or logistic regression analysis might be used to identify the classes.[77]

577. A design used in some time-use surveys asks the sampled person to complete a basic questionnaire and to record time use for sampled time slots (often a full day) in a diary or some other data-collection instrument. Given this design, there is the risk that some persons may respond to the basic questionnaire but not complete the time-use diary. A weighting class adjustment of w_{hij} for the missing time-use data has the potential to substantially reduce non-response bias in this case. Substantial bias reduction is possible if data from the basic questionnaire has variables highly correlated with time use that can be used to form the weighting classes. When many variables are available, the investigation of the most important ones by use of a search algorithm or similar technique as outlined earlier may be profitable.

578. Non-response adjustment classes, designed to compensate for persons who are sampled for multiple time units (for example, days) but respond only for some of these days, are an important case. One option is to form weekday and weekend day classes so that the adjustments are separate for these classes. An extension of this option might be to form classes by day of the week and season of the year, if the sample sizes in each of the classes are sufficient. If substitute days are allowed in the survey, then these substitutes should be treated as if they were observed values in the weighting so as to avoid overadjustment for the missed periods. Another option is to

---

[77] Brick and Kalton (1996) describe some of these options.

impute for the missing days with data from other responses in the household or from the same person. Essentially, this approach treats the missing days as item non-response rather than unit non-response. The advantages and disadvantages of imputation for this type of non-response are examined later on in this chapter.

3. Post-stratification-type adjustments

579. Post-stratification of the weights to known population totals is another standard weighting procedure in many household surveys. A more inclusive term for this type of adjustment is *calibration estimation*. Calibration to known population totals is used to reduce coverage bias, to compensate partially for non-response bias that is not dealt with in non-response weighting, and to make the estimates consistent with known totals. It also reduces the sampling error for estimates that are highly correlated to the known control totals. Post-stratification is a simple, one-dimensional method of calibration. Raking is a technique for extending the idea to two or more dimensions. We will begin with post-stratification and then discuss raking because of its potential importance in time-use surveys.

(a) Post-stratification[78]

580. In many countries, the total number of people by age, sex, region or some other categories is known from a recent census or projections from the census. For ease of illustration, suppose that the totals are known by sex, where N_f is the number of females

and N_m is the number of males in a country. The post-stratification factor for females is:

$$A_f = \frac{N_f}{\sum_{(hi)j \in resp} w'_{(hi)j} \delta_f(j)} \tag{4}$$

and the post-stratification factor for males is:

$$A_m = \frac{N_m}{\sum_{(hi)j \in resp} w'_{(hi)j} \delta_m(j)} \tag{5}$$

where $w'_{(hi)j}$ is the non-response adjusted weight for person j, $\delta_f(j)$ is equal to one if respondent j is a female and to zero otherwise. Likewise, $\delta_m(j)$ is equal to one if respondent j is a male and to zero otherwise, and the sum of the weights in the denominators is over all responding persons. The non-response adjusted weight for all responding females is multiplied by A_f to give the post-stratified weight, while the weight for responding males is multiplied by A_m. The considerations about the minimum number of responses per class, the size of the adjustments, and the methods for constructing the classes discussed in the non-response section apply to the development of the post-stratification classes.

581. The control totals for time-use studies are different from the totals used in typical household surveys. If the analysis is of person/days, then the control totals should also be expressed in this metric. For example, the post-stratification adjustment factor for female/person days is:

$$A_f = \frac{365 \cdot N_f}{\sum_{(hij)k \in resp} w'_{(hij)k} \delta_f(j)} \tag{6}$$

---

[78] The literature dealing with post-stratification types of adjustments tends to be more technical than some of the references mentioned previously. The articles by Deville and Särndal (1992) and Lundström and Särndal (1999) are technical but useful. Djerf (1997) discusses the effects of the adjustment on some of the estimates.

where $w'_{(hij)k}$ is the non-response adjusted weight for person j for time period k and $\delta_f(j)$ is as defined above, and the sum of the weights in the denominators is over all responding person/day records. The numerator in this case is the number of female person/days in the year.

(b) Raking

582. When population totals are available for several variables, it may not be possible to form the full cross-classification of these variables because the data may not be collected or tabulated that way. Even if such a complete classification is available, the potential for using all the variables for post-stratification is limited because the number of respondents in each class should be sufficiently large, as discussed above. Raking is an attractive alternative to post-stratification because it makes it possible to take advantage of all of the auxiliary variables available.

583. Raking can be thought of as a multivariate extension of post-stratification. Suppose there are three variables or dimensions for which control totals exist, say sex, age and region. The weights are raked to these three dimensions by first post-stratifying the non-response adjusted weights to sex as described above. The weights from this step are then post-stratified to the age categories. The weights from this step are then post-stratified to the regional totals. When all the raking variables have been adjusted once, the first raking iteration is complete. At the end of the first iteration, the sum of the weights exactly matches the region control totals, but probably will not be exactly equal to the sex or age totals. By repeating this iterative process several times (for example, the next step would be to post-stratify the weights from the regional post-stratification to the sex control totals), the weights generally converge in the sense that they will not change appreciably after further adjustments. The weights from this process are the final raked weights and the sum of the weights classified by any of the raking variables should approximately equal the control totals.

584. Problems sometimes arise with raking, but often they can be avoided by taking simple precautions. The control totals must be consistent in the sense that the sum of the number of persons by sex must equal the sum of the persons by age and by region in the example given above. Missing values for the variables in the sample corresponding to the control totals should be eliminated, possibly by imputing for the missing items. The variables should be measured in the same way in the time-use survey as they are measured in producing the control totals. The recommended minimum number of respondents in each class for every raking variable (for example, both females and males) is often set at about 40. Sometimes, the same variable is used as a component in more than one dimension and this may cause problems in certain cases. For example, one dimension of raking might have classes formed by crossing sex and age categories and another dimension might have classes formed by crossing sex and region. This approach may have merit, but it can also cause convergence problems.

585. If raking until full convergence is not feasible because of computational limitations, it is possible to reduce the number of iterations (this is sometimes called incomplete raking). In this case, the order of the raking may be important. For example, suppose that in the above example the process is stopped after one iteration. The sum of the weights should exactly equal the regional controls but not the sex or age controls. If one set of controls is considered to be more important, then the final adjustment should be for this control variable.

586. When the control totals can be cross-classified, it is then possible to either post-

stratify or rake the weights. If the number of control variables is very limited and the number of respondents in each cell of the full cross-classification of these variables is large enough, then post-stratification is generally the better method. When more variables are available or many of the cells in the cross-classification have a small number of respondents, then raking has an advantage. Even when raking is done, it may be possible to improve the adjustment by cross-classifying some variables to create the levels of a raking dimension. For example, suppose that there are important time-use differences between young males and young females. Creating a raking dimension with levels defined by the age/sex cross-classification is better than having separate age and sex raking dimensions.

587. The special value of raking for time-use surveys is due to the natural control totals that are available for the time dimension. For example, the numbers of weekdays and weekend days in the year are known, the numbers of specific days of the week are known, and the number of days by month and season are known. These variables can all be used in raking when the weights are expressed in person/days. The importance of having control totals that are person/days was described for post-stratification.

588. As an example of raking to the time dimension, suppose the year has 261 weekdays and 104 weekend days and we wish to control to these counts. If the time use of males and that of females differ by weekday and weekend day, then the time dimension should be crossed with sex to improve the estimates. In this case, the sex/time dimension has four levels: female weekdays ($261 N_f$), female weekend days ($104 N_f$), male weekdays ($261 N_m$) and male weekend days ($104 N_m$). Similarly, age categories might be crossed

with the number of seasons. For example, if there were 90 days in the winter, then the first level would be young person-winter days ($90 N_y$, where N_y is the number of young persons in the population).

589. The importance of raking is evident because controlling the time dimension potentially increases the number of levels of each of the standard demographic variables. This increase in levels is problematic with post-stratification because of the limits on the sample sizes in each cell of the cross-classification. Even when there are very few demographic variables available for post-stratification, raking should be considered in order to take fuller advantage of the time variables. For example, suppose the only known demographic control total for a country is the total population, N. Raking by day of the week (each of the 7 levels being N times the number of days of the week in the year) and month of the year might still be beneficial. In this case, carrying out even a single raking iteration provides valuable control of the estimates by these important time dimensions.

590. As noted above, the post-stratification or raking scheme must be consistent with the sample design. This relationship is enforced by such requirements as the need for a minimum number of respondents in each level for all the control variables. For example, unless there are enough observations for each day of the week, the weights cannot be raked to this dimension.

4. Adjustments for variability of weights

591. If the weighting procedures such as those discussed above result in substantial variations in weights, then the estimates might have larger-than-desired sampling errors or be more likely to be highly influenced by a small number of observations. For these reasons the

135

weights, and in particular the adjustments to the weights for non-response and post-stratification, should be evaluated at each stage, and methods to reduce the variation should be considered.

592. Recommendations on specific procedures for reducing the variability of the weights are difficult to formulate. Nevertheless, because of the importance of dealing with this issue in time-use surveys, some guidance is provided in the present section. Techniques that can be used to identify situations where the variation in weights might be sufficient to require adjustments are also presented.

(a) Sources of variation in estimation weights

593. Any stage of sampling or estimation can produce variation in the weights. The best defense against excessive variation is the application of good sample design principles and effective data-collection procedures. For example, suppose the number of eligible persons per household varies substantially and the sample design calls for selecting one person per household. The weight for a person from a household with five eligible persons will be five times the weight for a person sampled from a household with only one person. Selecting two persons from households with larger numbers of eligible persons can substantially reduce the variation in weights. Similarly, achieving high and consistent response rates from different types of households and persons minimizes the possibility that non-response adjustments will cause large variations in the weights.

594. Even when the design and execution of the sample are well done, variations in the weights may need to be addressed. A common circumstance is that a combination of factors causes the product of the base weights and

non-response adjustments to have more than expected variability. Again, consider the situation in which one person is sampled in a household, noting that similar problems can occur when more than one person is sampled. The person-level weights in households with many eligible persons are relatively large and, if non-response is above average for these households, the product of the inverse selection probability weights and non-response adjustments may cause the weights for these cases to be comparatively large.

(b) Dealing with excessive variation: trimming

595. One option for dealing with excessive variation in the weights is to trim the weights for the set of respondents with the largest weights. Other methods could be considered, but trimming is simple and directly addresses the weight variation problem.[79] Trimming involves truncating the weights and possibly redistributing the sum of the weights that were trimmed to other responding cases. The redistribution of weights may not be necessary if post-stratification or raking to control totals is used later in the weighting process. For example, suppose the non-response-adjusted weights for any person sampled from households with more than five eligible persons are the largest weights and it is decided to trim these weights. The weights for persons sampled from households with six or more persons would be trimmed to a specified maximum number, and the difference between the weights prior to trimming and those after trimming could be redistributed to the sampled persons from households with fewer than five persons. Since trimming does result in biases in the estimates, the implications of trimming

---

[79] Kish (1992) provides the rationale and some of the methods for examining excessive variation in the weights. Potter (1990) covers trimming and other measures used to reduce the variability in the weights.

need to be evaluated in each particular case. The effect of trimming in this example would be to reduce the estimated average size of households and any characteristics associated with household size would also be biased.

596. Before presenting guidelines for trimming, rules of thumb for recognizing situations in which the variability in the weights might be large enough for trimming to be considered are examined. All these rules of thumb should be applied within classes or strata of the sample. In other words, if persons are sampled at different rates by region, then the exploration for outlying weights should be done within the region. A common way of doing this is to restrict the investigation to weight adjustments rather than the overall product of the weights, although this practice might not reveal all the extreme weights.

597. A simple method of identifying excessive variation in weights is to plot the weights or the weight adjustments. Since large weights cause the biggest problem, trimming may be needed if the weights for a small percentage of the cases are much larger than the weights for the vast majority of the cases. For example, weights that are three or four times the average weight are good candidates for trimming. The same information may be obtained by sorting the weights from largest to smallest. If there are a few cases with weights that are much larger than the average weight, trimming should be considered. Another approach is to monitor the coefficient of variation (CV) of the weights at each stage of weighting. If the CV goes up substantially at a stage (say, by a factor of 20 per cent or more), then the weighting adjustments should be carefully examined to determine if large differential factors are being introduced at that stage. The plotting of the weights is a technique that can be used for this evaluation. If weights are trimmed at some stage of weighting, comparing the CV of the weights before and after trimming can help evaluate the effectiveness of the trimming. If the CV of the weights after trimming is less than 10 per cent smaller than the CV before trimming, then the trimming procedure is probably not very effective.

598. Some guidelines for trimming are presented next. Remember that these are only guidelines and the weights for any particular application should be carefully examined before trimming is used. The guidelines are:

- Trim weights only when the benefits from trimming are clear.
- The need for trimming should be examined within classes or strata with approximately the same sampling rate.
- The number of cases trimmed should be minimized.
- Consider the bias introduced by trimming and examine redistributing the trimmed weights in such a way as to minimize this bias.

599. The examination of the variation in weights for time-use surveys is especially important because it involves sampling over the time dimension in addition to the sampling and weighting issues faced in standard household surveys. For example, if a day of the week is used in the raking step and the response rate for Sunday is much lower than it is for other days of the week, the raked weights may be subject to large variations. In this case, it may be appropriate to collapse some days of the week for the raking to avoid the relatively large weights. If only a few of cases have large weights for Sundays, then trimming may be the better choice. In this case, the Sunday weights might be redistributed to other Sunday cases or other weekend cases to minimize the bias from the trimming, under the assumption that time use on the weekend is different than it is on weekdays.

C. Imputation versus non-response adjustments

1. Case of missing diary days

600. Imputation is another method of accounting for missing data in time-use surveys. Imputation is most often used to replace missing values for specific items when the sampled person has responded to most of the items in the survey. Because imputation replaces missing values on an item level, it may be more effective at reducing bias owing to non-response than weighting non-response adjustments that are carried out at the case level.[80]

601. Time-use surveys in which sampled persons are asked to report on more than one day present additional challenges for imputation. For example, suppose a person has reported time use for one sampled day but not for another. One option is to impute the missing day by filling it in with the reported data from the same person. This may appear attractive since the donor[81] in this case certainly matches on many of the key variables that would be used to define imputation classes. However, weighting for the missing day rather than imputing it is, in general, the recommended approach. For example, if the missing period is a weekend day and the reported period is a weekday, then simply imputing the missing period might be a very poor strategy. In fact, it is easy to see that the imputation strategy given above is equivalent to doubling the weight of the reported time period (assuming the two time periods have the same weight). A better procedure might be to create weighting classes that distribute the weight for the missing time period more smoothly over a group of records that have the same characteristics.

2. Case of person non-response

602. The same types of decisions arise when multiple persons are sampled within a household and some of the sampled persons respond and others do not. The approach of imputing the missing data using donors from the same household is often ineffective. For example, if one person spends a lot of time in caring for the children, imputing these same time-use data for other adults in the household is unwise. Again, weighting is often a better way of dealing with this type of missingness.

D. Generating estimates of time use

603. In the present section, a simplified illustration of how the weighting and estimation procedures discussed above can be utilized in the analysis of time-use survey data is presented. Illustrations of country practices (Australia, Canada and New Zealand) are reported in annex 13.

604. In the discussion that follows, assume that the estimation methods outlined earlier have been implemented and an analysis file that contains the items collected in the survey, imputed as needed, along with the adjusted survey weights and the data needed for computing variances are included in the file. For purposes of estimating time use using data collected on reported time periods, the analysis file should be constructed so that each time period corresponds to a record on the file.[82]

---

[80] Meekers (1991) examines the effect of imputation procedures on specific estimates.
[81] The "donor" is the record that supplies the value that is imputed to the "recipient" record that is missing. See chapter VIII.

---

[82] A detailed discussion of file structures is covered in chapter VIII.

1. Estimation at the person/day level

605. For ease of presentation, the fully adjusted weight for person j and time period k is written as w'_{jk}—the subscripts for PSU and household are suppressed. It is also assumed that each sample time period is of a fixed duration, say, one day, for illustration. With this structure, survey estimates can similarly be produced in most common sample designs.

(a) Estimation of totals

606. Estimates of totals for the entire population or for subgroups of the population are easily produced from a file with the structure described above. For example, the total time spent by all eligible persons working for pay may be estimated as:

$$\hat{y} = \sum_{j,k} w'_{jk} y_{jk} \qquad (7)$$

where y_{jk} is the proportion of a day spent working for pay by person j in time period k. (Note that y_{jk} is a proportion because each time period is one day, as assumed above. Other options are possible, such as having y_{jk} be the number of hours in the time period, but the approach given is simpler.) In this case, any missing values for y_{jk} have been imputed.

If the values are missing and not imputed, then the totals will be underestimated.

607. An estimate of a total for a subgroup, say the total time spent by all eligible persons working for pay in region r of the country, is:

$$\hat{y}_r = \sum_{j,k} w'_{jk} y_{jk} \delta_j \quad (\text{region} = r) \qquad (8)$$

where

$$\delta_j (\text{region} = r) = \begin{cases} 1, \text{if person } j \text{ lives in region } r \\ 0, \text{otherwise} \end{cases}$$

(b) Estimation of means, proportions and ratios

608. Given the file structure described above, estimates of means, proportions and ratios can also be easily developed with a file of this structure. Continuing the previous example, an estimate of the mean time spent working for pay by eligible persons in region r is given by

$$\hat{\bar{y}} = \frac{\sum_{j,k} w'_{jk} y_{jk} \delta_j (\text{region} = r)}{\sum_{j,k} w'_{jk} \delta_j (\text{region} = r)} \qquad (9)$$

This statistic is also an estimate of the proportion of time spent working for pay by persons in region r. It is valuable to remember that a proportion is a special case of estimating a mean. In fact, a mean is a special case of estimating a more general ratio in most multi-stage samples. An example is the ratio of the mean time spent by men working for pay to the mean time spent by women working for pay in region r. An estimate of the ratio is given by

$$\hat{q}_r = \frac{\dfrac{\sum_{j,k} w'_{jk} y_{jk} \delta_j (\text{region} = r) \delta_j (\text{male})}{\sum_{j,k} w'_{jk} \delta_j (\text{region} = r) \delta_j (\text{male})}}{\dfrac{\sum_{j,k} w'_{jk} y_{jk} \delta_j (\text{region} = r) \delta_j (\text{female})}{\sum_{j,k} w'_{jk} \delta_j (\text{region} = r) \delta_j (\text{female})}} \qquad (10)$$

609. When estimating means, proportions and ratios, the effect of missing item responses is not as simple as with estimates of totals. For example, consider estimating the mean

time spent working for pay by eligible persons in region r where y_{jk} is the proportion of all the *reported* time slot data. This estimate of the mean may be either an overestimate or an underestimate. If the missing time slot data are imputed with good predictors as the imputation class variables, then the bias due to the item non-response may be smaller than if the data were left missing. The same issues arise with other estimates of proportions and ratios.

2. Estimation at the person and household levels

610. In time-use surveys with both a basic questionnaire and a diary, it is not uncommon to produce estimates of both persons and person/days. The description above relates to person/days but can easily be transformed to apply to estimates of characteristics of persons by using data from the basic questionnaire. For example, an estimate of the total number of persons who work for pay in region r of the country is

$$\hat{t}_r = \sum w_j'' \delta_j(region = r)\delta_j(\text{work for pay}) \quad (11)$$

where w_j'' is the adjusted weight for person j and

$$\delta_j(\text{work for pay}) = \begin{cases} 1, & \text{if person } j \text{ works for pay} \\ 0, & \text{otherwise} \end{cases}$$

611. The analysis file in this case should contain one record for each responding person with the adjusted person weight, irrespective of the number of time periods the person reports. The same procedure also applies for household-level estimates if a household-level file and weight are created.

612. Confusion occurs in some analyses when data are collected at multiple levels, such as household, person and time period. The problem occurs when analysts try to characterize an entire unit using data reported from a subset. For example, it is clearly incorrect to state that the household has no persons who are female because only the sampled person is male. The same problem occurs if estimates of the percentage of persons who engage in some category of time use are characterized by virtue of an activity they performed on a specific day. In other words, it is incorrect to state that a sampled woman does not spend any time caring for children just because she did not report this activity for the sampled day. An appropriate analysis for this should be at the unit of analysis for which the data are collected. In this case, the statistic should be at the person/day level and the estimate is the percentage of time women spend in childcare.

613. To avoid this type of problem, it is suggested that only the weight that is appropriate at a certain level of analysis be included. Therefore, only a person/day weight would be included in the analysis file that contains the data for each sampled day. Another file with a person weight could be developed for estimating person-level characteristics. This suggestion also helps to eliminate the confusion that sometimes occurs when a data file has more than one weight.

X. PREPARATION OF SURVEY OUTPUTS

614. Information collected from surveys are organized and summarized in statistical tables. The main statistical tables are produced from the analysis files created at the data-processing stage of a survey. Statistical summaries represent estimates of population characteristics; in the case of time-use surveys, the main focus concerns people's activities during the course of the 24-hours of a day, the duration of the activities and the time at which they take place. Typically, estimates are expressed as functions of population totals, for example: total number of hours spent on an activity; number of persons participating in an activity (participants); average number of hours spent on an activity by participants; proportion of time spent on an activity per day.

615. Formats and contents of statistical tables are defined by the tabulation plan of the survey. Time-use statistics in the table are generated using the estimation procedures defined for the survey.

A. Key survey outputs

616. Specifications for the statistical tables can be described in terms of analysis variables (for example, activity, location, other context variables), classification variables (for example, sex, age) and key statistics (for example, total time spent by the population on an activity). The choice of variables and statistics as well as the level of detail depends on the analytical objectives of the survey. Such analysis may be at the household level, person level or person/day level. The present section discusses key statistics needed for most general types of analyses on how people spend their time. A basic tabulation plan for generating these statistics is suggested.

1. Key time-use statistics

617. Most of the analyses of time-use data are based on six types of time-use measures:[83]

(a) Average time the survey population spent on a specified activity.

(b) Average time spent on a specified activity by those who did engage or participate in the activity.

(c) Average duration of an episode of a specified activity.

(d) Average number of episodes of a specified activity reported by the survey population.

(e) Average number of episodes of a specified activity reported by participants in the activity.

(f) Participation rate or proportion of persons in the survey population who participated in a specified activity.

618. The basic units of analysis of these time-use measures are the activity and the episode. These measures are essentially means or proportions taken over two groups of persons—the survey population, and the participants or the subset of the population who engaged in the specified activity. The total number in the survey population remains constant while the total number of participants changes depending on the activity. Table 17 highlights the differences in the resulting statistics by presenting the measures in terms of their numerators and denominators.

---

[83] These indexes are described by Philip Stone in the chapter entitled "Analysis of time-budget data" in Szalai, ed. (1972), p. 100.

Table 17. Six types of time-use measures

Denominator	Numerator		
	Total duration of activity	Total number of episodes of activity	Total number of persons performing activity
Total number of persons (population)	(1) $\dfrac{duration}{all\ persons}$	(4) $\dfrac{episodes}{all\ persons}$	(6) $\dfrac{doers}{all\ persons}$
Total number of persons performing activity (doers/participants)	(2) $\dfrac{duration}{doers}$	(5) $\dfrac{episodes}{doers}$	-
Total number of episodes of activity	(3) $\dfrac{duration}{episodes}$	-	-

Source: United Nations (1978).
Note: A hyphen (-) means data not applicable

619. The measures can refer to different temporal units such as an "average" day in a week, an "average" week in a year, an "average" weekday, an "average" weekend. Averages may also pertain to a week, season/quarter or a year depending on the time sample and estimation objectives of the survey.

620. Table 18 shows how these time-use measures may appear in an analysis table. In this table, the survey population consists of persons aged 15 years or over. According to this table, the average time spent in paid work and related activities by all females aged 15 years or over—measure (1)—is 2.8 hours per day. This average includes the females in the survey population regardless of whether they participated in paid work. On the other hand, focusing exclusively on the group of the females who engaged in paid work and related activities (participants), one finds that on average these women spent 7.7 hours per day —measure (2)—engaged in these activities.

621. In addition to the six measures described above, diary data may be used to describe the "daily rhythm" of the population. This description is based on statistics that show what the population is doing at a given point in time, that is to say, the proportion of the population engaged in the different activities during a certain point in time. When these statistics are available for the whole day (for example, each hour or each half-hour of the 24-hour day) for a set of activity categories, patterns of the sequence in which activities occur and times at which specific types of activities usually occur can be discerned and analysed. For example, analysis of the 1979 Time Use Survey of Finland provides the following description of the daily rhythm during the hours from 11.30 p.m. to 8.00 a.m.

622. "The peak for sleeping *on weekdays* ranges between 11.30 p.m. and 5.00 a.m., when more than 90 per cent of the population is asleep. From 1 to 2 per cent of the population work at night. At 6.00 a.m., two thirds of the population is still asleep, but at 7.00 a.m., only less than a quarter and at 8.00 a.m. less than 10 per cent are not up. At 6.00 in the morning less than 10 per cent, at 7.00 a.m. nearly 30 per cent and at 8.00 a.m. up to 55 per cent of the population are on the way to work or already at work or study." [84]

[84] Niemi, Kiiski and Liikkanen (1981), p. 19.

Table 18. **Average time spent on various activities[a] for the population aged 15 years or over and participants showing participation rate by sex, Canada, 1998**

Activity group	Population 15+			Participants			Participation rate		
	Total	Male	Female	Total	Male	Female	Total	Male	Female
	Hours per day			Hours per day			Percentage		
Total work	7.8	7.8	7.8	8.0	8.0	7.9	98	97	99
Paid work and related activities	3.6	4.5	2.8	8.3	8.8	7.7	44	51	36
Unpaid work	3.6	2.7	4.4	3.9	3.2	4.6	91	87	96
Personal care	10.4	10.2	10.6	10.4	10.2	10.6	100	100	100
Free time	5.8	6.0	5.6	5.9	6.1	5.7	97	97	97

Source: Statistics Canada (1999b), table 1.

[a] Averaged over a seven-day week

2. Basic tabulation plan for analysing time-use data

(a) Specifications for analysis and classification variables

623.   Basic tables for analysis are specified in terms of: (a) analysis variables, (b) classification variables and (c) time-use measures.

624.   The key analysis variable is of course the activity. Activity may be defined in terms of main, secondary or simultaneous activities. Most standard statistical reports on time-use present tables on time spent in main activities; in addition, separate tables for secondary activities may also be prepared.

625.   Context variables (location of activity; persons present, for example, "with whom"; purpose of the activity, for example, "for whom"; whether activity is paid or unpaid) are also typically analysed in combination with duration and activity, for example, time spent together by parents and children or by spouses; time spent in the house; time spent on unpaid housework.

626.   Classification variables are used for defining the domains of study. These variables may be at the person level or at the household/family level. Relevant classification variables are those that define subgroups that are expected to differ substantially with regard to the use of time and those that are highly relevant in the policy issues under study. The Expert Group Meeting on Methods for Conducting Time-Use Surveys recommended the following minimum list of classification variables at the person level: age, sex, marital status, and work situation (employment status, class of worker) (United Nations, 2000).

627.   Sex and age are two essential classification variables in the analysis of time-use data; thus, sex by age groupings should constitute basic domains of study. While there is no international standard classification for age groups, data on age are most commonly collected according to single years of age and tabulated and published in five-year age groups (0-4, 5-9, 10-14 etc.) These five-year age groups are considered appropriate for indicators known to exhibit patterns associated with life-cycle variations. Other groupings are useful depending on the analysis but can be derived from these basic groups. For example, the group classified as "youth" represents ages 15-24 (sometimes subdivided into ages 15-19 and 20-24). "Elderly" usually corresponds to age group 60+. However, for analyses concerned specifically with issues of ageing such as care for the elderly, this grouping can be further subdivided into 60-69 (representing a relatively active and self-sufficient period)

and 70+ (representing the onset of disability, greater ill health and smaller incomes). For women, the 15-49 (or 15-44) age group is significant, as it corresponds to the reproductive period of life; and the ages above this group are the post-reproductive. For analyses focusing on economic activity, ages 15-59 may be considered the ages that are most active. One should consider, however, the age groupings as defined by the labour-force statistics of the country.[85]

628. For some types of analysis (for example, studies on intra-household allocation), household-related variables such as presence of children, family type (or household composition) and household income are important. Information on household durables is needed for explaining time-use patterns of activities that are related to their presence or absence in the household (United Nations, 2000).

(b) Table specifications

629. In this discussion it is useful to distinguish three types of tables, normally working tables, simultaneous activity tables and thematic tables.[86]

Working tables

630. Working tables are the core tabulations from which various analytical tables may be derived. These tables report the duration or proportion of time spent in each category of a comprehensive list of activities. Duration can be expressed in terms of total time or average time.

631. In preparing the tabulation plan, a major decision that needs to be made is the

level of aggregation or disaggregation to be used in the tables. In this regard, it is suggested to initially use the most detailed level of classification used in coding the activities. Broader aggregations may be needed for purposes of the analysis and these may be obtained by grouping the appropriate detailed activities. The Ås framework, for example, has been traditionally used in general analyses of time-use patterns as well as in analyses that focus on free time. The tabulation categories of the proposed International Classification of Activities for Time-Use Statistics, on the other hand, is useful for analyses involving paid and unpaid work.[87] Final published tables may also have to include less detailed activity descriptions owing either to financial constraints or to considerations of precision of estimates (see discussion in chap. X).

632. It is suggested that, at the minimum, the working tables use the sex-age cross-classifications as basic domains of study. As explained above, measures based on the total population are interpreted differently from those based on participants/doers; thus, tables referring to the survey population and those referring to participants/doers should be prepared separately. Tables should also report the number in the population or the number of participants to which the activities pertain.

633. Figure 8 illustrates the format of a core working table with main activity as the analysis variable. The working table would utilize the most detailed level of the activity classification. The tables should show both the time-use measure and the number of persons in the population (for population-based tables) or the number of participants (for participant-based tables). Published tables of aggregate statistics may be derived by

---

[85] These age groupings are as discussed in (United Nations, 1997b), pp. 35-36.
[86] This discussion follows Horrigan and others (1999).

---

[87] See chapter XIII for further discussion on tabulation categories for specific frameworks of analyses.

aggregating time-use measures in terms of higher levels of the activity classification. Suggested formats for publication tables are shown in annex 14.

634. A series of tabulations with this basic format can be generated for various classification variables, both person and household, including demographic and employment characteristics. In addition to tabulations for main activities, a set of tabulations for secondary activities can also be generated. Working tables using other analysis variables (for example, context variables) can also be produced using this basic format; in this case, categories of the context or other analysis variables replace the activity list in figure 8.

635. Countries have traditionally presented time-use data separately for main activities and secondary activities. In these tables, activities reported as simultaneously engaged in are separated out or prioritized into main and secondary, as discussed in chapter VIII. For this approach to be valid for analytical purposes, it is essential that the total time spent in all activities equals a 24-hour day. The issue then becomes how to divide up the time between simultaneously performed activities.

Figure 8. **Illustration of basic working table: total time[a] in a week[b] spent working in various main activities[c] by participants,[d] by sex and age[e]**

Main activity	Total			Women			Men		
	All ages	Age 1	... Age n	All ages	Age 1	... Age n	All ages	Age 1	... Age n

01. Work for corporations, quasi-corporations, Government, NPIs
    Time spent
    Number of participants									

02. Work for households in primary production activities
    Time spent
    Number of participants
    ⋮									

15. Personal care and maintenance
    Time spent
    Number of participants									

[a] Total time is the key statistic used in this illustration. Other measures that could be used instead of total time are proportion of time or average time.

[b] One week is the temporal unit used in this illustration. Other examples of temporal units are specific days of the week (for example, Sunday, Friday), weekday, weekend etc.

[c] This illustration uses the major divisions of the trial ICATUS to identify main activity groups. Other listing of activities can be used as long as they are exhaustive and mutually exclusive.

[d] Any time-use table should specify whether the data refer to the survey population or to participants/doers. If survey population is chosen as the unit of analysis, the tabulation can be simplified by reporting survey population only once, appropriately disaggregated by age and sex.

[e] Basic classification variables are sex and age groups, as shown here. Age groupings should exhaust the entire age range covered in the survey population.

Box 7.	Method for dividing time spent among several simultaneous activities
1.	Divide the time spent by the number of activities [a]
2.	Make use of the respondent's distinction between primary and secondary activities to determine the fraction of time that is allocated to each activity [b]
3.	Allocate the time spent in simultaneous activities according to the time spent in those activities as sole (not simultaneous) activities [c]

Source: Horrigan and others (1999).

[a] Using the example above, the one-hour block of time would be divided into 0.5 hours of watching television and 0.5 hours of childcare. This approach is simple, and the total time spent in all activities will add up to a 24-hour day. The obvious drawback is that there is no theoretical justification for allocating equal amounts of time to each of the individual activities.

[b] For example, 60 per cent of the time could be allocated to the primary activity and 40 per cent allocated to the secondary activity. This approach has the advantage of using information on which activity the respondent considers to be more important. Furthermore, the fractions could be made to depend on the specific activities in question. However, there is no theoretical justification for the 60-40 allocation—or any other predetermined allocation.

[c] To illustrate, suppose that for the diary day, the individual reports two hours watching television as a sole activity and one hour providing childcare as a sole activity. Then two thirds of the time spent watching television and providing childcare (simultaneously) would be allocated to watching television and one third would be allocated to providing childcare. There are two drawbacks to this approach: the day may not be representative and some activities may not be observed as sole activities. Both of these drawbacks can be overcome by dividing the sample into mutually exclusive and exhaustive demographic cells and using cell averages to allocate time to the individual activities. For example, suppose that the simultaneous activities pertain to a man aged 35-44 years and that the survey estimates that over the course of a year, men aged 35-44 years spend an average of 600 hours watching television as a sole activity and 300 hours providing childcare as a sole activity. Based on this division, two thirds of all time spent simultaneously watching television and providing childcare would be allocated to watching television and the remaining one third would be allocated to providing childcare.

636. Suppose that a respondent reports one hour of watching television as a primary activity and providing childcare during that same hour (that is to say, suppose the respondent was engaged in a secondary activity providing one hour of passive childcare while the child was taking a nap). A simple and straightforward approach to allocating time to the two activities is to count both activities as lasting one hour each. However, when the time spent in all activities is added up the daily total will exceed 24 hours.

637. Using the above example without loss of generality, three methods that could be used to allocate the time spent in these simultaneous activities into two individual activities without total time exceeding 24 hours are described in box 7.

638. In the third approach, the demographic cells would be ideally defined as accurately as possible. When there are not enough observations in a given cell, the next level of aggregation could be used. Further research would be required to determine the most appropriate time period and level of demographic detail, and the most appropriate method of aggregation when cells are too small.

639. An alternative that can be considered in tabulating activities is to separate out all activities performed singly (sole activities) from simultaneously performed activities. In this case, the main activity list would consist of sole activities and combinations of activities that are done simultaneously. The advantage of this type of table is that all hours in a week, weekday or weekend are accounted for and time spent in multiple activities is not counted in multiple categories.[88] Moreover, the problem discussed earlier of total time

---

[88] Horrigan and others (1999).

146

exceeding 24 hours does not occur. Figure 9 shows a modified working table that implements this concept. To simplify matters, the table suggests that only total time spent on all simultaneous activities be reported; thus, there is only one row associated with these activities and the various possible combinations are not shown. Details can be analysed using separate simultaneous activity tables as described below.

Figure 9.   Illustrative format of basic working table with main activities classified into "sole" and "simultaneous" activities: proportion of time[a] in a 24-hour day[b] spent in various activities[c] by participants,[d] by sex and age[e]

Activity	Total			Women			Men		
	All ages	Age 1	... Age n	All ages	Age 1	... Age n	All ages	Age 1	... Age n
Time spent in sole activities[f]									
01. Work for corporations, quasi-corporations, Government, NPIs Time spent Number of participants									
02. Work for households in primary production activities Time spent Number of participants :									
15. Personal care and maintenance Time spent Number of participants									
Time spent in all simultaneous activities[g]									

[a] Proportion of time is the key statistic used in this illustration. Other measures that could be used instead of proportion of time are total time or average time.

[b] A 24-hour day is the temporal unit used in this illustration. Other examples of temporal units are a week, weekday, weekend etc.

[c] This illustration uses the major divisions of the trial ICATUS to identify activity groups. Other listing of activities can be used as long as they are exhaustive and mutually exclusive.

[d] Any time-use table should specify whether the data refer to the survey population or to participants/doers. If the survey population is chosen as the unit of analysis, the tabulation can be simplified by reporting survey population only once, appropriately disaggregated by age and sex.

[e] Basic classification variables are sex and age groups, as shown here. Age groupings should exhaust the entire age range covered in the survey population.

[f] Referring to time spent in activities that were performed singly or not simultaneously with other activities.

[g] Referring to activities that were performed simultaneously. Time spent in all simultaneous activities is aggregated.

640. Simultaneous activity tables break down the time spent doing simultaneous activities in more detail. These tables show which activities are typically carried out together. Figure 10 offers an example of a table format for this type of tabulation which is a cross-tabulation of primary and secondary activity. At the minimum, the simultaneous activity tables should show the pair of activities occurring most often. A series of tabulations with this format can be produced for sex, age and other classification variables.

Figure 10. Format of simultaneous activity tables: total time[a] in a 24-hour day[b] spent in simultaneous activities,[c] by primary and secondary activity[d] by classification variable

Primary activity	No simultaneous activity	Secondary activity								
		1	2	3	4	5	6	7	8	9
Total										
1										
2										
3										
4										
5										
6										
7										
8										
9										

[a] Total time is the key statistic used in this illustration. Other measures that could be used instead of total time are proportion of time or average time.

[b] A 24-hour day is the temporal unit used in this illustration. Other examples of temporal units are a week, weekday, weekend etc.

[c] Referring to activities that were done simultaneously. Time spent is presented here for each combination of primary and secondary activities.

[d] This illustration uses nine numerical categories to identify activity groups. Other listing of activities can be used as long as they are exhaustive and mutually exclusive.

641. Finally, thematic tables focus on specific activities of interest such as SNA work, unpaid housework, childcare, travelling, waiting time etc. For example, a thematic table on childcare (see figure 11) would sum time spent in childcare activities by adding time spent doing childcare as a sole activity as well as time spent doing childcare in combination with any other activities.

642. A special type of a thematic table is that for analysing the daily rhythm of the population. Information on the daily rhythm of the population is usually presented in graphs (see annex 15). The underlying statistics are cumulative percentages; for example, for a particular time of the day, the percentage of the population recorded as eating is added to percentage sleeping and so on until all activities that are recorded for that particular time are accounted for.

B. Computation of sampling variances

643. The estimates produced from a time-use survey have many important uses. Because these estimates may influence policy decisions, the precision of the statistics should be estimated. The statistics from the survey may differ from the population characteristics because only a sample of all the persons and time periods are surveyed. This type of error is called sampling error and it can be estimated from the data collected in the survey itself. Other sources of error, generically called non-sampling errors, will also cause the estimates to differ from the population characteristics. Non-sampling errors, as mentioned in previous chapters, arise from sources such as non-response, respondents not understanding the questions, the influence of the interviewers, the errors made in coding the responses and processing the data etc. The present section

covers only sampling errors and how they can be estimated from the survey data; non-sampling errors are discussed in chapter XI.

644. Sampling error is a measure of how much the estimate from a sample may deviate from the population quantity. It is the square root of the variance of the estimate and is used to form confidence intervals that provide practical bounds for the likely range within which the population characteristic is likely to fall. In simple random samples, the sampling error of a mean or total decreases with the square root of the sample size. With the more complex designs and estimates typical of time-use surveys, this simple relationship between size of the sample and the sampling error does not hold. Sample design features such as deviations from equal probabilities of selection and clustering typically cause the sampling errors to be larger than they would be in simple random samples. The complexity of the sample designs also makes it more difficult to compute sampling errors analytically[89] and increases the need for generalized variance estimation techniques as well as the use of specialized variance estimation software.

1. Variance estimation methods

645. When simple random samples are used, the variances for linear estimates (for example, proportions, means, totals) can be computed analytically using formulae provided in standard sampling textbooks. These analytic formulae are of limited utility in time-use surveys because these surveys rarely, if ever, rely on simple random samples. Even the more complex analytic formulae discussed in textbooks on survey designs are seldom very

useful in practice; instead, approximation methods are more commonly used to compute variances of estimates in such designs. Two such methods—linearization and replication—are briefly described below.

(a) Linearization approach

646. The linearization approach is an approximate variance estimator that can be used when the estimator is not a simple mean or total or when the sample design is not a simple random sample. Since most estimates, including subgroup means and proportions, are ratios, the linearization method is appropriate for these estimates. This technique essentially uses a direct variance estimator but replaces the non-linear estimator with its linear approximation. The linear estimator is the first order term of the Taylor series expansion of the function (for example, the function is a ratio for a subgroup proportion). Taylor series expansion is a standard tool in mathematics for approximating a non-linear function.[90]

647. Even after the non-linear function is replaced by its linear approximation, the problem of estimating the variance of a linear statistic from a complex sample design remains. In most complex samples, the ultimate cluster variance estimator[91] is used for this purpose. The ultimate cluster variance estimator is a great simplification because variances can be estimated without having to compute sums of squares for each stage of the sample design. The ultimate cluster variance estimator is a simple function of sums of squares of estimates computed at the PSU level. Information about the design for lower

[89] Most sampling texts cover variance estimation to some extent. The book by Wolter (1985) is devoted to this topic and includes detailed discussions on all the methods presented here. Other useful references on variance estimates from sample surveys are Verma (1993) and Kish, Groves and Krotki (1976).

[90] The application of Taylor series expansion to variance estimation in sample surveys is described in some detail in Wolter (1985).
[91] Kalton (1979) covers the ultimate cluster variance estimator and its assumptions in detail.

Figure 11. Illustrative format of thematic table: average[a] time in a week[b] spent by the survey population[c] caring for own children[d] as the sole activity and simultaneous with other activities,[e] by sex and age[f]

Hours spent	Total	Women	Men
Total population			
Time spent caring for own children			
As sole activity[g]			
Simultaneously with other activities[h]			
Activity 1			
Activity 2			
⋮			
Activity 10			

[a] Average time is the key statistic used in this illustration. Other measures that could be used instead of average time are proportion of time or total time.

[b] One week is the temporal unit used in this illustration. Other examples of temporal units are specific days of the week (for example, Sunday, Friday), weekday, weekend etc.

[c] Any time-use table should specify whether the data refer to the survey population or to participants/doers. If participants/doers are chosen as the unit of analysis, the tabulation should report the number of participants, appropriately disaggregated by age and sex, for each activity.

[d] This illustration uses "caring for own children" as the main activity. Other examples could be television viewing, travel and waiting.

[e] This illustration uses ten hypothetical activities. Other listing of activities can be used as long as they are exhaustive and mutually exclusive.

[f] Basic classification variables are sex and age groups, as shown here. Age groupings should exhaust the entire age range covered in the survey population. Other examples are employment status, number of children, presence or absence of household durables etc.

[g] Referring to cases where the activity of interest is reported as not having been performed simultaneously with something else.

[h] The activity list covers all activities performed simultaneously with the activity of interest.

levels of the sample is not needed. This method requires either small sampling fractions or with replacement sampling of the first-stage sampling units. However, this assumption is nearly always satisfied in time-use surveys of the general population. Software available for implementing this method is discussed later in this section.

(b) Replication

648. Another way of producing an approximate variance estimator is replication, where subsamples are drawn from the sample and the statistics are computed from each subsample. Different ways of subsampling from the full sample correspond to different replication methods. The subsamples are called replicate samples and the statistics computed from each replicate sample are called replicate estimates. Popular methods of replication corresponding to different replicate samples are:

– The jackknife.
– Balanced repeated replication (BRR).
– The bootstrap.

The jackknife method is discussed in detail below to illustrate the basic ideas behind replication methods.

649. Suppose the population characteristic θ is the mean time spent by women in labour-force activities. The estimate of θ is defined as

$$\hat{\theta} = \frac{\sum w_{jk} y_{jk} \delta_j \,(female)}{\sum w_{jk} \delta_j \,(female)} \qquad (1)$$

where y_{jk} is the time spent in labour-force activities by person j in time period k, and $\delta_j(female) = 1$ if person j is female and zero otherwise. To derive the estimator $\hat{\theta}^{(p)}$ with sample data, let $\hat{\theta}^{(p)}$ be the same function of the n units when unit p is deleted from the sample. Since each of the n units can be deleted in turn, there are n different subsamples or replicates and hence n different replicate estimates. The jackknife variance estimator is defined as

$$\hat{V}_{JK} = \frac{n-1}{n} \sum_{p=1}^{n} (\hat{\theta}^{(p)} - \hat{\theta})^2 \qquad (2)$$

650. In the special case of the sample mean from a simple random sample selected with replacement, the jackknife variance estimator is equivalent to the standard analytic variance estimator (this is also true for the linearized variance estimator) (Wolter, 1985, p. 166). With more complex designs, the method of replicate variance estimation is the same except that the unit dropped for the replicate, instead of being a single sampled case, includes all the observations from an entire PSU. The replication variance estimator assumes *with replacement sampling* of first-stage sampling units or small sampling fractions.

651. The general formula for the variance estimate by means of replication is

$$\hat{V}(\hat{\theta}) = \sum_{p=1}^{L} c_p (\hat{\theta}^{(p)} - \hat{\theta})^2 \qquad (3)$$

where L is the number of replicates, c_p is a factor associated with replicate p that is determined by the replication method, and the

other terms are as defined above. For example, with jackknifing, $c_p = \frac{n-1}{n}$ for all replicates, while for BRR $c_p = \frac{1}{L}$ for all replicates.

2. Generalized variances

652. Direct estimates of variances are not the only way to assess the reliability of estimates from sample surveys. Another option that is sometimes employed in multi-purpose surveys such as time-use surveys involves computing direct estimates of variances with linearization or replication and producing a model that predicts the variance estimates for other estimates. This approach of modelling variance estimates is called *generalized variance estimation*.

653. One reason for generalizing variance estimates is that it limits the computational effort required in reporting, especially when many estimates are produced from the survey. Once the generalized variance model and parameters of the model have been developed, the variance estimates for other statistics can be approximated from the model with little additional computation. The generalized variance model also may be included in publications so that data users can approximate the sampling errors for the statistics in the report. Secondary data analysts may use the generalized variance models to estimate the sampling errors for statistics that can be derived from the publications, such as ratios of reported totals.

654. Another reason for modelling variance estimates is to reduce the variability in the variance estimates themselves. Variances computed from sample surveys are estimates and generally they have relatively large variances themselves. Some have suggested that modelled variance estimates smooth out this variability and may even produce a better

estimate of the variance than the direct estimate.

655. Variances are not modelled themselves in most applications because variances depend on the units of measurement. For example, the variance of a statistic based on daily time usage will be very different from the same statistic based on weekly usage. As a result, models are created for quantities that are related to variances but that are invariant with respect to the measurement unit. One such quantity is the design effect (deff); another is the rel-variance.

(a) Modelling design effects

656. A common approach is to model design effects (deff), where the deff is the ratio of the variance computed from the survey to the variance that would have arisen if the sample had been a simple random sample. Since the deff is a ratio of variances, it is not dependent on the units of measurement. The deff represents the effect of the sample design and estimation method on the variance of the estimate. If the deff is one, then the survey procedure gives a variance that is equal to the variance that would be expected from a simple random sample. In complex time-use surveys, deffs are usually greater than one because clustering and differential sampling rates tend to increase the variance of estimate.[92]

657. A simple model that is frequently applied in surveys entails computing the average deff and using it to approximate the variance for other statistics. For example, suppose a time-use survey has an average deff of 2.5 and an approximate variance is needed for an estimated proportion of 40 per cent computed from a sample size of 500. If a simple random sample had been used, the variance would have been 4.8 per cent (40 per cent x 60 per cent ÷ 500). Multiplying the simple random sample estimate by the average deff gives an approximate variance of 12 per cent (2.5 x 4.8).

658. The average deff is determined by calculating direct estimates of deffs (the variance is computed using linearization or replication and then dividing by the expected simple random sampling variance) for a number of statistics from the survey. These estimated deffs are then averaged. A better procedure in most cases is to take the square root of the deff and average it rather than the deff itself because the deffs are not very robust. Another improvement in the average deff approach is to compute average deffs for different subgroups of the population so that the deffs are more representative of the deffs for estimates from the subgroup.[93]

(b) Modelling rel-variances

659. A second approach is to model the *rel-variance* of an estimate rather than the variance, again because the rel-variance is invariant with respect to the measurement unit. The rel-variance is the variance of the estimate divided by the square of the estimate. The rel-variance is the square of a better-known statistic, the *coefficient of variation (CV)*. In this approach, the rel-variance of an estimate is modelled in a relationship such as

$$RV(\hat{y}) = a + \frac{b}{\hat{y}} \qquad (4)$$

where $\hat{y}$ is the survey estimate of a total and a and b are parameters of the model. The parameters of the model are fitted using regression methods (weighted least squares is a

---

[92] Kish (1995) discusses deffs and the relationships between them. Kish (1992) also gives reasons why deffs tend to be greater than one in sample surveys.

[93] Verma and Lê (1996) discuss detailed methods of approximating variances of estimates using design effects, including those described in this chapter.

popular choice).   As with the average design effect method, variations such as having different models for subgroups of the population may be helpful if the rel-variances are more homogeneous within the subgroups.[94]

660.   Variance estimation for the 1999 New Zealand Time Use Survey used three different methodologies (Statistics New Zealand, 1999) to estimate relative sampling errors. The first method used was the jackknife variance estimation using a replicated sampling procedure. This jackknife methodology was used in 10 of the main statistical tables. The second method used was that of modelling relative sampling errors using the magnitude of the relative sampling errors calculated with the jackknife method above as a basis. This was used to produce relative sampling errors for 16 tables. Some differences exist between the jackknife relative sampling errors and the modelled sampling errors, even for cells that contain the same information but are in different tables such as totals. Estimates of counts that are based on the calibration variables (ethnicity, labour force, age by sex and weekday/weekend) have zero relative sampling error associated with them. However, owing to the nature of the models, this will not be true in the tables where modelled sampling errors are used. For cells where the jackknife and modelled sampling errors are both available, the jackknife sampling errors are the best estimate. For the third group of tables, a well-fitting model could not be produced, although the model is considered accurate enough to identify those cells that are likely to be unreliable. These cells are flagged as "^^" indicating that the relative sampling error is estimated to be 50 per cent or more. The estimates in these tables are not accompanied by a corresponding relative sampling error table.

C.   Statistical estimation software

661.   The production of estimates can be accomplished through most statistical software packages that contain the features for handling survey data and weights. Many tabulation procedures exist that support this. Since sampling errors of the estimates are also needed, the statistical software packages developed for this purpose should also be considered. Variance estimation software produces both the estimates and the variance of the estimates for most types of statistics. Virtually all of such packages produce the statistics described above.[95]

662.   One issue to keep in mind in estimation and analyses with imputed data is that the variance of the estimates derived from these packages will treat the imputed data as if they were real observations. The effect is to underestimate the variance of the estimate. The bias tends to be larger when more data are imputed. This is another rationale for making sure that the data collected in the first place are as complete as possible.

663.   All software for variance estimation requires that key data about the sample design are included in the analysis file. With linearization, the minimum data items needed

---

[94] A discussion of this method of generalizing variances for the United States Current Population Survey is available in chapter 14 of the document at http://www.bls.census.gov/cps/tp/tp63.htm.

[95] Lepkowski and Bowles (1996) review variance estimation software in an article in *The Survey Statistician*, the newsletter of the International Association of Survey Statisticians. The article is available at http://www.fas.harvard.edu/~stats/survey-soft/survey-soft.html. This uniform resource locator (URL) also contains links to many variance estimation software packages. Some of the packages are available at no cost. Brogan (1998) describes some of the problems that arise when the appropriate methods of variance estimation such as those included in these packages are not used.

on each data record are the stratum and PSU from which the unit was sampled, along with the estimation weight. With just these three items on the same analysis record with the variables collected in the time-use survey, ultimate cluster variance estimates can be computed.

664. Software packages for replication methods operate in two different ways with respect to the data items needs on the file. One approach is to include stratum and PSU identifiers on the data file; the software then uses the identifiers to create the replicate samples, the replicate estimates, and the variance estimates. Another approach avoids including stratum and PSU identifiers on the analysis files. The identifiers are used to create replicate weights for each record and these replicate weights are then stored on the analysis file. Once this is done, only the replicate weights are used in subsequent analysis and production of variance estimates.[96]

---

[96] Rust and Rao (1996) describe the creation and use of replicate weights.

Part Four

Review and dissemination of time-use data

XI. QUALITY REVIEW OF TIME-USE DATA

665. The review process to assess data quality involves evaluating the final survey product in terms of the accuracy and reliability and general usability of the data, in light of the objectives of the survey. The findings of this review, when properly disseminated, allow users to make more informed interpretations of the survey results. Data quality evaluations also benefit the statistical agency in a number of ways. To the extent to which errors can be traced to specific steps in the survey process, these evaluations can be used to improve the quality of the next time-use survey as well as other similar surveys. Issuing statements relating to the quality of data produced by a statistical survey is encouraged as standard statistical practice. In view of the complex factors that affect the quality of time-use data, such statements for a national time-use survey are especially instructive.

666. Much of the information needed to evaluate data quality needs to be collected while the survey is being implemented; thus, it is important to make the planning of the review part of the overall survey planning process. In planning the review, it is important to consider users' needs to assess the degree to which errors in the data restrict uses of these data and to acknowledge that few users are in a position to assess the accuracy of the data produced. On the one hand, the statistical office needs to take on the responsibility of conducting the data quality evaluations required to measure and assess survey data errors and to disseminate the results of these evaluations to its users in a timely and understandable fashion. On the other hand, users of the results, both internal and external to the statistical office, need to be involved in setting the objectives of the review programme and, where possible, in the evaluation process itself.

667. With the wide range of potential sources of errors in surveys and the corresponding effects on the survey data and estimates, it is not generally feasible to provide a comprehensive set of measures of data quality. Rather, the data quality review should aim at identifying the most important sources of error and provide quantitative measures where possible or qualitative descriptions otherwise. The desired result is a balanced and informative discussion on specific sources of error and bias. Survey managers need to determine the appropriate level and intensity of evaluation for the survey. Factors to consider in making these decisions include: the uses and users of the data; the potential error and its impact on the use of the data; the variation in quality over time; the cost of the evaluation relative to the overall cost of the survey; the potential for improvement of quality, efficiency or productivity of statistical operations; the utility of data quality measures to users and their ease of interpretation; and whether the survey will be repeated or not (Statistics Canada, 1998b, p. 51, para 1).

A. Elements of a quality review of time-use survey results

668. Survey results should be reviewed prior to dissemination and publication to detect and measure errors in the data and inconsistencies in the tabulations. These will provide bases for making corrections and adjustments where possible and preparing appropriate explanations on data limitations to be included in reports that guide users in interpreting the results. Basic elements of a quality review of survey data in general are described in the present section; specific applications to time-use data are also discussed.

1. Data quality issues

669. Quality of survey data is assessed in relation to the extent to which errors occur. As in any survey, sources of error in a time-use survey are described in terms of the components of total survey error—sampling and non-sampling errors. There is an extensive technical literature on survey errors and this *Guide* does not go into a detailed discussion of the topic in general; rather, it highlights quality issues specific to time-use data. These issues are discussed in parts two and three in relation to measures that can be taken at the design stage (for example, mode of data collection, questionnaire design, sample design) as well as the operational and processing stages (for example, quality control procedures) to minimize the errors. This section discusses methods for identifying the nature and measuring the magnitude of these errors.

(a) Sampling error

670. Sampling error (or sampling variability) occurs when the results of the data collection are based on a sample of the population rather than the entire population. Statistics from time-use surveys may differ from population characteristics because only a sample of all the persons and time periods are surveyed. Factors that affect the magnitude of sampling error include the sample design, sample size and population variability (see chap. VI).

671. Standard measures of sampling error are the *standard error* and the *relative standard error* or coefficient of variation which is the standard error expressed as a percentage of the estimate to which it relates. One rule of thumb that may be used in assessing data quality in terms of standard errors is the following: when a sampling error is more than 33 1/3 per cent of the estimate

itself, it is considered to be too unreliable to be published; when the sampling error is between 16 2/3 and 33 1/3 per cent, such estimates should be used with caution; and, estimates with a sampling error of less than 16 2/3 per cent can be used without restriction (Statistics Canada, 1998c).

672. A rule of thumb based on relative standard errors is the following: only estimates with relative standard errors less than 25 per cent are considered sufficiently reliable for most purposes; estimates with relative standard errors between 25 and 50 per cent should be used with caution; and estimates with relative standard errors greater than 50 per cent are too unreliable to be published (Australian Bureau of Statistics, 1992, p. 28, para. 4).

(b) Non-sampling errors

673. The major sources of non-sampling error are: (a) *missing data* due to coverage errors and both unit and item non-response; and (b) *measurement errors* derived from response errors and processing (coding and data entry) errors. It is often difficult to detect and to quantify the extent of these errors.

Coverage errors

674. Coverage errors arise when there are differences between the target population and the surveyed population; these differences generally arise from omissions, erroneous inclusions and duplications in the frame used to conduct the survey. In time-use surveys, coverage errors pertain not only to the populations of households and individuals but also to coverage of time as defined by the design of the time sample. For instance, the target population of days for a time-use survey may be all the days in the year but some days may be excluded from the population of days sampled for the survey. These exclusions may

be made because of practical difficulties in obtaining time-use data from survey respondents for those days (for example, Christmas Day, New Year's Day) and/or because activities on these days are extremely atypical (for example, a fiesta, a wedding or an accident during the designated day for reporting).

675. Since coverage errors affect every estimate produced from the survey, they are one of the most important types of error. These errors may lead to either a positive or negative bias in the data and the effect can vary for different subgroups of the population. For example, institutional populations or geographical areas that are too costly to cover may be excluded. To the extent that the excluded population differs from the rest of the target population (for example, in respect of time-use patterns), the estimates will be biased.

676. When the number of units excluded from the population is small, the biases introduced in the estimates will generally also be small in magnitude. However, when responses to some of the survey questions are highly correlated with characteristics of the groups excluded, the magnitude of the biases may be more significant.

677. Coverage ratios obtained by comparing survey estimates of population subgroups like those for age, race or sex with population estimates from an independent source (for example, census, post-enumeration surveys) provide indicators of the extent of non-coverage. Studies that measure only the level of non-coverage provide no information on the bias for individual survey estimates. Adjusting estimates by post-stratification or calibration aims to reduce non-coverage bias but does not eliminate it. Studies of subsamples can provide evidence of non-

coverage bias but their sizes are generally too small to use for estimation (Kalton, 2000).

Non-response errors

678. Non-response errors occur when: (a) population units in the sample fail to respond (unit non-response); or (b) when a responding unit fails to provide complete responses to the data items in the survey (item non-response). In household surveys, unit non-response occurs when sample households and/or individuals are not contacted or refuse to participate in the survey. In time-use surveys, unit non-response may also occur at the diary level, that is to say, when a sampled individual fails to fill-out a diary for the assigned diary or designated day. Likewise, item non-response occurs when data collected—whether in the household and individual questionnaires or in a diary—are not complete. Non-response causes an increase in variance, due both/either to the decrease in the effective sample size and/or to the use of imputation, and may cause a bias if the non-respondents and respondents differ with respect to the characteristics of interest such as patterns of daily activity. The magnitude of the bias depends upon these differences and the level of non-response.

679. Response rates at the household, individual and diary days levels are basic indicators of level of unit non-response and are computed from survey information. These rates should be reported for the total sample and for major survey domains. Response criteria would need to be defined to determine when a non-response occurs; to be classified as responding, the degree of item response or partial response (where a sufficiently accurate response is obtained for only some of the data items required for a respondent) must meet some threshold level below which the response would be rejected and considered unit non-response (where the sampled person or

household is classified as not having responded at all).

680. To calculate response rate at the household level, it would be useful to first classify each sample household into eligibility classes based on the definition of the scope and coverage of the survey. An example of a set of eligibility classes is the following:

- *Ineligible contact.* Sample household is contacted but does not contain any eligible respondents.
- *Eligible non-responding.* Sample household contains at least one eligible respondent but none are interviewed or all eligible respondents fail to complete a diary according to a satisfactory standard.
- *Eligible responding.* Sample household contains at least one eligible respondent with at least one of the eligible respondents completing a diary and a personal questionnaire according to a satisfactory standard.
- *Unknown eligibility.* No information on eligibility can be obtained for a sample household because it was not contacted or the contact person refused to complete the household form.

Given these eligibility classes, response rate at the household level is the number of eligible responding households divided by the total number of households. It is also useful to further subdivide "eligible non-responding" households into "partly responding" and "fully non-responding".

681. Response criteria at the person level can be similarly constructed. For example, in a survey where an eligible person needs to complete a personal questionnaire and two 24-hour diaries, response categories may be defined as follows:

- *Responding.* Respondent with a completed personal questionnaire and both diaries have at least 18 hours (or a specified minimum) coded.
- *Non-response.* Respondent with no personal questionnaire completed or with one diary completed but with fewer than 18 hours (or a specified minimum) coded.

Non-response may be further subdivided according to the reason for incomplete forms; for example, refusal, non-contact.

682. Since differences between respondents and non-respondents can cause biases in the estimates, it is important to try to determine if such differences exist. Intensive follow-up studies of subsamples of non-respondents can be useful; responses of the non-respondents who eventually responded during a follow-up provide the basis for comparison. It is, however, generally easier to compare the characteristics of the respondents and the non-respondents to see to what extent there are differences at the level of known characteristics. Information on known characteristics can be obtained from the survey frame or from earlier rounds of the data collection, if available. For item non-response, respondents and non-respondents are compared in terms of their responses to other survey items. When it is not possible to quantify accurately the nature and extent of the differences between respondents and non-respondents in the survey, every effort needs to be made to reduce the level of non-response.

683. There are, in general, two methods of compensating for non-response: sampling weight adjustment and imputation (Kalton and Kasprzyk, 1986). Weighting adjustments aim to reduce non-response bias but do not eliminate the bias. When such adjustments are made, estimates of the variances of survey

estimates should incorporate their effects. Imputation may reduce non-response bias but cannot eliminate it; imputation effects should be incorporated into variance estimation. (See chaps. VIII and IX for additional discussion on weighting adjustments and imputation.)

Measurement errors

684. Two types of measurement errors are response errors and processing errors. *Response errors* occur when the response received differs from the "true" value. These errors may be caused by the respondent, the interviewer, the questionnaire, or the mode of data collection. Such errors may be random in nature, or they may introduce a systematic bias into the results. *Processing errors* may occur at the stages of data editing, coding, capture, imputation and tabulation. As in response errors, processing errors can result in either a variance or a bias.

685. Sources of response and processing errors in time-use surveys are summarized below. Measures for minimizing them are discussed in parts two and three of this *Guide*.

— *Reporting variability*. There may be considerable variations in descriptions of activities provided by respondents in diaries—in the level of detail or in the number of activities. One person may report "reading", another "reading a newspaper", for example; or one might give details about peeling vegetables, cutting meat and baking, whereas another might report only "cooking" or might even say just "housework". The result would be inconsistencies in the way the activities are coded.

— *Classifying activities*. Two basic sources of response and coding errors are: (a) the report by a respondent reports as a single activity of what is actually a combination of activities and

(b) the use of different levels of detail in describing an activity (for example, actual motions, intent or purpose, function) so that consistency in coding becomes dependent on having sufficient information on these dimensions for classifying the activity. A time slot with combined activities leads to less accurate and inconsistent coding of activities in general and problems in differentiating primary from secondary activities in particular. The fact that an activity may be described at different levels and thus may be coded in different ways has implications for the principles and structure of the activity classification used for the survey (also see part five for additional discussion).

— *Reporting of simultaneous activities*. Questionnaire design has an impact on the number of simultaneous activities reported. For example, in the 1987 Pilot Time Use Survey of Australia, it was observed that the use of only one column in the diary to report all activities resulted in considerable inconsistency in the recording of simultaneous activities. In addition, some activities (for example, childcare/minding; care for sick, disabled and elderly) were typically not reported as well with only one column as with two separate columns to differentiate primary from secondary activities.

— *Erroneous reporting and/or coding of sequential activities as simultaneous activities*. In using fixed time intervals, the length of interval has an effect on frequency of this type of problem: longer intervals may lead to more errors of this nature.

— *Omitted activities*. Many activities are likely to be omitted from the diaries and thus underestimated. Among these are background activities such as passive childcare, smoking, drinking, eating, and travel.

– *Pervasive activities*. A respondent may be engaged in an activity for a long interval of time but will not report this consistently in the diary. For example, childcare/child minding may take place throughout the whole day while the respondent is engaged in various other specific activities; the other activities might be reported as they occur, but childcare would only be reported sporadically in the diary.

686. Response errors are measured through studies of validity and reliability. The objective of a validity study for a time-use survey is to determine the extent to which activities recorded in the diary correspond to actual behaviour. The basic design of the study involves comparing activity data from the time-use survey with results that are assumed to be more valid. For example, Robinson (1985) describes two validity studies. One compared time diary activities with activities reported by respondents when they were alerted to the need to record the activity by a "beeper" device; the second study compared time diary activities with those reported by respondents when they were quizzed in greater detail about all their activities during a particular "random hour" during the 24-hour recording period (Robinson, 1985, p. 33).

687. The objective of reliability studies is to determine whether the time-use survey methods produce equivalent aggregate results when applied to equivalent samples. In these studies, time-use diary results using different methods are compared. Re-interview studies constitute a class of evaluation methods where subsamples of the original survey sample are selected for validity studies that measure response bias and for reliability studies that measure response variance. For example,

Robinson described a study where activities reported by a subsample of the survey on the day prior to the interview and those reported on the day after the interview were compared.

688. Coder error studies are designed to measure coding error bias and variance. Bias is measured by comparing responses with "true" values generated by using higher-quality interviewers or expert coders; variance is estimated by independent replications of data-collection methods or repeat independent codings by different coders.

2. Some quality review procedures

(a) Types of data quality evaluation methods

689. Two general types of data quality evaluation methods can be distinguished: *certification* or *validation methods* and *sources of error studies* (Statistics Canada, 1998b, p. 50, paras. 3-4).

690. Certification or validation is the process of reviewing the survey data prior to official release to ensure that grossly erroneous data are not released, or to identify data of marginal quality. Certification methods are often employed along with an interpretative analysis of the data. Certification usually has to be completed within tight time constraints; thus, methods used are ones that can be implemented quickly. Standard validation methods include calculation and review of indicators of data quality and both internal and external consistency checks on the data. In addition, debriefings with staff involved in the collection and processing, especially editing and coding, of the survey data can reveal operational and processing events that led to data errors. Checks of the "reasonableness" of survey results by knowledgeable subject-matter experts may supplement these standard methods; in some countries, however, such subjective reviews by experts may be the

primary or most feasible method for an initial and quick review of time-use survey results.

691. Sources of error studies are designed to provide quantitative information on specific sources of error in the data. As described in the previous section, total survey error is decomposed into sampling and non-sampling errors, and specific study as are designed to measure the extent of component errors—for example, post-enumeration studies to measure coverage errors; intensive follow-up studies to measure non-response bias; and re-interview studies for measuring response bias, response variance and coder variance. These studies are very useful in improving survey estimates and subsequent survey design and implementation. Statistical offices need to make decisions about the degree of research to be undertaken based on budget and time constraints, use of the data and the risk of errors or bias. Because of their generally complex nature, the results of these studies often become available only after the official release of the data.

(b) Review of quality of time-use data

692. Standard measures of quality for survey data have been defined and discussed in the previous section; these include coverage ratios, response rates, edit and imputation rates, and measures of sampling error. As part of the review of data quality of a time-use survey, these measures need to be computed and interpreted in relation to their effect on the use of survey estimates. For example, a time-use survey designed to estimate child labour by collecting diary information from young children may result in high non-response and/or response errors. Children may be unable to provide the survey information, resulting in underestimates of their work activities.

693. In addition to these standard measures, there are some indicators of quality specific to

time-use survey data collected from diaries. Five such measures are:

– Number of activities or episodes/events reported.
– Variety of activities reported.
– Number of simultaneous/secondary activities reported.
– Number of time intervals accounted for.
– Number of starting times that are rounded up.

694. In interpreting these measures, the rules of thumb are summarized by Juster (1985, p. 66) as follows: "Other things equal, it seems reasonable to assume that a less valid diary will tend to have fewer activities reported by the respondent, a smaller variety of activities reported, fewer secondary activities reported, more diary time reported as 'not ascertained' and more activities reported as beginning exactly on the hour or half hour." Juster qualifies this assertion by noting that the assessment of quality by means of these measures is complicated by other non-quality considerations such as the sociodemographic characteristics of the respondent and various behavioural and situational influences.

695. Number and variety of activities reported, number of secondary activities reported and number of time intervals of activities are measures of reporting detail of a diary; more detail is an indicator of better reporting. Survey quality is assessed by taking the averages over all diaries and comparing them with known results from similar surveys. In the case of average number of activities, 20 activities per day is a minimum reporting standard. In the case of number of secondary activities, the focus is on possible indications of underreporting of typically omitted and pervasive activities. The number of time intervals accounted for and the proportion of activities reported as beginning exactly on the

hour or half-hour are indicators of accuracy in reporting: the lower the values the lower the accuracy.

(c) Consistency checks

696. Tabulations are typically reviewed from the standpoint of internal consistency and validity. Usual checks include ensuring that individual lines or columns add up to marginal and overall totals, that rates are accurately computed, and that the same item is consistent from table to table.

697. For time-use data, there is a consensus among experts that in recording daily time use, total time allocated to activities must add up to 1,440 minutes per day. This means that for a 24-hour diary approach, the survey instrument design must be such that all activities within the 24-hour period are accounted for. Thus, when tabulations are compiled in terms of totals or averages per day, a basic consistency check is that totals across activities should sum to 1,440 minutes per day or 168 hours per week. Tabulations showing deviations from this should be reviewed with the objective of finding explanations for them and making adjustments, where possible. A basic reason why the average number of hours reported per day may be more than 24 is that multiple activities were reported in a single time interval; these activities may then be coded separately and a "double-counting" of time will occur.

(d) Comparisons based on known patterns and previous findings

698. Another basis for judging the reasonableness of the data would be to check results against certain expected patterns in time-use allocation. For example, omitting activities may lead to unexpected patterns for activities such as eating and personal care. Likewise, the treatment of *pervasive activities* may lead to tabulations showing minimal time

spent on childcare or childminding. In these cases, there may be a need to review the coding results of individual diaries. Also, there are expected differences between women and men in time spent on specific types of activities such as childcare, housework and employment; where simultaneous activities are recorded, there are certain combinations of activities that are expected to occur relatively frequently. Tabulations from the survey data can be evaluated against such expected patterns and marked deviations from such patterns could signal the need to review and find explanations.

699. In comparing the results of the current survey with existing data from another survey, data selected for making the comparisons should be drawn from comparable populations as closely as possible. Comparisons may be made of activity data by sex, day of the week, location or other characteristics. Indicators that may be compared are: mean duration of time allocated to an activity over the population and for participants; and participation rates or the proportion of the population engaging in an activity. It should be noted that not all categories of activities may be comparable owing to differences in the methodology or changes in the classification codes used.

(e) Comparability over time

700. Another quality review procedure consists in assessing the consistency of the time-use patterns estimated from the survey data against the results from similar studies with a previous reference period.

701. The procedure could consist in comparing mean durations of time allocated to major activity groups by sex, age groups, day of the week, and other relevant analysis variables. Mean duration over the population, mean duration for participants and

participation rates are three measures that could be compared.

702. In making the necessary comparisons, one would need to account for the effects of differences in methodology, coverage, concepts and definitions, and classifications. For example, in comparing time allocation patterns for two time periods, problems in the data may be indicated by inexplicable differences in the time allocation patterns between the two periods. If a change in methodology affects comparability from one time period to another, a quantitative estimate of this effect should be made whenever possible.

(f) Comparability with other data sources

703. Another way of assessing data quality is by comparing the survey results with existing (external) knowledge coming from other time-use studies relevant to the country, including studies of other countries with similar conditions to the home country's. For example, as discussed above, a basic measure of the quality of time-use data is the average number of episodes reported per respondent. This number can be calculated for different subgroups, for example, sex and age groups, and then compared with results from past studies. If the average number of episodes (total and for subgroups) of the survey is relatively fewer compared with known results that have been identified as acceptable bases for comparisons, one must first try to determine whether there are explanations for the difference based on differences in survey design and population coverage. Differences not explained by these factors would then provide an indication of the relative quality of the data. The same kind of evaluation can be performed for the other quality indicators discussed above.

(g) Expert judgement

704. If it is not possible to conduct intensive data quality evaluations or generate quantitative measures of errors for reasons of timeliness, cost or technical feasibility, it is suggested that a data quality rating of the time-use survey based on expert judgement or subjective analysis be attempted. The statistical office and time-use experts can work together in making such an assessment and producing a statement of data quality based on such a discussion.

B. Using results of data quality review

705. Quantitative measures and qualitative assessments that result from the review of data quality can be used to adjust survey estimates, guide users in the analysis and interpretation of survey data, and improve the quality of succeeding surveys.

706. The timeliness of the results of data quality evaluation is as important as the timeliness of the data themselves. The ideal situation occurs when the results of a data quality evaluation are of sufficient quality and timeliness to be used to improve the actual data that are released; for example, the results of a coverage measurement study might be used to offset coverage differences between the frame and the target population. Where this is not feasible, then the evaluation results need to be at least timely enough to assist users in their analysis of the data and to help survey design staff improve on aspects of the survey that were pinpointed to be major sources of errors (Statistics Canada, 1998b, p. 50, para. 7).

1. Adjustment of survey results

707. The question often arises whether adjustments should be made in survey results to correct obvious deficiencies. As discussed

above and in chapter IX, it may be possible to reduce to a limited extent bias due to coverage and non-response errors by adjusting estimates using appropriate adjustment factors. For example, adjustment factors for non-response bias can sometimes be developed from re-interview studies or record checks. These factors can theoretically be applied to the original survey results to reduce evident biases.

708. Where the survey estimates are so deficient as to be misleading, the case for making adjustments is stronger than in situations where the differences are moderate. Measurement studies are often based on small samples because of costs and may be subject to appreciable sampling errors as well as other problems such as conceptual and matching difficulties in validity and reliability studies (United Nations, 1984, para. 8.33).

709. An alternative to applying adjustment factors to survey estimates that are considered unreliable is to suppress the information with an explanation as to why it is being withheld. Another procedure is to allow the unadjusted survey estimates to stand but to provide as much information as possible in the technical appendices of publications on the estimated magnitudes of various kinds of errors based on results of data review studies.

710. As noted in chapter VIII, errors that cannot be resolved from other information on the questionnaires can be treated in two different ways: one approach is to allow the errors to remain, which usually requires provision for "unknown" categories in the tabulations; the other approach is to "impute" values to replace the erroneous or missing information. In cases where serious discrepancies observed in the course of internal or external checks cannot be fully explained, a further examination of the survey procedures is in order. The possibility may be investigated of failings in the computer

programs or other tabulation specifications or even some consistent errors made in coding or other manual operations (see also chap. VIII). It may even be possible to detect a consistent and correctable error made by an individual interviewer. Where operational errors are found, they should be corrected to the extent possible, even if this requires some delay in publication. A preliminary release can be issued, omitting those parts subject to correction. If evident errors are not found, the best course may be to issue the original data but include some caveats in the text of the reports concerning unusual patterns.

2. Guide in analysis

711. Evaluation results are important in guiding analysts in interpreting the survey data and in advising and perhaps cautioning others in their use of the statistics. Generally, by taking the initiative in evaluating its survey results, a statistical agency can often silence unreasonable criticism by outside interests that are not satisfied with the survey findings.

712. Information on item errors can affect various publication decisions. If the errors are especially numerous in a given item, for example, that item can be suppressed in the publication (that is to say, not shown), with a footnote explaining the reason for suppression. (Note: Another reason for suppression, disclosure control, will be discussed in chap. XII). Where imputation is used, the extent of imputation can also be specified through explanatory notes in statistical tables.

713. Information on sampling errors (standard error, relative standard error, coefficient of variation) needs to be provided to users. One way of doing this without having to incorporate all sampling error measures in tabulations is by indicating in the publication those estimates for which standard errors are relatively high and not including those estimates with standard errors that are

much too high. For example, estimates with relative standard errors outside the range considered sufficiently reliable for most purposes can be included in publications with a footnote cautioning users that the estimates are subject to high relative standard errors (for example, between 25 and 50 per cent). Estimates with relative standard errors that are considered way too high (for example, 50 per cent or higher) can be excluded from the published output but made available upon request.

714.   The issuance of a "quality statement" about a statistical survey is encouraged as standard practice.   The statement includes information on quality indicators and results of evaluations.   An illustration of the basic content of such a statement is shown in annex 17.

3. Methodological development

715.   Information obtained from an evaluation programme should aid in detecting those aspects of the survey operation that clearly require attention and improvement.

716.   Data evaluation will usually confirm the need for material improvements in survey methodology.   Evaluations may indicate the existence or even the magnitude of deficiencies but not usually the manner in which improvements may be achieved.   It is only through an organized research and development effort that such advances are ordinarily possible.

717.   As discussed in various parts of this *Guide*, methodological research and development in time-use surveys can encompass a wide range of issues.   For instance, data collection is an ongoing major focus of such efforts in the field of time-use research.   Alternative approaches in the use of time diaries, differences in concepts and wording of questions for obtaining data on context variables and simultaneous activities are some of the areas that need further work.   Understanding the impact of differences in data-collection methods (for example, stylized questions versus diaries, multi-purpose versus independent surveys) and choice of respondents are also important considerations for methodological analysis.   Alternative sampling (for example, time sampling) and estimation procedures including methods of adjustment for non-response also constitute important research objectives in the use of time diaries. Data-processing issues, such as manual versus machine editing, coding activities, different approaches to imputation, and the like, also call for exploration. Activity classification also entails issues that need to be studied.

718.   The extensive need for methodological research and development often places a strain on statistical resources, perhaps even more in terms of technical personnel than in terms of money.   As a result, there is sometimes a tendency to assign a lower priority to this activity and to view it as one that is to be accomplished if and when time and money are left over from the operational programme. This is an unfortunate approach, as an adequate research and development programme can pay important dividends from the standpoint not only of quality but also of efficiency of operations.

XII. DISSEMINATION OF TIME-USE DATA

719. As discussed in chapter I, most countries have undertaken the collection of time-use data for use in public policy advocacy in respect of a wide range of issues covering quality of life, gender and work, and caregiving, among others. As mentioned in part one, time-use statistics allow for:

– Measurement and analysis of quality of life or general well-being based on time-use patterns and trends of the population.
– Analyses of policy implications of development planning issues.
– Measurement and valuation of unpaid work (domestic and volunteer work) and development of satellite household production accounts.
– Improvement of estimates of paid and unpaid work.

720. Target audiences may vary widely in their knowledge of social and economic affairs as well as in their knowledge of data analysis methods. Thus, in analysing, presenting and disseminating time-use data, statistical offices need to know the audience and the issues of concern to them. For example, in addressing the importance of integrating paid and unpaid work into national policies, the United Nations Development Programme (UNDP) has recognized the need for and supported the development and testing of models for analysing, presenting and disseminating results of time-use data directed at policy makers (United Nations Development Programme, 1999).

721. To be able to meet the varying requirements for measurement and valuation and oftentimes complex analyses required to assess policy issues, survey results need to be made available to users as microdata, macrodata and metadata (see annex 18 for definitions of micro-, macro- and meta-data) and in suitable combinations of different formats and media for dissemination. The statistical office will need to assess the suitability of these differing modes of dissemination to meet the differing capabilities of users for data handling, analysis and interpretation. Finally, in optimizing access to time-use data, the statistical office is responsible for ensuring that the confidentiality and privacy provisions of official data collection are maintained. This is especially an issue for time-use data since many of the complex analyses undertaken by users require access to microdata files containing information on individuals.

A. Modes of dissemination

722. Standard media for disseminating survey information to users are: electronic formats and paper or hardcopy formats. Survey information may also be made available through telephone, fax or e-mail responses to a special request; a public speech or presentation; and television or radio interviews.

723. A data dissemination programme for a survey would typically utilize a combination of electronic media and paper-based media. Major selection criteria that can be used for determining which media would be appropriate include: timeliness, target audience and its intended use of the documents or data files, size of files, hardware and software requirements, and costs for producing data products and costs to the users.

1. Dissemination through print publications

724. Paper-based media include various types of print publications (preliminary

168

releases covering main findings, standard statistical tabulations, technical reports) and news or press releases.

725. Time-use survey results have traditionally been disseminated on paper-based media. The technical report and topical analyses from the 12-country multinational studies of the 1970s were in fact published as a book.[97] National statistical offices often publish statistical tabulations with a basic analysis of the key statistical indicators of time use. Some countries prepare an initial executive summary-type publication with three or four main tabulations highlighting the major findings of the survey. Detailed analyses on topics related to the specified survey objectives have also been prepared and published either by the statistical office or in collaboration with researchers. User's guides detailing the methodology and classification and providing information on quality indicators as well as means of accessing survey microdata have also been prepared by some countries. Annex 2 provides information on country publications on time-use surveys.

726. Print publications are disseminated by statistical offices through various channels. Complimentary copies are usually given to government agency users including legislators and policy makers as well as users and researchers who have been instrumental in the development and implementation of plans and analytical objectives for the survey.

727. Time-use data publications can be made available to the public through sales outlets. However, often only a limited number

of copies of print publications are produced, usually owing to financial constraints.

2. Electronic dissemination

728. Electronic media include Internet publications on web sites; online or remote access to macrodata and microdata databases; online publications or Internet-based publications which may have the same contents as the print publications presented as web pages or downloadable versions; downloadable macrodata and microdata files in various formats; and computer-based media such as diskettes and CD-ROMs. Microdata in the form of unidentifiable unit records are stored in standardized electronic form, for example, as relational tables in relational databases or as so-called flat files.

729. Electronic dissemination of statistical data increases efficiency since it widens access to data of a broader variety of users; leads to faster transfer of statistical data from producer to users; reduces the burden on users to re-enter data especially when large data sets are involved; and expands the ability of the user to analyse data. Electronic media forms may be grouped into two key types of data storage methods—on-line transmissions (for example, e-mail, Internet) and recorded media (for example, optical discs such as CD-ROM, diskettes, magnetic tapes).

(a) Internet technology and websites

730. Internet technology is one of the most important developments in the dissemination of statistical information. Electronic mail or e-mail, web sites, the file transfer protocol (FTP) server, browsers and mailing software are the main functional features of Internet technology which are increasingly being used for disseminating information and providing access to data from surveys.

731. A web site can be used as a distribution channel of information from a survey with the

---

[97] Szalai, ed., *The Use of Time: Daily Activities of Urban and Suburban Populations in Twelve Countries* (1972). This book was published by Mouton, The Hague; the European Coordination Centre for Research Documentation in Social Sciences sponsored the project

following contents: fixed statistical tables; Web-readable format and/or a downloadable version of the print publication or sections of it. Statistical websites also provide access to microdata databases although there are alternative means of offering access to users such as physical data or research centres providing restricted access (access to microdata is discussed in the next section.). Metadata would also have to be available to assist users in searching data, in understanding the content of the survey data on the web site and in identifying contacts with the responsible department in the statistical office for further assistance.

732. National statistical offices that have downloadable versions of print publications in their time-use surveys include Canada, Australia and New Zealand. The United Nations Statistics Division maintains a web site on time-use surveys (http://unstats.un.org/unsd/methods/timeuse) which contains metadata information on methods and classifications of national time-use surveys including downloadable versions of manuals for methods and classifications and survey instruments.

733. Documents may be stored on the Web in a number of formats. The two main formats for documents on the Internet are Hyper-Text Mark-up Language (HTML) and Extensible Mark-up Language (XML), both of which are suitable for browsing. Documents may also be stored on the Internet in a format specific to an application. That such a document can be accessed only on a computer on which the required application has been installed may limit the accessibility of the document. A general advantage of application-oriented formats is that a document is usually fully contained in a single file, ensuring the integrity of the downloaded version. Examples of application-oriented formats are read-only, word processor, spreadsheet and database formats. The United Nations Statistics

Division web site on time use makes use of a combination of HTML and application-specific formats.

(b) Providing access to microdata

734. There are different systems for providing access to microdata; these include public use files, remote access and research data centres (United Nations Economic Commission for Europe and Eurostat, 2001b). Protecting confidentiality of responses is a major consideration for this mode of dissemination; issues and measures for dealing with them are discussed in the next section.

Public use microdata files

735. Public use microdata files are microdata with personal identifiers removed that are released to the public for research and analytical purposes after being subjected to procedures that limit the risk of disclosure (see next section for discussion on disclosure methods). Public use microdata files substantially enhance the analytical value of the data, particularly time-use diary data. Annex 19 provides an illustration of a user's guide to public use microdata files from a time-use survey whose purpose is to ensure their proper use.

736. Public use microdata files of national and special time-use surveys for 21 countries (Australia, Austria, Belgium, Bulgaria, Canada, Czechoslovakia, Denmark, Finland, France, Germany, Hungary, Italy, Israel, Netherlands, Norway, Peru, Poland, Sweden, United Kingdom, United States and Yugoslavia) have been made accessible through the Multinational Time Use Study (MTUS) collaborative project of four universities in Canada, the United Kingdom and Australia. People and agencies responsible for collecting national sample time-use surveys or other large scale time-use studies are invited to deposit data with MTUS. Some data may be accessed by any interested

user. Other data may be accessed only by authorized academic users. Any researcher wishing to use the MTUS data should complete the general registration form, and apply to the original data producers for permission to use the restricted data sets.

737. As part of the harmonization of time-use surveys, Eurostat is considering the setting-up of a common database for microdata from the various national time-use surveys in order for data to be made more widely available, with direct access to the data restricted by means of research contracts stipulating the conditions of data use and access.

Remote access

738. Remote electronic access allows researchers access to a richer base of survey microdata without compromising the confidentiality of the data. The aim is to increase the analytical scope of the data and to simplify procedures for special or customized tabulations. One way of doing this involves the e-mailing by users of special compute programs to the statistical office, which are used to analyse data from the master data files; however, outputs are vetted for confidentiality before being e-mailed to users. The success of such a system is contingent on several factors, including the availability of good survey documentation that users would use as the basis for specifying tabulation requirements, the ability to run a variety of softwares that users may submit programs for, and a fast turnaround time (United Nations Economic Commission for Europe and Eurostat, 2001b).

Restricted access sites

739. Some researchers need more information than is available in the released microdata. Restricted access sites are secure sites where researchers may go to access confidential data. These sites can be located either at the statistical agency or at an external

approved location. An approved user may access the data at these restricted sites for approved statistical purposes only. While at the site, they can apply standard statistical softwares and also run their own application programmes there (United Nations Economic Commission for Europe and Eurostat, 2001a).

3. Other modes of dissemination

740. Print and broadcast media or "the press" are both users and modes of disseminating survey data. Thus, contacts with media serve two purposes: to make statistics available and known to the media and to give the media open and clear information about the work of the statistical office. In the dissemination of statistical information, relations with media representatives should be characterized by promptness, openness and accessibility, while taking into account provisions regarding confidentiality and security. Press releases may be faxed or sent through an e-mail subscriber list. Press briefings, news conferences, question-and-answer briefs, TV and radio briefings are also traditional means of providing information to the media. In addition to these traditional means, web sites are increasingly being used as the basis for communication via the Internet with the media.

741. Some of the special uses of the time-use results may require special modes of dissemination. For example, workshops for disseminating time-use survey results were organized in India, Mongolia and South Africa with the objective of highlighting policy implications of the data.

B. Issues in dissemination of time-use data

1. Disclosure control and confidentiality

742. To make statistical data both relevant and accessible to users, it is essential that the

statistical office ensure privacy of respondents by making it impossible to identify the respondent from the resulting statistical data and by preventing the unintentional disclosure of confidential data. These needs create a fundamental tension in the mission of statistical agencies. On the one hand, the agency is charged with collecting high-quality data to inform national policy and enable statistical research which necessitates dissemination of both macrodata and microdata. On the other hand, the agency is also charged with protecting the confidentiality of survey respondents which has an effect on the quality of data that is made accessible to users. The trade-off dilemma, which could be stated as "protecting confidentiality (avoiding disclosure) but optimizing access, has become more complex as both technological advances and public perception have altered in this information age" (Conference of European Statisticians, 2001).

743. By combining legal, methodological and technical tools, a statistical office can both increase the availability and accessibility of statistical data, particularly microdata, for a wide range of statistical usages and improve confidentiality protection to the benefit of the respondents (United Nations Economic Commission for Europe and Eurostat, 2001c).

744. Legal tools such as confidentiality laws alone may no longer suffice in the wake of new events such as technological change, especially computational progress, and changes in public attitudes towards the privacy and confidentiality of their records. Events that are likely to influence the perception of confidentiality are the increasing importance of administrative data, the increasing use of the Internet by statistical agencies to disseminate information, an increasing demand for microdata by academic researchers, and an increasing demand for timely, relevant information by policy makers.

745. Methodological and technical tools include disclosure control methods and software systems for implementing them. *Disclosure control* refers to measures taken to protect statistical data in such a way as not to violate confidentiality requirements as prescribed or legislated. The goal is to solve the problem of how to publish and release as much detail in these data as possible without disclosing information on individuals. Disclosure control methods make a distinction between data constituting aggregate estimates from survey responses and unit record files or microdata that refer to individuals.

746. Methods for reducing the disclosure risk in statistical tables include:

– Suppression of individual values or *cell suppression* on the basis of a "sensitivity" criterion for identifying cells in the table that have high risks of disclosure.

– Table redesign such as changing the row and column definitions by collapsing categories or by regrouping the category values.

– Perturbing data through the addition of noise to the microdata used for generating the table or the addition of noise to the tabular data, such as rounding.

747. In the case of microdata releases, individual records rather than aggregated data are being published, and confidentiality provisions generally require that no individual on a microdata file be identifiable. There are two general methods to control the disclosure risk for microdata files:

– Data reduction methods, including sampling, ensuring that the populations for certain identifiable groups are sufficiently large, making the variable categories coarser, top and bottom coding, removing some of the variables from some respondents, and removing the respondents from the file.

- Data modification methods, including adding random noise to the microdata, data swapping, replacing small groups with average values, and deleting information from some respondents and replacing it with imputed values.

748. The Federal Statistical Office of Germany (Holz, 1999) used direct measures and modifications for anonymization of the 1998 German Time Use Survey for purposes of producing public use files as follows:

- Existing identification numbers, auxiliary variables (for example, dates of interview), and month of birth of respondents were deleted.
- The public use file was constructed from a randomly selected subsample from the masterfile. In order not to destroy the household structure, the subsample was drawn at the household level and not at the person level. In this way, information about the daily time use of each member of a subsampled household was included in the public use file.
- The order in which records for subsampled households were included in the file was rearranged. This minimized the possibility of tracking specific records based on the order in the master file.
- Area-related variables were ranked according to importance to analysis by deleting those variables that increased chances of identifying respondents. Area-related variables included regions, States, communities, size and population, settlement structures, population density. The community code was deleted.
- Variable values with an extremely low frequency count were presented in a less detailed and more aggregated

form. Data on income and occupation were made available in highly aggregated classes.

2. Documentation

749. Documentation constitutes a record of the survey, including the data produced and the underlying concepts, definitions and methods used in the production of the data. It also includes descriptions of influences affecting comparability of data and of data quality. Good documentation is complete, concise and precise, up to date, well organized and easily retrievable. Effective presentation of results is an important part of documentation.

750. Documentation may be multimedia (for example, paper, electronic, visual) and different documentation may be prepared for different audiences and purposes.

751. In documenting time-use surveys, a main consideration is the building up of the body of knowledge needed for improving methods, classifications and implementation of the survey. Thus, documentation should include not only what decisions were made in the course of planning and implementation of the survey, but also the reasons why they were made. Documentation should also inform users of what was done in order to provide a context for effective and informed use of the data. The essential points to be included in a documentation system are:

- *Objectives*: Include information on the objectives and uses of the data as well as objectives for timeliness, frequency and data quality targets. Although these may have changed as work proceeded on the survey (for example, owing to budgetary constraints, perceived feasibility, results of new pilot studies, or new technology), these changes need to be documented because they are reflected in the design of the questionnaire and the analysis of test results.

– *Content*: Include the questionnaires used and concepts and definitions. To facilitate integration with other sources, use standardized concepts, questions, processes and classifications. Mention the role of advisory committees and users.

– *Tests*: Describe cognitive tests, field tests or pilot surveys, and report on results as to how specifications were met.

– *Methodology*: Set out design alternatives. Deal with issues such as target population, frame, coverage, reference period, stratification, sample design, sample size and selection, collection method and follow-up procedures for non-response, estimation, imputation, benchmarking and revision, confidentiality, and evaluation. Emphasize different aspects for different readers. Provide a consolidated document on technical issues for professionals. Provide a methodological overview.

– *Systems*: Include documentation of data files (capture method, layouts, explanation of codes, basic frequencies, edit procedures), systems documentation (construction, algorithms, use, storage and retrieval) and monitoring reports (time spent including location, trouble areas, scheduling of runs to determine if processing was on time).

– *Operations*: Include or cite references for training manuals, operator and interviewer manuals, feedback and debriefing reports.

– *Implementation*: Document operations, with inputs and outputs clearly specified. Attach schedules for each implementation step.

– *Quality control*: Include the instructions and/or a manual for supervisors and verifiers.

– *Data quality*: For general use, include coverage, sampling error, non-sampling error, response rates, edit and imputation effect and rate, comparability over time and with other data, validation studies and any other relevant measures specific to the particular statistical activity. Describe any unexpected events affecting data quality (for example, floods, high non-response). For technical users, include total variance or its components by source, non-response and response biases, and the impact and interpretation of seasonal adjustment.

– *Resources*: List the actual resources consumed, as a function of time. Account for all expenditures in terms of money and time. Comment on expenditures versus budgets.

– *References*: Organize and document references (theoretical and general papers and documents relevant to, but not produced by, the project).

3. Preservation of time-use data

752. Although survey data may be collected to meet certain immediate objectives, their usefulness does not normally end at that point. For instance, many of the important analytical uses of and interests in time-use data take considerable time to develop and would warrant maintaining the necessary outputs from the survey to accommodate these future requirements. In addition, because of the great cost and effort usually expended to collect data on time use and the rare opportunities (so far) to collect them, the preservation or archiving of time-use data is especially important. Thus, provisions for the archiving of time-use data should be addressed during the planning phase of the survey.

753. Historically, the sheer bulk of the material involved and the space limitations for storage were the characteristic problems associated with decisions on the preservation of statistical information from surveys. Advances in information technology, however, have greatly expanded the alternatives for dealing with these problems. With the availability of tools not only for archiving but also for making such archives accessible to users, preservation of statistical data is now undertaken as one of the major functions of national statistical offices.

754. Because the usefulness of time-use data is enhanced by opportunities for time-series analysis and cross-country comparability, time-use researchers have advocated for the preservation of diary data from time-use surveys as well as accessibility not only at the local level but also at regional and international levels. For example, the MTUS microdata files described earlier serve as archives of the Multinational Time Use Studies of the 1970s and the current and past surveys of the 23 countries that have made these files accessible to the project.

755. As a rule, to preserve time-use data, all print publications produced (standard reports, media releases etc.) should be retained in hard-copy format along with the electronic print file, as may be applicable. Customized output generated on an ad hoc basis to meet client requests should also be retained because of its potential future value beyond the immediate use for which it was prepared. It is possible that some summary data and commentary may be published only on the Internet and not through the print media; in this case, an electronic copy of this information should be retained in secure form with corresponding metadata.

756. Unit data files are the raw data "transcribed" from an original source document (form or questionnaire); these are the basis for generating microdata files. Data files are built up from the original data provided by survey respondents. However, in the process of validating this, information changes or edits may be made to correct errors and inconsistencies, and statistical techniques applied to impute for missing data. It can happen that different versions of a unit record file are used at different stages of the statistical publication process. It may therefore be desirable to keep more than one version of a unit data file if there are statistically significant differences affecting the published results. It is also desirable to flag imputed information and retain documentation of editing and imputation rules to assist in the interpretation of unit-level results. Unit data files from time-use surveys should be retained because of the historic value of the data as well as their "rarity" value—they are invariably the only data set available on the topic.

757. Although most information needed for statistical analysis is captured electronically from a paper questionnaire or time diary, the forms themselves may often contain respondent's comments that are not always captured as part of the unit record data file. This information may be helpful in interpreting the data supplied, and there is merit in retaining the questionnaire (or a computer image of it) at least until current period processing is complete or, in the case of panel surveys, until the next corresponding period data is processed. The retention of some completed questionnaires may also assist in the redesign of surveys by highlighting problems that respondents had in interpreting questions. Retention of a sample of such forms until the next redesign of the survey is also recommended.

Part Five

Classification of activities for time-use statistics

XIII. PROPOSED INTERNATIONAL CLASSIFICATION OF ACTIVITIES FOR TIME-USE STATISTICS

758. The present chapter discusses the purpose and nature of the proposed International Classification of Activities for Time-Use Statistics (ICATUS),[98] the principles used in constructing the classification and the structure and coding system adopted for it. It discusses major considerations in applying the classification, including guidance on how the classification can be adapted by countries for their use both in data collection and in tabulation and analysis. A comparison of the proposed ICATUS and the Eurostat classification is also discussed briefly. The detailed ICATUS appears in annex 21.

A. Purpose and nature of the classification

759. The proposed ICATUS is intended to be a standard classification of all activities that the general population may spend time on during the 24 hours of a day. Its main purpose is to provide a set of activity categories that can be utilized in producing meaningful statistics on time use. These have to be meaningful in relation to the broad range of objectives of national time-use studies as well as cross-national and cross-temporal comparative studies on time use.

760. The ICATUS is intended to serve as a standard activity classifications for time-use statistics applicable to both developing and developed countries. It builds on existing national and regional classifications and a consideration of the experiences of both developed and developing countries in constructing and applying activity classifications for collecting and analysing time-use data.

761. A main objective in the development of the ICATUS is to enable statisticians and researchers to delineate more precisely the boundaries of economic and non-economic activities and productive and non-productive activities and to measure all forms of work including unremunerated work. Certain types of unremunerated work such as subsistence agriculture as well as work for small family enterprises are included in the System of National Accounts (SNA) and should not be considered as unpaid housework. While the ICATUS draws on the main existing classifications of time-use activities, it separates out into a cluster of categories the economic activities of households. Specifically, it distinguishes between the production of *goods* either for income or for own final use and the production of *services* for income. This permits a clear delineation of activities that are important in developing countries within a classification that covers the circumstances of both developed and developing countries.

762. The proposed ICATUS is designed to be consistent with existing standard classifications in labour and economic statistics; the underlying objective is the integration of time-use statistics with official social and economic statistics. The set of activity categories for productive activities are defined in relation to concepts of employment, economic activity and occupation; the ICATUS utilizes definitions and categories used in the SNA and the standard economic classifications—the International Clas-

---

[98] This is a draft classification for trial use. The classification will be placed on the web site of the United Nations Statistics Division for further discussion.

sification of Status in Employment (ICSE), the International Standard Industrial Classification of All Economic Activities (ISIC) and the International Standard Classification of Occupations (ISCO).

763. The ICATUS seeks to provide data that can be linked to official statistics emanating from the SNA and labour statistics frameworks. This is especially critical where time-use data are used in estimates of household production in satellite accounts that extend measurement of gross domestic product (GDP) to include non-SNA production. Furthermore, by giving relatively more weight to productive activities, it allows for an analytical framework that can generate indicators of welfare and quality of life with both economic and social dimensions.

764. The degree of detail required in the classification of type of daily human activity differs from country to country. Differences in the historical, cultural, economic and geographical circumstances result in differences in the degree of elaboration that various countries may find necessary or feasible to achieve for their data on time use. The level of detail required for purposes of international comparison is generally lower than that needed for national analysis. Section E of this chapter discusses how the proposed ICATUS can be used for national purposes.

B. Concepts and definitions

1. Production, productive activities and work

765. Daily activities can be categorized into those that are considered productive and those that are "not productive", that is to say, *personal activities*. "Productive" activities are those that can be associated with the concept of "work". In relation to the objectives of time-use data collection and an activity

classification, it is important to define what constitutes production, productive activities and work activities and to differentiate these from personal activities.

(a) Production boundaries

General production boundary

766. An activity is said to be productive or fall within the "general production boundary" if its performance can be delegated to another person and yield the same desired results; activities that fit this description are said to satisfy the "third-person criterion". Production, in this context, is an activity carried out under the control and responsibility of an *institutional unit*[99] that uses input of labour, capital, and goods and services to produce output of goods and services. There must be an institutional unit that assumes responsibility for the process and owns any goods produced as outputs or is entitled to be paid, or otherwise compensated, for the services provided (Commission of the European Communities and others, 1993, para. 6.15).

767. Productive activities included in the SNA framework are a smaller set or subset of the general productive activities. The distinction is made between two main types of production:

–   Within the SNA production boundary.
–   Outside the SNA production boundary but within the general production boundary, or non-SNA production.

---

[99] An *institutional unit* is "an economic entity that is capable, in its own right, of owning assets, incurring liabilities and engaging in economic activities and in transactions with other entities" (Commission of the European Communities, International Monetary Fund, Organisation for Economic Co-operation and Development, United Nations and World Bank, 1993, para. 4.2).

SNA production boundary

768.   Activities within the "SNA production boundary" comprise production of goods or services supplied or intended to be supplied to units other than their producers, own-account production of all goods retained by their producers (including all production and processing of primary products, whether for the market, for barter or for own consumption), own-account production of housing services by owner-occupiers and of domestic and personal services produced in a household by paid domestic staff (Commission of the European Communities and others, 1993, para. 6.18).   SNA production *excludes* all household activities that produce domestic or personal services for own final consumption within the same household, except the services produced by employing paid domestic staff.

769.   Non-SNA production within the general production boundary, on the other hand, include domestic and personal services produced and consumed *within* the same household (except those produced by paid domestic staff (Commission of the European Communities and others, 1993, paras. 6.17 and 6.20), including cleaning, servicing and repairs; preparation and serving of meals; care, training and instruction of children; care of the sick, infirm and elderly; transportation of members of the household or their goods etc.; as well as unpaid volunteer services to other households, community, neighbourhood associations and other associations.[100]

(b)   The concept of work

770.   The term "work" has numerous interpretations and meanings depending on the context.   In a general sense, work has been defined as "any conscious, purposeful activity which with satisfaction serves the material and spiritual needs of the individual and community" (Anderson, 1961).   In the ICATUS, a person performing any kind of productive activity—whether within the SNA production boundary or not—is said to be "working" or spending time on "work" activities.   The ICATUS, however, differentiates between work in relation to SNA production (*SNA work*) and work in relation to non-SNA production (*non-SNA work*).

771.   Persons are said to be engaged in SNA work if and only if "they contribute or are available to contribute to the production of goods and services falling within the SNA production boundary" (Hoffmann, 1990, p. 14); they are also said to be "economically active" or engaged in an economic activity.[101] Production activities that are non-SNA, on the other hand, are referred to as "non-economic activities" or non-SNA work.   As described above, these consist of the set of activities that are, in relation to national accounts and labour-force estimation, "unvalued" and "invisible" unpaid domestic and volunteer work; these are the object of measurement and valuation in satellite accounts on household production.

2.   Non-productive   or   personal activities

772.   For purposes of classifying activities, the ICATUS uses the dichotomy of productive and non-productive activities.   The basic idea, drawn from the "third-party" criterion is that an activity is considered productive if it can be delegated to someone else or if it yields an output that is capable of being exchanged

[100] Note that unpaid volunteer work in institutions producing goods and services with employed workers and community-organized major construction, inter alia, of roads, dams, wells etc., are, however, SNA activities.

[101] This concept of economic activity is the basis for definitions of the economically active population, employment and unemployment in the international recommendations on labour-force statistics as well as estimates of production reflected in the GDP.

(Eurostat, 1999, p. 22); otherwise, it is considered non-productive.

773. Activities performed for personal maintenance and care such as eating, drinking, sleeping, exercising etc. are non-productive or *personal activities*: these cannot be delegated to a person other than the one benefiting from them. Similarly, activities associated with socializing, entertainment, participation in sports, hobbies and games, and use of mass media are considered non-productive activities.

774. Education or learning activities includes time spent in full-time and part-time classes, special lectures, laboratories, examinations, homework, leisure and special interest classes, travel related to education and all other forms of active study. Education, skills acquisition and related activities are considered personal activities: from the perspective of the student/pupil, studying is a consumption activity because it is not possible to delegate to someone else.[102]

775. In general, the third-person criterion when applied yields the desired delineation between productive and personal activities. However, the following main issues and exceptions apply:

– Although it is also true that personal services provided to oneself such as washing, dressing, putting on make-up and shaving can be provided by a third party, these are also treated as non-productive activities. It has been argued that these are generally not bought from the market or that they

conform to normal adult behaviour and so are generally not delegated to others (Eurostat, 1999, p.22). On the other hand, bathing a child and dressing a disabled person are considered productive activities.

– Shopping for and availing oneself of services are generally considered productive. Exceptions are receiving medical and personal care services (for example, a haircut) which are considered non-productive activities, as these cannot be delegated to a person other than the one benefiting from them.

– Some activities that are productive are sometimes perceived as personal because of the attachment of emotional or subjective values to the activity. For instance, baking a cake is productive regardless of the purpose of doing so but baking a birthday cake for one's child may be perceived as a personal activity rather than a productive activity because of the symbolic personal value (love) attached to it. Both cases are productive activities, however, according to the third-person criterion (Eurostat, 1999, p. 22).

– An activity can be perceived as work by one individual but as leisure by another based on whether the person "likes" or enjoys performing the activity; fishing and hunting are examples of such activities. Whether the person doing the activity likes it or not or derives utility from it or not is irrelevant from the economic point of view.

776. In addition, travelling is classified according to the purpose of the trip. Travel in relation to performing a productive activity is seen as productive while travel in relation to personal activities is considered personal.

---

[102] Educational activities are sometimes treated as productive activities because they lead to an accumulation of knowledge or skills and represent a part of time invested in human capital and thus have economic consequences. (Harvey and Olomi, 1997, pp. 8-9).

C. Principles used for constructing the classification

777. Underlying principles that guided the construction of the proposed ICATUS are the following: (a) it must be flexible enough to be applicable to the identified analytical objectives of time-use studies as well as other potential uses for statistics on time use; (b) it must have a balanced and comprehensive coverage of all groups of activities which reflects the structure of distribution of time over activities in the general population (for example, productive and personal; formal employment and informal employment); (c) it must be detailed enough to identify separately activities of important subpopulations (for example, women, children, elderly), yet not so detailed as to become operationally unwieldy (inter alia, by overburdening respondents and creating difficulty in coding); and (d) it should not deviate significantly from classification schemes of historic data sets and national and regional listings that have undergone cycles of testing, use and review.

778. The ICATUS groups activities into three hierarchic levels. Specific criteria used in defining the various categories of activities are described below.

1. Main categories

779. The first criterion for differentiating between activities is with respect to the relationship they bear to the production boundary of the SNA. On this basis, three types of activities are defined:

–   Activities performed in relation to production within the SNA production boundary, that is to say "SNA work" activities.

–   Activities performed in relation to production activities within the general production boundary but outside the SNA production boundary, or "non-SNA work" activities.

–   Activities that are not considered production activities, namely personal activities.

These three types of activities are allocated into main categories based on several criteria.

(a) "SNA work" activities

780. SNA work activities are first distinguished based on the institutional unit in which production takes place. All work-related activities in relation to a person's employment in *corporations/quasi-corporations, non-profit institutions,* or *government* are combined into one main category, P1, representing all types of "formal sector" work.

P1. Formal employment or work in "formal enterprises" consists of provision of labour inputs to production of goods and production of services that are typically associated with working for pay or profit even though this pay or profit may not actually be realized in the given reference period, regardless of occupation, status in employment, contractual arrangements, economic activity etc., in corporations, quasi-corporations, cooperatives, commercial farms, and non-profit institutions.

781. Work activities in relation to *household production*[103] are delineated on the basis of the

---

[103] Usage of the term "household production" is as defined in the 1993 SNA and refers to production activities engaged in by members of household unincorporated market enterprises and household unincorporated enterprises producing for own final use. Informal sector enterprises are part of household unincorporated market enterprises. Household members engaged in production for own final use "work" in household enterprises. See also section E of this chapter.

character of the goods and services produced by the activities undertaken, as illustrated below:

P2. Production of goods by households for income or for own final use (either for consumption or for gross capital formation) or for both, including employment in the informal sector.[104]

Primary production of goods

- Production of agricultural products and their subsequent storage; gathering of berries or other uncultivated crops; forestry; woodcutting and the collection of firewood; hunting and fishing.
- Production of other primary products such as salt; mining and quarrying; cutting peat; collecting and supply of water.

Non-primary production of goods

- Processing of agricultural products; production of grain by threshing; production of flour by milling; tobacco preparing and curing; curing of skins and production of leather; production and preservation of meat and fish

products; preservation of fruit by drying, bottling etc.; production of dairy products such as butter or cheese; production of beer, wine or spirits; production of baskets or mats.
- Weaving cloth; dressmaking and tailoring; production of footwear; production of pottery, utensils or durables; making furniture or furnishings; crafts-making; making bricks, tiles, hollow blocks.

P3. Paid construction activities and construction for own capital formation.

- Construction of own house.
- Major home improvements and repairs.
- Community-organized construction and major repairs of roads, buildings, dams, bridges.

P4. Providing services for income, including employment in the informal sector.

- Food vending and trading.
- Repairing, installing and maintaining durable goods.
- Providing business, professional, social, personal care services.
- Transporting goods and passengers.
- Providing paid domestic services (includes employment in households as domestic help: gardener, chauffeur, utility person, maid).

782. The resulting main divisions in the ICATUS for SNA work activities are as follows:

01. Work for corporations/quasi-corporations, non-profit institutions, and government.

02. Work for household unincorporated enterprises in primary production activities (activities carried out in

---

[104] According to the definition in the resolution concerning statistics of employment in the informal sector of the 15th International Conference of Labour Statisticians, January 1993, the informal sector is "regarded as a group of production units which, according to the definitions and classifications provided in the United Nations System of National Accounts (Rev.4), form part of the household sector as household enterprises or, equivalently, unincorporated enterprises owned by households" (para. 6(1)). "The informal sector is defined irrespective of the kind of workplace where the productive activities are carried out, the extent of fixed capital assets used, the duration of the operation of the enterprise (perennial, seasonal or casual), and its operation as a main or secondary activity of the owner" (para. 6 (3)).

relation to agriculture, forestry, hunting, fishing, mining and quarrying).

03. Work for household unincorporated enterprises in non-primary production activities (activities carried out in manufacturing of goods).

04. Work for household unincorporated enterprises in construction activities (activities carried out in construction work).

05. Work for household unincorporated enterprises providing services for income (activities carried out in relation to providing services for income).

(b) "Non-SNA" work activities

783. Non-SNA work activities are delineated in terms of whether they are done for household members or for members of other households or the community. This differentiation identifies volunteer work activities that fall under non-SNA production separately.[105] Non-SNA work performed for one's own household is part of household production in the general sense. An illustration of the main categories for classifying non-SNA work activities is given below.

P5. Providing unpaid services for own final use.

Domestic services for own final use within household

–   Cleaning, decoration and maintenance of the dwelling occupied by the household, including small repairs.

----

[105] The term "volunteer work" is generally used to refer to unpaid work activities and can encompass SNA or non-SNA production as well as market or non-market.

–   Cleaning, servicing and repair of household durables or other goods, including vehicles used for household purposes.
–   Preparation and serving of meals.
–   Transportation of members of the household or their goods.

Unpaid caregiving services to household members

–   Care, training and instruction of children.
–   Care of sick, infirm or old people.

P6. Providing unpaid domestic services, caregiving services and volunteer services to other households, community, non-profit institutions serving households (NPISH).

–   Informal help to neighbours and relatives.
–   "Informal/unorganized" volunteer and community work through; neighbourhood and informal community associations.
–   "Formal/organized" volunteer and community work through the Red Cross, welfare organizations, professional organizations, churches, clubs and other non-profit institutions serving households (NPISH).

784. "Volunteer work" is the one category of work that can be either SNA or non-SNA. All volunteer work producing goods (including community-organized major construction, inter alia, of roads, dams, wells etc.) is classified as SNA work. Unpaid volunteer work in non-household institutions producing services with employed workers also comprises SNA work activities. On the other hand, unpaid volunteer services to other households, to the community (except organized major construction as noted above), to neighbourhood associations, and to other

informal associations are non-SNA work activities. The resulting major divisions in the ICATUS for non-SNA work are:

06. Work providing unpaid domestic services for own final use within household

07. Work providing unpaid caregiving services to household members.

08. Work providing community services and help to other households.

(c) Personal activities

785. Personal activities are distinguished according to: (a) the nature of the activity (for example, learning, socializing, meeting physiologic needs); and (b) participation of others (for example, watching sports versus participating in sports; attending a stage play versus acting or participating, as a hobby, in a stage play). Applying these criteria results in the following major divisions of activities:

09. Learning.

10. Socializing and community participation.

11. Attending/visiting cultural, entertainment and sports events/venues.

12. Engaging in hobbies, games and other pastime activities.

13. Indoor and outdoor sports participation.

14. Use of mass media.

15. Personal care and maintenance.

2. Divisions and groups

786. Activities within the broad categories are further distinguished by their allocation into *divisions*. In defining specific groups under the divisions, the basic criterion is that of universality or frequency and regularity of occurrence; that is to say, if there are specific types of activities that are known to be typical for or prevalent in most countries, then these are listed at the most detailed level. In some divisions, no specific groups have been defined because it is recognized that there would be too much country variation if activities were listed at that level of detail.

787. Another consideration in forming separate divisions or groups is the importance of the particular set of activities in relation to the objectives of time-use surveys—in the case of this classification, a more comprehensive measurement of work. Thus, divisions pertaining to SNA work activities in households highlight those economic activities that are typically undertaken as part of own household production and those associated with the informal sector.

D. Structure and coding system of the classification

788. The proposed ICATUS has been developed to a detailed six-digit coding scheme following a hierarchy. The first level consists of 15 major divisions as indicated in the previous section. These 15 categories are given two-digit codes from 01 to 15. The second level consists of divisions within the major divisions; these are assigned three-digit codes. The third level consists of groups within divisions; these are assigned four-digit codes. The fourth level consists of classes within groups that are assigned five-digit codes, while the fifth level consists of sub-classes that are assigned six-digit codes. Higher levels provide more detailed activities. Each major division consists of three or more divisions of which there are 54 in all. These divisions are further divided into a total of 92 groups. There are 200 classes and 363 sub-classes.

789. Activities at the division level comprise: (a) core activities pertaining to the category; and (b) non-core or related activities. Travelling is uniformly treated as a "related activity" at the division level within a category. Some categories include divisions comprising additional "other related" activities.

790. A "not elsewhere classified (n.e.c.)" division is included in all major divisions to be used for specific activities that clearly fall within the major division but do not correspond to any of the pre-defined divisions of activities. In addition, each major division and division includes a *not fully defined (n.f.d)* code; these are for activities that have been described vaguely or in too general a sense so that there is not enough information to be able to classify them into any of the divisions.

791. The structure of the classification up to the division level is detailed in annex 20 and summarized below.

1. Major divisions 01 to 05

792. For the major divisions covering SNA work activities (01-05), core activities are defined as those activities that are engaged in as part of performing one's job or as part of "working time". Related activities are those that are conceptually related within the labour-force statistics framework (looking for work, training and studies at work) even though these are not SNA production activities.

793. Categories corresponding to SNA work activities (major divisions 01 to 05) are uniformly structured as follows:

– Core activities, consisting of work activities.

– Related activities, consisting of activities related to looking for work/setting up a business.
– Travel.

794. Work in "formal" sector enterprises (major division 01) covers work as part of both "main job" and "other jobs". To be consistent with the definition of working hours used in the labour statistics framework, the work activities of apprentices, interns and those in related positions and activities performed during short breaks at work are also classified in this major division. Other activities that occur in the workplace in formal sector enterprises outside of the usual working time constitute another division in this major division. The desired result is for major division 01 to represent a complete coverage of activities that occur in the workplace.

795. Major division 01 also includes activities pertaining to "short breaks and interruptions from work" as part of working time and activities pertaining to "other breaks". However, such activities are not separately identified for work carried out in household enterprises. The reason for this is that it is assumed that working time arrangements in household unincorporated enterprises are generally less structured or more flexible compared with those in the formal sector. Thus, activities associated with such breaks from work are classified in the corresponding divisions and not within the major division.

2. Major divisions 06 to 08

796. Major divisions corresponding to non-SNA work (Major divisions 06 to 08) have the following uniform structure:

– Core activities, consisting of work activities.

- Related activities (for major division 08 only).
- Travel.

Working time activities constitute the core activities for each of these categories. In addition, major division 08 (Providing community services and help to other households) allocates one division for non-core or related activities.

3. Major divisions 09 to 15

797. Major divisions corresponding to personal or non-productive activities have the following uniform structure:

- Core activities, consisting of activities specific to the category.
- Related activities (for major division 09 only).
- Travel.

Core activities constitute all divisions in these categories except for major division 09 (Learning) which allocates one division for non-core or related activities.

E. Application of the classification

1. Adapting the classification to country situations

798. The proposed ICATUS has been developed for use in planning and implementing data collection on time use as well as in the processing and analysis of the resulting data.

799. The character and definition of categories of the ICATUS can serve as a guide to countries developing an activity classification for the first time, or to those revising an existing one. A number of countries (see annex 2) have utilized the ICATUS in this way.

800. The proposed ICATUS does not supersede national classifications, but provides a framework for the international comparison of national statistics. Where national classifications differ from the international classification, this comparability may be achieved by regrouping figures obtained under national classifications, provided all the elements required for such a rearrangement are obtainable from the national statistics.

801. In order to attain international comparability, it is suggested to all countries that they adopt, to the extent that individual requirements permit, the same general principles and definitions in their activity classification schemes, as set out in this chapter. As a result, it should be feasible to rearrange national classifications to fit the requirements of the international standard by combining entire categories of the national classifications. This, however, is not always feasible because certain classes at the most detailed level may not be distinguished in the classifications of some countries.

802. While the ICATUS aims for international comparability, its main feature is its usefulness in developing a framework for a comprehensive measurement of work. The data obtained through this classification will be useful in: (a) the assessment of national labour inputs into production of goods and services, (b) the compilation of household satellite accounts and, (c) the analysis of time use within the framework of the SNA. This system is especially useful for developing countries that may lack labour-force or expenditure surveys and may need to use a single national survey to address many different research and policy issues.

803. The proposed ICATUS does not intend to fully break open the "black box" of time spent in paid employment (particularly in the formal sector), although it does provide more

detailed specifications of economic work activities based in the household. Thus, it can be applied only on a very limited basis for the purpose of generating statistics on working time and working time arrangements.

804. The detail required for an activity classification for time use such as the present one may differ from country to country and, in many cases, the focus may be on a subset of the divisions covered by this classification. Given differences in the scope of activities and interests, this classification serves as a framework from which varying levels of detail may be derived.

805. Most of the currently used activity classification systems have evolved from the original structure developed for the Multinational Time Use Project of the 1960s. These include both national classifications and the regional Eurostat activity classification. It is very likely that countries with years of experience with their own time-use coding schemes, as well as fully developed national statistical survey programmes to address specific research needs, will continue to use these. Since the proposed ICATUS maintains consistency with these schemes, they share many similarities. It is hoped that these countries review their classifications and suitably revise them to strive for even more harmonization with the ICATUS.

806. On the other hand, for countries that lack the infrastructure required to develop and maintain their own activity classification or who are venturing for the first time into the conduct of a national survey on time use, it is suggested that the ICATUS be adopted mainly with such minimal modifications as may be found suitable.

807. To make possible the conversion of a national activity classification to the proposed ICATUS, the categories at the most detailed

level of classification in the national scheme should coincide with, or be subdivisions or combinations of, the individual groups of the ICATUS. In other words, each most detailed category of the national classification should not, in general, cover portions of two or more divisions. Where the categories represent combinations of two or more entire groups, they should in general be part of the same division, as appropriate.

Retaining categories

808. An important phase in the process of further developing the proposed ICATUS is the accumulation and evaluation of country experiences in constructing activity classifications in general and in adapting the ICATUS in particular. Comparability at the main category levels is ideal in order to evaluate these results. It is also recommended that the three-digit divisions be retained to the extent possible.

Expansion or contraction

809. Since there may be few countries in the world in which all categories of the proposed ICATUS are equally important, it may be expanded or contracted, depending on the social, cultural and economic situation of the country.

810. Some countries will find that the ICATUS is much more elaborate or has much more detail than required in respect of the objectives of the survey. For example, the detailed categories for shopping activities may not be relevant either for the survey purpose or for actual situations in the country. Respondents, for example, may either not specify the goods and services being purchased or purchase them at the same time as other "general goods". A related observation is that some activities that are considered important in the ICATUS may not

be important or even applicable to the country. For example, laws may prohibit or heavily restrict the manufacture, selling or drinking of alcoholic beverages; thus, corresponding activities will not be common or relevant in these countries.

811.   The ICATUS may be contracted by combining the groups of selected divisions into fewer or less detailed groups or by entirely telescoping groups into divisions. It may be desirable or necessary to combine different groups of the ICATUS. This may be because the kinds of activity segregated by selected groups of ICATUS are not important enough in a given country. A related case is where an activity listed in the ICATUS at the six-digit level is considered important enough in a country to be elevated to the five-digit level. For example, a specific type of craft-making may be much more common than others listed at the six-digit level under ICATUS code 03114.

812.   On the other hand, for some types of activities considered important to specific country situations, the ICATUS categories may be too aggregated. In such cases, countries can expand the groups of activities under the three-digit divisions to take into account the need for greater detail. In doing so, it is suggested that, to the extent possible, the three-digit levels of the ICATUS be maintained, although countries may add new groups, or even five-digit classes and six-digit sub-classes within groups, as may be needed.

813.   In order to preserve comparability with the ICATUS, the more detailed classes should be delineated so that they may be aggregated to divisions or major divisions without changing the existing relationships.

814.   There may be certain activities that very few people engage in or that are relatively unimportant to the analytical framework representing the objectives of the data collection which do not fall under any other defined group. The creation of a "not elsewhere classified" (n.e.c.) division provides for capturing these activities without creating a separate subcategory. This solution can reduce the costs of developing and implementing the classification without any significant impact on its utility. Another reason for defining n.e.c. divisions is that, at the design stage, not all activities may have been taken into account or new activities may appear after the classification has been adapted.

815.   It should be noted that n.e.c. divisions, when injudiciously applied at the coding stage, may result in loss of information on the nature of specific activities and in practical applications of the classification, and may be abused as "dump divisions" for inadequately described activities. For inadequately defined activities, the use of a "not fully defined" or n.f.d. division is recommended.

2. Need for contextual information

816.   Some dimensions of the context in which activities are carried out are built into the classification. The need for supplementary questions in the data-collection instrument to capture the additional information should be considered. (See the discussion on contextual variables in part two.) The need for the various types of information may arise under the following circumstances:

–   Categories of work activities are delineated in relation to the institutional type of the producer unit, that is to say, in relation to whether it is a household enterprise or non-household enterprises. Thus, there is a need for information on the institutional unit where production takes place.

– Categories of work activities are defined in terms of type of economic activities as defined in industrial classifications for economic activities. Thus, there is a need to obtain this information in order to be able to classify the activity.

– Category 01 activities are generally paid except possibly in the case of "unpaid" contributing family workers and apprentices. To determine whether work is paid or unpaid, additional information will need to be collected.

– Category 02 activities may be paid or unpaid but "Paid domestic services" is defined as a specific division.

– Unpaid domestic work and caregiving activities are categorized separately depending on "for whom" the activity is done—whether it is for own household members (major divisions 06 and 07) or for others (major division 08). A contextual variable on "for whom" may be needed to be able to accurately classify the activity.

– Activities generally associated with unpaid volunteer work are placed in major division 08. The divisions are delineated in relation to whether the volunteer work is informal help to other households or with a formal entity. A "for whom" context variable may be needed to make the distinction.

– Travel and waiting are classified according to the main purpose or activity for which they are needed, for example, whether they are in relation to work, to attending a sports event or to carrying out household maintenance activities. Thus, information on the purpose for travelling or waiting is needed.

– Computer technology is given some prominence with separate divisions (12133, 1414) defined. This is another implicit use of contextual information

(technology used) in defining divisions and groups.

3. Treatment of simultaneous and "pairs" of activities

817. The ICATUS list of activities describes single activities. However, two or more activities may be performed in parallel or simultaneously. Further, some pairs of activities may be intrinsically linked and for all practical purposes constitute a single activity. In applying the classification, countries will have to determine how these activities are to be recorded and coded.

818. When activities occur simultaneously, countries have a choice as to whether they will record only one (the main or primary activity) or whether they will record both. A basic consideration is the survey objective. If both activities are equally important in relation to the survey objectives, then information on both activities should be recorded and the survey instrument designed accordingly so as not to lose the information on both activities. Childcare is the classic example of an activity that commonly occurs simultaneously and is treated as a secondary activity. Interest in the activity is often the reason why surveys are designed to capture simultaneous activities.

819. If it is not important to be able to separately code both activities in the pair, such as eating and drinking, then coding rules would have to specify which activity will be coded. The rule may specify that the less disaggregated level into which both activities may fall should be used for coding, if applicable. Or, a prioritization rule will need to be specified. (Note that the draft classification includes "passive" childcare as a division to ensure that this activity is not automatically paired with any other activity; it can also be considered a primary activity in case simultaneous activities are recorded and a prioritization is made).

820. Examples of "pairs" of activities that it is generally not practical to record separately are eating and drinking; talking/conversing in relation to work, in attending meetings, or at social events; watching video or listening to the radio strictly in relation to studying. Countries may consider including these types of pairs of activities in the classifications or defining priority rules for dealing with them.

821. Waiting for transport and the consequent travelling are a pair of activities that can be treated in two ways, again, depending on the objective of the survey. Specific objectives related to provision of public services, for example, would find a separate analysis of waiting time and travel time useful. Waiting time that goes with the use of various types of services, such as public-health services or other government services, can be treated similarly.

822. Another special "pair" of activities is related to lunch breaks at work. The ICATUS suggests that lunch breaks are to be classified under major division 01 (and would thus be reflected under "work") if only primary activities are recorded. However, if the survey records simultaneous activities, then "lunch break at work" is to be treated as a secondary activity and the specific activities undertaken during the break (for example, eating, shopping, a business meeting) are to be recorded as the main activity.

823. Prioritization of activities can be carried out at the recording or data-collection stage or at the coding stage, depending on the design of the survey. When carried out at the data-collection stage, both interviewers and respondents (especially in the case of the "leave-behind" diary method) would need to know the prioritization rules. This is especially critical when the survey collects information on only one (primary) activity or when the survey collects information on simultaneous activities where a primary activity and a secondary activity need to be specified. In survey designs where simultaneous activities are not delineated as primary or secondary at the recording stage, such a delineation would need to be achieved at the coding stage.

4. Implications for data collection

824. For countries conducting their first time-use survey, a compromise may need to be made between the degree of comprehensiveness and the ease in the use of the classification. As mentioned above, to be able to use the classification even at the most aggregate level, there would be a need to obtain additional information in the form of a contextual variable or through probing questions.

825. For some countries, especially those where labour-force statistics are still being developed and experience in collecting data on the informal sector may be limited, it may be difficult to distinguish the different types of SNA work for coding purposes even at the major division level. For example, respondents may not be able to tell whether they are engaged in the formal sector. It may be better to ask for information on individual's place of work and use this as the basis for coding rather than leave the decision to either investigator or respondent.

826. On the other hand, countries requiring more detailed specification of the activities may adapt this classification for their purposes by adding groups or defining classes under groups using five-digit or six-digit codes. Countries should note, however, that, because of the complexities of collecting and analysing time-use data, too much detail may result in overburdening respondents, lengthening time spent in data collection, and complicating the coding process.

Table 19. Tabulation categories using the Ås framework

Types of time	ICATUS major divisions	
Necessary time	15	Personal care and maintenance
Contracted time	**Work for:**	
	01	Corporations, quasi-corporations, government, NPIs
	Work for household unincorporated enterprises in:	
	02	Primary production activities
	03	Non-primary production activities
	04	Construction activities
	05	Providing services for income
	09	Learning
Committed time	**Work:**	
	06	Providing unpaid domestic services for own final use within household
	07	Providing unpaid caregiving services to household members
	08	Providing community services and help to other households
Free time	10	Socializing and community participation
	11	Attending/visiting cultural, entertainment and sports events/venues
	12	Engaging in hobbies, games and other pastime activities
	13	Indoor and outdoor sports participation
	14	Use of mass media

827. Countries may also need to provide operational definitions for some of the concepts used in the classification. Important examples are: household unincorporated enterprise, community, and non-profit institutions including NPISH.

5. Applications to tabulation and analysis

828. The 15 major divisions of the classification are intended to serve as general tabulation categories for type of activity. These major divisions are meaningful for most analyses that look at patterns in the allocation of time by type of activities by sex, age group, and geographical location. Further disaggregation at the three- or four-digit levels provide sufficient detail for analyses focusing on specific types of activities within these major divisions.

829. In the other direction, it may be desirable to utilize less detailed categories for some types of analyses. By providing for three levels of classification (major divisions, divisions and groups), the proposed ICATUS furnishes a framework for comparable classifications of data at different levels of detail. The 15 major divisions can be meaningfully aggregated in relation to analyses such as those focused on indicators of free time, SNA and non-SNA work, and paid and unpaid work.

(a) Tabulation categories based on the Ås framework

830. An example of this is provided by the fourfold typology of time developed by Dagfinn Ås (1978), based on the ideas of V.D. Patrushev. This approach has been used in analysing and reporting the results of many time-use studies. The framework identifies all time as either: (a) *necessary time* serving basic physiologic needs, (b) explicitly *contracted time* related to gainful employment and school attendance, (c) *committed time* to which one is obligated, but for which a substitute service could be purchased or (d) *free time* which remains when the other three types have been accounted for. Table 19 illustrates how the

major divisions of the ICATUS can be further aggregated using this framework.

(b) Tabulation of major divisions based on the SNA framework

831. Analyses that focus on issues related to paid and unpaid work and valuation of unpaid work have used tabulation categories that show aggregates of SNA work activities, non-SNA work activities and non-productive activities. As already discussed earlier in this section, the ICATUS major divisions provide a structure that is consistent with the SNA framework and thus facilitate tabulation in this respect. A basic tabulation plan that reflects this is shown in table 20. It should be noted, however, that for SNA work categories (major divisions 01-05), some of the activities are not generally regarded as constituting productive time; these include time allocated to travel or waiting not directly related to the productive activity, looking for work, and long breaks. For purposes of general time-allocation analysis, the distinction need not be made; however, for purposes of valuation in satellite household accounts, countries may choose to subtract such time from estimates of productive time.

(c) Analysing household production

832. The structure of the ICATUS categorizes SNA work activities engaged in by individuals into two major groups in relation to the institutional unit that produces the output: activities performed by individuals as household members that input into household production, and activities performed by individuals that input into production of units belonging to sectors other than the household sector. Thus, the basic tabulation categories based on the SNA framework shown in table 20 can be further expanded for the purpose of analysing aspects of household production—differentiating, for example, between SNA and non-SNA production or between market and non-market production. For this application, there would be a need to assess the activities in major divisions 02 to 05 at the three-digit levels and to combine them into the appropriate categories. Depending on the analysis required, additional information about the activities might be needed, for example, whether production is market or non-market. Relevant concepts are discussed below.

Households as producers

833. Household production may be described as being inclusive of those activities that are "carried on, by and for the members, which activities might be replaced by market goods, or paid services, if circumstances such as income, market conditions, and personal inclinations permit the service being delegated to someone outside the household group" (Reid, 1934 as cited in Quizon, 1978). Activities performed by household members for household production are classified in the ICATUS into the two broad categories of SNA production or work and non-SNA production or work.

SNA household production

834. In the SNA, household production "takes place within enterprises that are directly owned and controlled by members of households, either individually or in partnership with others" (Commission of the European Communities and others, 1993, para. 4.139). An important distinction is that when "members of households work as employees for corporations, quasi-corporations or government, the production to which they contribute takes place outside the household sector" (ibid.) The concept of the household as a producer refers to production by "household unincorporated enterprises". Such production can either be market production or non-market production.

Table 20. Tabulation of major divisions using the SNA framework

Type of activity	ICATUS major divisions	
SNA work	**Work for:**	
	01	Corporations, quasi-corporations, government, NPIs
	Work for household unincorporated enterprises in:	
	02	Primary production activities
	03	Non-primary production activities
	04	Construction activities
	05	Providing services for income
Non-SNA work	**Work:**	
	06	Providing unpaid domestic services for own final use within household
	07	Providing unpaid care-giving services to household members
	08	Providing community services and help to other households
Non-productive	09	Learning
	10	Socializing and community participation
	11	Attending/visiting cultural, entertainment and sports events/venues
	12	Engaging in hobbies, games and other pastime activities
	13	Indoor and outdoor sports participation
	14	Use of mass media
	15	Personal care and maintenance

835. *Household unincorporated market enterprises* produce goods or services for sale or barter on the market. "They can be engaged in virtually any kind of productive activity—agriculture, mining, manufacturing, construction, retail distribution or the production of other kinds of services. They can range from single persons working as street traders or shoe cleaners with virtually no capital or premises of their own to large manufacturing, construction or service enterprises with many employees" (ibid., para. 4.144). They also include unincorporated partnerships engaged in producing goods or services. Some of the outputs of these market producers may be retained for consumption by members of the household to which the owner of the enterprise belongs. "Informal sector enterprises" are part of household unincorporated market enterprises.

836. When household members are engaged in the production of goods and services for own final use, they are said to be carrying it out for *household unincorporated enterprises producing for own final use*. Such enterprises are engaged in non-market production and may consist of the following (ibid., paras. 4.148-4.149):

– Subsistence farmers or others engaged in the production of agricultural goods for their own final consumption.

– Households engaged in the construction of their own dwellings or other structures for their own use, or on structural improvements or extensions to existing dwellings or structures.

– Households engaged in the production of other goods for their own consumption such as cloth, clothing, furniture, other household goods, foodstuffs (other than meals for immediate consumption).

– Households producing domestic services for their own consumption by employing paid staff.

– Households producing housing services for their own consumption.

– Households producing goods on a volunteer (unpaid) basis.

– Households producing services on a volunteer (unpaid) basis in non-household units such as NPIs, schools, hospitals that produce services with employed workers.

- Groups of households that engage in the communal construction of buildings, roads, bridges etc. for their own individual or community use for which services are not paid.

837. Enterprises producing goods may sell any output that is surplus to their own requirements, but if they regularly sell most of their output they should be treated as market producers.

Non-SNA household production

838. Non-SNA household production activities relate to two types of activities:

- Production of domestic services for own final use by household members without pay (see, for example, major divisions 06 and 07).
- Production of unpaid services by household members for other households or institutional units (see, for example, major division 08).

Market and non-market production

839. Production results in *outputs* of goods and services. An output can be classified as *market* or *non-market*. In the SNA framework, market output is "output that is sold at prices that are economically significant or otherwise disposed of on the market, or intended for sale or disposal on the market" (Commission of the European Communities and others, 1993, para. 6.45).[106] Non-market output consists of output produced for own

final use by household unincorporated enterprises (including subsistence production), goods produced for own gross fixed capital formation by enterprises, and "goods and individual or collective services produced by NPISHs or government that are supplied free, or at prices that are not economically significant, to other institutional units or the community as a whole." (ibid., para. 6.49).

840. Depending on the type of output, producers can be classified as market or non-market producers; correspondingly, production can be either market or non-market. In terms of institutional units, market producers are financial and non-financial corporations, quasi-corporations, and unincorporated household enterprises. Non-market producers, on the other hand, are general government; households producing for own final use or for own fixed capital formation are also non-market producers. While NPISHs and NPIs mainly financed by government are non-market producers, other types of NPIs may be market or non-market producers depending on their purpose.

841. In the estimation of GDP, the SNA accounts for all market production and the non-market production of the government sector and non-profit institutions producing goods and services with employed workers. All other non-market production is not valued in the SNA.

(d) Analysing paid and unpaid work

842. The distinction between paid and unpaid work is important in many of the important analytical uses of time-use data discussed in part one of this *Guide*. This distinction is basic to characteristics of SNA work and non-SNA work activities and is thus made both explicitly (for example, paid domestic services) and implicitly in the major divisions of the ICATUS.

---

[106] Prices are said to be *economically significant* when they have a significant influence on the amounts the producers are willing to supply and on the amounts purchasers wish to buy" (Commission of the European Communities and others, 1993, para. 6.45).

Table 21. Relationship between producers and work

Production/ Institutional unit	Market		Non-market				
			Household		NPI		Government
	Corporation, quasi-corporation	Household Unincorporated enterprise	Own-account, goods	Own-account, services	With employed worker	NPISH	General government, national and subnational
Work	SNA	SNA	SNA	Non-SNA	SNA	Non-SNA	SNA
Paid	Employment with compensation	Compensation as employee; mixed income*			Employment with compensation; volunteer with allowance		Employment with compensation; elective position
Unpaid (in GDP)		Incorporated in mixed income* of household	Incorporated in mixed income* of household				
Unpaid (not in GDP)				Equivalent to value of services	Free volunteer services	Free volunteer services	

Source: H. Arboleda *"Time use data and valuation of unpaid work"* unpublished document (2001).
Mixed income is the surplus or deficit accruing from production by unincorporated enterprises owned by households; it implicitly contains an element of remuneration for work done by the owner, or other members of the household, that cannot be separately identified from the return to the owner as entrepreneur but excludes the operating surplus coming from owner-occupied dwellings (Commission of the European Communities and others, 1993, para. 7.8).

843. An individual is said to be engaged in a paid work activity if the individual receives compensation or remuneration, in cash or in kind, for the work done. Labour input into activities within the SNA production boundary has corresponding compensation, regardless of whether the worker is actually paid or not. Labour input that is actually paid is valued and recorded in the SNA as compensation. Compensation may be in the form of wages and salaries, commission from sales, payments by piecerate, bonuses or in-kind payment such as food, housing or training.

844. *Unpaid work* activities can belong to one of five types:

– Work performed by an *unpaid family worker*.[107]

– Unpaid work performed in the production of goods by households for own final use including subsistence production.
– Unpaid volunteer services for NPIs producing goods and services with employed workers.
– Unpaid work performed in the production of services by households for own final use.
– Unpaid volunteer services for NPISHs.

It is important to note that the first three types of unpaid work activities are SNA production activities. Further, the first two types of activities are theoretically included in the estimation of GDP although, in practice, they may be underestimated owing to lack of data;

---

[107] In the 1993 International Classification of Status in Employment (ICSE), unpaid family workers are referred to as *contributing family workers*. They engage in SNA production activities for a household unincorporated enterprise owned by a household member but do not receive compensation.

the value of unpaid volunteer services for NPIs is not, however, included in GDP estimation.

845.   Table 21 summarizes the relationships between producers and work that are relevant to the conceptual framework of the ICATUS and that have been discussed in this section. Work activities are performed by institutional units and the resulting outputs may be market or non-market. All market outputs are a result of SNA productive activities but there are work activities within the SNA production boundary that result in non-market outputs. Non-SNA work results in non-market production. Value of all paid work (all paid work are SNA work) as well as unpaid SNA work is included in GDP estimates; households account for all unpaid SNA work and its value are imputed as part of mixed income of the household. All non-SNA work is excluded from GDP estimation; in addition, some volunteer work is included in the SNA production boundary but is not valued in GDP.

Table 22.   Comparison of the main categories of the ICATUS and Eurostat classifications

ICATUS Major Divisions		EUROSTAT	
		1	Employment
01	Work for corporations, quasi-corporations, government, NPIs		
02	Primary production activities		
03	Non-primary production activities		
04	Construction activities		
05	Providing services for income		
09	Learning	2	Study
		3	Household and family care
06	Work providing unpaid domestic services for own final use within household		
07	Work providing unpaid care-giving services to household members		
08	Work providing community services and help to other households	4	Volunteer work and meetings
		5	Social life and entertainment
10	Socializing and community participation		
11	Attending/visiting cultural, entertainment and sports events/venues		
12	Engaging in hobbies, games and other pastime activities	7	Hobbies and games
13	Indoor and outdoor sports participation	6	Sports and outdoor activities
14	Use of mass media	8	Mass media
15	Personal care and maintenance	0	Personal care
	Incorporated in respective main categories	9	Travel and unspecified time use

198

F. Relationship to the Eurostat Activity Coding List

846. The proposed ICATUS is intended to provide a means for cross-national comparative studies. Similarly, the Eurostat Activity Coding List was developed with the objective of increasing comparability of the time-use data collected in European Union member countries and Eastern European (PHARE) countries. Just as it benefited from previous experiences, the Multinational Comparative Time-Budget Research Project, and country modifications in Europe (18 countries tested the draft Eurostat), Canada and Australia, the proposed ICATUS has benefited from the experience in developing the Eurostat activity list. There is in fact a strong correspondence between the two classifications (see annex 22 for details). The correspondence at the major division level (one-digit code for Eurostat, two-digit code for the ICATUS) is shown in table 22.

847. In general, the major divisions of the ICATUS correspond to one of the one-digit codes of the Eurostat list. The ICATUS has more main categories corresponding to the one-digit Eurostat codes for employment, household and family care and social life and entertainment. Almost all of the activities at the division level and two-digit level of both lists are also similar; the major differences are the following:

- All activities regarded as work activities are classified in a single one-digit code in the Eurostat list: work is generally associated with formal employment; the ICATUS has five major divisions for work, with one major division associated with formal employment.
- The ICATUS classifies activities that could conceptually fall under either SNA or non-SNA work as SNA work;

some of these activities are classified as non-SNA work in the Eurostat classification and are placed under "Household and family care". Examples include: (a) collecting water and gathering firewood; (b) preserving and baking for household consumption; (c) producing handicraft and textiles; (d) gardening; and (e) tending of domestic animals.

- In both classifications, "Major construction for own final use" such as construction of a house and major repairs are treated as SNA work; however, this activity is classified under "Household and family care" in the Eurostat classification, with an accompanying explanation.
- "Hunting and fishing, picking berries, mushrooms and herbs" are classified under SNA work activities in the ICATUS but as "Productive exercise" under "Sports and outdoor activities" in the Eurostat list.
- All study or learning activities not related to paid study for work are classified as study, specifically free-time study, in the Eurostat list; courses in relation to sports and hobbies are classified in the ICATUS under their respective categories and not under the main category of learning.
- Religious activities related to individual practices are categorized under personal care in the ICATUS but are classified as participatory activities under volunteer work and meetings in the Eurostat list.
- Receiving personal and medical services are activities classified under personal care and maintenance in the ICATUS but are classified as shopping and services activities under "Household and family care" in the Eurostat list.

- "Resting" is classified under social life and entertainment in the Eurostat list but is classified under personal care in the ICATUS.
- Travel activities are listed as divisions within the associated main categories of the ICATUS; the Eurostat list has a one-digit code for travel, with travel activities classified by purpose.

ANNEX 1. ILLUSTRATIVE LISTING OF OBJECTIVES FOR NATIONAL TIME-USE DATA COLLECTION

Country	Survey	Objectives
Australia	1997 Time Use Survey	– Measure the daily activity patterns of people in Australia to establish current Australian time-use profile – Study the differences in patterns of paid work and unpaid household and community work by sex and other characteristics – Make comparisons with the 1992 survey to identify changes in patterns of time use
Benin	1998 Time Use Survey	– Obtain information on gender differences in time-use
Canada	1998 General Social Survey Cycle 12	– Gather data on social trends in order to monitor changes in Canadian society over time – Provide information on specific social issues of current or emerging interest – Provide information in support of policy-making: child tax benefits, pension plans and health-care programmes
Dominican Republic	1995 National Time Use Survey	– Evaluate the magnitude of unpaid work – Analyse the participation of women and men in unpaid work – Identify the variables that are related to unpaid work
Guatemala	Guatemala 2000 National Survey of Living Conditions	– Provide policy-relevant data on living conditions in Guatemala for use by the Government in designing a poverty alleviation strategy – Explore more fully issues of labour behaviour, how government policies can be developed regarding development of employment programmes, infrastructure needs etc
India	1998 Time Use Survey	– Evolve a methodology to estimate labour force/ workforce in the country and to estimate the value of unpaid work in the economy in a satellite account – Infer policy/programme implications from the analysis of the data on (a) distribution of paid and unpaid work among men and women in rural and urban areas, (b) nature of unpaid work of women including the drudgery of their work and (c) sharing of household work by men and women for gender equity – Analyse the time-use pattern of the individuals to understand the nature of their work so as to draw inference for employment and welfare programmes for them – Analyse the data of the time-use pattern of the specific section of the population such as children and women to draw inferences for welfare policies for them – Collect and analyse the time-use pattern of people in

203

Country	Survey	Objectives
		the selected States in India in order to have comprehensive information about the time spent by people on marketed and non-marketed economic activities covered under the 1993-SNA, non marketed non-SNA activities covered under the general production boundary, and personal care and related activities that cannot be delegated to others – Use the data in generating more reliable estimates on work force and national income as per 1993 SNA, and in computing the value of unpaid work through separate satellite account
Lao People's Democratic Republic	1998 Expenditure and Consumption Survey: Time Use Module	– Measure productivity in farming, mainly rice cultivation – Measure labour-input work in small-scale businesses and the informal sector
Mexico	1998 Survey on Time Use	– Know different activities that people perform during the day – Know the period of time that household members dedicate to different activities during the day
Mongolia	Time Use Survey, 2000	– Collect data on gender inequality and women's unpaid work. – Collect data on employment and informal sector to come up with realistic assessment of employment.
Morocco	1997/98 National Survey on Women's Time Budget	– Examine how women participate in economic life through an in-depth analysis of the different aspects of women's work – Examine how sociocultural norms and practices constrain total participation of women in economic life – Quantify and describe in detail the different tasks preformed by women in order to better understand their nature and conditions – Determine which factors influence women's contribution to development and, inversely, the effect of this contribution on demographic, economic and sociocultural factors
New Zealand	1999 Time Use Survey	– Determine how people aged 12 years or over allocate their time to various activities – Determine whether significant differences in time use exist between different population groups – Provide data to significantly improve national accounts estimates of the contribution to GDP of the domestic services of households industry and the employment contribution to GDP in the NPISHs
Occupied Palestinian Territory	Time Use Survey, 1999-2000	– Provide statistical data on the time spent by people and types of activities they engage in, as relevant to policy- and decision-making, including: statistics on time spent on paid and unpaid work, time spent by the unemployed searching for jobs, leisure pursuits, caring

Country	Survey	Objectives
		for children and the elderly, information on the hidden economy
Oman	Overall Monitoring of Annual National Indicators Survey, 1999	– Measure the individual's use of time for social and economic analysis, for example, productivity, informal sector size, women's economic activities
Republic of Korea	1999 Time Use Survey in the Republic of Korea	– Estimate what people do, how they spend their time, what everyday life looks like, how much time is spent on gainful employment, unpaid work, leisure activities, personal activities, how population groups and countries differ in these respects – Provide basic data and new information about the volume and pattern of unpaid women's household work – Deduce policy implications from the result of the time-use survey such as sharing of household work by men and women for gender equity, and spreading of paid and unpaid work in rural areas
South Africa	Time Use Survey, 2000	– Measure and analyse time spent from day to day by different individuals – Provide new information on the division of both paid and unpaid labour between women and men and other groupings – Incorporate unpaid work in satellite accounts – Gain more insight on the reproductive and leisure activities of household members – Gain more understanding of productive activities such as subsistence work, casual work and work in the informal sector

ANNEX 2. DESIGN SPECIFICATIONS OF TIME-USE SURVEYS IN SELECTED COUNTRIES: 1995-2000

AUSTRALIA	
Title of survey:	1997 Australia Time Use Survey
Reference period:	No information available
Source:	Time Use Survey, Australia—Confidentialised Unit Record File. 1997. Information paper. Australian Bureau of Statistics. Canberra.
Survey design:	Independent survey
Survey objectives:	– To measure the daily activity patterns of people in Australia in order to establish current Australian time-use profile – To study the differences in patterns of paid work and unpaid household and community work, by sex and other characteristics – To make comparisons with the 1992 survey so as to identify changes in patterns of time use
Method of data collection:	Self-completed 24-hour diary
Survey instrument	
Description	Open diary with chronological recording of activities
Recording of simultaneous activities	One secondary activity
Context variables collected (for what purpose, for whom, with whom, location, paid/unpaid etc.)	For whom; communication/technology used; physical location; spatial location; mode of transport; with whom
Activity classification:	1997 Australian Time Use Activity Classification: three-digit level; 10 major groups; 69 two-digit-level groups
Time sample:	Covers whole year on a periodic (quarterly) basis; each respondent provides data for specified two consecutive days; all days of the week surveyed in equal proportions; school and public holidays represented in approximately same proportion as occurred during the year
Sample selection:	
Reference population	National; household population (excluding 175,000 persons living in remote or sparsely settled parts of Australia); all household members aged 15 years or over, with some exceptions
Sampling procedure	All eligible household members in about 4,100 sample households were selected, yielding about 14,300 diary days
Response rate:	72 per cent household response rate; 84 per cent individual response rate

BENIN	
Title of survey:	1998 Time Use Survey
Reference period:	March-April 1998
Source:	*Méthodologie et Résultats. Enquête Emploi du Temps ou Bénin, 1998.*
Survey design:	Module of semestral household survey on labour, income and social indicators in urban areas; independent survey on time use and education in rural areas.
Survey objectives:	To obtain information on gender differences in time use
Method of data collection:	Face-to-face recall interview
Survey instrument:	
Description	"Light" time diary with 62 activities pre-listed as rows and time line in 15-minute increments starting from 4 a.m. as columns
Recording of simultaneous activities	Each pre-listed activity that occurs in a given 15-minute interval is recorded by placing an "x" in the appropriate cell. Simultaneous activities are indicated by encircling the "x"
Context variables collected (for what purpose, for whom, with whom, location, paid/unpaid etc.)	None
Activity classification:	62 activities pre-listed in survey instrument
Time sample:	Single period covered; each respondent provides data for one day; respondent diary days are distributed so that each day of the week is uniformly represented
Sample selection:	
Reference population	National; urban/rural; persons 6-65 years of age
Sampling procedure	All eligible persons in sample households were covered: 5,834 persons from 1,787 households in urban area; 6,770 persons from 1,419 households in rural areas
Response rate:	No information available

CANADA

Title of survey:	GSS 1998 - Cycle 12—Time Use Survey
Reference period:	February 1998-January 1999
Source:	Time Use Surveys: User's Guide. General Social Survey (GSS) 1998
Survey design:	Independent module
Survey objectives:	– Gather data on social trends in order to monitor changes in Canadian society over time – Provide information on specific social issues of current or emerging interest
Method of data collection:	Recall interview using computer-assisted telephone interview
Survey instrument:	
Description	Twenty-four-hour retrospective diary covering 4 a.m. to 4 a.m.
Recording of simultaneous activities	None
Context variables collected (for what purpose, for whom, with whom, location, paid/unpaid etc.)	Location; with whom; for whom
Activity classification:	1998 Time Use Classification of Canada
Time sample:	Covers whole year (February 1998-January 1999) on a continuous (monthly) basis; sample is evenly distributed over 12 months to represent seasonal variation; sample represents each day of the week: respondents are assigned one designated day
Sample selection:	
Reference population	National (excluding respondents of the Yukon, Nunavut and Northwest Territories); households population; all persons aged 15 years or over
Sampling procedure	Household sample was selected using the Elimination of Non-Working Banks technique of Random Digit Dialling; one eligible person per household was selected to provide data on time use
Response rate:	77.6 per cent overall response rate

208

DOMINICAN REPUBLIC

Title of survey:	1995 National Time Use Survey
Reference period:	June-December 1995
Source:	Unpublished documents. International Research and Training Institute for the Advancement of Women (INSTRAW)
Survey design:	Independent survey
Survey objectives:	– Evaluate the magnitude of unpaid work – Analyse the participation of women and men in unpaid work – Identify the variables that are related to unpaid work
Method of data collection:	Combination face-to-face recall interview and direct observation
Survey instrument:	
Description	Main instrument for recording activities is 5 a.m. to 5 a.m. time diary; activity recording is per 15-minute intervals; post-coding. Household questionnaire lists household members and obtains information on whether children work and who the principal decision maker is
Recording of simultaneous activities	Secondary activity is recorded
Context variables collected (for what purpose, for whom, with whom, location, paid/unpaid etc.)	Where, for what purpose; paid/unpaid for both principal and secondary activities
Activity classification:	One hundred and seventeen activity codes
Time sample:	Seasonal variation in agriculture is captured by using crops as stratification variable in selecting households and spacing interviews over seven months; each respondent provides diary data for one day; respondent diary days are distributed so that each day of the week is represented in the survey
Sample selection:	
Reference population	National; urban/rural Persons aged 10 years or over
Sampling procedure	All eligible household members in 1,500 sample households were covered
Response rate:	Overall response rate of 84.4 per cent, 79.7 per cent in urban areas and 88.6 per cent in rural areas

FINLAND

Title of survey:	The Finnish Time Use Survey, 1999/2000
Reference period:	March 1999-February 2000
Source:	Statistical Office of the European Communities. Unpublished report, 2000
Survey design:	Independent survey
Survey objectives:	No information available
Method of data collection:	Computer-assisted face-to-face interview
Survey instrument:	
Description	Full 24-hour diary with 10-minute intervals. Separate diaries for adults and children aged 10-14 years. An extra example with fewer activities is given to the elderly, unemployed etc. Household and individual questionnaires
Recording of simultaneous activities	Secondary activity is recorded
Context variables collected (for what purpose, for whom, with whom, location, paid/unpaid etc.)	With whom; location. Location is coded based on activity description.
Activity classification:	National adaptation of Eurostat Activity Classification
Time sample:	The survey participants record their time use on one weekday and on one weekend day. Those in gainful employment also keep a week's schedule on their working hours during seven days. All members of the household keep their diaries on the same days. The sample is allocated to survey weeks and diary days uniformly giving the same number of household for each week. Postponement of diary days is allowed for maximum two weeks
Sample selection:	
Reference population	Population aged 10 years or over
Sampling procedure	The survey covered 4,800 households, whose members (11,000 individuals) represent the population aged 10 years or over. The sampling design is single-stage cluster sampling where households serve as a cluster and persons are elementary units. The Population Register is used as a basis for selecting a sample of persons, whose households form the study sample. All members of the household are enumerated
Response rate:	Non-response in the household interview during the first half of the survey period was 34 per cent, which was in line with other recent household surveys in Finland. Main reason for non-response was refusal. Four per cent of the household members were non-respondents in the individual interview. After the individual interview, 11-12 per cent of the interviewed household members did not fill in the diaries

GUATEMALA

Title of survey:	Living Standards Measurement Study Survey Guatemala 2000 National Survey of Living Conditions
Reference period:	
Source:	Informal report prepared by D. Steele, LSMS Office-World Bank, from the Expert Group Meeting on Methods for Conducting Time-use Surveys (United Nations, 2000)
Survey design:	Module on time use in multi-purpose surveys
Survey objectives:	– To provide policy-relevant data on living conditions in Guatemala for use by the Government in designing a poverty alleviation strategy – To explore more fully issues of labour behaviour, how households make decisions regarding trade-offs, and how government policies can be developed regarding development of employment programmes, infrastructure needs etc.
Method of data collection:	Face-to-face recall interview
Survey instrument:	
Description	The Guatemala household questionnaire is a multi-topic questionnaire which includes modules on housing, social capital, languages spoken, health, education, migration, economic activity, fertility, time use, household enterprises, household expenditures, agricultural activities, and credit/savings. The time module includes stylized questions about the time spent on 22 specific activities, and a question on "other" activities, and requires that the total time sum to 24 hours. In addition, in several of the other modules there is information collected on how long it takes to travel to services (school, health facilities) and how long people had to wait for services
Recording of simultaneous activities	Respondents are asked which activities were performed at the same time
Context variables collected (for what purpose, for whom, with whom, location, paid/unpaid etc.)	The module itself does not include questions about the context in which the time was spent; however, information from the other modules could be used with respect to some of the activities to provide contextual information
Activity classification:	Information is collected on: employment activities (paid work, unpaid work, making clothes for family members, taking care of animals, repairs to house, commuting time); education (class time); housework (cleaning, cooking, washing, taking out trash, collecting water or fuel, taking care of children, purchases); pay for services; other (personal care, leisure, community service, eating, sleeping); and others. Total of 22 activities
Time sample:	Single period. Information about the day prior to the interview
Sample selection:	
Reference population	All household members aged 7 years or over. The sample for the survey is nationally representative and is representative at the urban/rural level.

The sample is also representative of the five main ethnic groups in the country.

Sampling procedure   The time-use module was administered in one quarter of the interviewed households to all members age 7 years or over

Response rate: Not available

INDIA	
Title of survey:	1998 Time Use Survey
Reference period:	July 1998-June 1999
Source:	Pandey and Hirway (2000)
Survey design:	Independent survey
Survey objectives:	– To develop a conceptual framework and a suitable methodology for designing and conducting time-use studies in India on a regular basis. Also, to evolve a methodology to estimate labour force/workforce in the country and to estimate the value of unpaid work in the economy in a satellite account
	– To infer policy/programme implications from the analysis of the data on: (a) distribution of paid work among men and women in rural and urban areas, (b) nature of unpaid work of women including the drudgery of their work and (c) sharing of household work by men and women for gender equity
	– To analyse the time-use pattern of the individuals to understand the nature of their work so as to draw inferences for employment and welfare programmes for them
	– To analyse data on the time-use pattern of the specific section of the population such as children and women to draw inferences for welfare policies for them
	– To collect and analyse information on the time-use pattern of people in the selected States of India in order to have comprehensive information about the time spent by people on marketed and non-marketed economic activities covered under the general production boundary and on personal care and related activities that cannot be delegated to others
	– To use the data in generating more reliable estimates on workforce and national income as per the 1993 SNA, and in computing the value of unpaid work through separate satellite accounts
Method of data collection:	Face-to-face recall interview
Survey instrument:	
Description	Main instrument for recording activities is a 4 a.m. to 4 a.m. time diary for a normal day, a weekly variant day and an abnormal day (where applicable); activity recoding is per one-hour intervals; actual time use in minutes is recorded; pre-coding. Household questionnaire lists household members and obtains detailed information on work and whether member participates in decision-making
Recording of simultaneous activities	All activities that occur within the one-hour interval are recorded; multiple activity indicator identifies simultaneous activities
Context variables collected (for what purpose, for whom, with whom, location, paid/unpaid etc.)	Location (whether within or outside the household); whether paid and mode of payment

Activity classification:	Nine major groups; 16 two-digit subgroups; 176 activities
Time sample:	Covers whole year on a periodic (quarterly) basis; each respondent provides diary data for three types of days in a week—normal, abnormal, "weekly variant"
Sample selection:	
Reference population	National as represented by six States selected on basis of geographical dispersion (region) and likely differentiation in work patterns such as in rural/urban areas, tribal/industrial areas
	Persons aged 6 years or over
Sampling procedure	All eligible household members in 18,591 sample households were covered
Response rate:	99.8 per cent household response rate

LAO PEOPLE'S DEMOCRATIC REPUBLIC	
Title of survey:	Expenditure and Consumption Survey: Time Use Module, 1997-1998
Reference period:	No information available
Source:	*The 'light' time diary approach.* Paper prepared by K. Rydenstam (2000)
Survey design:	Independent survey
Survey objectives:	– To measure productivity in farming, mainly rice cultivation – To measure labour-input work in small-scale businesses and the informal sector
Method of data collection:	Recall interview
Survey instrument:	
Description	"Light" time diary with 21 activities pre-listed as rows and timeline in 30-minute increments starting at 4 a.m. as columns; additional information is recorded for the economic activities and for travel
Recording of simultaneous activities	No recording of simultaneous activities
Context variables collected (for what purpose, for whom, with whom, location, paid/unpaid etc.)	None
Activity classification:	Twenty-one activities pre-listed in survey instrument
Time sample:	Covers the entire year; each respondent provides diary data for one day; each day of the week is uniformly represented; enumerator selects the diary day
Sample selection:	
Reference population	National; household population Persons aged 10 years or over
Sampling procedure	Size: 8,882 eligible respondents from one randomly selected person per sample household
Response rate:	Non-response rate is negligible

MEXICO	
Title of survey:	1998 Survey on Time Use
Reference period:	No information available
Source:	*Country report.* Paper prepared by P. Mendez for the Expert Group Meeting on Conducting Time-use Surveys (United Nations, 2000)
Survey design:	Module of National Income and Expenditure Survey (NIES)
Survey objectives:	– To know different activities that people perform during the day – To know the period of time that household members dedicate to different activities during the day
Method of data collection:	Face-to-face recall interview
Survey instrument:	
Description	Open diary; total time spent on each reported activity is recorded
Recording of simultaneous activities	Parallel activity and total time spent were recorded
Context variables collected (for what purpose, for whom, with whom, location, paid/unpaid etc.)	Location; with whom
Activity classification:	Fourteen major groups; 68 subgroups
Time sample:	Single period covered
Sample selection:	
Reference population	National; household population Persons aged 8 years or over
Sampling procedure	All eligible respondents of the 12,000 sample households of NIES
Response rate:	Non-response index is negligible

MONGOLIA

Title of survey:	Time Use Survey, 2000
Reference period:	June 2000
Source:	*Country report on Time Use Survey, 2000.* Paper prepared by Y. Noov for the Expert Group Meeting on Conducting Time-use Surveys (United Nations, 2000)
Survey design:	Independent survey
Survey objectives:	– To collect data on gender inequality and women's unpaid work – To collect data on employment and informal sector to come up with realistic assessment of employment
Method of data collection:	Combination of recall interview and self-completed diary
Survey instrument:	
Description	Main instrument for recording activities is a 24-hour full time diary divided into 10-minute intervals Household and individual questionnaire obtained information on education, marital status and employment
Recording of simultaneous activities	Primary and secondary activities in two separate columns
Context variables collected (for what purpose, for whom, with whom, location, paid/unpaid etc.)	Where/what transport; with whom; paid/unpaid
Activity classification:	Adaptation of United Nations trial classification; extension to three-digits
Time sample:	Single period covered; two thirds of respondents are assigned two diary days and one third of respondents are assigned three diary days; all days of the week are covered uniformly
Sample selection:	
Reference population	National; urban/rural; household population; persons aged 12 years or over
Sampling procedure	Size: 2,753 eligible respondents from 1,086 randomly selected households; all eligible respondents in sample household were selected
Response rate:	82.1 per cent of respondents

MOROCCO	
Title of survey:	1997/98 National Survey on Women's Time Budget
Reference period:	16 June 1997-15 June 1998
Source:	*Condition socio-economique de la femme au Maroc. Enquête nationale sur le budget temps des femmes 1997/98. Rapport de Synthèse*, vol. 1. *Les emplois du temps de la femme au Maroc. Enquête nationale sur le budget temps des femmes 1997/98. Rapport de Synthèse*, vol. 2.
Survey design:	Independent survey
Survey design and objectives:	– To examine how women participate in economic life through an in-depth analysis of the different aspects of women's work – To examine how sociocultural norms and practices constrain total participation of women in economic life – To quantify and describe in detail the different tasks performed by women in order to better understand their nature and conditions – To determine which factors influence women's contribution to development and, inversely, the effect of this contribution on demographic, economic and socio-economic factors
Method of data collection:	Recall interview and observation; repeated visits per day
Survey instrument:	
Description	Twenty-four-hour open diary with start and end times of main activity recorded; total time spent in hours and minutes recorded; Household, individual and community background questionnaires
Recording of simultaneous activities	Parallel activity is recorded
Context variables collected (for what purpose, for whom, with whom, location, paid/unpaid etc.)	Location; for whom/purpose
Activity classification:	Four-digit classification: nine major groups, thirty-six two-digit groups
Time sample:	Covers whole year to account for seasonal variations in women's economic activity; designated days were assigned so that each day of the week would be uniformly allocated to total number of sample diaries
Sample selection:	
Reference population	National; urban/rural; household population Female household members aged 15-70 years
Sampling procedure	Size: 2,776 female household members were randomly selected from 4,487 sample households
Response rate:	Not available

NEW ZEALAND	
Title of survey:	Time Use Survey
Reference period:	1998/1999
Source:	New Zealand Time Use Survey Users' Guide. 1999. Statistics New Zealand
Survey design:	Independent survey
Survey objectives:	– To determine how people aged 12 years or over allocate their time to various activities – To determine whether significant differences in time use exist between different population groups – To provide data to significantly improve national accounts estimates of the contribution to GDP of the domestic services of households industry and the employment contribution of GDP to NPISHs
Method of data collection:	Self-completed 48-hour diary
Survey instrument:	
Description	Forty eight-hour time diary, set out in five-minute intervals, to record activities and context variables; household questionnaire; individual questionnaire.
Recording of simultaneous activities	All simultaneous activities are recorded in a separate column in the diary
Context variables collected (for what purpose, for whom, with whom, location, paid/unpaid etc.)	Location and mode of travel; for whom; paid/unpaid
Activity classification:	Four-digit classification: eleven two-digit major groups, sixty seven three-digit groups
Time sample:	Sample primary sampling units (PSUs) were allocated evenly across the 12 months of the survey period in such a way as to minimize the influence of seasonal effects on time-use estimates. The sample was balanced across weeks in quarters and days in a week
Sample selection:	
Reference population	National (people living on offshore islands, except the Waiheke Island, excluded); Maori/non-Maori; household population; household members aged 12 years or over
Sampling procedure	Size: 7,200 sample households were selected from the 752 Household Economic Survey (HES) Primary Sampling Units (PSUs). An additional 150 screening PSUs were selected to ensure that the sample had a sufficient number of Maori
Response rate:	Overall response rate of 72 per cent

219

Title of survey:	Living Standards Measurement Study Survey
	Nicaragua 1998 Living Standards Measurement Study Survey
Reference period:	No information available
Source:	Informal statement prepared by D. Steele, LSMS Office-World Bank
Survey design:	Time-use module in multi-purpose survey
Survey objectives:	– To provide policy-relevant data on living conditions in Nicaragua for use by the Government in designing a poverty alleviation strategy
	– To explore more fully issues of labour behaviour, how households make decisions regarding trade-offs, and how government policies can be developed regarding development of employment programmes, infrastructure needs etc.
Method of data collection:	Interview with all household members aged 6 years or over
Survey instrument:	
Description	The Nicaragua household questionnaire was a multi-topic questionnaire which includes modules on housing, social capital, languages spoken, health, education, migration, economic activity, fertility, time use, household enterprises, household expenditures, agricultural activities, and credit/savings. The time module included stylized questions about the time spent on 22 specific activities and a question on "other" activities, and required that the total time sum to 24 hours. In addition, in several of the other modules there was information collected on how long it takes to travel to services (school, health facilities) and how long people had to wait for services
Recording of simultaneous activities	Respondents are asked which activities were performed at the same time
Context variables collected (for what purpose, for whom, with whom, location, paid/unpaid etc.)	The module itself did not include questions about the context in which the time spent, however, information from the other modules could be used with respect to some of the activities to provide contextual information
Activity classification:	Information was collected on: employment activities (paid work, unpaid work, making clothes for family members, taking care of animals, repairs to house, commuting time); education (class time); housework (cleaning, cooking, washing, taking out trash, collecting water, collecting fuel, taking care of children, purchases); personal activities (eating, sleeping, personal care, leisure, seeking health care); social activities (weddings, funerals, family visits, community service)
Time sample:	Single period. Information about the day prior to the interview
Sample selection:	
Reference population	All household members aged 6 years or over. The sample for the LSMS survey is nationally representative and is also representative at the urban/rural level.
Sampling procedure	The time-use module was administered in one half of the interviewed households to all members aged 6 year or over
Response rate:	No information available

220

OCCUPIED PALESTINIAN TERRITORY

Title of survey:	Time Use Survey, 1999-2000
Reference period:	8 May 1999-7 May 2000
Source:	*Time Use Survey: a Palestinian example.* Paper prepared by S. Al-Asi for the Expert Group Meeting on Conducting Time-Use Surveys (United Nations, 2000)
Survey design:	Independent survey
Survey objectives:	To provide statistical data on the time spent by people and types of activities they engage in, as relevant to policy- and decision-making, including: statistics on time spent on paid and unpaid work, time spent by the unemployed searching for jobs, leisure pursuits, caring for children and the elderly, information on the hidden economy
Method of data collection:	Self-completed 24-hour diary
Survey instrument:	
Description	Main instrument for recording activities is a time diary from 12 midnight to 12 midnight; activity recording is per 30-minute interval during the night and 15-minutes interval during the day; post-coding Household questionnaire includes questions on participation in leisure and culture-related activities
Recording of simultaneous activities	Only main activity recorded
Context variables collected (for what purpose, for whom, with whom, location, paid/unpaid etc.)	Paid/unpaid; with whom; where: location and transport
Activity classification:	United Nations trial classification: ten major groups; eighty two-digit groups
Time sample:	Covers whole year on a continuous basis: each respondent provides diary data for one day; respondent diary days are distributed so that total survey data covers one whole year; total daily sample of 11 households
Sample selection:	
Reference population	All persons aged 10 years or over
Sampling procedure	From 4,019 sample households, one male and one female eligible member were randomly selected for the survey for a total of 8,038 respondents
Response rate:	4 per cent non-response rate

OMAN

Title of survey:	Overall Monitoring of Annual National Indicators Survey, 1999
Reference period:	May 1999-April 2000
Source:	*The overall monitoring of annual national indicators. 1999.* Technical report. Statistics Sweden
Survey design:	Module of Household Expenditure and Income Survey (HEIS)
Survey objectives:	To provide statistical data on the time spent by people and types of activities they engage in, as relevant to policy- and decision-making, including: statistics on time spent on paid and unpaid work, time spent by the unemployed searching for jobs, leisure pursuits, caring for children and the elderly, information on the hidden economy
Method of data collection:	Self-completed diary for literate persons; recall interview for non-literate persons
Survey instrument:	
Description	"Light" time diary with 23 activities pre-listed as rows and time line in 15-minute increments starting with 4 a.m. as columns
Recording of simultaneous activities	None
Context variables collected (for what purpose, for whom, with whom, location, paid/unpaid etc.)	None
Activity classification:	Twenty three activities listed in survey instrument
Time sample:	Covers whole year on a periodic monthly basis: each respondent provides diary data for one day randomly selected during the third week of data collection for HEIS
Sample selection:	
Reference population	National; urban and rural; household population Persons aged 15 years or over
Sampling procedure	All eligible persons in subsample of 50 per cent of the 4,148 sample households of HEIS
Response rate:	95 per cent non-response rate

REPUBLIC OF KOREA

Title of survey:	1999 Time Use Survey in the Republic of Korea
Reference period:	2-14 September 1999
Source:	Country report. Paper presented by A. Schon (2000)
Survey design:	Independent survey
Survey objectives:	– To estimate what people do, how they spend their time, what everyday life looks like, how much time is spent on gainful employment, unpaid work, leisure activities, personal activities, how population groups and countries differ in these respects
	– To provide basic data and new information about the volume and pattern of the unpaid women's household work
	– To deduce policy implications from the results of the time-use survey such as sharing of household work by men and women for gender equity, and spreading of paid and unpaid work in rural area
Method of data collection:	Combination of self-complied diary and interview from background questionnaires
Survey instrument:	
Description	Main instrument for recording activities was a full-time diary starting from 0 a.m. to 24 p.m.; 10-minute fixed-time interval
	Household and individual questionnaires
Recording of simultaneous activities	Secondary activity is recorded
Context variables collected (for what purpose, for whom, with whom, location, paid/unpaid etc.)	Location; with whom (for eating activities only); for whom (for family care activities only); paid/unpaid (for work in the family business, work on family farm, work on family farm and garden not for sale)
Activity classification:	Nine major groups (one-digit); forty two-digit groups
Time sample:	The survey participants record their time use on one weekend and on one weekday. Those in gainful employment also keep a week's schedule on their working hours during seven days. All members of the household keep their diaries on the same days. The sample is allocated to survey weeks and diary days uniformly giving the same number of households for each week. Postponement of diary days is allowed for the maximum of two weeks
Sample selection:	
Reference population	National; household population
	Persons aged 10 years or over
Sampling procedure	All eligible respondents in 17,000 sample households were selected yielding a total of 46,109 sample respondents
Response rate:	94.7 per cent of sample population

Title of survey:	Time Use Survey 2000
Reference period:	February-October 2000
Source:	*Time Use Survey, 2000.* Paper prepared by Y. Mpetsheni and D. Budlunder for the Expert Group Meeting on Conducting Time-Use Surveys (United Nations, 2000)
Survey design:	Independent survey
Survey objectives:	– To measure and analyse time spent from day to day by different individuals;
	– To provide new information on the division of both paid and unpaid labour between women and men and other groupings
	– To incorporate unpaid work in satellite accounts
	– To gain more insight on the reproductive and leisure activities of household members
	– To gain more understanding of productive activities such as subsistence work, casual work and work in the informal sector
Method of data collection:	Face-to-face recall interview
Survey instrument:	
Description	Main instrument for recording activities is a 4 a.m. to 4 a.m. time diary; activity recording is per 30-minute intervals; up to three activities per 30-minute interval are recorded; post-coding. Household questionnaire asks who is the main person responsible for doing housework; individual questionnaire obtains information on number of children and detailed information on work, and asks respondents to classify business as formal/informal
Recording of simultaneous activities	Simultaneous activities are recorded; no prioritization of activities into primary, secondary or tertiary
Context variables collected (for what purpose, for whom, with whom, location, paid/unpaid etc.)	Location; purpose of travel
Activity classification:	Adoption of United Nations trial classification: 10 major groups; some changes in two-digit level of group 1; three-digit level extensions for specific country situations
Time sample:	Covers whole year on a periodic basis; design calls for all days of the week to be uniformly represented by allocating interview days to enumerators accordingly; each respondent provides diary data for one day
Sample selection:	
Reference population	National; urban/rural; settlement types (urban formal, urban informal, rural commercial farms, rural other/tribal areas) Persons aged 10 years or over
Sampling procedure	Two eligible household members are randomly selected for each sample household; planned total size is 10,800 dwelling units; all households in a sample dwelling unit are selected
Response rate:	84 per cent response rate

SWEDEN

Title of survey:	The Swedish Time Use Survey 2000
Reference period:	2000-2001
Source:	Statistical Office of the European Communities. Unpublished report. 2000
Survey design:	Independent survey
Survey objectives:	No information available
Method of data collection:	"Leave behind" diary approach; interviews for individual and household data
Survey instrument:	
Description	Full time diary with 10-minute intervals; household and individual questionnaires
Recording of simultaneous activities	Secondary activity is recorded
Context variables collected (for what purpose, for whom, with whom, location, paid/unpaid etc.)	With whom, location
Activity classification:	European Time Use Survey (ETUS) and the Swedish activity code system used in 1990-1991 survey
Time sample:	The survey covers 12 months. Two diary days, a weekday and a weekend day, are randomly selected. Designated diary day approach
Sample selection:	
Reference population	Persons aged 20-64 years
Sampling procedure	The unit of study is a combination of the individual and the household. A sample of 5,500 individuals; single mothers are overrepresented; spouses for a subsample of individuals
Response rate:	No information available

225

ANNEX 3. EXAMPLES OF COUNTRY CODES FOR "LOCATION/MODE OF TRAVEL"

AUSTRALIA	
Location	
Field 1: Physical location	**Field 2: Spatial location**
0 Undescribed/ not specified	0 Undescribed/moving between indoors and outdoors
1 Own house	1 Indoor
2 Someone else's house	2 Outdoor
3 Workplace if outside home (includes farm)	3 In transit
4 Public area, for example, street, town hall, public gardens, church	4 Waiting – indoors
5 Commercial and service area for example, bank, shop, office (other than 6 and 7)	5 Waiting – outdoors
6 Establishment for leisure, culture, sports activities	
7 Eating and drinking locale (excluding work canteen etc.)	
8 Educational establishment	
9 Country, bush, beach	

Mode of transport

00	Not applicable
01	Train
02	Bus
03	Ferry/tram
04	Taxi
05	Car, van, truck as driver
06	Car, van, truck as passenger
07	Motorbike, scooter
08	Bicycle
09	Walking
98	Transport used, not specified
99	Other n.e.c.

CANADA	
Place	**In transit**
1 Respondent's home	5 Car (driver)
2 Workplace	6 Car (passenger)
3 Other place (including park, neighborhood)	7 Walk
	8 Bus and subway (includes streetcars, commuter trains or other public transit)
	9 Bicycle
	10 Other (for example, airplane, train, motorcycle)

DOMINICAN REPUBLIC

Donde realizo las actividades

1	Su hogar
2	Hogar de otros personas
3	Lugar de trabajo
4	Escuela/universidad
5	Centros de salud
6	Restaurantes, cafes, discotecas, parques, gimnasios y afines
7	Calle
8	Supermercado/colmado

EUROSTAT

Location and mode of transport

00	Unspecified location
10	Unspecified location (not travelling)
11	Home
12	Second home or weekend house
13	Working place or school
14	Other people's home
15	Restaurant, cafe or pub
19	Other specified location (not travelling)
20	Unspecified private transport mode
21	Travelling on foot
22	Travelling by bicycle
23	Travelling by moped, motorcycle or motorboat
24	Travelling by passenger car
25	Travelling by lorry, van or tractor
29	Other specified private travelling mode
30	Unspecified public transport mode
31	Travelling by taxi
32	Travelling by bus or coach
33	Travelling by tram or underground
34	Travelling by train
35	Travelling by aeroplane
36	Travelling by boat or ship
39	Other specified public transport mode
40	Unspecified transport mode

INDIA

Location

1	Within household
2	Outside household

MEXICO

En que lugar

1	Dentro de la vivienda
2	Fuera de la vivienda

MOROCCO

Lieu de l'occupation

1	Domicile
2	Ailleurs

NEW ZEALAND

Where the activity was done		Mode of travel	
01	At home	08	Travelling by foot or bicycle, for example skateboard, Rollerblade
02	Other people's home	09	Travelling by private transport, for example car, motorbike, van
03	Workplace or place of study		
04	Public or commercial or service area, for example street, shop	10	Travelling by public transport, for example bus, ferry, train, plane, taxi
05	Bush, beach or wilderness	11	Travelling, but mode of travel not stated
06	*Marae* (meeting house) or other site of cultural significance to Maori, for example *urupa* (burial ground)		
07	Other area, for example church, sports club room		

REPUBLIC OF KOREA

Location		Mode of travel	
0	Outside home (for example, workplace, school, other person's home etc.)	2	Travelling on foot
		3	Travelling by urban bus
1	Home	4	Travelling by subway
		5	Travelling by taxi
		6	Travelling by passenger car
		7	Travelling by bicycle, motorcycle, commuter bus, school bus etc.
		8	Travelling by train, suburban bus, long-distance bus
		9	Others (for example, truck, cultivator, airplane, boat etc.)

SOUTH AFRICA

Location code 1		Location code 2	
1	Own dwelling	1	Inside
2	Someone else's dwelling	2	Outside
3	Field, farm or other agricultural workplace	3	Travelling on foot
4	Other workplace outside private dwelling	4	Travelling by private transport (car, van, motorcycle)
5	Educational establishment		
6	Public area, in other words, not in private dwelling, workplace or educational establishment	5	Travelling by taxi (kombi (minibus) or other)
		6	Travelling by train
7	Travelling or waiting to travel	7	Travelling by bus
8	Other (specify)	8	Travelling by bicycle
		9	Travelling by other means (specify)

ANNEX 4.   EXAMPLES OF COUNTRY CODES
FOR "WITH WHOM"

AUSTRALIA		
With whom: relationship		**With whom: age**

With whom: relationship			With whom: age	
0	Undescribed		0	Undescribed/not applicable
1	Spouse		1	Children 0-4
2	Other family (excluding spouse) living in household		2	Children 5-11
			3	Children 12-14
3	Family living outside household		4	Adults 15-59
4	Friends/neighbours/acquaintances		5	Adults 60+
5	Children of friends/neighbours			
6	Colleagues			
7	Shop personnel/service providers			
8	Crowd			
9	No one			
10	Non-family household member			

CANADA		
Living in the household:		**Living outside the household:**

Living in the household:			Living outside the household:	
1	Alone		6	Child(ren) of the respondent under age 15
2	Spouse/partner		7	Child(ren) of the respondent aged 15 years or over
3	Child(ren) under age 15			
4	Parent(s) or parent(s)-in-law		8	Parent(s) or parent(s) in-law
5	Other member(s) (including children aged 15 years or over)		9	Other family member(s)
			10	Friend(s)

EUROSTAT	
1	Alone
2	Children up to age 9 living in the household
3	Other household members
4	Other persons known to the respondent

JAPAN	

With whom:

1	Alone
2	With family members
3	With classmates or colleagues
4	With other persons

MEXICO	

Personas presentes:

1	Con personas que viven con usted en la misma vivienda
2	Con personas que no viven con usted en la misma vivienda
3	Con personas que viven y no viven con usted en la misma
4	Solo(a)

ANNEX 5.   EXAMPLES OF COUNTRY CODES FOR "FOR WHOM"

AUSTRALIA	
For whom:	
00	Undescribed/ not specified
01	Self
02	Children
03	Family – own household – well
04	Family – other household – well
05	Family – other household – sick, frail, disabled
06	Pet
07	Group household – well
08	Group household – sick, frail, disabled
09	Friend/neighbour – well
10	Friend/ neighbour – sick, frail, disabled
11	Work
12	Community – sports
13	Community – arts
14	Community health and welfare
15	Community education/youth
16	Community religious
17	Community emergency services
18	Community other
19	Other person/group n.e.c.

DOMINICAN REPUBLIC	
Para quien realizo actividades:	
1	Si misma (o)
2	Otros/as integrantes del hogar
3	Su hogar/familia
4	Otros hogares
5	Su hogar y otros hogares
6	Partido, iglesia, club y otras organizaciones sociales o comunitarias
7	El mercado
8	Empleadores(as)/patrones(as)
9	Sin respuesta

NEW ZEALAND

For whom the activity was done:

1   Own household (including self)

   11   Household child n.f.d.
         111   Household child 0-4
         112   Household child 5-13
   12   Household adult n.f.d.
         121   Household adult – well (with no disability)
         122   Household adult – temporarily ill or injured (illness or injury effects expected to last less than six months
         123   Household adult – has disability (limitation or condition lasting or expected to last six months or more)

2   Another household or individual

   21   Non-household child n.f.d.
         211   Non-household child 0-4
         212   Non-household child 5-13
   22   Non-household adult n.f.d.
         221   Non-household adult – well (with no disability)
         222   Non-household adult – temporarily ill or injured (illness or injury effects expected to last less than six months
         223   Non-household adult – has disability (limitation or condition lasting or expected to last six months or more)

3   Maori-based committee, organization, grouping etc.

4   Non-profit organization (excluding Maori-based committee, organization, grouping etc.)

   41   Disability support and health-related services
   42   Social support and assistance to individuals and *whanau* (extended family or support group)/families, including information and advice services
   43   Education
   44   Community safety and protection, and general community benefit
   45   Leisure and recreation including sports, arts and culture
   46   Member benefit groups, that is to say, organizations whose primary focus is the benefit or advancement of the members (not included in one of the above categories)

5   Employer

ANNEX 6. PROBES FOR CONTEXTUAL INFORMATION

Night of day two: 10 pm - 1 am

If you were doing a number of things at once, e.g. making a snack and talking to a friend and listening to the radio, be sure to write them all in.

What were you doing?	What else were you doing at the same time?	Where were you OR How were you travelling?

10.00pm
.05
.10
.15
.20
.25
.30
.35
.40
.45
.50
.55
11.00
.05
.10
.15
.20
.25
.30
11.30
.35
.40
.45
.50
.55
midnight
.05
.10
.15
.20
.25
12.30
.35
.40
.45
.50
.55
1.00am

Use these lines for any notes you want to make

Interviewer Use Only

HOUSEHOLD MEMBER

child aged | 14+ sick or disabled
0 - 4 | 5 - 13 | Put in L or S

1 During this time, were you responsible for anyone who lives in your household, who could not be left alone? Don't count paid work.

☐ yes → Fill in columns to show the age of person looked after and when. If person aged 14 or over, put: L for illness/disability lasting six months or more, and S for one lasting less than six months

☐ no

2 Were you responsible for anyone who doesn't live in your household, who could not be left alone? Don't count paid work.

☐ yes → Fill in table and mark diary later.

responsible		age		# 14+ put in L or S
from	until	0 - 4	5 - 13	

☐ no

3 If respondent was asleep for whole three hours, go to next page.

4 Were you doing anything you were paid for, or anything that was part of your paid job(s), regardless of whether you were paid for it or not?

☐ yes → Make sure it's clear which activity. Put J if necessary.

☐ no

5 If respondent was working in their job for the whole 3 hours, go to next page.

6 Did you do anything, without pay, for or through any organisation or group, for example, a marae, club, school, church or community group?

☐ yes → Make sure it's clear which activity it is. Ask which organisation/group and put code on entry (see separate sheet).

☐ no

7 Was there anything you did for a person, without pay, because they were sick or had a disability?

☐ yes → Go to 8

☐ no → Go to 9

8 Does that person live in this household?

☐ household member → Only mark if activity is physical care, or something that people usually do for themselves. Make sure it's clear which activity was done for the person. Unless clear from earlier entry, put L or S (see question).

☐ not household member → If childcare, mark it OTH and put age-group of child (0-4 or 5-13). Otherwise, make sure all are marked OTH to show they were done for others. Also put L or S (see question).

9 During this time, were you doing anything else you were not paid for, for anyone who does not live in your household?

☐ yes → If childcare, mark it OTH and put age-group of child (0-4 or 5-13). Otherwise, make sure all these things are marked OTH FAV to show they were done for others, but not because they were sick/disabled.

☐ no

Source: Statistics New Zealand (1998a).

ANNEX 7. SAMPLE PAGE IN A STYLIZED ANALOGUE OF A TIME DIARY REFORMAT

HOUSEHOLD MAINTENANCE

I D C O D E	11. Did you spend time yesterday collecting water? YES...1 NO...2 (→12)	How much time did you spend? HOURS MINUTES	12. Did you spend time yesterday collecting firewood? YES...1 NO...2 (→13)	How much time did you spend? HOURS MINUTES	13. Did you spend time yesterday shopping for food, clothing, household items? YES...1 NO...2 (→14)	How much time did you spend? HOURS MINUTES	14. Did you spend time yesterday child caring (exclusive of pregnancy) YES...1 NO...2 (→15)	How much time did you spend? HOURS MINUTES	15. Did you spend time caring for the sick? YES...1 NO...2 (→16)	How much time did you spend? HOURS MINUTES
1										
2										
3										
4										
5										
6										
7										
8										
9										
10										
11										
12										

Source: Harvey and Taylor (2000).

ANNEX 8. ILLUSTRATION OF HINDSIGHT QUESTIONS AS PART OF A TIME DIARY

TS/98/03

Reference number

R | | | | | |

Person number

| |

Appointment time:

| |

Questions for interviewers to ask at the end of the diary days

1 During the seven days ending today, did you eat any meals at a cafe or restaurant, or eat any takeaways that needed no cooking?

1 ☐ yes
2 ☐ no

2 If any children aged 13 or less living in household, ask this question. Otherwise go to 3.
During the two diary days, was anyone paid for an hour or more, to look after any of the children who live in the household?

1 ☐ yes
2 ☐ no

3 If employed ask this question. Otherwise go to 5.
During the two diary days, did you go on any training courses which were paid for by your employer?

☐ yes → Go to 4
☐ no → Go to 5

4 Did you write it / them in the diary?

☐ yes
☐ no → Go back and write in the training courses so the coders can identify them.

Showcard 5

5 During the last four weeks, have you done any of the things listed on this card?

1 ☐
2 ☐
3 ☐
4 ☐
5 ☐
6 ☐
7 ☐
8 ☐ What was that? | |
0 ☐ None of these

Time Use Survey
48-hour diary

to be filled in from 4 am on day one, which is

Day | | Date | |

all through day two, which is

Day | | Date | |

until 4 am on day three, which is

Day | | Date | |

The information you provide in this diary will be used only for statistical purposes. Your information remains confidential to Statistics New Zealand and is protected by the Statistics Act 1975.

Len Cook
Government Statistician

Please look after your diary and keep it with you.

234

Source: Statistics New Zealand (1998a).

ANNEX 9. SAMPLE SELF-REPORT FORM

Box 1 Typical Experiential Sampling Method Response Form

Date: _____ Time Beeped: _____ am/pm   Time Filled Out: _____

AS YOU WERE BEEPED:

What were you thinking about? _____

Where were you? _____

What was the main thing you were doing? _____

Who were you with?
- _____ Spouse/Partner
- _____ Your children
- _____ Other
- _____ Alone
- _____ Friends/neighbors

	Not at all	Somewhat	Quite	Very Much
How well were you concentrating?				
Was it hard to concentrate?				
Were you in control of the situation?				
How pressed for time were you?				

Describe how you felt as you were beeped (answer all):

	Very	Quite	Some-what	Neither/not sure	Some-what	Quite	Very	
Alert								Drowsy
Happy								Sad
Irritable								Cheerful
Energetic								Tired
Upset								Calm
Active								Passive
Worried								Carefree
Excited								Bored
Confused								Clear
Relaxed								Tense
Good								Bad

	0	1	2	3	4	5	6	7	8	9	
Time was passing	Slowly										Fast
Challenges of the activity:	Low										High
Your skills, knowledge, or competence in the activity:	Low										High
Do you wish you had been doing something else?	Not at all										Very much
How free were you to choose what you were doing?	Not at all										Very much
How interested were you in what you were doing?	Not at all										Very much

Did you do it because:
- _____ You had to
- _____ You wanted to
- _____ There was nothing else to do
- _____ Other _____

Did you feel any of the following states as you were beeped?

	Not at all	Somewhat	Very much
Physical fatigue			
Mental fatigue			
Headache			
Physical discomfort, stiffness, body aches			

Great thoughts, wise cracks: _____

235

ANNEX 10.   ANNOTATED TRAINING SCHEDULE FOR DATA COLLECTION ON AND CODING OF TIME-USE ACTIVITIES

SESSION ONE

DAY ONE

08h00-08h20 Introduction to the time-use study

08h20-08h40 Introductions

New trainees to give their name and province and to say what previous experience they have had of surveys. Other participants to introduce themselves. Everyone makes themselves labels. Facilitator gives outline of programme for rest of training.

08h40-09h10 Ground rules

Hand out fieldworker's manual, participant's manual and one copy of questionnaire. Participatory exercise developing norms and values to set ground rules for workshop. First write down in participant's manual then develop full group list on flip chart. (Further ideas in facilitator's manual.)

09h10-09h30 Explanation of conventions

Explain what different questions look like, for example, font, multi- or single mention, and so on; and how to mark (circle) questions. Read through this part of manual together. Point to a few questions in questionnaire and ask individuals to say whether read-out or not.

09h30-10h15 Household questionnaire

Read carefully through each question. Ask trainees to look at the translation into their own language and discuss any queries or observations.

Tea

10h30-10h50 Who is a household member

Explanation and group exercise. Emphasize that no substitution is allowed in selecting dwelling units. Emphasize possibility of more than one household at a dwelling unit. Emphasize domestic workers. Read through appropriate definitions in manual. Do exercise in participant's manual. (Answers in facilitator's manual.)

10h50-11h10 Relationships

Explain and then do exercise in participant's manual. (Answers in facilitator's manual.) Emphasize that it is the relationship of the selected person to all other household members.

11h10-11h40 Household questionnaire fishbowl

Exercise in which one trainee interviews another trainee on the household questionnaire. The "respondent" to be briefed, privately, that he or she is to act the part of a busy, employed person who does not want to give up the time and then, on agreeing, is suspicious and says that some items of information are "private". Other trainees observe and note comments in their participant's manual, and then contribute their observations and suggestions. Participants can

Source: 2000 South Africa Time Use Survey, unpublished training document.
Note: The first session will cater to all new fieldworkers, provincial coordinators and provincial survey managers. The second session will cater to both new and old fieldworkers.

also suggest ways to deal with the difficulties that occurred.

11h40-12h25 Demographic questionnaire

Go through individual demographic questionnaire, again comparing with translations. Pay particular attention to work questions—different types of work, work status, occupation and industry. Pay particular attention to skips. Stress that fieldworker must not make assumptions about the respondent, but rather follow the questions as set.

12h25-12h45 Demographic questionnaire fishbowl

Choose two other trainees to be in the fishbowl, or ask for volunteers. "Respondent" to be briefed, privately, that he/she is to act the part of a young, school-going, unmarried person 11 years of age. Other participants write comments and suggestions in their manuals and then pool them.

Lunch

13h15-14h15 Time-use diary

Explain how the core of the diary works. Read through the relevant part of the manual. Include the section on simultaneity and on location. Stress the importance of asking and filling in these details during the interview. Stress the importance of asking for multiple activities. Show example of correctly completed diary.

14h15-14h30 Location exercise

Do exercise in participant's manual. (Answers in facilitator's manual.)

14h30-14h45 Diary questionnaire

Work through the questions before and after the diary as with the household and demographic questionnaires.

14h45-15h15 Paired participant diaries

Trainees pair off and one in each pair fills in the diary for the other about the previous day. Concentrate on describing activity simultaneous and location columns. (Facilitators collect the diaries, study them and provide feedback in later session.)

15h15-16h00 In-house practical

Fieldworker trainees fill in a household questionnaire, demographic questionnaire and diary for a staff member at Stats SA. Participants give the completed diaries to each other for scrutiny and comment. Participants then hand the diaries in for scrutiny and comment by coordinators and facilitators.

Tea available from 15h45

DAY TWO

08h00-08h30 Feedback on the two exercises

Group discussion on experience of interviewing and difficulties. Provincial coordinators to take notes and stress these points during later training.

08h30-09h00 Introducing yourself

Participatory exercise on how an interviewer should introduce him/herself to the respondent. Give participants copies of the introductory letter.

09h00-09h45 Choosing respondents

Explain and then do exercise in participant's manual. (Answers in facilitator's manual.)
During these sessions, coordinators provide written (or oral if necessary) feedback to participants on the paired and Stats SA diaries.

Tea

10h00-11h00 Activity coding

Explain activity coding by going through coding list, first category by category, and then item by item. Then explain coding index. Pay particular attention to the "work" categories 1 to 3, and read through explanation of "establishment" in manual.

11h00-12h00 Coding exercises

Do exercise in participant's manual. This is an exercise primarily to check codes but also includes reminders as to (a) things that should provoke prompting during interviewing and (b) incorrect ways of filling in a diary. Stress that the examples were done by inexperienced fieldworkers who made a lot of mistakes! In particular, proper diaries should contain more multiple activities. (Answers in facilitator's manual.)

12h00-12h45 Coding of own diaries

Trainees code the diaries from in-house practice and interviewing of each other.

Lunch

13h15-14h00 Group coding checks

Trainees divide into groups and check each other's coding.

14h00-15h00 Group checking of question-naires

Trainees go back into same groups. Each person must check the questionnaires of at least three other trainees, noting mistakes in skips, relationship etc.

Tea

15h00-15h30 Discussion of common mistakes

Plenary discussion of common errors found in questionnaires.

15h30-16h00 Wrap-up and completion of evaluation forms

Hand out evaluation form. Participants to fill them in before leaving.

SESSION TWO

DAY ONE

08h00-08h15 Introductions

Each person says his or her name, and what he or she feels most and least confident about in respect of the time-use fieldwork. Hand out participants' manuals. Stress the importance of improving the response rate. Describe the outline of the programme for the next two days.

08h15-08h45 Ground rules

Hand out fieldworker's manual, participant's manual, one copy of questionnaire and relevant translations. Participatory exercise developing norms and values to set ground rules for workshop. (Facilitator's manual has ideas.)

08h45-09h15 The control page

Hand out examples of HH1, HH2 and HH3. Explain how to use them. Discuss on how to give full physical description. Do exercise in which each person writes a description of one other participant. Ask a few participants to read out what they have written. Then draw out principles of describing and discuss differences between describing a person and describing a household. Stress that no substitution is allowed. Stress that fieldworkers must check for multiple households at a dwelling unit.

09h15-09h45 Household questionnaire

Go through. Concentrate on skips. Emphasize that set translations **must** be used throughout.

09h45-10h15 Who is a household member

Explanation and group exercise. Emphasize possibility of more than one household at a dwelling unit. Emphasize domestic workers. Read through appropriate definitions in manual. Do exercise in participant's manual. (Answers in facilitator's manual.)

Tea

10h30-11h00 Relationships

Get group member to explain to other members and test them. Do exercises in participant's manual. (Answers in facilitator's manual.)

11h00-11h30 Household questionnaire fishbowl

Exercise in which one trainee interviews another on the household questionnaire. The "respondent" to be briefed, privately, to be a domestic worker who is living on her employer's premises.

11h30-11h50 Demographic questionnaire

Go through individual demographic questionnaire, again concentrating on difficult parts: different types of work, work status, occupation and industry. Pay particular attention to skips. Stress that **all** of the seven types of work count as work. Stress that fieldworker must not make assumptions about the respondent, but rather follow the questions as set.

11h50-12h15 Work exercises

Ask group members to find problems with responses on work in previous seven days, occupation, industry and status in the participant's manual. (Possible responses in facilitator's manual.)

12h15-12h45 Demographic questionnaire fishbowl

Choose two other trainees to be in the fishbowl, or ask for volunteers. "Respondent" to be briefed, privately, with respect to the fact that she is a retrenched factory worker, who is doing "char" (domestic) work for other households in between looking for another factory job.

Other participants write comments and suggestions in their manuals and then pool them.

Lunch

13h15-14h00 Time use diary

Explain how the core of the diary works. Look at the example of a correctly completed diary in the participant's manual. Read through the relevant part of the manual. Include the section on simultaneity and on location, and stress that these questions must be asked and filled in during the interview. Stress the importance of asking for multiple activities. Stress the importance of starting on the first line of each time period. Stress that there must be at least one activity for each time period.

14h00-14h30 Location exercise

Do exercise in participant's manual. (Answers are in facilitator's manual.) Then get participant's to ask each other how they would code different difficult situations.

14h30-15h00 Diary questionnaire

Work through and translate the questions before and after the diary as with the household and demographic questionnaires.

Tea

15h15-15h45 Introducing yourself

Participatory exercise on how an interviewer should introduce him/herself to the respondent. Give participants copies of the introductory letter. Stress the importance of this introduction.

15h45-16h15 Choosing respondents

Explain and then do exercise in participant's manual. (Answers are in facilitator's manual.)

DAY TWO

08h00-12h00 Practice in the field

Participants go to nearby PSUs for field practice. Each trainee goes to a single household for which they fill in the household questionnaire, a single demographic questionnaire and one diary. Facilitators check the questionnaires as each trainee finishes. Check includes who should have been chosen as respondents if this had been the first interview. Participants code the activities in their diary.

Lunch

13h00-13h30 Discussion on field practice

Participants describe experiences. Discuss common problems. Facilitators discuss common problems found in diaries.

13h30-14h30 Group coding checks

Trainees divide into groups and check each other's coding. Each person to check at least three others.

14h30-15h00 Difficult codes

Do exercise, in participant's manual, on more difficult aspects of coding, for example, travel

and location, "work", childcare, and who does what for whom. (Answers in facilitator's manual.)

Tea

15h15-16h00 Administration and logistics

Go through administrative details and logistics. Talk about team and field organization. Talk about days of work, compulsory work on weekends, and quotas for diaries. Explain the information that they will need to give to supervisors each day. Fill out contracts. Hand out name badges etc.

16h00-16h15 Final evaluation

Hand out evaluation. Participants to fill it in before they leave.

SESSION FOR SUPERVISORS

16h15-17h00 Roles and duties

Go through manual pointing out different sections.

Hand out dwelling unit selection forms and revise how these work.
Plan how each team will do its work, its route through the PSUs and where they will sleep over.

Discuss transport rules.
Review the different things that supervisors must check for, reading through manual on this topic.

17h15-17h30 Closure

Discuss any other concerns that supervisors raise.

ANNEX 11. DEVELOPMENT OF CODING INDEX FOR ACTIVITY CLASSIFICATION[a]

What is a coding index?

The process of coding the descriptions of activities written in the time-use diaries involves the task of matching the verbatim responses against the entries in the coding index, to find the appropriate codes. Thus, the coding index is the key instrument for this matching process. The index can take the physical form of durable printed publications, loose-leaf binders, computer printouts or machine-readable files within a computer system, and the matching can be carried out by a person, namely, the coder, by a computer or through interaction between the coder and a computer.

It is important to recognize that a coding index is different from the list of groups specified in the classification. The titles chosen for those groups are designed to be as descriptive as possible for the group content, given that only a few words may be used. Only a few of these titles will correspond to the terms used by individuals when asked about their daily activities.

Since it must be in place before the coding operations start, the coding index has to be constructed in anticipation of the most likely forms of verbatim descriptions of activities. To achieve this, the index needs to be based on responses in actual diary entries that may be obtained in pre-tests and pilot surveys. An initial simple list may be constructed from the activity descriptions in the classification and further refined using actual responses such as the list shown in table A1 below.

At the start of the survey operations, the coding indexes must be assumed to be incomplete, and provisions must be made to update them during the whole period of the coding operation, and with more new items early in the process. The updating should be an extension of the query resolution process in the sense that the nature and outcome of resolved queries should be made available to all coders as soon as possible, in case they encounter the same type of response. The best approach is to issue new versions of the coding indexes as frequently as they may be needed (this would depend on the volume of new unaccounted-for responses). Note that to issue a complete, new version of a coding index is better than to issue additions to the index, because the new entries will belong in different places in the index and the coders will have to transfer the information from the note on additions into the main coding index, with the danger that they will be making mistakes. New, complete versions of the coding indexes issued frequently in the first weeks of the coding operation will also reduce the danger that individual coders will keep their own notes on the coding of particular responses. Such notes can easily be the source of systematic differences between coders in coding responses not reflected in the initial version of the coding indexes.

Source: Hoffmann (2001), pp. 18-33.

[a] The present annex is based mainly on experience from English-speaking industrialized countries, because the limited documentation readily available on the development and use of coding indexes and coding procedures has mainly originated in such countries. Knowledge of the experience with coding in other languages and settings in limited and it is therefore difficult to say to what extent the documented English experience is transferable to other languages and cultures. However, the suggestions below provide a starting point for work and experiments with the coding of responses in other languages.

Developing and updating the coding index

The process of developing and updating a coding index for a classification of activities should be viewed as one part of the general process of maintaining and updating the classification. When the material to be included in the coding index of occupations is being organized, the first issue concerns the structure of the index itself. Basically, the choice is between two different approaches: (a) all-inclusive and (b) structured. In the all-inclusive approach, every distinct type of response found in the process of coding should, in theory, have an entry in the index. An advantage of this approach is that it may be possible for coders to find even rare or obscure activities listed in the index. The main disadvantage is that the size of the index may become very large and its sheer size may slow down the process of searching for the "right" entry in the index, and thereby slow down the coding, whether the coding is done manually or is computer-assisted. Also, large verbatim indexes may create the impression that coding is a simple task, involving a straightforward matching between a response and an index entry. However, no matter how large the index experiences with coding, indexes for occupations show that a significant proportion of responses fail to match the index entries exactly, and for those one has to use rules and/or judgement to make the "best" match.

A structured index does not try to reflect every possible response, but the entries are accompanied with instructions to the coder on how to break down the available response into functional (key) words and qualifying nouns or adjectives for an effective search for the most appropriate code. The primary entries in the index are the functional words. If a functional word in itself is not sufficient to uniquely identify the group, an appropriate qualifying word (or phrase) must be added to distinguish between the possible alternatives having the same functional word. If this is not sufficient to resolve all ambiguities, second- or higher-order qualifying words should be used. The structured coding index will normally have a much smaller number of index entries than a complete listing index. This is the result both of the restriction of the index to functional words when possible and of the use of "(except above)" instructions. They allow the exclusion from the index of a large number of responses where the qualifying words are immaterial for the selection of the correct group. A structured coding index is alphabetically arranged in terms of functional words.

The advantages of having a structured coding index are twofold. First, it helps the coder search for index entries in a way that is consistent with the coding rules. Second, it speeds up the task of coding by restricting the number of entries the coder has to search through in the index, because of the smaller number of entries. The simple coding index in table A1 is an illustration of a structured index.

Using the coding indexes

Coding can be seen as a process where the task of the coder is to "translate" the information provided by the recorded responses into the most appropriate code in the relevant classification structure. The main tools for this translation are the coding indexes and the coding instructions, including instructions on when a response should be treated as a query to be resolved by supervisors or expert staff. The instructions should specify:

(a)   How this translation process should be carried out.

(b)   What items to look for in the relevant response and in what order; what type of ancillary information to use from other responses.

(c)   When the use of such ancillary information is permissible and how to use it.

Ideally the coding index should have been constructed to reflect and support the use of these instructions. Some responses simply cannot be coded to a detailed activity group. This will normally be for one of the following reasons:

(a)   The response may be vague, that is to say, it may not contain enough information to be coded according to the coding index and coding rules.

(b)   The response may be precise, but may use descriptions that do not correspond to any of the index entries.

In order to keep to manageable proportions the number of queries that the supervisors and expert coders must handle, the coding index and the coding instructions should be designed to guide the coders with respect to the most common of such cases. The simplest solution will be to specify that the response should be coded to a "default" group.

There is a real danger that before they even try to find a precise code, coders may use "default" groups as "dump groups" for responses that are difficult to code. Some coding operations therefore have tried to keep the coders ignorant of the possibility of using such codes and only allowed them to be used by better-trained supervisors. However, this strategy may create a morale problem among the coders, and place a very large query burden on the supervisors. It may therefore be better to monitor carefully the use of default codes by the coders. Asking them to record the index item number selected as most valid for the response, rather than the code given by this item, may also restrain the temptation to "code by memory".

The fully specified responses that are not adequately covered by the classification and the coding index should always be handled by expert coders. Their appearance should be recorded carefully, both to ensure consistent treatment of equal cases and because these cases represent an important source of information on the updating of the coding index as well as of the classification itself. These cases can be handled either by using the priority rules specified for the classification or by assigning them to an appropriate group for activities "not adequately described" by the classification. As indicated, the latter solution should be used only by expert coders. It is important to note that these groups are not the same as the "not elsewhere classified" (n.e.c.) groups of the classification. Great care must be taken not to create confusion in respect of the two types of group.

Table A1.   Simple coding index for the ICATUS

Code	Description
ASK	Arrive (This is instantaneous action. Ask what rest of period spent on)
12111	Attend/art class as extra-mural activity
09111	Attend/art class as part of school curriculum
15152	Attend/church
15142	Attend/clinic
11113	Attend/concert
01115	Attend/course of work-related training for formal sector
04114	Attend/course of work-related training for informal construction work
03118	Attend/course of work-related training for informal non-primary work
02118	Attend/course of work-related training for informal primary sector

Code	Description
05170	Attend/course of work-related training for informal services
083002	Attend/court case as witness
10122	Attend/funeral, non-religious
082	Attend/meeting
15152	Attend/religious service
091111	Attend/school
091111	Attend/university, technikon or college
10122	Attend/wedding, non-religious
061111	Bake/for household use
031122	Bake/for income-earning purposes
071111	Bathe/child from household
08116	Bathe/child not from household
071211	Bathe/other adult from household
08117	Bathe/other adult not from household
15131	Bathe/self
15141	Be looked after by household member
061119	Boil water/for cooking, drinking, making tea or coffee
061125	Boil water/not for cooking
071211	Braid hair of other person/not to earn income
15131	Braid hair/own
0514	Braid hair/to earn income in informal sector
01111	Bring back livestock from fields/as worker on commercial farm
02112	Bring back livestock from fields/household's farming activities
15131	Brush teeth
06121	Buy goods/for home or personal use
03121	Buy goods/for home production
ASK	Buy goods/to resell or to use in paid work: code according to type of work
071111	Change nappy/of household baby
10111	Chat
061111	Check if pots ready
01111	Check livestock/as paid worker on commercial farm
02112	Check livestock/household's farming activities
12113	Choir practice/not religious
15152	Choir practice/religious
02114	Chop wood/part of collecting fuel
051111	Clean/chickens for selling after cooking
031111	Clean/chickens for selling uncooked
071111	Clean/child from household
08116	Clean/child not from household
061111	Clean/food for cooking
0516	Clean/house paid as domestic worker
061121	Clean/own house unpaid
061122	Clean/yard or garden
02122	Close/stall where sell clothes sewn by self
051121	Close/stall where sell other things

Code	Description
051113	Close/stall where sell food prepared by others'
021128	Collect/cow dung
08131	Collect/door to door for charity
021142	Collect/imifino (wild spinach)
061227	Collect/pension (from government)
021143	Collect/wood
02122	Collect/work equipment for clothes stall
03112	Collect/work equipment for food processing
02122	Collect/work equipment for food stall
02122	Collect/work equipment for other stall
04111	Collect/work equipment for repair work (informal sector): ask type for sixth digit
1513	Comb own hair
08121	Cook/for community celebration or funeral
0516	Cook/paid work as domestic worker
061111	Cook/unpaid in own home
05141	Cut hair/to earn income, informal sector
031133	Cut, make and trim (CMT)
10112	Dance/as part of socializing
12113	Dance/dancing lesson
ASK	Deliver goods to customers: classify according to type of work
061112	Dish up food
0912	Do homework
071111	Dress/child from household
08116	Dress/child not from household
1513	Dress/self
151211	Drink/as part of meal
151212	Drink/as part of snack
15122	Drink/not with meal or snack
ASK	Drive: classify according to purpose of travel
1512	Eat
101122	Entertain visitors
01111	Feed animals/as worker on commercial farm
021121	Feed animals/as part of household farming activity
061161	Feed animals/pets
071111	Feed child/from household
08116	Feed child/not from household
07113	Fetch child/member of household
08116	Fetch child/non-member of household
02117	Fetch water
021143	Fetch wood
01111	Fix equipment/as part of formal sector job
05121	Fix equipment/to earn income, informal sector
101122	Friend visits
02111	Garden/for household consumption or income-earning purposes
061124	Garden/for leisure

Code	Description
1513	Get dressed
ASK	Go back home: classify according to purpose of journey
102	Go to meet someone
08112	Go to shop/shopping time (ask more detail for sixth digit)
062	Go to shop/travel time
15111	Go to sleep
ASK	Go to taxi rank; station: classify according to purpose of journey
1513	Go to toilet
013	Go to work/formal sector
033	Go to work/informal sector
10112	Greet
1513	Groom self
13113	Gym
061142	Hang washing to dry
15141	Have a haircut
061119	Heat water/as part of cooking
061125	Heat water/non-cooking purposes
08116	Help/child not of household with homework
071121	Help/child of household with homework
08111	Help/neighbour with task
061143	Iron
061112	Lay table
15161	Lie in bed/not sleeping: omit this code if other simultaneous activity
061119	Light fire/as part of cooking
061125	Light fire/non-cooking purposes
14132	Listen/to music
14131	Listen/to radio
08117	Look after adult/not of household
07121	Look after adult/of household
08116	Look after child/not of household
07111	Look after child/of household, active care: ask type for sixth digit
07114	Look after child/of household, not active, keep an eye on only
01111	Look after livestock/as worker on commercial farm
02112	Look after livestock/as part of household farming activity
01201	Look for work/formal sector
061121	Make bed
031145	Make clay pots to sell
061111	Make fire/as part of cooking
061125	Make fire/non-cooking purposes
061145	Mend clothes
07111	Nurse baby/of household
061144	Pack away clothes
061113	Pack away dishes
ASK	Pack away work tools/equipment: code according to type of work activity
061151	Pay electricity account

Code	Description
12131	Play/alone
13	Play/sport: ask type for third digit
1213	Play/TV game
12134	Play/with other person or people
061145	Polish shoes
15151	Pray/alone
15152	Pray/as part of group
061111	Prepare food
ASK	Prepare for bed: ask what activities involved
02122	Prepare goods for selling/clothes made by self
02122	Prepare goods for selling/food or drink prepared by self
02122	Prepare goods for selling/not food, drink or clothes made by self
061142	Put washing on the line
061227	Queue for pension
15151	Read bible
14111	Read book
14112	Read newspaper
15161	Relax/alone: omit code if doing anything else simultaneously
10112	Relax/together with person/people
041113	Repair house/as income-earning activity
01111	Repair house/as part of formal sector job
061131	Repair house/as part of home upkeep
15161	Rest: omit code if doing anything else simultaneously
ASK	Return: code according to purpose of journey
0912	Revise schoolwork
13112	Ride bicycle/not for travel purposes
01111	Sell/as part of formal sector job
05112	Sell/clothes made by others
02122	Sell/clothes made by self
05112	Sell/door to door
05112	Sell/food or drink prepared by others
02122	Sell/food or drink prepared by self
061112	Serve food
01111	Sew/as home-based worker for a factory
03113	Sew/for own use
031133	Sew/for selling, informal sector
06122	Shop: what shopped for will give sixth digit
1513	Shower
02112	Slaughter livestock/for own use
01111	Slaughter livestock/for selling, commercial farm or abattoir
02112	Slaughter livestock/for selling, household farm
15111	Sleep/main sleep of day
15112	Sleep/nap
15162	Smoke
061111	Soak samp and beans

Code	Description
101112	Speak on phone
10112	Spend time with person: ask for detail for sixth digit
091111	Study/at educational institution
0912	Study/at home, homework
0913	Study/at home, not related to school, technikon, college or university attendance
14143	Surf the Internet
0516	Sweep room/paid work as domestic worker
061121	Sweep room/unpaid work in own home
061122	Sweep yard
071232	Take older person to clinic
10111	Talk with friends
01114	Tea break/at work
061121	Tidy/room
051123	Trade/in street
ASK	Travel: consult coding list for travel code in category related to purpose of travel
1513	Undress/self
142	Visit/library
101123	Visit/someone
ASK	Wait: code as activity for which waiting
13111	Walk/for pleasure or exercise
ASK	Walk/to go somewhere: code according to purpose of travel
071111	Wash/baby of household
061133	Wash/car
061141	Wash/clothes
061113	Wash/dishes
061141	Wash/laundry
071111	Wash/nappies of household baby
1513	Wash/self
11131	Watch/live sport
061111	Watch/pots
14121	Watch/TV
14122	Watch/video
061124	Water plants/decorative plants
021114	Water plants/part of market gardening
01113	Work/as apprentice or intern
0516	Work/as domestic worker
ASK	Work/for own pocket, informal sector: ask type of work
01111	Work/for profit (as employer/self-employed) in a formal establishment
01111	Work/for wage or salary in formal sector
04111	Work/on public works programme
01111	Work/unpaid in formal business

ANNEX 12.   ILLUSTRATION OF MARKED EPISODES IN A DIARY

Time, am	What were you doing? Record your main activity for each 10-minute period from 07.00 to 10.00 am!		What else were you doing? Record the most important parallel activity		Were you alone or together with somebody you know? Mark 'yes' by crossing			
	Only one main activity on each line! Distinguish between travel and the activity that is the reason for travelling. Do not forget the mode of transportation. Distinguish between first and second job, if any				Alone	Children up to 9 living in your household	Other household members	Other persons that you know
07.00-07.10	Woke up the children	381				☒	☐	☐
07.10-07.20	Had breakfast	021	Talked with my family	511 →		☒	☒	☒
07.20-07.30	-"-	→	-"-	831	☒	☒	☒	☐
07.30-07.40	Cleared the table	313	Listened to the radio			☐	☐	☐
07.40-07.50	Helped the children dressing	381	Talked with my children	383 →		☒	☐	☐
07.50-08.00	Went to the day care centre, by foot	938	-"-		☒	☒	☐	☒
08.00-08.10	By bus to job	913	Read the newspaper	811	☒	☐	☐	☐
08.10-08.50	By bus to job	913	-"-	811	☒	☐	☐	☐
08.20-08.30	Regular work (first job)	111			☒	☒	☐	☐
08.30-08.40					☒	☐	☐	☐
08.40-08.50					☒	☐	☐	☐
08.50-09.00					☒	☐	☐	☐
09.00-09.10					☒	☐	☐	☐
09.10-09.20					☒	☐	☐	☐
09.20-09.30					☒	☐	☐	☐
09.30-09.40					☒	☐	☐	☐
09.40-09.50					☒	☐	☐	☐
09.50-A.00					☒	☐	☐	☐

Source: Eurostat (2000a).

249

What were you doing?
Record your main activity for each 10-minute period from 10.00 am to 01.00 pm!

Only one main activity on each line!
Distinguish between travel and the activity that is the reason for travelling.
Do not forget the mode of transportation.
Distinguish between first and second job.

What else were you doing?
Record the most important parallel activity.

Were you alone or together with somebody you know?
Mark 'yes' by crossing

Time, am-pm	Main activity	code	Parallel activity	code	Alone	Children up to 9 living in your household	Other household members	Other persons that you know	
10.00-10.10	Break: had coffee	112	Talked with a colleague	021	☐	☐	☐	☒	13
10.10-10 20	Regular work (first job)	111			☒	☐	☐	☐	
10 20-10 30					☒	☐	☐	☐	
10 30-10 40					☒	☐	☐	☐	
10 40-10 50					☒	☐	☐	☐	
10 50-11 00					☒	☐	☐	☐	
11 00-11 10					☒	☐	☐	☐	
11 10-11 20					☒	☐	☐	☐	
11 20-11 30					☒	☐	☐	☐	
11.30-11 40	Lunch break: had lunch in the canteen	021	Talked with colleagues	131	☐	☐	☐	☒	
11 40-11 50					☐	☐	☐	☒	
11 50-12 00					☐	☐	☐	☒	
12.00-12 10	Lunch break: went to the supermarket, by foot	936			☒	☐	☐	☐	21
12.10-12 20	Lunch break: bought food	361			☒	☐	☐	☐	16
12.20-12 30	Lunch break: went back to work, by foot	936			☒	☐	☐	☐	21
12.30-12 40	Regular work (first job)	111			☒	☐	☐	☐	13
12 50-01 00					☒	☐	☐	☐	

What were you doing?

Record your main activity for each 10-minute period from 04.00 pm to 07.00 am!

Only one main activity on each line!
Distinguish between travel and the activity that is the reason for travelling
Do not forget the mode of transportation.
Distinguish between first and second job, if any

What else were you doing?

Record the most important parallel activity.

Were you alone or together with somebody you know?

Mark "yes" by crossing

Time, pm	What were you doing?	What else were you doing?	Alone	Children up to 9 living in your household	Other household members	Other persons that you know	
04.00-04.10	913 Bus from work to the day care centre	371 Planned a birthday party for my son →	☒	☐	☐	☐	32
04.10-04.20	→		☒	☒	☐	☐	
04.20-04.30	384 Talked with the child minder	381 Helped the children dressing	☐	☒	☐	☒	19
04.30-04.40	938 Went to the grocery, by foot	383 Talked with my children	☐	☒	☐	☐	21
04.40-04.50	361 Bought food for my family and my neighbour	425	☐	☒	☐	☐	19
04.50-05.00	936 Went home by foot		☐	☒	☐	☐	21
05.00-05.10	425 Delivered food to my neighbour		☒	☒	☐	☒	14
05.10-05.20	324 Put own food in fridge		☐	☐	☐	☐	11
05.20-05.30	311 Cooked supper	831 Listened to the radio	☐	☐	☒	☐	
05.30-05.40	311	831	☐	☒	☒	☐	
05.40-05.50	021 Had supper	511 Talked with my family	☐	☒	☒	☐	
05.50-06.00		→	☐	☐	☐	☐	
06.00-06.10	313 Cleared the table	→	☒	☒	☒	☐	
06.10-06.20	531 Had a rest		☒	☐	☒	☐	
06.20-06.30	821 Watched TV with my children	333	☐	☒	☒	☐	
06.30-06.40			☐	☒	☒	☐	
06.40-06.50			☐	☐	☐	☐	
06.50-07.00			☐	☐	☐	☐	

821 Knitted

ANNEX 13. ILLUSTRATIONS OF ESTIMATION PROCEDURES FOR TIME-USE SURVEYS

Illustration 1. 1992 Time Use Survey, Australia: two person-days[*]

Estimates obtained from the survey were derived using a complex ratio estimation procedure. This ensures that survey estimates conform to an independently estimated distribution of the total population by quarter, sex, age, employment and region (rather than by the sex, age, employment and region within the sample itself). The survey was conducted over four fortnightly periods in 1992, from 24 February to 7 March, from 25 May to 6 June, from 28 September to 10 October, and from 23 November to 5 December. Estimates were made to conform to the population distributions of the time frames.

Benchmarks

Population estimates are produced monthly by the ABS (spell out the acronym). Benchmarks are derived from these for the monthly labour-force survey. For the quarter-age-sex-employment-region (capital city/rest-of-State) benchmarks for the Time Use Survey, the average of the two labour-force benchmarks surrounding each collection period were used. Population benchmarks were adjusted to take into account those population groups out of the survey scope.

Weights

To obtain person-based estimates, expansion factors or "weights" were inserted into the responding person's records to enable the data to be expanded to provide estimates relating to the whole population within the scope of the survey. The weights applied were based initially on the probability of selection which varied depending on the State/Territory of enumeration. An adjustment based on quarter-age-sex-employment-region bench-marks was then made to these weights to ensure that the estimated population distribution from the survey conformed to the population distribution of the benchmarks. As the weighted unit was the person-day, further proportional adjustment was made for weekday and weekend. (See appendix below for a description of the estimation formula used.)

When data from person records were combined to form household data, the weight of those units was the "harmonic mean" of the weights of the members of that unit.

The estimation procedure was designed to adjust estimates in such a way as to reduce non-response bias by adjusting the weights of responding persons' records in each quarter-age-sex-employment-region cell to compensate for underenumeration in that cell.

Appendix. Estimation formula

Estimates at national levels

National estimates were formed by producing estimates at region level (capital city/rest of state) and then adding to national level.

Weights used for this type of benchmark were derived from population benchmarks showing number of persons (N) in each part of State, cross-classified by quarter (collection period), age, sex and whether employed.

---

[*]*Source*: Australian Bureau of Statistics (1992), pp. 36-59.

The weights were calculated at the diary level rather than at the respondent level. Thus, each respondent had two weights, corresponding to the first and second diary day respectively. Type of day, whether weekday or weekend, was a further weighting variable. The number of diary day responses is represented by (n).

The weight w for a person-day record I for a responding individual in quarter q, of age a and sex s, employment status e, region r and day type z was determined using the following formula:

$$w_{qaserz} = \begin{cases} 5/7 \dfrac{N_{qaser}}{n_{qaserz}}, & \text{if } z = \text{weekday} \\[2em] 2/7 \dfrac{N_{qaser}}{n_{qaserz}}, & \text{if } z = \text{weekend day} \end{cases} \quad (1)$$

where:

N_{qaser} = number of persons in the quarter, age group, sex, employment group and region

n_{qaserz} = number of respondents in the quarter, age group, sex, employment group, region and type of day

The total estimate for region r for the variables X_c, M_c and N_c could then be obtained in the following way:

(a) X_c = total number of hours spent on activity A, by persons in classification c, on an "average day".

Estimate of:

$$X_c = \hat{X}_c = \sum_a \sum_s \sum_e \sum_z w_{qaserz} \sum_i x_{cqaserzi} \quad (2)$$

(b) M_c = number of persons in classification c participating in activity A on an "average day"

Estimate of:

$$M_c = \hat{M}_c = \sum_a \sum_s \sum_e \sum_z w_{qaserz} \sum_i m_{cqaserzi} \quad (3)$$

(c) N_c = number of persons in classification c

Estimate of

$$N_c = \hat{N}_c = \sum_a \sum_s \sum_e \sum_z w_{qaserz} n_{cqaserz} \quad (4)$$

(d) $\overline{X}_c = \dfrac{X_c}{M_c}$ = average number of hours spent, per participating person in classification c, on activity A on an "average day"

Estimate of $\overline{X}_c = \dfrac{\hat{X}_c}{\hat{M}_c} \quad (5)$

National estimates were then obtained by adding the region estimates.

Illustration 2. 1998 General Social Survey (GSS)—Time Use: Sample one respondent per household; one-person day[*]

There are two microdata files from which GSS Cycle 12 estimates can be made. The **Main file** contains summary time use information from 10749 respondents. It also contains the questionnaire responses obtained from these respondents. The **Time-use episode file** contains information describing the details of the 221105 time-use episodes reported by these respondents. Questionnaire information was not collected for those respondents who refused to complete a full diary.

When analysing GSS Cycle 12 data, it is necessary to use one of the weighting factors WGHTFIN on the Main file and WGHTEPI on the Time Use Episode file. WGHTFIN indicates the number of persons in the population that a record on the Main file represents, while WGHTEPI indicates the number of time-use episodes that a record on the Episode file represents.

In the last GSS Time Use survey, Cycle 7, there were also two weights: one to be used for estimates not based on the episode data, and one for estimates that used the episode data. In Cycle 7, the time-use diaries were collected only for a subsample (owing to non-response to the diary section of the questionaire). To account for this subsampling of episodes, the episode weights were larger than the person weights (in the same way that the person weights differed from the household weights to account for the sampling of only one respondent per household). In this GSS cycle, there was no subsampling of time-use episodes; GSS Cycle 12 collected data for all time-use episodes during the reference day for all respondents. Since there was no subsampling, the weight for each episode was the same as the weight for the respondent by whom it was reported.[a]

The Time Use Episode file is structured differently from the Main file in that there are multiple time-use episode records for each respondent. Each time use episode is a separately identified record, with each respondent having on average 21 episode records. This introduces additional complexity in applying the weights correctly.

Weighting

We view each cycle of the General Social Survey as being composed of a number of independent surveys: one per collection month. Wherever possible, therefore, we weight each monthly survey independently so that the data collected for each month contribute to the estimates in proportion to the Canadian population for that month. Where the sample size for a particular month is not large enough, the records for two or more months are grouped together at certain stages of the weighting process.

A self-weighting sample design is one for which the weights of each unit in the sample are the same. The GSS sample for Cycle 12 was selected using the Elimination of Non-Working Banks (ENWB) sampling technique, which has such a design, with each household within a stratum having an equal probability of selection. This probability is equal to:

---

[*]*Source*: Statistics Canada. (1999a), pp. 8-17.

[a] In the last GSS Time Use survey, Cycle 7, diaries were collected only for a subsample (owing to non-response to the diary section of the questionnaire) and thus the weight for the Cycle 7 Time use Episode file differed from that for the Cycle 7 Main file.

$$\frac{\text{Number of telephone numbers}}{\text{sampled within the stratum}} \tag{6}$$
$$\frac{\text{Total number of possible}}{\text{telephone numbers within the stratum}}$$

(The total number of possible telephone numbers for a stratum is equal to the number of working banks for a stratum times 100.)

Where possible, each survey month was weighted independently. This was done in an attempt to ensure that each survey month contributed appropriately to estimates. If monthly sample sizes were not large enough, two or more survey months were combined in certain steps of the weighting.

1. Basic weight calculation

Each working (in-service) telephone number (responding and non-responding) in the random digit dialing (RDD) sample was assigned a weight equal to the inverse of its probability of selection. This weight was calculated independently for each stratum-month group as follows:

$$\frac{\text{Number of possible telephone numbers}}{\text{in each stratum - month group}} \tag{7}$$
$$\frac{}{\text{Number of sampled telephone numbers}}$$
$$\text{in each stratum - month group}$$

2. Non-response adjustment

Weights for responding telephone numbers were adjusted to represent non-responding telephone numbers. This was done independently within each stratum-month group. Records were adjusted by the following factor:

$$\text{Factor 1} = \frac{\begin{array}{c}\text{Total of basic weights of all}\\\text{telephone numbers in}\\\text{each stratum - month group}\end{array}}{\begin{array}{c}\text{Total of basic weights of responding}\\\text{telephone numbers in}\\\text{each stratum - moth group}\end{array}} \tag{8}$$

Non-responding telephone numbers were then dropped.

3. Household weight calculation

The weight from step 2 was used as an initial household weight. For households with more than one residential telephone number[b] (that is to say, not used for business purposes only), this weight was adjusted downward to account for the fact that such households had a higher probability of being selected. The weight for each household was divided by the number of residential telephone numbers that serviced the household.

$$\text{Factor 2} = \frac{1}{\begin{array}{c}\text{Number of non - business}\\\text{telephone numbers}\end{array}} \tag{9}$$

This produces a household weight = Basic Weight * Factor 1 * Factor 2.

4. Person weight calculation

A person weight was then calculated for each person who responded to the survey, by multiplying the household weight for that person by the number of persons in the household who were eligible to be selected for the survey (that is to say, the number of persons aged 15 years or over).

This produced a person weight = Basic Weight * Factor 1 * Factor 2 * Number of eligible household members

5. Adjustment of person weight to external totals

The person weights were adjusted several times using a raking ratio procedure. This procedure ensures that, based on the survey's

---

[b] Less than 6 per cent of the households in the sample had more than one non-business telephone number.

total sample, estimates produced that should match certain external reference totals do indeed match them. Three sets of external references were used for this survey, all of them population totals: for stratum by month, for age-sex group by province, and for day of the week by province by month.

It should be noted that persons living in households without telephone service are included in the external references though such persons were not sampled.

(a)   Regional office (RO) - stratum - month adjustment

An adjustment was made to the person weights on record within each stratum per month in order to make population estimates consistent with projected population counts. This was done by multiplying the person weight for each record within the stratum by the following ratio:

$$\frac{\text{Projected population count} \atop \text{for the RO - stratum - month}}{\text{Sum of the person weights} \atop \text{for the RO - stratum - month}} \qquad (10)$$

When sample sizes were small, adjacent months' data for the same stratum were combined before this adjustment was made.

(b)   Province - age - sex adjustment

The next weighting step was to ratio-adjust the weights to agree with projected province-age group-sex distributions. Projected population counts were obtained for males and females within the following sixteen age groups:

15-19	20-24	25-29	30-34
35-39	40-44	45-49	50-54
55-59	60-64	65-69	70-74
75-79	80-84	85-89	90+

For each of the resulting classifications, the person weights for records within the classification were adjusted by multiplying by the following ratio:

$$\frac{\text{Projected population count for} \atop \text{the province - age - sex group}}{\text{Sum of the person weights of records for} \atop \text{the province - age - sex group}} \qquad (11)$$

where

Projected population count =

$$\qquad (12)$$

$$= \frac{\sum\limits_{\text{Feb 1998}}^{\text{Jan 1999}} \begin{array}{l} \text{Projected population count for} \\ \text{province - age - sex group} \end{array}}{12}$$

When sample sizes were small, adjacent age group data for the same province and sex were combined before this adjustment was made.

(c)   Province - day of the week (designated day) - month adjustment

Time-use information was collected from respondents for a selected day of the week so that each day would have an approximately equal number of respondents. An adjustment was made to the person weights on records within each province, selected day of the week, and month of collection to ensure that population estimates would represent each day of the week. The adjustment was effected by multiplying the person weight for each record within the province - day of the week - month combination by the following ratio:

$$\frac{\text{Projected population count for} \atop \text{the province - day - month}}{\text{Sum of the person weights for} \atop \text{the province - day - month}} \qquad (13)$$

where

Projected population count =

$$\text{(14)}$$

$$= \frac{\text{Projected population count for province - month}}{7}$$

(d)   Raking ratio adjustments

The weights of each respondent were adjusted several times using a raking ratio procedure. This procedure ensured that estimates produced for RO - stratum - month, province - age group - sex and province - day of the week - month totals would agree with the projections. This adjustment was made by repeating steps (a), (b) and (c) of the weighting procedures until each repetition of the step made a minimal adjustment to the weights.

6. Final person weight

The weight produced at the end of (5) is the final person weight WGHTFIN placed on the Main file and on the Episode file.

7. Episode weight

In GSS-7, diaries were collected from only 90 per cent of the respondents who provided otherwise usefully complete data. Thus, many time-use variables and all the episode data were available only for a subsample of respondents, so a second weight (TIMEWGT) was needed to account for this subsampling, and this was the weight to be used when using the Time-use episode file. In GSS-12, there was no such subsampling, so the weight that should be used with episode data had the same value as the person weight; it did, however, have a different interpretation: weighting up to a total over time-use episodes rather than over persons, so it was given a different name, WGHTEPI. It is only on the Time-use episode file.

Illustration 3. 1999 New Zealand Time Use Survey: two persons per household; two person/days per person[*]

Weighting

Each responding adult was assigned a unique survey weight to be used in the calculation of survey estimates. The two most important functions of these weights were:

- To produce unbiased survey estimates by taking account of the varying probabilities of selection among members of the sample population.
- To "rate up" the sample data to total population size, enabling simple calculation of estimates of population counts of given time-use breakdowns.
- The weighting process for the Time Use Survey included three main steps.
- Adjustment for probability of selection.
- Adjustment for non-response.
- Calibration of sample totals to population benchmarks.

Adjustment for probability of selection

Each selected person in "eligible responding" households was assigned a selection weight reflecting his or her inverse probability of selection into the TUS sample. The method of calculating these weights differed for Maori and non-Maori because of the screening sample.

Adjustment for non-response

An adjustment to the selection weight was made to allow for the non-response in the Time Use Survey. These adjustments were

made by estimation group. There were five estimation groups: three in the core sample based on geographical locations, and two in the screening sample based on ethnic density. Every eligible responding individual had their weight increased, depending on the rate of non-response that occurred in their particular estimation group.

Calibration of sample totals to population benchmarks

The purpose of this stage was to ensure that the sample data totals matched known population benchmarks.

The benchmarks used were:

- Age (12-14, 15-24, 25-34, 35-44, 45-54, 55-64, 65-74, 75+) by sex.
- Ethnicity (Maori, non-Maori).
- Labour-force status (employed, not employed, that is to say, those unemployed plus those not in the labour force) for people aged 15+.

In addition, benchmarks ensured that five-sevenths of the data related to weekdays and two-sevenths of the data related to weekends.

The age by sex and ethnicity benchmarks were obtained from Census 1996 data, adjusted for births, deaths and migration. The labour-force benchmarks were obtained from Household Labour-Force Survey data for the four quarters during which the Time Use Survey data was collected.

Producing estimates

The final weights created after calibration were then used to produce the estimates of interest. There were three different types of estimates:

---

[*] *Source*: Statistics New Zealand (1999), pp. 16-22.

– Average minutes per day in activity X (for example, necessary time) for people in subpopulation Y (for example, males aged 15-19).

– Total number of people in subpopulation Y with characteristic K (for example, multiple jobs).

– Participants: average minutes per day in activity X amongst subpopulation Y.

Estimates were formed as follows:

– For each person in subpopulation Y, sum the number of minutes each person in the subpopulation spends on activity X, multiply this by the person's weight. Sum this over all people in subpopulation Y. This total is then divided by the sum of the weights for all people in subpopulation Y to produce the average minutes.

– Sum the weights for each person in subpopulation Y with characteristic K.

– For each diary day (belonging to a person in subpopulation Y), sum the number of minutes spent on activity X on that day and multiply by the person's weight. Sum this over all diary days belonging to a person in subpopulation Y. This total is then divided by the sum of the weights for each diary day on which there were non-zero minutes spent on activity X by a person in subpopulation Y. (Note: each person may contribute up to two diary days to this estimate.)

Estimates of population sizes

Separate tables provide selected estimates of population sizes derived from the Time Use Survey. Accompanying tables provide relevant relative sampling errors for these estimates. The tables show that the size of the survey population—the civilian, usually resident, non-institutionalized population aged

12 years or over residing in private households—is estimated to be 30,032,740 people. This figure, together with analyses by variables such as sex, age and Maori/non-Maori, provides useful background to the time-use statistics themselves. For example, when considering the average time spent by women aged 35-44 on education and training, it is useful to know how many women aged 35-44 there are.

Basic measures estimated

Average minutes per day on activity z (averaged over the whole population):

$$\frac{\sum_i^n w_i \sum_j^{d_i} t_{ijz}}{\sum_i^n w_i d_i} \qquad (15)$$

where t_{ijz} is the number of minutes recorded by respondent i on day j on activity z; d_i is the number of diary days recorded by respondent i (Note: This should be two most of the time but may occasionally be one); w_i is the weight associated with respondent i; and n is the number of eligible respondents in the sample.

Participants: average minutes per day on activity z

"Participants: average minutes per day" is the average time spent on an activity on days on which people reported doing that activity. This is calculated from the total time spent on activity z divided by the total number of days people spent participating in activity z.

The figures do not represent an average per participant (that is to say the total time spent on a particular activity divided by the number of people who participate in that activity). This is because we do not have a count of all participants. We collected data for only a two-day period and therefore do not know about people who may have participated in an activity on their non-diary days. The formula is as follows:

$$\frac{\sum\limits_{i}^{n^z} w_i \sum\limits_{j}^{d_i^z} t_{ijz}}{\sum\limits_{i}^{n^z} w_i d_i^z} \qquad (16)$$

where t_{ijz} is the number of minutes recorded by respondent i on day j on activity z; d_i^z is the number of diary days where respondent i recorded non-zero time spent on activity z; w_i is the weight associated with respondent i; and n^z is the number of eligible respondents in the sample who recorded time on activity z.

ANNEX 14. SUGGESTED TABLES FOR TIME-USE DATA

Table A2. Average time per day spent on various activities for the population, by sex and age, cross-classified by {individual-level/household characteristic}[a]

Primary activity[b]	Total population			Women				Men			
	All ages	Age group[c]		All ages	Age group			All ages	Age group		
		<15	15-59	60 and over		<15	15-59	60 and over		<15	15-59	60 and over
	(hours per day)			(hours per day)				(hours per day)			
Total											
01. Work for corporations, quasi-corporations, Government, NPIs											
02. Work for households in primary production activities											
03. Work for households in non-primary production activities											
04. Work for households in construction activities											
05. Work for households providing services for income											
06. Work providing unpaid domestic services for own final use within household											
07. Work providing unpaid domestic services to household members											
08. Work providing community services and help to other households											
09. Learning											
10. Socializing and community participation											
11. Attending/visiting cultural, entertainment and sports events/venues											
12. Engaging in hobbies, games and other pastime activities											
13. Indoor and outdoor sport participation											
14. Use of mass media											
15. Personal care and maintenance											
Category 1 of characteristic (as for "Total")											
Category 2 of characteristic (as for "Total")											
...											
Last category of characteristic (as for "Total")											

[a] Including: (a) urban/rural; (b) educational attainment; (c) marital status; (d) labour-force status; (e) household composition; (f) income; (g) presence/absence of appliances.

[b] Estimates are based on primary or main activities only. Tabulation categories are those defined in the ICATUS.

[c] Age groups may be further broken down into five-year groups.

Table A3. Average time per day spent on various activities for the population, by sex and age, cross-classified by urban/rural

Primary activity [a]	Total population				Women				Men			
	All ages	Age group [b]			All ages	Age group			All ages	Age group		
		<15	15-59	60 and over		<15	15-59	60 and over		<15	15-59	60 and over
	(hours per day)				(hours per day)				(hours per day)			
Total												
01. Work for corporations, quasi-corporations, Government, NPIs												
02. Work for households in primary production activities												
03. Work for households in non-primary production activities												
04. Work for households in construction activities												
05. Work for households providing services for income												
06. Work providing unpaid domestic services for own final use within household												
07. Work providing unpaid domestic services to household members												
08. Work providing community services and help to other households												
09. Learning												
10. Socializing and community participation												
11. Attending/visiting cultural, entertainment and sports events/venues												
12. Engaging in hobbies, games and other pastime activities												
13. Indoor and outdoor sport participation												
14. Use of mass media												
15. Personal care and maintenance												
Urban (as for "Total")												
Rural (as for "Total")												

[a] Estimates are based on primary or main activities only. Tabulation categories are those defined in the ICATUS.

[b] Age groups may be further broken down into five-year groups.

262

Table A4. Average time per day spent on various activities for participants, by sex and age, cross-classified by {individual-level/household characteristic} [a]

Primary activity [b]	Total population				Women				Men			
	All ages	Age group [c]			All ages	Age group			All ages	Age group		
		<15	15-59	60 and over		<15	15-59	60 and over		<15	15-59	60 and over
	(hours per day)				(hours per day)				(hours per day)			
Total												
01. Work for corporations, quasi-corporations, Government, NPIs												
02. Work for households in primary production activities												
03. Work for households in non-primary production activities												
04. Work for households in construction activities												
05. Work for households providing services for income												
06. Work providing unpaid domestic services for own final use within household												
07. Work providing unpaid domestic services to household members												
08. Work providing community services and help to other households												
09. Learning												
10. Socializing and community participation												
11. Attending/visiting cultural, entertainment and sports events/venues												
12. Engaging in hobbies, games and other pastime activities												
13. Indoor and outdoor sport participation												
14. Use of mass media												
15. Personal care and maintenance												
Category 1 of characteristic (as for "Total")												
Category 2 of characteristic (as for "Total")												
...												
Last category of characteristic (as for "Total")												

[a] Including: (a) urban/rural; (b) educational attainment; (c) marital status; (d) labour-force status; (e) household composition; (f) income; (g) presence/absence of appliances.

[b] Estimates are based on primary or main activities only. Tabulation categories are those defined in the ICATUS.

[c] Age groups may be further broken down into five-year groups.

Table A5. Average time per day spent on various activities for participants, by sex and age, cross-classified by urban/rural

Primary activity [a]	Total population				Women				Men			
	All ages	Age group [b]			All ages	Age group			All ages	Age group		
		<15	15-59	60 and over		<15	15-59	60 and over		<15	15-59	60 and over
	(hours per day)				(hours per day)				(hours per day)			
Total												
01. Work for corporations, quasi-corporations, Government, NPIs												
02. Work for households in primary production activities												
03. Work for households in non-primary production activities												
04. Work for households in construction activities												
05. Work for households providing services for income												
06. Work providing unpaid domestic services for own final use within household												
07. Work providing unpaid domestic services to household members												
08. Work providing community services and help to other households												
09. Learning												
10. Socializing and community participation												
11. Attending/visiting cultural, entertainment and sports events/venues												
12. Engaging in hobbies, games and other pastime activities												
13. Indoor and outdoor sport participation												
14. Use of mass media												
15. Personal care and maintenance												
Urban (as for "Total")												
Rural (as for "Total")												

[a] Estimates are based on primary or main activities only. Tabulation categories are those defined in the ICATUS.

[b] Age groups may be further broken down into five-year groups.

264

Table A6. Participation rates on various activities, by sex and age, cross-classified by {individual-level/household characteristic} [a]

Primary activity [b]	Total population			Women			Men		
	All ages	Age group [c] (percentage)		All ages	Age group (percentage)		All ages	Age group (percentage)	
		<15	15-59	60 and over		<15	15-59	60 and over		<15	15-59	60 and over
Total									
01. Work for corporations, quasi-corporations, Government, NPIs									
02. Work for households in primary production activities									
03. Work for households in non-primary production activities									
04. Work for households in construction activities									
05. Work for households providing services for income									
06. Work providing unpaid domestic services for own final use within household									
07. Work providing unpaid domestic services to household members									
08. Work providing community services and help to other households									
09. Learning									
10. Socializing and community participation									
11. Attending/visiting cultural, entertainment and sports events/venues									
12. Engaging in hobbies, games and other pastime activities									
13. Indoor and outdoor sport participation									
14. Use of mass media									
15. Personal care and maintenance									
Category 1 of characteristic (as for "Total")									
Category 2 of characteristic (as for "Total")									
...									
Last category of characteristic (as for "Total")									

[a] Including: (a) urban/rural; (b) educational attainment; (c) marital status; (d) labour-force status; (e) household composition; (f) income; (g) presence/absence of appliances.

[b] Estimates are based on primary or main activities only. Tabulation categories are those defined in the ICATUS.

[c] Age groups may be further broken down into five-year groups.

265

Table A7. Participation rates on various activities for participants, by sex and age, cross-classified by urban/rural

Primary activity[a]	Total population				Women				Men			
	All ages	Age group[b]			All ages	Age group			All ages	Age group		
		<15	15-59	60 and over		<15	15-59	60 and over		<15	15-59	60 and over
		(percentage)				(percentage)				(percentage)		
Total												
01. A work for corporations, quasi-corporations, Government, NPIs												
02. Work for households in primary production activities												
03. Work for households in non-primary production activities												
04. Work for households in construction activities												
05. Work for households providing services for income												
06. Work providing unpaid domestic services for own final use within household												
07. Work providing unpaid domestic services to household members												
08. Work providing community services and help to other households												
09. Learning												
10. Socializing and community participation												
11. Attending/visiting cultural, entertainment and sports events/venues												
12. Engaging in hobbies, games and other pastime activities												
13. Indoor and outdoor sport participation												
14. Use of mass media												
15. Personal care and maintenance												
Urban (as for "Total")												
Rural (as for "Total")												

[a] Estimates are based on primary or main activities only. Tabulation categories are those defined in the ICATUS.

[b] Age groups may be further broken down into five-year groups.

266

Table A8. Average minutes per day spent on various activities as sole primary and simultaneous activities, by sex and age groups, cross-classified by urban/rural

Activity group[a]	Total population				Women				Men			
	All ages	Age group[b]			All ages	Age group			All ages	Age group		
		<15	15-59	60 and over		<15	15-59	60 and over		<15	15-59	60 and over
		(percentage)				*(percentage)*				*(percentage)*		
Total												
01. Work for corporations, quasi-corporations, Government, NPIs												
Sole primary												
Simultaneous with other activities												
02. Work for households in primary production activities												
Sole primary												
Simultaneous with other activities												
03. Work for households in non-primary production activities												
Sole primary												
Simultaneous with other activities												
...												
15. Personal care and maintenance												
Sole primary												
Simultaneous with other activities												
Urban (as for "Total")												
Rural (as for "Total")												

[a] Estimates are based on primary activities performed alone (sole primary) and primary activities performed simultaneously with other activities. Tabulation categories are those defined in the ICATUS.
[b] Age groups may be further broken down into five-year groups.

Table A9. Average minutes per day spent on various activities performed simultaneously, by sex and age groups, cross-classified by {individual-level/household characteristic} [a]

Activity combination [b]	Total population				Women				Men			
	All ages	Age group [c]			All ages	Age group			All ages	Age group		
		<15	15-59	60 and over		<15	15-59	60 and over		<15	15-59	60 and over
	(percentage)				(percentage)				(percentage)			
Total												
01. Work for corporations, quasi-corporations, Government, NPIs												
Simultaneous with:												
Work for households in primary production activities												
Work for households in non-primary production activities												
Work for households in construction activities												
Work for households providing services for income												
Work providing unpaid domestic services for own final use within household												
Work providing unpaid domestic services to household member												
Work providing community services and help to other households												
Learning												
Socializing and community participation												
Attending/visiting cultural, entertainment and sports events/venues												
Engaging in hobbies, games and other pastime activities												
Indoor and outdoor sport participation												
Use of mass media												
Personal care and maintenance												
...												
15. Personal care and maintenance												
Simultaneous with:												
Work for corporations, quasi-corporations, Government, NPIs												
Work for households in primary productive activities												
Work for households in non-primary production activities												
Work for households in construction activities												
Work for households providing services for income												

268

Work providing unpaid domestic services for own final use within household		
Work providing unpaid domestic services to household members		
Work providing community services and help to other households		
Learning		
Socializing and community participation		
Attending/visiting cultural, entertainment and sports events/venues		
Engaging in hobbies, games and other pastime activities		
Indoor and outdoor sport participation		
Use of mass media		
Category 1 of characteristic (as for "Total")		
Category 2 of characteristic (as for "Total")		
…		
Last category of characteristic (as for "Total")		

[a] Including: (a) urban/rural; (b) educational attainment; (c) marital status; (d) labour-force status; (e) household composition; (f) income; (g) presence/absence of appliances. Tabulation categories are those defined in the ICATUS.
[b] Estimates are based on combinations of activities performed simultaneously with a primary activity.
[c] Age groups may be further broken down into five-year groups

ANNEX 15. GRAPHS OF "DAILY RHYTHM"

Figure 4.

ACTIVITIES AT DIFFERENT HOURS OF THE DAY

WEEKDAYS

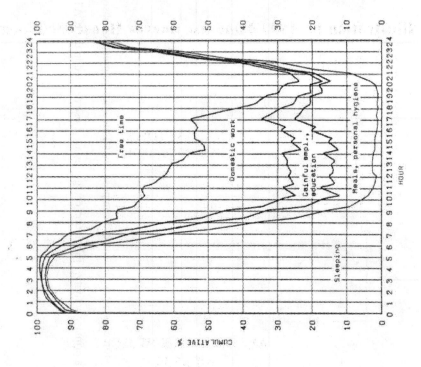

Figure 5.

ACTIVITIES AT DIFFERENT HOURS OF THE DAY

SATURDAYS

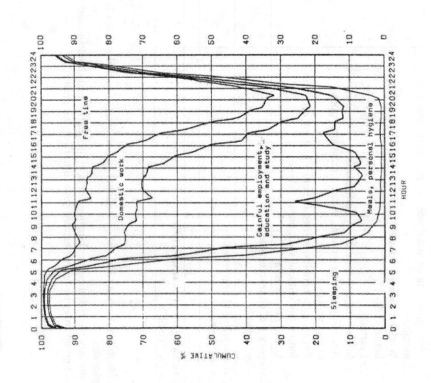

270

ANNEX 16.   SAMPLE TIME-USE SURVEY INSTRUMENTS

Illustration 1.   1997 Time Use Survey Household Form, Australia

IN CONFIDENCE
HOUSEHOLD FORM

Australian
Bureau of
Statistics

| Workload | PSU | Block | Dwelling | Household |

Address

Further Identification

Phone number
....

IF THE NEED ARISES
MAY WE PHONE YOU?

Yes ☐
No ☐

AUSTRALIAN BUREAU OF STATISTICS

TIME USE SURVEY

DETAILS OF CALLS									
	1st CALL	2nd CALL	3rd CALL	4th CALL	5th CALL	6th CALL	7th CALL	8th CALL	9th CALL
DAY & DATE									
TIME OUT									
TIME IN									
TOTAL									

APPOINTMENTS etc.   Primary Approach Letter: Yes ☐   No ☐

Source: Australian Bureau of Statistics (1996a).

<table>
<tr><td colspan="2">USUAL RESIDENTS</td></tr>
</table>

USUAL RESIDENTS

WHAT ARE THE NAMES OF ALL THE PEOPLE WHO
<u>USUALLY</u> LIVE HERE STARTING WITH THE
HEAD OF HOUSEHOLD?

    Complete Columns A to I

    Ask coverage for all usual residents

    Record coverage in Column J

VISITORS

WILL ANYONE ELSE BE STAYING HERE TONIGHT?
    Complete Columns A and B

2. Ask coverage for visitors and record in Column J

    Complete Cols C to I for visitors in on coverage

<u>COVERAGE FOR USUAL RESIDENTS</u>

1. WILL ANY OF THESE PEOPLE BE STAYING
    AWAY TONIGHT?
       Yes - Ask Q2 for each such person AND
            INCLUDE all others URs

       No - INCLUDE all URs

2. HAS ... BEEN AWAY FOR ALL OF THE TIME
    FROM .... UNTIL NOW?
       Yes - Go to Q3

       No - INCLUDE

3. WILL .... BE AWAY FOR ALL OF THE TIME
    FROM NOW UNTIL ....?
       Yes - EXCLUDE

       No - INCLUDE

COVERAGE FOR VISITORS

4. DOES .... USUALLY LIVE IN A PRIVATE
    DWELLING?
       Yes - Ask Q5

       No - INCLUDE

5. HAS ... BEEN AWAY FOR FROM ... USUAL
    RESIDENCE FOR ALL OF THE TIME FROM
    .... UNTIL NOW?
       Yes - Go to Q6

       No - EXCLUDE

6. WILL .... BE AWAY FROM ...... USUAL
    RESIDENCE FOR ALL OF THE TIME FROM
    UNTIL ....?
       Yes - INCLUDE

       No - EXCLUDE

	A NAME	B PERSON TYPE	C RELATIONSHIP		D SEX	E AGE	F MARITAL STATUS
			WHAT IS ... RELATION- SHIP TO THE HEAD OF THE HOUSE- HOLD?	(ARE THERE ANY (OTHER) STEP, DE FACTO OR IN-LAW RELATION- SHIPS WITHIN THE HOUSE- HOLD?)		WHAT WAS .... AGE LAST BIRTHDAY?	WHAT IS ... MARITAL STATUS? Married = 1 De facto = 2 Separated = 3 Divorced = 4 Widowed = 5 Never
Person No.	Surname Other	UR = 1 VIS = 2	To Head	Within Household	Male = 1 Female = 2		Married = 6
01							
02							
03							
04							
05							
06							
07							
08							
09							
10							

SCOPE EXCLUSIONS   *(enter '2' in Column J)*

- Overseas visitors (i.e., people whose usual place of residence is outside Australia)
- Non-Australian diplomat, non-Australian diplomatic staff and non-Australian members of their household
- Members of non-Australian defence forces stationed in Australia and their dependents
- Children aged 0-14

	G	H	I	J	K		L
	COUNTRY OF BIRTH	YEAR ARRIVAL	EDUCATION ATTENDANCE	SCOPE AND COVERAGE	SCHEDULE/ DIARY		HOUSEHOLD TYPE CODE
	IN WHICH COUNTRY WAS ... BORN?	WHAT YEAR DID ... ARRIVE IN AUST?	*Age 15 to 24 only* IS ..... IN FULL-TIME SECONDARY OR TERTIARY EDUCATION? Secondary = 1 Tertiary = 2 No = 3	In on scope and coverage = 1 Out on scope= 2 Out on coverage = 3	*Leave blank if person is out on scope or coverage* Complete = 1 Incomplete = 2 Schedule /Diary not obtained = 3		*Interviewer:* *When editing, tick Household Type Code. Code Household Type on the basis of Usual Residents only; ignore visitors.* 1. Person living alone .... ☐ 1 2. Married or de facto couple only............................. ☐ 2 3. Married or de facto couple living only with their unmarried child(ren) aged 15 or over.................... ☐ 3 4. Married or de facto couple living only with their child(ren) aged 0-14 .... ☐ 4
					Schedule	Diary	
Person No.							5. Married or de facto couple living only with their child(ren) aged 0-14 and their unmarried child(ren) aged 15 or over.............. ☐ 5
01							
02							
03							6. One person living only with his/her unmarried child(ren) aged 15 or over .. ☐ 6
04							
05							7. One person living only with his/her child(ren) aged 0-14 .... ☐ 7
06							
07							8. One person living only with his/her child(ren) aged 0-14 and his/her unmarried child(ren) aged 15 or over......................... ☐ 8
08							
09							
10							9. All other household......... ☐ 9

RESPONSE REPORT

INITIAL STATUS			INTERVIEWER TO COMPLETE
FULLY RESPONDING	01	All schedules and diaries fully complete for all persons in on scope and coverage.	☐ 01
NON RESPONSE			
	02	Full refusal } *Complete a Refusal Report Form*	☐ 02
	03	Part refusal }	☐ 03
	04	Full non-contact	☐ 04
	05	Part non-contact	☐ 05
	06	Language problems	☐ 06
	07	Death/illness	☐ 07
			Record full details below
SAMPLE LOSS			
	08	All persons out on scope / coverage	☐ 08
	09	Vacant dwelling	☐ 09
	10	Dwelling under-construction, converted to non-dwelling, derelict, demolished or listed in error	☐ 10
OFFICE USE ONLY		Final Status *(enter code)*	☐☐

DETAILS OF CODES 04-10

274

Illustration 2. 1999 New Zealand Time Use Survey Household Questionnaire

Household Questionnaire

1998

30   31

July

Sun	Mon	Tue	Wed	Thu	Fri	Sat
			1	2	3	4
5	6	7	8	9	10	11
12	13	14	15	16	17	18
19	20	21	22	23	24	25
26	27	28	29	30	31	

September

Sun	Mon	Tue	Wed	Thu	Fri	Sat
		1	2	3	4	5
6	7	8	9	10	11	12
13	14	15	16	17	18	19
20	21	22	23	24	25	26
27	28	29	30			

November

Sun	Mon	Tue	Wed	Thu	Fri	Sat
1	2	3	4	5	6	7
8	9	10	11	12	13	14
15	16	17	18	19	20	21
22	23	24	25	26	27	28
29	30					

1999

January

Sun	Mon	Tue	Wed	Thu	Fri	Sat
					1	2
3	4	5	6	7	8	9
10	11	12	13	14	15	16
17	18	19	20	21	22	23
24	25	26	27	28	29	30
31						

March

Sun	Mon	Tue	Wed	Thu	Fri	Sat
	1	2	3	4	5	6
7	8	9	10	11	12	13
14	15	16	17	18	19	20
21	22	23	24	25	26	27
28	29	30	31			

May

Sun	Mon	Tue	Wed	Thu	Fri	Sat
						1
2	3	4	5	6	7	8
9	10	11	12	13	14	15
16	17	18	19	20	21	22
23	24	25	26	27	28	29

1. Do you, or anyone else who lives here, own this house / flat?

Tick 'Yes' even if it is owned with a mortgage or only partly owned.

1 ☐ Yes → *Go to 2*

2 ☐ No → *Go to 3*

2. Do you, or anyone else who lives here, make mortgage payments for this dwelling?

1 ☐ Yes → *Go to 4*

2 ☐ No → *Go to 4*

3. Do you, or anyone else who lives here, pay rent to the owner (or to their agent) for this house / flat?

1 ☐ Yes

2 ☐ No

4. Do you have any of the following in your household? Don't count any that are not in working order.

1 ☐ a telephone?

2 ☐ a microwave oven?

3 ☐ a dishwasher?

4 ☐ an automatic washing machine?

5 ☐ a clothes dryer?

6 ☐ a fridge or fridge/freezer?

7 ☐ a separate freezer?

8 ☐ a sewing machine?

9 ☐ a motor or electric lawn mower?

10 ☐ a television set?
   → How many? ☐

11 ☐ a video recorder / player?
   → How many? ☐

0 ☐ *none of the above*

5. Is there a computer in this house / flat?

1 ☐ Yes → *Go to 6*

2 ☐ No → *Go to 8*

6. Does it have a modem?

1 ☐ Yes

2 ☐ No

7. Does it have an internet connection?

1 ☐ Yes

2 ☐ No

8. Does anyone in this household have a motor vehicle available for their use?

Tick 'No' if vehicle is not in working order, or is used only for business / farm work.

1 ☐ Yes

2 ☐ No

9. In the past **seven days**, has anyone been paid to do any household cleaning or laundry for this house / flat?

1 ☐ Yes → *Go to 10*

2 ☐ No → *Go to 11*

10. Was anyone who <u>doesn't live here</u> paid to do that?

1 ☐ Yes

2 ☐ No

11. In the past **four weeks**, has anyone been paid to do any gardening or lawn-mowing for this house/flat?

1 ☐ Yes

2 ☐ No → *No more questions*

12. Was anyone who <u>doesn't live here</u> paid to do that?

1 ☐ Yes

2 ☐ No

End of Household Questionnaire

Source: Statistics New Zealand. (1998b).

Illustration 3.   1997 Time Use Survey Individual Questionnaire, Australia

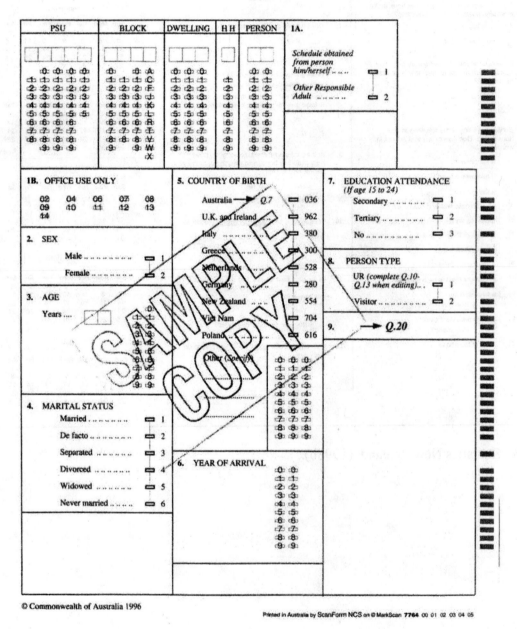

TUS

SCS26

IN CONFIDENCE

TIME USE SURVEY
1997

Source: Australian Bureau of Statistics. (1996b).

2

HOUSEHOLD TYPE		
1 *(Nothing further)* ..	▭	1
2	▭	2
3	▭	3
4	▭	4
5	▭	5
6 *(Complete Q.12)* ..	▭	6
7 *(Complete Q.12)* ..	▭	7
8 *(Complete Q.12)* ..	▭	8
9 *(Nothing further)* ..	▭	9

Husband *(Complete Q.13)*	▭	1
Wife *(Nothing further)*	▭	2
Son/daughter *(Nothing further)*	▭	3

Father/mother	▭	1
Son/daughter *(Nothing further)*	▭	2

If Household Types 2, 3 or 6 in Q.10 nothing further

If Household Type 4, 5, 7, or 8 in Q.10, enter number of children aged 0 to 14 years

1 2 3 4 5 6 7 8 9

14. OFFICE USE ONLY

A HH Type 9 Relationship	B Family Number	C Children 0-14 years
1 2 3 4 5 6 7 8 9	1 2 3 4 5 6 7 8 9	1 2 3 4 5 6 7 8 9

UR CHILDREN 0-14 YEARS

D Age	E Sex	F Age	G Sex	H Age	I Sex
0 0 1 1 2 3 4 5 6 7 8 9	male ▭ 1 female ▭ 2	0 0 1 1 2 3 4 5 6 7 8 9	male ▭ 1 female ▭ 2	0 0 1 1 2 3 4 5 6 7 8 9	male ▭ 1 female ▭ 2

J Age	K Sex	L Age	M Sex	N Age	O Sex
0 0 1 1 2 3 4 5 6 7 8 9	male female	0 0 1 1 2 3 4 5 6 7 8 9	male ▭ 1 female ▭ 2	0 0 1 1 2 3 4 5 6 7 8 9	male ▭ 1 female ▭ 2

15.

A UR Scope/ Coverage Exclusion	B Compulsion Queried	C Diary Status	D Schedule Initial Response
1 2	1 2	1 2 3 4 5 6 7 8 9	1 2 3 4 5

E Incomplete Schedule	F Income	G	H I J
1 2 3 4 5 6 7 8 9	1	0 1 2 3 4 5 6 7 8 9	0 0 0 1 1 1 2 2 2 3 3 3 4 4 4 5 5 5 6 6 6 7 7 7 8 8 8 9 9 9

SAMPLE COPY

277

20. I AM NOW GOING TO ASK YOU SOME QUESTIONS ABOUT ..... LANGUAGE AND EDUCATION.

WHAT LANGUAGE DID .... <u>FIRST</u> SPEAK AS A CHILD?

English	1201
Italian	2401
Greek	2201
Cantonese	7101
Mandarin	7104
Arabic	4202
German	1301
Vietnamese	6302
Spanish	2303
Polish	3602

Other (Specify) ....

21. WHAT LANGUAGE DOES ... USUALLY SPEAK IN THIS HOUSEHOLD?

English	1201
Italian	2401
Greek	2201
Cantonese	7101
Mandarin	7104
Arabic	4202
German	1301
Vietnamese	6302
Spanish	2303
Polish	3602

Other (Specify) ....

22. *Sequence Guide*

. If respondent's mother is a usual resident .... → *Q.24*   1

. Otherwise .... → *Q.23*   2

23. IN WHICH COUNTRY WAS ... MOTHER BORN?

Australia	036
U.K. and Ireland	962
Italy	380
Greece	300
Netherlands	528
Germany	280
New Zealand	554
Viet Nam	704
Poland	616

Other (Specify) ....

24. *Sequence Guide*

. If respondent's father is a usual resident .... → *Q.26*   1

. Otherwise .... → *Q.25*   2

25. IN WHICH COUNTRY WAS ... FATHER BORN?

Australia	036
U.K. and Ireland	962
Italy	380
Greece	300
Netherlands	528
Germany	280
New Zealand	554
Viet Nam	704
Poland	616

Other (Specify) ....

278

ATION   4

Sequence Guide

. If still at school (code '1' in Q.7)
.... → Q.49 1

. Otherwise.............. → Q.27 2

AT WHAT AGE DID .... LEAVE SCHOOL?

Never went to school → Q.31 01

Under 14 years ...... → Q.31 02

14 years .... → Q.31 03

15 years 04

16 years 05

17 years 06

18 years 07

19 years 08

20 years 09

21 years and over 10

DID .... COMPLETE THE HIGHEST YEAR OF SECONDARY SCHOOL?

Yes .... → Q.31

No 2

Sequence Guide

. If respondent aged 25 years or more (see Q.3) .... → Q.31

. Otherwise............. → Q.30

WHAT WAS THE HIGHEST LEVEL OF SCHOOLING THAT .... COMPLETED?

Year 12 or equivalent 1

Year 11 or equivalent 2

Year 10 or equivalent 3

Other 4

(SINCE LEAVING SCHOOL,) HAS .... COMPLETED A TRADE CERTIFICATE, DIPLOMA, DEGREE OR ANY OTHER EDUCATIONAL QUALIFICATION?

Yes 1

No .... → Q.39 2

---

32. *Interviewer:* Show PINK Prompt Card A

WHICH OF THESE BEST DESCRIBES THE HIGHEST QUALIFICATION .... HAS COMPLETED?

Secondary School Certificate 01

Nursing Qualification → Q.36 02

Teaching Qualification
.... → Q.38 03

Trade Certificate/Apprenticeship 04

Technician Cert./Advanced Certificate 05

Certificate other than above
.... → Q.34 06

Associate Diploma .. → Q.34 07

Undergraduate Diploma
.... → Q.34 08

Bachelor Degree 09

Post-graduate Diploma 10

Masters Degree/Doctorate 11

---

33. → Q.39

---

34. **HOW LONG DOES THAT (CERTIFICATE/ DIPLOMA) TAKE TO COMPLETE, STUDYING FULL-TIME?**

Less than 1 semester 1

1 semester to less than 1 year 2

1 year to less than 3 years 3

3 years or more...... 4

---

35. → Q.39

---

36. *Interviewer:* Show BLUE Prompt Card B

WHICH OF THESE GROUPS BEST DESCRIBES THAT NURSING QUALIFICATION?

Group ..... [ ] 0
1
2
3
4
5
6
7
8
9

---

37. → Q.39

---

38. *Interviewer: Show YELLOW Prompt Card C*

WHICH OF THESE GROUPS BEST DESCRIBES THAT TEACHING QUALIFICATION?

Group .. .. □   1 2 3 4 5 6 7

39. IS .... CURRENTLY TAKING ANY COURSE OF STUDY AT A SCHOOL OR ANY EDUCATIONAL INSTITUTION?

Yes 1
No .... → Q.49   2

40. IS .... DOING THIS COURSE FULL-TIME, PART-TIME OR BY CORRESPONDENCE?

Full-time 1
Part-time 2
Correspondence 3

41. IS .... CURRENT STUDY BEING DONE TO OBTAIN A TRADE CERTIFICATE, DIPLOMA, DEGREE OR ANY OTHER EDUCATIONAL QUALIFICATION?

Yes 1
No .... → Q.49   2

42. *Interviewer: Show PINK Prompt Card A*

WHICH OF THESE BEST DESCRIBES THE QUALIFICATION .... IS CURRENTLY STUDYING?

Secondary School Certificate ... 01
Nursing Qualification → Q.46   02
Teaching Qualification → Q.48   03
Trade Certificate/Apprenticeship   04
Technician Cert./Advanced Certificate   05
Certificate other than above. → Q.44   06
Associate Diploma.... → Q.44   07
Undergraduate Diploma → Q.44   08
Bachelor Degree   09
Post-graduate Diploma   10
Masters Degree/Doctorate   11

43. → Q.49

44. HOW LONG DOES THAT (CERTIFICATE/DIPLOMA) TAKE TO COMPLETE, STUDYING FULL-TIME?

Less than 1 semester 1
1 semester to less than 1 year 2
1 year to less than 3 years 3
3 years or more 4

45. → Q.49

46. *Interviewer: Show BLUE Prompt Card B*

WHICH OF THESE GROUPS BEST DESCRIBES THAT NURSING QUALIFICATION?

Group .. .. □□   00 01 2 3 4 5 6 7 8 9

47. → Q.49

48. *Interviewer: Show YELLOW Prompt Card C*

WHICH OF THESE GROUPS BEST DESCRIBES THAT TEACHING QUALIFICATION?

Group .. .. □   1 2 3 4 5 6 7

49. I WOULD NOW LIKE TO ASK YOU ABOUT THE WEEK STARTING MONDAY THE .... AND ENDING LAST SUNDAY THE .... THAT IS, LAST WEEK.

50. LAST WEEK, DID .... DO ANY WORK AT ALL IN A JOB, BUSINESS OR FARM?

Yes ...... → Q.53   1
No 2
Permanently unable to work ...... → Q.77   3

51. LAST WEEK, DID .... DO ANY WORK WITHOUT PAY IN A FAMILY BUSINESS?

Yes ...... → Q.53   1
No 2

52. DID .... HAVE A JOB, BUSINESS OR FARM THAT .... WAS AWAY FROM BECAUSE OF HOLIDAYS, SICKNESS OR ANY OTHER REASON?

Yes 1
No ...... → Q.68   2

6

5. DID .... HAVE MORE THAN ONE JOB (LAST WEEK)?

Yes .. .. ▭ 1

No .. .. ➝ *Q.55* ▭ 2

6. I WOULD NOW LIKE TO ASK YOU ABOUT THE JOB IN WHICH ....USUALLY WORKS THE MOST HOURS.

7. WHAT KIND OF WORK DOES .... DO?

(*Title*)..........................

....

....

(*Main tasks / duties*)..............

....

....

```
:0: :0: :0:
:1: :1: :1: :1:
:2: :2: :2: :2:
:3: :3: :3: :3:
:4: :4: :4: :4:
:5: :5: :5: :5:
:6: :6: :6: :6:
:7: :7: :7: :7:
:8: :8: :8: :8:
:9: :9: :9: :9:
```

8. (IN THAT JOB,) DOES .... WORK —

FOR AN EMPLOYER FOR WAGES OR SALARY? .. .. ➝ *Q.59* ▭ 1

IN .... OWN BUSINESS WITH EMPLOYEES? .. .. ▭ 2

WITH NO EMPLOYEES? .. .. ▭ 3

WITHOUT PAY IN A FAMILY BUSINESS? .. .. ➝ *Q.59* ▭ 4

WHAT ARE .... WORKING ARRANGEMENTS?

Payment in kind .. ➝ *Q.59* ▭ 5

Unpaid voluntary work .. .. ➝ *Q.68* ▭ 6

9. IS .... BUSINESS A LIMITED LIABILITY COMPANY?

Yes .. .. ▭ 1

No .. .. ▭ 2

10. WHAT IS THE FULL NAME AND ADDRESS OF .... BUSINESS?

....

....

.... ➝ *Q.60*

11. WHO DOES .... WORK FOR? (Name/*Full* address)

```
:0: :0: :0:
:1: :1: :1:
:2: :2: :2:
:3: :3: :3:
:4: :4: :4:
:5: :5: :5:
:6: :6: :6:
:7: :7: :7:
:8: :8: :8:
:9: :9: :9:
```

....

....

....

....

60. WHAT KIND OF INDUSTRY, BUSINESS OR SERVICE IS CARRIED OUT AT THAT ADDRESS?

....

.... ➝ *Q.62*

61. OFFICE USE ONLY

Sector Code

```
:1:
:2:
:9:
```

62. DOES .... DO ANY WORK AT HOME IN THAT JOB?

Yes .. .. ▭ 1

No .. .. ➝ *Q.64* ▭ 2

63. DOES .... USUALLY WORK MORE HOURS AT HOME THAN AWAY FROM HOME?

Yes .. .. ▭ 1

No .. .. ▭ 2

Same number of hours at home/ away from home .. .. ▭ 3

64. *Sequence Guide*

If away from work last week (code '1' in Q.52) .. .. .. ➝ *Q.66* ▭ 1

Otherwise .. .. ➝ *Q.65* ▭ 2

65. ON WHICH DAYS DID .... WORK LAST WEEK (IN ALL JOBS)?

	MON *a*	TUES *b*	WED *c*	THU *d*	FRI *e*	SAT *f*	SUN *g*
Yes	▭ 1	▭ 1	▭ 1	▭ 1	▭ 1	▭ 1	▭ 1
No	▭ 2	▭ 2	▭ 2	▭ 2	▭ 2	▭ 2	▭ 2

66. HOW MANY HOURS A WEEK DOES ....USUALLY WORK IN (ALL) .... JOB(S)?

Hours .. .. ..

Less than one hour/ no hours .. .. ➝ *Q.68* ▭ 99

```
:0: :0:
:1: :1:
:2: :2:
:3: :3:
:4: :4:
:5: :5:
:6: :6:
:7: :7:
:8: :8:
:9: :9:
```

67. ➝ *Q.77*

68. AT ANY TIME DURING THE LAST 4 WEEKS HAS .... BEEN LOOKING FOR FULL-TIME WORK?

Yes .. .. ➝ *Q.70* ▭ 1

No .. .. ▭ 2

281

7

69. AT ANY TIME DURING THE LAST 4 WEEKS HAS .... BEEN LOOKING FOR PART-TIME WORK?

Yes .. .. ▭ 1

No .. .. → Q.75 ▭ 2

70. AT ANY TIME IN THE LAST 4 WEEKS HAS ....

WRITTEN, PHONED OR APPLIED IN PERSON TO AN EMPLOYER FOR WORK? .. .. ▭ 01

ANSWERED A NEWSPAPER ADVERTISEMENT FOR A JOB? ▭ 02

LOOKED IN NEWSPAPERS?

Yes .. .. .. ▭

No .. .. ▭

CHECKED FACTORY OR COMMONWEALTH EMPLOYMENT SERVICE NOTICE BOARDS? .. .. ▭ 03

AT ANY TIME IN THE LAST 4 WEEKS HAS .....

BEEN REGISTERED WITH THE COMMONWEALTH EMPLOYMENT SERVICE? .. ... ▭ 04

CHECKED OR REGISTERED WITH ANY OTHER EMPLOYMENT AGENCY? .. .. ▭ 05

DONE ANYTHING ELSE TO FIND A JOB?

Advertised or tendered for work ▭ 06

Contacted friends/relatives ... ▭ 07

Other (Specify)
.... → Q.76B ▭ 08

Only looked in newspapers
.. .. → Q.76B ▭ 09

None of these .. .. → Q.76B ▭ 10

71. IF .... HAD FOUND A JOB COULD .... HAVE STARTED WORK LAST WEEK?

Yes.. .. .. ▭ 1

No .. .. → Q.77 ▭ 2

Don't know .. .. ▭ 3

72. WHEN DID .... BEGIN LOOKING FOR WORK?

Enter date ....

Less than 2 weeks.. .. ▭ 001

No. of weeks .. .. [ ]

73. HOW LONG AGO IS IT SINCE .... LAST WORKED FULL-TIME FOR TWO WEEKS OR MORE?

Enter date ....

Under 2 years (no. of weeks) .. .. ., [ ]

2 years or more ▭ 104

Never worked full-time for 2 weeks or more but has worked ▭ 998

Has never worked ▭ 999

74. → Q.77

75. EVEN THOUGH .... IS NOT LOOKING FOR WORK, WOULD .... LIKE A JOB?

Yes .. .. → Q.76A ▭ 1

Maybe, it depends .. → Q.76A ▭ 2

No .. .. → Q.77 ▭ 3

Don't know .. .. .. → Q.77 ▭ 4

SAMPLE COPY

282

WHAT ARE ALL THE REASONS .... IS NOT
LOOKING FOR WORK NOW?

WHAT ARE ALL THE REASONS .... HAS NOT
TAKEN ANY OTHER STEPS TO FIND WORK?

Has a job to go to	a	☐ 01

Personal reasons
Own ill health or disability ..	b	☐ 02
Pregnancy	c	☐ 03
Studying/returning to studies	d	☐ 04
Does not need to work	e	☐ 05
Give others a chance	f	☐ 06
Welfare payments/ pension may be affected ..	g	☐ 07
Moved house/holidays	h	☐ 08

Family reasons
Child care	i	☐ 09
Ill health of other than self ..	j	☐ 10
Other family considerations ..	k	☐ 11

Training Program
On a job-related training program	l	☐ 12

Believes no work available or couldn't find work because:
Employers think too young or too old	m	☐ 13
Lacks necessary schooling, training, skills or experience	n	☐ 14
Difficulties with language or ethnic background	o	☐ 15
No jobs - in locality/line of work	p	☐ 16
- in suitable hours	q	☐ 17
- at all	r	☐ 18
Other (Specify)		
....		
....	s	☐ 19
Don't know	t	☐ 20

---

77. *Interviewer*: Show GREEN Prompt Card D

CURRENTLY, WHAT IS .... MAIN ACTIVITY?

Working	☐ 01
Looking for work	☐ 02
Working in unpaid voluntary job..	☐ 03
Home duties	☐ 04
Child care	☐ 05
Studying	☐ 06
Retired	☐ 07
Voluntarily inactive	☐ 08
Own illness/injury	☐ 09
Own disability/handicap	☐ 10
Looking after ill/disabled/aged person..	☐ 11
Other (Specify).....................	☐ 12

78. THE NEXT FEW QUESTIONS ARE ABOUT VARIOUS SOURCES OF INCOME.

79. *Interviewer*: Show WHITE Prompt Card E

IN THE 1995-96 FINANCIAL YEAR DID .... RECEIVE INCOME FROM ANY OF THESE SOURCES?

Yes	☐ 1
No .. .. → Q.84	☐ 2

80. WHICH ONES?

Profit or loss from own business (excluding limited liability company(s) or share in a partnership)	a	☐ 1
Profit or loss from rental investment properties	b	☐ 2
Dividends	c	☐ 3
Interest	d	☐ 4

81. BEFORE TAX IS TAKEN OUT (BUT AFTER BUSINESS EXPENSES HAVE BEEN DEDUCTED), HOW MUCH DID .... RECEIVE FROM (THIS/THESE) SOURCE(S) IN THE 1995-96 FINANCIAL YEAR?

$

a [ ][ ][ ][ ][ ][ ]

Interviewer:
If respondent reports a loss mark the "loss" box and record the amount.

Don't know ▭ 999998

➔ *Q.83*

b Loss ▭ 1

82. ➔ *Q.84*

83. *Interviewer: Show PINK Prompt Card F*

BEFORE TAX IS TAKEN OUT (BUT AFTER BUSINESS EXPENSES HAVE BEEN DEDUCTED), IN WHICH OF THESE GROUPS WAS .... INCOME FROM (THIS/THESE) SOURCE(S) IN THE 1995-96 FINANCIAL YEAR?

Interviewer: If respondent reports a loss mark the "loss" box and record the appropriate category.

a Group Number [ ][ ]

Don't know ▭ 98

b Loss ▭ 1

84. *Interviewer: Show BLUE Prompt Card G*

DOES .... CURRENTLY RECEIVE INCOME FROM ANY OF THESE SOURCES?

Yes .... ▭ 1

No .... ➔ *Q.89* ▭ 2

---

85. WHICH ONES?

A wage or salary from an employer .... a	▭	1
A wage or salary from own limited liability company .... b	▭	2
Family Payment c	▭	3
Any other Government pension or allowance .... d	▭	4
Child support / Maintenance ..... e	▭	5
Superannuation / Annuity .... f	▭	6
Worker's Compensation / Accident or Sickness Insurance .... g	▭	7
Any other regular income ...... h	▭	8

86. BEFORE TAX IS TAKEN OUT, HOW MUCH DOES .... USUALLY RECEIVE FROM (THIS/THESE) SOURCE(S) IN TOTAL?

WHAT PERIOD DOES THAT COVER?

$ b

a [ ][ ][ ][ ][ ][ ]   Weeks [ ][ ] 1

Months [ ][ ] 2

Don't know ▭ 999998

➔ *Q.88*

87. ➔ *Q.89*

88. *Interviewer: Show PINK Prompt Card F*

BEFORE TAX IS TAKEN OUT, IN WHICH OF THESE GROUPS IS .... USUAL INCOME FROM (THIS/THESE) SOURCE(S) IN TOTAL?

Group Number [ ][ ]

Don't know ▭ 98

89. *Sequence Guide*

. If more than one income source reported (see Q.80 & Q.85)
.... ➔ *Q.90* ▭ 1

. Otherwise ... ... ➔ *Q.91* ▭ 2

WHAT IS .... MAIN SOURCE OF INCOME?

Profit or loss from own business or share in a partnership (excluding limited liability company(s)) ... ... ☐ 01

Profit or loss from rental investment properties ... ... ☐ 02

Dividends ... ... ☐ 03

Interest ... ... ☐ 04

A wage or salary from an employer ... ... ☐ 05

A wage or salary from own limited liability company ... ... ☐ 06

Family Payment ... ... ☐ 07

Any other Government pension or allowance ... ... ☐ 08

Child Support / Maintenance ... ... ☐ 09

Superannuation / Annuity ... ... ☐ 10

Worker's Compensation / Accident or Sickness Insurance ... ... ☐ 11

Any other regular income ... ... ☐ 12

Sequence Guide

. If receives Government pension/ allowance (Code '4' in Q.85) ... ... → Q.92 ☐ 1

. Otherwise ... ... → Q.94 ☐ 2

Interviewer: Show YELLOW Prompt Card H

DOES .... CURRENTLY RECEIVE ANY OF THESE PENSIONS OR BENEFITS?

Age pension ... ... ☐ 01

Service pension (DVA) ... ... ☐ 02

Disability Support pension / (Invalid pension) (DSS) ... ... ☐ 03

Widow allowance (DSS) ... ... ☐ 04

Wife pension ... ... ☐ 05

Carer pension ... ... ☐ 06

Sole Parent pension ... ... ☐ 07

Sickness allowance / Sickness benefit ... ... ☐ 08

Newstart allowance / Job Search allowance / Mature Age allowance/ Youth Training allowance ... ... ☐ 09

Special benefit ... ... ☐ 10

Partner allowance ... ... ☐ 11

None of these ... ... ☐ 12

93. *Interviewer:* Show GREEN Prompt Card I

DOES .... CURRENTLY RECEIVE ANY OF THESE?

Austudy / Abstudy ... ... *a* ☐ 1

Disability pension (DVA) ... ... *b* ☐ 2

War Widow's pension (DVA) ... ... *c* ☐ 3

Child Disability allowance ... ... *d* ☐ 4

Parenting allowance ... ... *e* ☐ 5

Overseas pension or benefit ... ... *f* ☐ 6

Other pension / benefit ... ... *g* ☐ 7

None of these ... ... *h* ☐ 8

94. *Sequence Guide*

. If respondent is responsible for child(ren) less than 12 (see HH) ... ... → Q.95 ☐ 1

. Otherwise ... ... → Q.112 ☐ 2

95. *Sequence Guide*

. If questionnaire of first parent/ guardian of those children ... ... → Q.96 ☐ 1

. Otherwise ... ... → Q.112 ☐ 2

96. *Interviewer:* Show WHITE Prompt Card J

IS/ARE ANY OF) ..... CHILD(REN) AGED LESS THAN 12 YEARS USUALLY CARED FOR AT ANY OF THESE PLACES?

Yes ... ... ☐ 1

No ... ... → Q.103 ☐ 2

Don't know ... ... → Q.103 ☐ 3

97. *Interviewer:* Show WHITE Prompt Card J

WHICH ONE(S)?

Before and After School Care ... *a* ☐ 1

Long Day Care Centres ... ... *b* ☐ 2

Family Day Care ... ... *c* ☐ 3

Pre-School ... ... *d* ☐ 4

Occasional Care ... ... *e* ☐ 5

Other (*Specify*) ... ... *f* ☐ 6

98. DO THEY USUALLY ATTEND EACH WEEK?

Yes ... ... ☐ 1

No ... ... → Q.103 ☐ 2

99. *Sequence Guide*

. If respondent responsible for only one child aged less than 12 years (see HF) .. .. ➤ *Q.101* ☐ 1

. Otherwise .. .. ➤ *Q.100* ☐ 2

---

100. WHICH CHILD USUALLY ATTENDS FOR THE MOST NUMBER OF HOURS A WEEK?

Child's Name:

....

---

101. *Interviewer:* Show WHITE Prompt Card J

HOW MANY DAYS EACH WEEK DOES (specify child from Q.100/ ..... CHILD AGED LESS THAN 12 YEARS) USUALLY ATTEND THESE PLACES?

Days .. .. ☐
1
2
3
4
5
6
7

---

102. HOW MANY HOURS A WEEK IN TOTAL DOES (specify child from Q.100/ ..... CHILD AGED LESS THAN 12 YEARS) USUALLY ATTEND THESE PLACES?

Hours .. .. ☐
0 9
1
2
3
4
5
6
7
8

---

103. *Interviewer:* Show PINK Prompt Card K

(IS/ARE ANY OF) ..... CHILD(REN) AGED LESS THAN 12 YEARS USUALLY CARED FOR BY ANY OF THESE PEOPLE?

Yes .. .. ☐ 1

No .. .. ➤ *Q.111* ☐ 2

Don't know .. .. .. ➤ *Q.111* ☐ 3

---

104. *Interviewer:* Show PINK Prompt Card K

WHICH PEOPLE?

Child's (step) brother / (step) sister .. .. a ☐ 1

Child's grandparents .. .. b ☐ 2

Child's other relative .. .. .. c ☐ 3

Other people .. .. d ☐ 4

Other organisation .. .. .. e ☐ 5

Child looks after self .. .. .. f ☐ 6

---

105. *Sequence Guide*

. If any of codes 1-4 marked in Q.104 .. .. ➤ *Q.106* ☐ 1

. Otherwise ... . ➤ *Q.111* ☐ 2

---

106. ARE THEY USUALLY LOOKED AFTER EACH WEEK?

Yes .. .. ☐ 1

No .. .. ➤ *Q.111* ☐ 2

---

107. *Sequence Guide*

. If respondent responsible for only one child aged less than 12 years (see HF).. .. .. ➤ *Q.109* ☐ 1

. Otherwise ... . ➤ *Q.108* ☐ 2

---

108. WHICH CHILD IS USUALLY LOOKED AFTER FOR THE MOST NUMBER OF HOURS A WEEK?

Child's Name:

....

---

109. *Interviewer:* Show PINK Prompt Card K

HOW MANY DAYS EACH WEEK IS (specify child from Q.108/ ..... CHILD AGED LESS THAN 12 YEARS) USUALLY LOOKED AFTER BY THESE PEOPLE?

Days .. .. ☐
1
2
3
4
5
6
7

---

110. HOW MANY HOURS A WEEK IN TOTAL IS (specify child from Q.108/ ..... CHILD AGED LESS THAN 12 YEARS) USUALLY LOOKED AFTER BY THESE PEOPLE?

Hours .. .. ☐☐
0 0
1 1
2 2
3 3
4 4
5 5
6 6
7
8
9

---

111. CAN ..... ARRANGE CHILD CARE AT SHORT NOTICE FOR EMPLOYMENT OR LEISURE REASONS?

Yes .. .. ☐ 1

No .. .. ☐ 2

Sometimes / usually .. .. ☐ 3

ABILITY   12

2. I WOULD NOW LIKE TO ASK ABOUT ANY CONDITIONS THAT .... MAY HAVE THAT HAVE LASTED, OR ARE LIKELY TO LAST FOR SIX MONTHS OR MORE.

3. *Interviewer:* Show BLUE Prompt Card L

DOES .... HAVE ANY OF THESE CONDITIONS?

Sight problems not corrected by glasses or contact lenses	*a*	☐	01
Hearing problems	*b*	☐	02
Speech problems	*c*	☐	03
Blackouts, fits or loss of consciousness	*d*	☐	04
Slow at learning or understanding things	*e*	☐	05
Limited use of arms or fingers	*f*	☐	06
Difficulty gripping things	*g*	☐	07
Limited use of feet or legs	*h*	☐	08
Nerves or emotional conditions which require treatment	*i*	☐	09
Any condition that restricts physical activity or physical work (eg back problems, arthritis)	*j*	☐	10
Any disfigurement or deformity	*k*	☐	11
Any mental illness which requires help or supervision	*l*	☐	12
Long term effects as a result of a head injury, stroke or other brain damage	*m*	☐	13
Treatment or medication for a long-term condition or ailment and is still restricted by that condition	*n*	☐	14
Any other long-term condition such as asthma, heart disease, Alzheimer's disease, dementia etc. which is restricting	*o*	☐	15
None of these .. → *Q.121*	*p*	☐	16

114. *Interviewer:* Show YELLOW Prompt Card M

BECAUSE OF THE CONDITION(S) YOU HAVE TOLD ME ABOUT, DOES .... <u>EVER</u> NEED <u>HELP OR SUPERVISION</u> WITH ANY OF THESE TASKS?

Personal care

Bathing / showering .. .. *a*	☐	1
Dressing or undressing	*b*	☐	2
Eating or feeding	*c*	☐	3
Using the toilet	*d*	☐	4
Bladder / bowel control ..	*e*	☐	5

Mobility

Moving around at home	*f*	☐	6
Moving around away from home	*g*	☐	7
Understanding / being understood in own language	*h*	☐	8
No .. .. → *Q.116*	*i*	☐	9

115. → *Q.118*

116. *Interviewer:* Show YELLOW Prompt Card M

BECAUSE OF THE CONDITION(S) YOU HAVE TOLD ME ABOUT, DOES .... <u>EVER</u> HAVE <u>DIFFICULTY</u> WITH ANY OF THESE TASKS?

Personal care

Bathing / showering .. .. *a*	☐	1
Dressing or undressing	*b*	☐	2
Eating or feeding	*c*	☐	3
Using the toilet	*d*	☐	4
Bladder / bowel control ..	*e*	☐	5

Mobility

Moving around at home	*f*	☐	6
Moving around away from home	*g*	☐	7
Understanding / being understood in own language	*h*	☐	8
No	*i*	☐	9

117. → *Q.121*

118. *Sequence Guide*

. If respondent lives alone → Q.121   ▭ 1

. Otherwise .... → Q.119   ▭ 2

---

119. IS THIS ASSISTANCE MAINLY PROVIDED BY SOMEONE IN THIS HOUSEHOLD?

Yes ....   ▭ 1

No .... → Q.121   ▭ 2

Does not receive assistance
.... → Q.121   ▭ 3

---

120. WHO IS THE MAIN PROVIDER OF THAT ASSISTANCE?

Person Number   ▭▭   0:0
1:1
2:2
3:3
4:4
5:5
6:6
7:7
8:8
9:9

---

121. *Sequence Guide*

. If respondent has a condition (see Q.113) .... → Q.122   ▭ 1

. If respondent aged 60 years or more (see Q.3) .... → Q.122   ▭ 2

. Otherwise .... → Q.123   ▭ 3

---

122. *Interviewer: Show GREEN Prompt Card N*

BECAUSE OF .... (CONDITION/AGE), DOES .... RECEIVE ASSISTANCE WITH ANY OF THE FOLLOWING TASKS?

Meal preparation .... a   ▭ 1

Laundry / linen .... b   ▭ 2

Light housework c   ▭ 3

Heavy housework .... d   ▭ 4

Home maintenance .... e   ▭ 5

Gardening / mowing .... f   ▭ 6

Transport .... g   ▭ 7

None of the above .... h   ▭ 8

---

123. THE FOLLOWING QUESTIONS ARE ABOUT HELP GIVEN TO PEOPLE LIVING SOMEWHERE ELSE.

---

124. *Interviewer: Show WHITE Prompt Card O*

DOES .... PROVIDE HELP WITH ANY OF THESE TASKS TO ANYONE LIVING OUTSIDE THIS HOUSEHOLD ON A REGULAR UNPAID BASIS?

Personal care .... a ▭ 01

Mobility .... b ▭ 02

Verbal communication .... c ▭ 03

Health care .... d ▭ 04

Home help .... e ▭ 05

Home maintenance .... f ▭ 06

Meals .... g ▭ 07

Personal affairs / supervising money matters .... h ▭ 08

Teaching everyday living skills (physical or mental) .... i ▭ 09

Transport .... j ▭ 10

None of these.. → Q.128 k ▭ 11

---

125. WHAT IS .... RELATIONSHIP TO THE PERSON .... HELPS (THE MOST)?

Spouse / de facto .... ▭ 1

Parent .... ▭ 2

Child .... ▭ 3

Grandparent .... ▭ 4

Grandchild .... ▭ 5

Brother / sister .... ▭ 6

Other family member .... ▭ 7

Non-family member .... ▭ 8

---

126. WHAT IS THE MAIN REASON .... PROVIDES HELP WITH THESE TASKS?

Long-term illness / disability .... ▭ 1

Old age .... ▭ 2

Other .... ▭ 3

IS .... THE MAIN PROVIDER OF HELP TO THAT PERSON?

Yes .... ☐ 1

No .... ☐ 2

Sequence Guide

. If first person interviewed in household .... → Q.129 ☐ 1

. Otherwise ... **no more questions** ◄ ☐ 2

Sequence Guide

. If any child(ren) under 15 years on HF .... → Q.130 ☐ 1

. Otherwise .... → Q.135 ☐ 2

Interviewer: Show BLUE Prompt Card L

DOES ANY CHILD UNDER 15 LIVING HERE HAVE ANY OF THESE CONDITIONS?

Yes .... ☐ 1

No .... → Q.135 ☐ 2

(HAS THIS/HAVE ANY OF THESE) CONDITION(S) LASTED, OR (IS IT/ARE THEY) LIKELY TO LAST 6 MONTHS OR MORE?

Yes .... ☐ 1

No .... → Q.135 ☐ 2

Interviewer: Show YELLOW Prompt Card M

(DOES THIS CHILD/DO THESE CHILDREN) RECEIVE MORE THAN USUAL ASSISTANCE WITH ANY OF THESE TASKS?

Yes .... ☐ 1

No .... → Q.135 ☐ 2

IS THIS ASSISTANCE PROVIDED BY ANYONE IN THE HOUSEHOLD?

Yes .... ☐ 1

No .... → Q.135 ☐ 2

WHO IS THE MAIN PROVIDER OF THAT ASSISTANCE?

Person Number ☐

135. THE FOLLOWING QUESTIONS ARE ABOUT ITEMS IN THIS HOUSEHOLD THAT AFFECT THE WAY PEOPLE SPEND THEIR TIME.

HOW MANY OF THE FOLLOWING ITEMS ARE THERE IN THIS HOUSEHOLD:-

a TELEVISIONS?

None .... ☐ 1
One .... ☐ 2
Two .... ☐ 3
Three or more .... ☐ 4

b MOTOR VEHICLES?

None .... ☐ 1
One .... ☐ 2
Two .... ☐ 3
Three or more .... ☐ 4

136. *Sequence Guide*

. If no televisions (Code '1' in Q.135a) .... → Q.138 ☐ 1

. Otherwise .... → Q.137 ☐ 2

137. ARE THERE ANY OF THE FOLLOWING ITEMS IN THIS HOUSEHOLD:-

PAY TV SUBSCRIPTIONS?
Yes .... ☐ 1
No .... ☐ 2

VIDEO CASSETTE PLAYERS / RECORDERS?
Yes .... ☐ 1
No .... ☐ 2

138. (ARE THERE ANY OF THE FOLLOWING ITEMS IN THIS HOUSEHOLD:-)

MICROWAVE OVENS?
Yes .... ☐ 1
No .... ☐ 2

DISHWASHERS?
Yes .... ☐ 1
No .... ☐ 2

289

c CLOTHES DRYERS?

    Yes ... ... ▭ 1

    No ... ... ▭ 2

d DEEP FREEZERS?

    Yes ... ... ▭ 1

    No ... ... ▭ 2

e ANSWERING MACHINES?

    Yes ... ... ▭ 1

    No ... ... ▭ 2

f FAX MACHINES?

    Yes ... ... ▭ 1

    No ... ... ▭ 2

g PERSONAL COMPUTERS?

    Yes ... ... ▭ 1

    No ... ... → Q.140 ▭ 2

139. (ARE THERE ANY OF THE FOLLOWING ITEMS IN THIS HOUSEHOLD:-)

    MODEMS?

    Yes ... ... ▭ 1

    No ... ... ▭ 2

140. (ARE THERE ANY OF THE FOLLOWING ITEMS IN THIS HOUSEHOLD:-)

    LAWNMOWERS OR WHIPPER-SNIPPERS?

    Yes ... ... ▭ 1

    No ... ... ▭ 2

141. I WOULD NOW LIKE TO ASK SOME QUESTIONS ABOUT THE USE OF TIME SAVING SERVICES.

IN THE LAST TWO WEEKS, HAS ANYONE IN THIS HOUSEHOLD USED ANY OF THE FOLLOWING SERVICES:-

a A DRY CLEANING, IRONING OR LAUNDRY SERVICE?

    Yes ... ... ▭ 1

    No ... ... ▭ 2

b A CLEANER OR SOMEONE TO DO THE HOUSEWORK?

    Yes ... ... ▭ 1

    No ... ... ▭ 2

c A GARDEN MAINTENANCE, LAWN MOWING, PRUNING OR RUBBISH REMOVAL SERVICE?

    Yes ... ... ▭ 1

    No ... ... ▭ 2

142. *Sequence Guide*

If code '1' in Q.141a, b, OR c ... ... → Q.143 ▭ 1

Otherwise ... ... → Q.145 ▭ 2

143. HAS ANYONE WHO LIVES OUTSIDE THIS HOUSEHOLD PAID FOR (THIS/THESE) SERVICE(S)?

    Yes ... ... → Q.145 ▭ 1

    No ... ... ▭ 2

144. WILL ANYONE WHO LIVES OUTSIDE THIS HOUSEHOLD PAY FOR (THIS/THESE) SERVICE(S)?

    Yes ... ... ▭ 1

    No ... ... ▭ 2

16

. I WOULD NOW LIKE TO ASK YOU ABOUT MEALS PURCHASED IN THE LAST TWO WEEKS. HOW MANY TIMES HAS ANYONE IN THIS HOUSEHOLD:-

a   BOUGHT TAKE-AWAY FOOD OR HAD FOOD DELIVERED FOR BREAKFAST, LUNCH OR DINNER?

Number (1-14) .. .. .. ☐☐

15 or more .. .. ☐ 15

Don't Know .. .. .. ☐ 98

Nil .. .. ☐ 99

b   BOUGHT BREAKFAST, LUNCH OR DINNER AT A RESTAURANT, CAFETERIA, CLUB OR FOOD COURT?

Number (1-14) .. .. .. ☐☐

15 or more .. .. ☐ 15

Don't Know .. .. .. ☐ 98

Nil .. .. ☐ 99

Interviewer: Code best description of structure containing household.

Separate house .. .. ☐ 01

Semi-detached/row or terrace house/town house
  - One storey .. .. ☐ 02

  - Two or more storeys .. .. ☐ 03

Flat attached to house .. .. ☐ 04

Other flat/unit/apartment
  - One or two storeys .. .. ☐ 05

  - Three storeys .. .. ☐ 06

  - Four or more storeys .. .. .. ☐ 07

Caravan/tent/cabin in a caravan park, houseboat in a marina, etc. ☐ 08

Caravan not in a caravan park, houseboat, etc. .. .. ☐ 09

Improvised home/campers out .. ☐ 10

House or flat attached to shop, office, etc. .. .. ☐ 11

No more questions ◀

Illustration 4. Excerpts from the computer assisted telephone interviewing (CATI) instrument for the Canadian 1998 Time Use Survey

Time Use
General Social Survey, Cycle 12

Confidential when completed. Collected under the authority of the Statistics Act, Revised Statutes of Canada, 1985, Chapter S19. STC/HFS-027-75095

INTRODUCTION

Date / Time stamp

INTRO_1   INTERVIEWER:

Repeat the introduction below if selected respondent is different from household respondent.

Hello, I'm..........from Statistics Canada. We are calling you for a study on the way Canadians spend their time.

All information we collect in this voluntary survey will be kept strictly confidential. Your participation is essential if the survey results are to be accurate.

(The next paragraph should be optional.)

My supervisor is working with me today and may listen to the interview to evaluate the survey.

MARSTAT Is {household member x}'s marital status .....

<1>   Living common-law?
<2>   Married?
<3>   Widowed?
<4>   Divorced?
<5>   Separated?
<6>   Single (never married)?

[CATI]:   If household roster members = 1, then [Go to INTRO_5Y], else do until all household roster members are completed, then [Go to INTRO_2]

[CATI]:   If age of household member is less than 15 years of age, then MARSTAT = 6 (Single, never married)

Page 1

Source: Statistics Canada (1998a)

292

INTRO_2 What is {household member x}'s relationship to {household member y}?

<2>   Husband/wife/spouse
<3>   Common-law partner
<4>   Son or daughter [Go to INTRO_3]
<10>   Father or mother [Go to INTRO_4]
<15>   Brother or sister
<20>   Grandchild
<21>   Grandfather or grandmother
<30>   Son-in-law or daughter-in-law
<31>   Father-in-law or mother-in-law
<32>   Brother-in-law or sister-in-law
<40>   Nephew or niece
<41>   Uncle or aunt
<42>   Cousin
<50>   Other relative
<60>   Non-relative
<70>   Same sex partner

[CATI]:   If value of y for {household member y} = total amount of household members and x = (y - 1), then [Go to INTRO_5Y], else return and select next member of roster.

INTRO_3 Is {household member x} the birth or step-child of {household member y}?

<5>   Birth child
<6>   Adopted child
<7>   Step-child
<8>   Foster child

[CATI]:   If value of y for {household member y} = total amount of household members and x = (y - 1), then [Go to INTRO_5Y], else return and select next member of roster.

INTRO_4 Is {household member x} the birth or step-father/mother of {household member y}?

<11>   Birth parent
<12>   Adoptive parent
<13>   Step parent
<14>   Foster parent

[CATI]:   If value of y for {household member y} = total amount of household members and x = (y - 1), then [Go to INTRO_5Y], else return and select next member of roster.

INTRO_5Y What is your year of birth? (year)

<1890-1982>

INTRO_5M   What is your month of birth? (month)

<01-12>

INTRO_5D What is your day of birth? (day)

<01-31>

[CATI - INTRO_6]: [Go to A0]

Section A: General Questions

A0   Date / Time stamp

A1   **I will start with a few general questions related to time.**

A2   **How often do you feel rushed? Would you say it is....**
Include times when being pressed for time was a positive stimulant as well as times the respondent felt stress because of the number of activities he/she had to do in a day.

<1>   **Every day?**
<2>   **A few times a week?**
<3>   **About once a week?**
<4>   **About once a month?**
<5>   **Less than once a month?**
<6>   Never?
<r>   Refused

A3   **Compared to five years ago, do you feel more rushed, about the same or less rushed?**

<1>   More rushed
<2>   About the same
<3>   Less rushed
<x>   Don't know
<r>   Refused

A4   **How often do you feel you have time on your hands that you don't know what to do with? Would you say it is....**
Exclude:
- times when the respondent chooses to do nothing;
- times when the respondent had to think for a few minutes about what to do next.

        Select •never• if the respondent can always think of something to do.
<1>   **Every day?**
<2>   **A few times a week?**
<3>   **About once a week?**
<4>   **About once a month?**
<5>   **Less than once a month?**
<6>   Never?
<r>   Refused

A5   **Do you feel that weekdays are just too short to do all the things you want ?**

<1>   Yes
<3>   No   Go to B0
<x>   Don't know   Go to B0
<r>   Refused   Go to B0

A6   **On which main activity would you choose to spend more time if you could?** (Only one
            activity)

<1>   Time with family (spouse, children, boy-friend - girl-friend)
<2>   Relaxation - personal time
<3>   Practising sports
<4>   Crafts or hobbies
<5>   Outdoor activities
<6>   Reading - writing
<7>   Studies
<8>   Work
<9>   Other   Go to A6S
<x>   Don't know
<r>   Refused

A6S   Specify <50 characters>

Section B: Time Use Diary

B0   Date / Time stamp

B1   We need accurate information on the way people use their time and the best way is to complete a diary listing of all of your activities over a 24-hour period. We start our diary at 4:00 in the morning because most of the people are asleep at that time.

Let me give you an example:

[CATI-B2]:   If RCHD = 1 and RSEX = 1 and RSPO = 1, then go to Example 2B
If RCHD = 1 and RSEX = 1 and RSPO = 1 and INTRO_2=70, then go to Example 2A
If RCHD = 1 and RSEX = 2 and RSPO = 1, then go to Example 2A
If RCHD = 1 and RSEX = 2 and RSPO = 1 and INTRO_2=70, then go to Example 2B
If RSPO = 1, then go to Example 1
Otherwise go to Example 3

B2a   EXAMPLE 1: (Respondent living with spouse with no children)
Yesterday morning I was asleep until 6:00. From 6:00 to 6:15 I got dressed. Then from 6:15 until 6:25 I made breakfast. From 6:25 to 6:35 I ate breakfast with my spouse.

B2b   EXAMPLE 2A: (Female respondent with spouse and children)
Yesterday morning I was asleep until 7:15. From 7:15 to 7:30 I got dressed. Then from 7:30 to 7:45 I made breakfast. Then I ate breakfast with my spouse and children until 8:10.

B2c   EXAMPLE 2B: (Male respondent with spouse and children)
Yesterday morning I was asleep until 7:15. From 7:15 to 7:30 I got dressed. Then from 7:30 to 7:45 I made breakfast. Then I ate breakfast with my spouse and children until 8:10.

B2d   EXAMPLE 3: (Person living alone or other situation)
Yesterday morning I was asleep until 8:30. From 8:30 to 8:40 I had a shower and got dressed. Then from 8:40 until 8:55, I made breakfast.

B3   **In this survey, you do not need to report activities of less than 5 minutes duration unless it involves travel or a change in who you are with.**
Let's begin.

Information to capture for each episode:

part a)
[CATI- if first activity - **On** - print designated day **at 4:00 a.m. what were you doing?**

or - if not first activity- **And then, what did you do?**]

[CATI: Use screen specified in Appendix D to capture the description of the activity]

[CATI: If first activity code = 450 then go to Exception 1 , otherwise go to (b)]

Exception 1

##ax   **What time did you fall asleep[reference day-1] night?**
     This question is asked in order to measure the amount of sleep on a given night. This would
     otherwise be missed as the designated day begins only at 4:00 a.m.
     <00:00-23:59>

##a1   Check 1:   00 •   first two numbers   •   23 et
                 00 •   last two numbers   •   59

     <x>   Don't know
     <r>   Refused

     [CATI- if first activity, impute b=0400] or
##b   **When did you start?**

     <00:00-23:59>

##b1   Check 1

##c   **When did this end?**

     <00:00-23:59>

##c1   Check 1
##c2   Check 2:   time in (c) • time in (b)
##c3   Checks 11
##c4   Checks 12
##c5   Checks 13
##c6   Checks 14
##c7   Checks 15

     [CATI - if c = 0400 and activity code= 450, then go to Exception 2, otherwise go to (d)]
     [CATI- if activity code = 001 or 002, then go to next episode]

Exception 2
##cx   **What time did you wake up ?**
     This question is asked in order to measure the amount of sleep on a given night. This would
     otherwise be missed as the designated day ends only at 4:00 a.m.
     <00:00-23:59>
     <x>   Don't know
     <r>   Refused

##c8   Check 1

     <x>   Don't know

<r>   Refused

##d   **Where were you? / Were you still...** (Accept only one answer)
PLACE
<1>   respondent's home
<2>   work place
<3>   someone else's home
<4>   other place (include park, neighbourhood)

OR IN TRANSIT:
<5>   car (driver)
<6>   car (passenger)
<7>   walk
<8>   bus & subway (includes street cars, commuter trains or other public transit)
<9>   bicycle
<10>   other (for example, airplane, train, motorcycle)

##d1   Check 3
##d2   Checks 17
##d3   Checks 18

[CATI - if activity code = 400, 450, 460 or 480 then go to next episode, part a]

##e   **Who was with you?/ Were you still ...** (Mark all that apply)]

<11 variables of 1 character>
<u>Living in the household</u>
<1>   alone
<2>   spouse/partner
<3>   child(ren) less than 15 years old Go to ##eC
<4>   parent(s) or parent(s) in-law
<5>   other member(s) (include children of 15 and older)
<u>Living outside the household</u>
<6>   child(ren) of the respondent less than 15 years old
<7>   child(ren) of the respondent 15 or older
<8>   parent (s) or parent(s) in-law
<9>   other family member (s)
<10>   friend(s)
<11>   other person(s)
<x>   Don't know
<r>   Refused
<0>   to continue
<b>   make a correction......Go to ##eb

##e1   Check 4: alone cannot appear with another category
##e2   Check 5: <2> should be consistent with household members list
##e3   Check 16: respondent cannot be alone for these activities

##e4   Check 7:   <3> should be consistent with the presence of children in the household
               [CATI - Go to ##ex]

##eb   **What do you want to erase?**

           <u>Living in the household</u>
           <1>   alone
           <2>   spouse/partner
           <3>   child(ren) less than 15 years old   Go to ##eC
           <4>   parent(s) or parent(s) in-law
           <5>   other member(s) (include children of 15 and older)
           <u>Living outside the household</u>
           <6>   child(ren) of the respondent less than 15 years old
           <7>   child(ren) of the respondent 15 or older
           <8>   parent (s) or parent(s) in-law
           <9>   other family member (s)
           <10>   friend(s)
           <11>   other person(s)
           <99>   all
           < 0>   none or continue

##eC   **Which ones ?**

           [CATI - Bring display 1 (children of the household)]
           <13 variables with 2 characters>
           <95>   All children of the respondent
           < b>   make a correction......Go to ##eB
           < 0>   to continue

##eB   **What do you want to erase?**

           <13 variables with 2 characters>

           <95>   All children of the respondent
           <99>   all
           < 0>   none or continue

           [CATI- ##ex -   if activity code = 660, Go to ##h2
                            if activity code = 671 to 678, Go to ##g2]
           [CATI - if activity code is one of the codes redlined in Appendix C, then go to next episode, part a]

##f   Many of our daily activities help persons living outside our own household. The following question is asked to determine how much informal support people provide to one another.
           Did this activity help a person outside your household or an organization?

           <1>   Person   Go to ##g2
           <2>   Organization   Go to ##h2

<3>   No   (Go to next episode, part a)
<x>   Don't know   (Go to next episode, part a)
<r>   Refused   (Go to next episode, part a)

##g2   **Was the person helped 65 years or older?** (If more than one, principal person helped.)

<1>   Yes
<3>   No
<x>   Don't know
<r>   Refused

##g3   **Does the person you helped have a long-term health or physical limitation?**
(Any conditions lasting or expected to last more than 6 months and which can be either chronic or permanent)

<1>   Yes
<3>   No
<r>   Refused

##h1   **What is this person's relationship to you ?**

<1>   Parent(s) or parent (s) in-law
<2>   Children of respondent living outside the household
<3>   Other member(s) of the family outside the household.
<4>   Friend(s)
<5>   Neighbour (s)
<6>   Co-worker(s)
<7>   Others
<x>   Don't know
<r>   Refused

[CATI - Go to next episode, part a]

##h2   **Was this organization mostly concerned with seniors, children, persons with disabilities or other?**

<1>   Seniors
<2>   Children
<3>   Persons with disabilities
<4>   Other
<x>   Don't know
<r>   Refused

[CATI- Go to next episode, part a]

End of loop: [CATI - Once the list of activities has been collected, do checks 8 and 9]

B4   Date/Time Stamp

[CATI - If status of diary is partial or complete, then go to section C; otherwise go to L35]

Section C: Questions about the Designated Day

CO   Date / Time stamp

C1a   **Of the activities you just reported, which one did you enjoy the most?**

          [CATI - Display list of activities]

          <0-60> (record the episode number from B3)   (Go to CATI- C2)

          Check 20

          <00>   None   (Go to CATI - C2)
          <95>   All

C1Ba   **Is there one in particular that you enjoyed?**
          (Interviewer: Probe the respondent for the most enjoyable activity)

C1Bb   <0-60> (record the episode number from B3)

          <95>   All

CATI - C2 If respondent has children less than 15 years old living in the household (RC15= 1), then go to
          C3, otherwise go to section D.

C3   **Looking after children is an activity that places many demands on our time, but which is
          often missed by the kind of diary we've just completed because we often do something
          else at the same time such as preparing meals or watching TV.**

C4   **When did your child/children wake up on (designated day) ?** (Children less than 15)
          (Interviewer: Record the time of the child who woke up first.)

          <00:00-23:59>

C4e   Check 1

          <s>   Child did not sleep in household ..
          <x>   Don't know
          <r>   Refused

C5   **When did your child/children go to sleep on** [CATI - Interviewer: print designated day]?
          (Children less than 15)

          (Interviewer: Record the time of the child who went to sleep last)

          <00:00-23:59>
C5e1   Check 1

Illustration 5. 1997 Time Use Survey Time Diary, Australia

In Confidence

**Australian
Bureau of
Statistics**

1997 Time Use Survey

Workload	PSU	Block	Dwelling	Household	Person

Time Use Diary

Day 1: [   ]   [   ]

Day 2: [   ]   [   ]
            (Day)   (Date)

Purpose of collection

.... has been included in a survey being conducted by the Australian Bureau of Statistics (ABS) to understand how people spend their time.

Confidentiality

The answers you provide will be treated confidentially. The ABS is required by the Census and Statistics Act 1905 to maintain the secrecy of all information provided to it. No information will be released in a way that would enable an individual or household to be identified.

Help available

Please complete this diary for both nominated days. If you have problems with filling in this diary, please contact the ABS office on ( ) ....

Due date

An ABS interviewer, ..., will return on .... (date) at ....(time) to collect this diary.

W. McLennan
Australian Statistician

Source: Australian Bureau of Statistics. (1996c).

Please complete these questions before you start.

1 How often do you feel rushed or pressed for time?

Tick one only

Always..........................	☐ 1
Often.............................	☐ 2
Sometimes......................	☐ 3
Rarely............................	☐ ► 4 (Go to 3)
Never.............................	☐ ► 5 (Go to 3)

2 What are all the reasons you feel rushed?

Trying to balance work and family responsibilities...........	☐ 1
Pressure of work/study..............	☐ 2
Demands of family..................	☐ 3
Take too much on/not good at managing time..................	☐ 4
Too much to do/too many demands placed on you.........	☐ 5
Other (please specify)...............	☐ 6

```
..................................
..................................
```

3 How often do you feel you have spare time that you don't know what to do with?

Always.....................................	☐ 1
Often......................................	☐ 2
Sometimes................................	☐ 3
Rarely....................................	☐ ► 4 (Go to 3)
Never.....................................	☐ ► 5 (Go to 3)

4 What are all the reasons you have spare time that you don't know what to do with?

Don't have enough money.............	☐ 1
Sick/injured/disabled..................	☐ 2
No friends of family life near me.....	☐ 3
No interests or hobbies.................	☐ 4
Lack of community facilities or services (e.g., pool, library)...............	☐ 5
Other (please specify).................	☐ 6

```
..................................
..................................
```

5 Please read the instructions on page 1 and complete the diary for the days indicated on the front cover.

An example of how to complete the diary is on pages 2&3.

Day 1
6 am –9 am

	1 What was your main activity? (Please record all activities, even if they only lasted a few minutes)	2 Who did you do this for? (e.g., self, family, work, friend, a charity, the community)	3 What else were you doing at the same time? (e.g., childminding, watching television, listening to the radio)	4 Where were you? (e.g., at work, home, on a bus, driving the car)	5 Who was with you at home, or with you away from home? (e.g., no-one, family, friends)
6.00	Sleep	Self	Passive child care	Home	Family
6.05					
6.10					
6.15	↓				
6.20	Toilet				
	Had shower				
6.25					
6.30	↓				
	Got dressed	↓			
6.35	Put on a load of washing	Family			
6.40	Made breakfast		↓		
			Talked to family		
6.45		↓			
6.50	Ate breakfast	Self	Read newspaper		
6.55					
7.00					
7.05	↓	↓	↓		
	Hung washing on line	Family	Nothing		
7.10	↓				
7.15		↓			
	Dressed children	Children	Talked to children		
7.20					
7.25	↓	↓	↓		
	Brushed hair, teeth, etc.	Self	Nothing		
7.30					
7.35					
7.40	↓	↓	↓		
	Packed children's bags	Children	Said goodbye to partner	↓	↓
7.45	Drove children to my mother's house		Talked to children	Driving Car	2 Children
7.50					
7.55					
8.00					
	↓	↓	↓	↓	↓
8.05	Greeted my mother	Self	Organising children	Mother's	Children and
8.10	Said goodbye to children		Nothing	↓	mother
8.15	Drove to work		Listening to radio	Car	No-one
8.20					
8.25					
8.30	↓	↓	↓	↓	
	Parked car and walked to work		Nothing	Street	↓
8.35					
	Working	Work		Work	Workmates
8.40					
8.45					
8.50					
8.55					
9.00	↓	↓	↓	↓	↓

305

Day 1   6 pm –9 pm

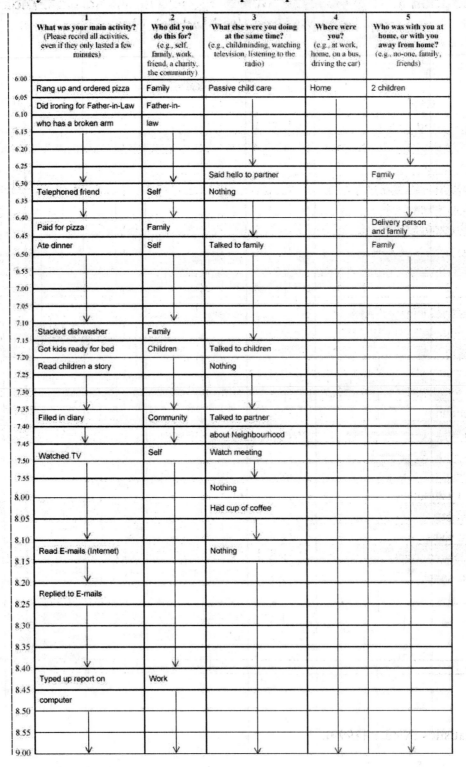

Time	1 What was your main activity? (Please record all activities, even if they only lasted a few minutes)	2 Who did you do this for? (e.g., self, family, work, friend, a charity, the community)	3 What else were you doing at the same time? (e.g., childminding, watching television, listening to the radio)	4 Where were you? (e.g., at work, home, on a bus, driving the car)	5 Who was with you at home, or with you away from home? (e.g., no-one, family, friends)
6.00	Rang up and ordered pizza	Family	Passive child care	Home	2 children
6.05	Did ironing for Father-in-Law	Father-in-			
6.10	who has a broken arm	law			
6.15					
6.20					
6.25			Said hello to partner		Family
6.30	Telephoned friend	Self	Nothing		
6.35					
6.40	Paid for pizza	Family			Delivery person and family
6.45	Ate dinner	Self	Talked to family		Family
6.50					
6.55					
7.00					
7.05					
7.10	Stacked dishwasher	Family			
7.15	Got kids ready for bed	Children	Talked to children		
7.20	Read children a story		Nothing		
7.25					
7.30					
7.35	Filled in diary	Community	Talked to partner		
7.40			about Neighbourhood		
7.45	Watched TV	Self	Watch meeting		
7.50					
7.55			Nothing		
8.00			Had cup of coffee		
8.05					
8.10	Read E-mails (Internet)		Nothing		
8.15					
8.20	Replied to E-mails				
8.25					
8.30					
8.35					
8.40	Typed up report on	Work			
8.45	computer				
8.50					
8.55					
9.00					

Illustration 6. 1999 Overall Monitoring of Annual National Indicators Survey (Time Use Module), Oman

Source: Statistics Sweden (1999).

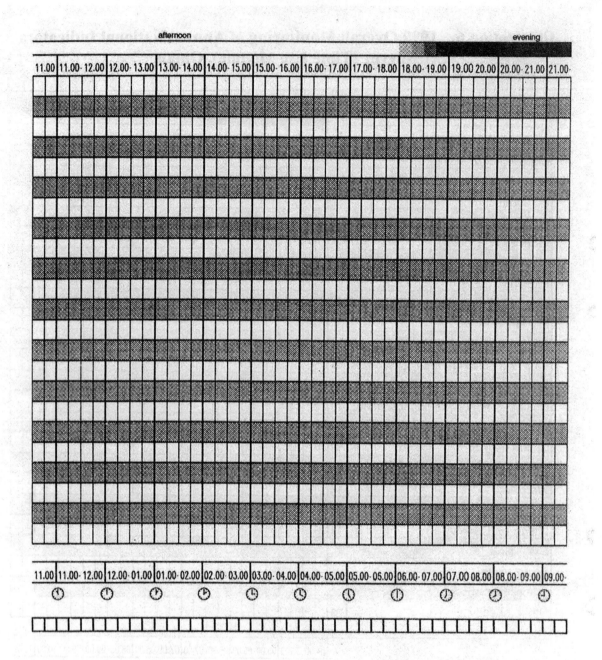

308

ANNEX 17. EXAMPLE OF A DATA QUALITY STATEMENT*

Statistics from the General Social Survey (GSS) databases are estimates based on data collected from a small fraction of the population (roughly one person in 2000) and are subject to error. The error can be divided into two components: sampling error and non-sampling error.

Sampling error is the difference between the estimate derived from a sample and the result that would have been obtained from a population census using the same data-collection procedures. For a sample survey such as the GSS, this error is estimated from the survey data. The measurement of error used is the standard deviation of the estimate. When a sampling error is more than 33 1/3 per cent of the estimate itself, it is considered to be too unreliable to be published. In such a case, the symbol "--" appears in statistical tables in place of the estimate. When the sampling error is between 16 2/3 and 33 1/3 per cent, the corresponding estimate is accompanied by the symbol "*" in a table. Such estimates should be used with caution. Finally, all estimates with a sampling error of less than 16 2/3 per cent can be used without restriction. All other types of errors, such as coverage, response, processing and non-response, are non-sampling errors. Many of these errors are difficult to identify and quantify.

Coverage errors arise when there are differences between the target population and the surveyed population. Households without telephones represent a part of the target population that was excluded from the surveyed population. To the extent that this excluded population differs from the rest of the target population, the estimates will be biased. Since these exclusions are small, one would expect the biases introduced to be small. However, since there are correlations between a number of questions asked on this survey and the groups excluded, the biases may be more significant than the small size of the groups would suggest.

Individuals residing in institutions were excluded from the surveyed population. The effect of this exclusion is greatest for people aged 65 years or over, for whom it approaches 9 per cent.

In a similar way, to the extent that the non-responding households and persons differ from the rest of the sample, the estimates will be biased. The overall response rate for the GSS was approximately 80 per cent.

Non-response could occur at several stages in this survey. There were two stages of information collection: at the household level and at the individual level. Non-response at the household level averaged 6 per cent. Non-response also occurs at the level of individual questions. For most questions, the response rate was high and, in tables, the non-responses generally appear under the heading "not stated".

While refusal to answer specific questions was very low, accuracy of recall and ability to answer some questions completely can be expected to affect some of the results presented in the subsequent chapters. Awareness of exact question wording will help the reader interpret the survey results.

Since the survey is cross-sectional, caution is required in making causal inferences about the association between variables. Observed associations may be a reflection of differences between cohorts, period effects, differences between age groups or a combination of these factors.

* *Source*: Statistics Canada (1998c).

ANNEX 18.   TECHNICAL NOTES ON MAJOR OUTPUTS FROM A TIME-USE SURVEY

Outputs from a statistical survey may be categorized in relation to the type of statistical data produced as microdata, macrodata and metadata.

Microdata: Microdata are data on the characteristics of units of a population, such as individuals or households. In time-use surveys utilizing time diaries and personal and household questionnaires, microdata files would consist of records for each person/diary containing: descriptions and/or codes of activity episodes and their corresponding characteristics such as beginning and ending times and context variables and derived variables such as duration, as well as the values of data items appearing in the personal and household questionnaires of the individual including demographic and economic characteristics.

Macrodata: Macrodata are derived from microdata by generating statistics on groups or aggregates, such as proportions, means, totals or frequencies specified by the tabulation plan and estimation procedures of the survey, or from tables produced on request to meet specific user requirements from the survey. Macrodata are the bases for the analyses and applications of survey data. Basic macrodata from time-use surveys include estimates of total time or mean time or proportion of time spent by type of activity or specified activity groups by sex and population subgroups and areas (see chap. X for detailed discussion of statistical measures from time-use surveys and recommended statistical tables.)

Metadata: Metadata are a special type of data intended to describe microdata, macrodata or other metadata. Statistical metadata may be classified according to sources and uses as follows: [a]

- *Definitional metadata*: information describing statistical units, populations, classifications, data elements, standard questions and question modules, collection instruments, and statistical terminology.
- *Procedural metadata*: information describing the procedures by which data are collected, processed, disseminated and archived.
- *Operational metadata*: information summarizing the results of implementing procedures, including measures of respondent burden, response rates, edit failure rates, costs and other quality and performance indicators.
- *Systems metadata*: information on locations, record layouts, database schemas, access paths used by programs.
- *Data set metadata*: a particular type of systems metadata comprising the minimal metadata required to describe, access, update and disseminate data sets, including title, textual description, data elements, data cell annotations and (optionally) population, source and topics. Data set metadata play a major role in dissemination and secondary analysis.

Metadata are essential to users in their search for data to find out which data are actually available and how they can be retrieved; they help users to understand meaning and

---

[a] Colledge and Boyko (2000).

310

limitations in the use of the data and to assess the reliability and the quality of the data. The degree of detail required depends on a user's statistical knowledge, informatics expertise, intended use of the data. The growth of statistical dissemination via Internet, for instance, leads to a higher demand for metadata, as the audience is not necessarily aware of the statistical context. At the same time, a higher degree of information is required to assess data quality and to help international comparability. [b] For purposes of illustration of considerations in addressing international comparability, the proposed set of metadata for a national time-use survey by the Harmonised European Time Use Surveys project is shown below: [c]

- Main concepts and definitions: population, household.
- Sample: sample size; coverage and sampling frame; sample design and selection.
- National versions of recommended harmonized survey forms.

- Data collection: fieldwork period; interviewers; contacts with the households; data collection work; response rates. Data quality: national activity coding list; coding staff; data checking and validation.
- Estimators: estimators; including calculation of weights, adjustment of weights, variances, formulae, data programs.
- Data on national contact persons.

Some other information that may be considered for country-specific metadata for time-use surveys are: description of interviewer recruitment process; mean number of households per interviewer in relation to period worked; mean duration of interviewer information to the respondent about the time diary; postponement of designated diary days; percentage of "right" days; distribution of diaries by days of the week; and coding, including training and supervising of coders, coding time per diary, checking of quality.

---

[b] Vale and Pellegrino (2000).
[c] Eurostat (2000b).

ANNEX 19.   EXCERPTS FROM CANADA GENERAL SOCIAL SURVEY CYCLE 12:   USER'S GUIDE

Table of Contents[*]

---

[*] This table of contents, which encompasses the entire Canada General Social Surveys Cycle 12: User's Guide and therefore does not apply to the contents of the present annex, is given for information only.

1. Introduction

This document is designed to enable interested users to access and manipulate the microdata file for the twelfth cycle of the General Social Survey, conducted from February 1998 through January, 1999. It contains information on the objectives, methodology and estimation procedures as well as guidelines for releasing estimates based on the survey.

This document gives a description on how to correctly use the microdata files. Appendices D and F contain the data dictionaries for the Main file and the Time-Use Episode file, respectively, which is the major part of this documentation package. The variance tables are in appendix A and the survey questionnaire, in appendix B. This package is available in machine readable form.

Excerpts from User's Guide

6.5. Amount of detail on microdata file

In order to guard against disclosure, the amount of detail included on this file is less than is available on the master file retained by Statistics Canada. Variables with extreme values have been capped and information for some variables have been aggregated into broader classes (for example, occupation, religion, country of birth).

The measures taken to cap, group or collapse data have been indicated in the data dictionary. Variables with a very limited number of observations or referring to small population areas have been excluded from the file.

7. Estimation

When a probability sample is used, as was the case for the GSS, the principle behind estimation is that each person selected in the sample "represents" (in addition to

himself/herself) several other persons not in the sample. For example, in a simple random sample of 2 per cent of the population, each person in the sample represents 50 persons in the population. The number of persons represented by a given person in the sample is usually known as the weight or weighting factor of the sampled person.

There are two microdata files from which GSS Cycle 12 estimates can be made. The **Main file** contains summary time-use information from 10,749 respondents. It also contains the questionnaire responses obtained from these respondents. The **Time Use Episode file** contains information describing the details of the 221,105 time-use episodes reported by these respondents. Questionnaire information was not collected for those respondents who refused to complete a full diary. For a description of the file layouts, contents and correct interpretation of data on the microdata file, users should refer to appendices D, E, F, G, H and N.

When analysing GSS Cycle 12 data, it is necessary to use one of the weighting factors WGHTFIN on the Main file and WGHTEPI on the Time Use Episode file. WGHTFIN indicates the number of persons in the population that a record on the Main file represents, while WGHTEPI indicates the number of time use episodes that a record on the Episode file represents. For example, using the Main file, the estimate of the number of Canadians aged 15 years or over who feel "trapped in a daily routine" (that is to say D2G = 1) is 8,859,095. This is the sum of WGHTFIN over all records on the Main file with D2G = 1. Using the Time Use Episode file, the estimate of the number of episodes of watching TV by Canadians 15 years of age and older in an average day is 33,559,271, the sum of WGHTEPI over all records on the Time Use Episode file with ACTCODE=911, 912, 913, or 914.

In the last GSS Time Use Survey, Cycle 7, there were also two weights, one to be used for estimates not based on the episode data and one for estimates that used the episode data. In Cycle 7, the time-use diaries were collected only for a subsample (owing to non-response to the diary section of the questionaire). To account for this subsampling of episodes, the episode weights were larger than the person weights (in the same way that the person weights differed from the household weights to account for the sampling of only one respondent per household (see sect. 7.1- 4)). In this GSS cycle, there was no subsampling of time-use episodes; GSS Cycle 12 collected data for all time use episodes during the reference day for all respondents. Since there was no subsampling, the weight for each episode is the same as the weight for the respondent by whom it was reported.[a]

The Time Use Episode file is structured differently from the Main file in that there are multiple time use episode records for each respondent. Each time use episode is a separately identified record, with each respondent having on average 21 episode records. This introduces additional complexity in applying the weights correctly. Users should refer to appendix N for the correct methods of using this file.

7.2. Weighting policy

Users are cautioned against releasing unweighted tables or performing any analysis based on unweighted survey results. As was discussed in sect. 7.1, there were several weight adjustments performed that depended on the province, stratum, age, sex and

reference day of the respondent. Sampling rates as well as non-response rates varied significantly from province to province and non-response rates varied with demographic characteristics. For example, it is known that non-respondents are more likely to be males and more likely to be younger. In the responding sample, 3.3 per cent were males between the ages of 15 and 19, while in the overall population, approximately 4.3 per cent were males between the ages of 15 and 19. Therefore, it is clear that unweighted sample counts cannot be considered to be representative of the survey target population.

7.4. Guidelines for analysis

As is detailed in section 4 of this document, the respondents from the GSS do not form a simple random sample of the target population. Instead, the survey had a complex design, with stratification and multiple stages of selection, and unequal probabilities of selection of respondents. Using data from such complex surveys presents problems to analysts because the survey design and the selection probabilities affect the estimation and variance calculation procedures that should be used.

The GSS used a stratified design, with significant differences in sampling fractions between strata. Thus, some areas are overrepresented in the sample (relative to their populations) while some other areas are relatively underrepresented; this means that the unweighted sample is not representative of the target population, even if there was no non-response. Non-response rates may vary by demographic group, making the unweighted sample even less representative.

The survey weights must be used when producing estimates or performing analyses in order to account as much as possible for the geographical over- and under-representation and for the under- or over- representation of

---

[a] In the last GSS Time Use survey, Cycle 7, diaries were collected only for a subsample (owing to non-response to the diary section of the questionnaire) and thus the weight for the Cycle 7 Time Use Episode file differs from that for the Cycle 7 Main file.

age-sex groups, months of the year, or days of the week in the unweighted file. While many analysis procedures found in statistical packages allow weights to be used, the meaning or definition of the weight in these procedures often differs from that which is appropriate in a sample survey framework, with the result that while in many cases the estimates produced by the packages are correct, the variances that are calculated are almost meaningless.

For many analysis techniques (for example linear regression, logistic regression, estimation of rates and proportions, and analysis of variance), a method exists that can make the variances calculated by the standard packages more meaningful. If the weights on the data, or on the subset of the data that is of interest, are rescaled so that the average weight is one (1), then the variances produced by the standard packages will be more reasonable; they still will not take into account the stratification and clustering of the sample's design, but they will take into account the unequal probabilities of selection. This rescaling can be accomplished by dividing each weight by the overall average weight before the analysis is conducted.

Section 8 describes sampling variability and data reliability in more detail and Appendix A gives a series of tables that can be used to estimate the sampling variability of many qualitative estimates of totals and proportions.

The calculation of variance estimates that are specific to a variable of interest requires detailed knowledge of the design of the survey; such detail cannot be given in this microdata file because of the risk of breaching confidentiality. Variances that take the sample design into account can be calculated for many statistics by Statistics Canada on a cost-recovery basis.

7.5. Methods of estimation and interpretation of estimates

Examples and interpretation:

(a) In 1998, 50.4 per cent of female (SEX = 2) Canadians aged 15 years of age or over (6.2 million) stated they felt more rushed compared with five years ago (A3 = 1).

(b) Fifty six per cent of Canadians aged 25 to 44 (2 # AGEGR 10 #.3) tend to cut back on their sleep when they need more time for other activities (D2C = 1).

(c) Seventy per cent of males (SEX = 1) aged 15 to 24 (AGEGR10 = 1) stated that during the past 12 months they had regularly participated in sports (J1 = 1) while only 46 per cent of females (SEX = 2) in the same age category took part regularly.

8. Release guidelines and data reliability

It is important for users to become familiar with the contents of the present section before publishing or otherwise releasing any estimates derived from the General Social Survey microdata files.

This section of the documentation provides guidelines to be followed by users. With the aid of these guidelines, users of the microdata files should be able to produce figures consistent with those produced by Statistics Canada and in conformance with the established guidelines for rounding and release. The guidelines can be broken into four broad sections: minimum sample sizes for estimates; sampling variability policy; sampling variability estimation; and rounding policy.

9. File structure

In view of the nature of the time use data, the microdata file consists of the two subfiles described below.

The **Main file** consists of one record per respondent. It contains well over 300 questionnaire-based variables. In addition, it summarizes the total time spent on the diary day on each category of activity, the 10 major categories, the 24 subcategories, total time spent at each location, total time spent with various persons, and time spent helping persons outside the household.

This is the most widely used file for time-use analysis. There are 10,749 records.

The **Time Use Episode file** consists of all episodes reported by respondents. Each respondent generated a variable number of records depending on the number of episodes reported. For each episode, there is information on the activity, start and end time, duration, location and an indication of who the respondent was with for that episode. New for Cycle 12, information on whom an activity helped is included for selected types of activities. There are 221,105 records.

There is minimal duplication across the two files. However, the variable CASEID can be used for linking respondent characteristics and other main file variables with the detailed

diary information on the Episode file. See appendix N for guidelines for using time-use data.

Special notes

The diary response determined whether or not a respondent was included in the file. Therefore, the respondent may have stopped responding at any point from section C of the questionnaire onwards. This methodological change may increase the rate of non-response to many questions and should be taken into account in any comparisons over time.

The sample and population counts for each variable in the data dictionaries are calculated from all respondents not only the ones specified in the coverage component of the description of the variable.

10. Additional information

Additional information about this survey can be obtained from the individuals listed below. Data from the survey are available through published reports, special request tabulations, and this microdata file. The microdata file is available from the Housing, Family and Social Statistics Division of Statistics Canada at a cost of $1,600.00. Tabulations can be obtained at a cost that will reflect the resources required to produce the tabulation.

ANNEX 20.   STRUCTURE OF THE TRIAL INTERNATIONAL CLASSIFICATION OF ACTIVITIES FOR TIME-USE STATISTICS (ICATUS)

01   **Work for corporations/quasi-corporations, non-profit institutions and government (formal sector work)**

011   **Core activities: working in "formal sector" employment**

   0111   **Working time in "formal sector" employment**

      01111   Working time in main job

      01112   Working time in other jobs

      01113   Working time as apprentice, intern and related positions

      01114   Short breaks and interruptions from work

      01115   Training and studies in relation to work in the "formal sector"

   0112   **Other breaks**

      01121   Idle time before/after work

      01122   Lunch break from work

012   **Related activities: looking for work/setting up business in the "formal sector"**

   0120   **Looking for work/setting up business in the "formal sector"**

      01201   Looking for work in the "formal sector"

      01202   Looking for/setting up business in the "formal sector"

013   **Travel related to work in the "formal sector"**

   0130   **Travel related to work in the "formal sector"**

      01300   Travel related to work in the "formal sector"

019   **Work in the "formal sector" n.e.c.**

   0190   **Work in the "formal sector" n.e.c.**

      01900   Work in the "formal sector" n.e.c.

02   **Work for household in primary production activities**

021   **Core activities: working time in primary production activities**

   0211   **Working time in primary production activities**

      02111   Growing of crops and trees; kitchen gardening

      02112   Farming of animals; production of animal products; animal husbandry services

      02113   Hunting, trapping and production of animal skins

		02114	Gathering of wild products, woodcutting and gathering firewood and other forestry activities
		02115	Fishing and fish/aquatic farming
		02116	Mining and quarrying
		02117	Collecting water
		02118	Training and studies in relation to work in primary production activities of households
		0211x	Working time in primary production activities n.f.d.
	0212		**Acquiring inputs/supplies and disposing of outputs used for primary production activities of households**
		02121	Purchasing/acquiring inputs/supplies used for primary production activities of households
		02122	Selling/disposing of outputs of primary production activities of households
022			**Related activities: looking for work/setting up business in primary production activities in household enterprise**
	0220		**Looking for work/setting up business in primary production activities in household enterprise**
		02201	Looking for work in primary production activities in household enterprise
		02202	Looking for/setting up business in primary production activities in household enterprise
023			**Travel related to primary production activities of households**
	0230		**Travel related to primary production activities of households**
		02300	Travel related to primary production activities of households
029			**Work for households in primary production activities n.e.c.**
	0290		**Work for households in primary production activities n.e.c.**
		02900	Work for households in primary production activities n.e.c.

03   Work for household in non-primary production activities

031			**Core activities: working time in non-primary production activities**
	0311		**Working time in non-primary production activities**
		03111	Processing of food products
		03112	Making of other food products and beverages
		03113	Making textiles, wearing apparel, leather and associated products
		03114	Craft-making using all types of materials
		03115	Tobacco preparing and curing
		03116	Making bricks, concrete slabs, hollow blocks, tiles etc.
		03117	Making herbal and medicinal preparations

		03118	Training and studies in relation to work in non-primary production activities of households
		0311x	Working time in non-primary production activities n.f.d.
	0312		**Acquiring inputs/supplies and disposing of outputs in non-primary production activities households**
		03121	Purchasing/acquiring inputs/supplies used for non primary production activities for households
		03122	Selling/disposing of outputs of non-primary production activities of households
032			**Related activities: looking for work/setting up business in non-primary production activities in household enterprise**
	0320		**Looking for work/setting up business in non-primary production activities in household enterprise**
		03201	Looking for work in non-primary production activities in household enterprise
		03202	Looking for/setting up business in non-primary production activities in household enterprise
033			**Travel related to non-primary production of household**
	0330		**Travel related to non-primary production of household**
		03300	Travel related to non-primary production of household
039			**Work for household in non-primary production activities n.e.c.**
	0390		**Work for household in non-primary production activities n.e.c.**
		03900	Work for household in non-primary production activities n.e.c.

04   Work for household in construction activities

041			**Core activities: working time in construction activities**
	0411		**Working time in construction activities**
		04111	Construction and repair for own capital formation
		04112	Construction and repair of buildings, roads, dams and other structures
		04113	Community-organized construction and major repairs of roads, buildings, bridges, dams etc.
		04114	Training and studies in relation to work in construction activities in household enterprise
		0411x	Working time in construction activities n.f.d.
	0412		**Acquiring inputs/supplies for construction activities for household production**
		04120	Purchasing/acquiring inputs/supplies for construction activities for household production

042			Related activities: looking for work/setting up business in construction activities in household enterprise
	0420		Looking for work/setting up business in construction activities in household enterprise
		04201	Looking for work in construction activities in household enterprise
		04202	Looking for work/setting up business in construction activities as household enterprise
043			Travel related to construction activities of households
	0430		Travel related to construction activities of households
		04300	Travel related to construction activities of households
049			Work for household in construction activities n.e.c.
	0490		Work for household in construction activities n.e.c.
		04900	Work for household in construction activities n.e.c.

05   Work for household providing services for income

051			Core activities: working time in providing services for income
	0511		Food vending and trading
		05111	Preparing and selling food and beverage
		05112	Petty trading, door-to-door vending, street vending, hawking
	0512		Providing repair, installation and maintenance services
		05121	Fitting, installing, tool-setting, maintaining and repairing tools and machinery
		05122	Repair of vehicles
		05123	Repair of personal goods
		05124	Repair of household goods
	0513		Providing business and professional services
		05131	Renting out rooms, sleeping space and associated work
		05132	Lending and collecting money; foreign exchange
		05133	Typing, word-processing, programming, encoding
		05134	Accounting, bookkeeping, legal and related services
		05135	Tutoring
		05136	Provision of medical and dental services
		05137	Provision of nursing/therapy services
	0514		Providing personal care services
		05141	Provision of personal care services
		05142	Provision of non-professional health-care

	0515		**Transporting goods and passengers**
		05151	Transporting goods
		05152	Transporting passengers
	0516		**Paid domestic services**
		05160	Providing paid domestic services
	0517		**Meetings/training and studies**
		05170	Training and studies related to work in service activities
	051x		**Working time in providing services for income n.f.d.**
052			**Related activities: looking for work/setting up business in service activities in household enterprise**
	0520		**Looking for work/setting up business in service activities in household enterprise**
		05200	Looking for work in service activities in service activities in household enterprise
053			**Travel related to providing services for income**
	0530		**Travel related to providing services for income**
		05300	Travel related to providing services for income
059			**Work for household providing services for income n.e.c.**
	0590		**Work for household providing services for income n.e.c.**
		05900	Work for household providing services for income n.e.c.

06 Providing unpaid domestic services for own final use within household

061			**Core activities: working time in providing unpaid domestic services for own final use**
	0611		**Unpaid domestic services**
		06111	Food management
		06112	Cleaning and upkeep of dwelling and surroundings
		06113	Do-it-yourself decoration, maintenance and small repairs
		06114	Care of textiles and footwear
		06115	Household management
		06116	Pet care
	0612		**Shopping**
		06121	Shopping for/purchasing of goods and related activities
		06122	Shopping for/availing of services and related activities
	061x		**Working time in providing unpaid domestic services for own final use n.f.d.**

062			Travel related to provision of unpaid domestic services
	0620		Travel related to provision of unpaid domestic services
		06200	Travel related to provision of unpaid domestic services
069			Unpaid domestic services n.e.c.
	0690		Unpaid domestic services n.e.c.
		06900	Unpaid domestic services n.e.c.

07 Providing unpaid caregiving services to household members

071			Core activities: working time providing unpaid caregiving services to household members
	0711		Childcare
		07111	Caring for children/physical care
		07112	Teaching, training, helping children
		07113	Accompanying children to places
		07114	Minding children (passive care)
	0712		Adult care
		07121	Caring for adults/physical care
		07122	Caring for adults/emotional support
		07123	Accompanying adults to places
	071x		Working time providing unpaid caregiving services to household members n.f.d.
072			Travel related to unpaid caregiving services to household members
	0720		Travel related to unpaid caregiving services to household members
		07200	Travel related to unpaid caregiving services to household members
079			Providing unpaid caregiving services to household members n.e.c.
	0790		Providing unpaid caregiving services to household members n.e.c.
		07900	Providing unpaid caregiving services to household members n.e.c.

08 Providing community services and help to other households

081			Core activities: working time providing community services and help to other households
	0811		Unpaid help to other households
		08111	Household maintenance and management as help to other households
		08112	Shopping for/purchasing of goods and services as help to other households

		08113	Construction, renovation and repairs of dwellings and other structures as help to other households
		08114	Repairs of consumer and household goods as help to other households
		08115	Unpaid help in business/farm and employment as help to other households
		08116	Childcare as help to other households
		08117	Adult care as help to other households
		08118	Transportation assistance to other households
	0812		**Community-organized services**
		08121	Community organized work: cooking for collective celebrations etc.
		08122	Work on road/building repair, clearing and preparing community land, cleaning (streets, markets etc.)
		08123	Organizing and work on community-based assistance to villages, other sublocations
		08124	Organizing and work on community-based assistance to families and individuals
	0813		**Organized unpaid volunteer services**
		08131	Volunteer work for organizations (not directly for individuals)
		08132	Volunteer work through organizations (extended directly to individuals)
	081x		**Working time providing community services and help to other households n.f.d.**
082			**Related activities: attendance in meetings**
	0820		**Attendance in meetings**
		08200	Attendance in meetings
083			**Related activities: other community services**
	0830		**Other community services**
		08300	Involvement in civic and related responsibilities
084			**Travel related to community services and help to other households**
	0840		**Travel related to community services and help to other households**
		08400	Travel related to community services and help to other households
089			**Community services and help to other households n.e.c.**
	0890		**Community services and help to other households n.e.c.**
		08900	Community services and help to other households n.e.c.

09   Learning

091			**Core activities: time spent in learning activities**
	0911		**General education**
		09111	School/ university attendance

		09112	Breaks/waiting at place of general education
		09113	Self-study for distance education course work (video, audio, online)
	0912		**Homework, course review, research and activities related to general education**
		09120	Homework, course review, research and activities related to general education
	0913		**Additional study, non-formal education and courses during free time**
		09130	Additional study, non-formal education and courses during free time
	0914		**Career/professional development training and studies**
		09140	Career/professional development training and studies
	091x		**Learning n.f.d.**
092			**Related activities: other activities carried out in relation to learning activities**
	0920		**Other activities carried out in relation to learning activities**
		09200	Other activities carried out in relation to learning activities
093			**Travel related to learning**
	0930		**Travel related to learning**
		09300	Travel related to learning
099			**Learning activities n.e.c.**
	0990		**Learning activities n.e.c.**
		09900	Learning activities n.e.c.

10 Socializing and community participation

101			**Core activities: time spent in socializing and community participation**
	1011		**Socializing and communication**
		10111	Talking, conversing
		10112	Socializing activities
		10113	Reading and writing mail
		10114	Unsocial/antisocial/negative social activities
		1011x	Socializing and communication n.f.d.
	1012		**Participating in community cultural/social events**
		10121	Participating in community celebrations of cultural/historic events
		10122	Participating in community rites/events (non-religious) of weddings, funerals, births and similar rites-of-passage
		10123	Participating in community social functions (music, dance etc.)
		1012x	Community participation n.f.d.

102			**Travel related to socializing and community participation**
	1020		**Travel related to socializing and community participation**
		10200	Travel related to socializing and community participation
109			**Socializing and community participation n.e.c.**
	1090		**Socializing and community participation n.e.c.**
		10900	Socializing and community participation n.e.c.

11   Attending/visiting cultural, entertainment and sports events/venues

111			**Core activities: time spent attending cultural, entertainment and sports events**
	1111		**Attendance at organized/mass cultural events**
		11111	Visit museum, art gallery, historical/cultural park, heritage site
		11112	Attendance at movies/cinema
		11113	Attendance at theatre, opera, ballet, concerts
		11119	Attendance at other specified mass cultural events
	1112		**Attendance at parks/gardens, shows**
		11120	Attendance/visit to zoo, animal park, botanic garden, amusement centre, fairs, festivals, circus, animal shows, plant shows
	1113		**Attendance at sports events**
		11131	Attendance at professional sports events
		11132	Attendance at amateur sports events
	111x		**Attendance at cultural, entertainment and sports events n.f.d.**
112			**Travel related to attending/visiting cultural, entertainment and sports events/venues**
	1120		**Travel related to attending/visiting cultural, entertainment and sports events/venues**
		11200	Travel related to attending/visiting cultural, entertainment and sports events/venues
119			**Attending/visiting sports, entertainment and cultural events/venues n.e.c.**
	1190		**Attending/visiting sports, entertainment and cultural events/venues n.e.c.**
		11900	Attending/visiting sports, entertainment and cultural events/venues n.e.c.

12   Hobbies, games and other pastime activities

121			**Core activities: hobbies, games and other pastime activities**
	1211		**Visual, literary and performing arts (as hobby) and related courses**
		12111	Visual arts

	12112	Literary arts
	12113	Performing arts (dance, music, theatre)
	1211x	Visual, literary and performing arts n.f.d.
1212		**Technical hobbies and related courses**
	12120	Technical hobbies and related courses
1213		**Playing games and other pastimes and related courses**
	12131	Solo games
	12132	Card games, board games
	12133	Computer games (including arcade and video games)
	12134	Social/group games
	12135	Gambling
	1213x	Playing games and other pastimes n.f.d.

122   Travel related to hobbies, games and other pastimes

1220		**Travel related to hobbies, games and other pastimes**
	12200	Travel related to hobbies, games and other pastimes

129   Hobbies, games and other pastimes n.e.c.

1290		**Hobbies, games and other pastimes n.e.c.**
	12900	Hobbies, games and other pastimes n.e.c.

13   Indoor and outdoor sports participation and related courses

131   Core activities: time spent participating in sports and outdoor activities

1311		**Participating in sports**
	13111	Walking and hiking; jogging and running
	13112	Biking, skating, skateboarding
	13113	Aerobics, yoga, weight-training and other fitness programmes
	13114	Ball games, individual sports
	13115	Ball games, team sports
	13116	Water sports
	13117	Winter/ice/snow sports
	13118	Contact sports
1312		**Camping and other outdoor activities**
	13121	Camping
	13122	Horseback-riding
	13123	Pleasure drives; sightseeing

	131x		**Indoor and outdoor sports participation n.f.d.**
132			**Travel related to indoor and outdoor sports participation and related courses**
	1320		**Travel related to indoor and outdoor sports participation and related courses**
		13200	Travel related to indoor and outdoor sports participation and related courses
139			**Indoor and outdoor sports participation and related courses n.e.c.**
	1390		**Indoor and outdoor sports participation and related courses n.e.c.**
		13900	Indoor and outdoor sports participation and related courses n.e.c.

14   Mass media

141			**Core activities: time spent using mass media**
	1411		**Reading**
		14111	Reading books
		14112	Reading periodicals
		14119	Reading other specified materials
		1411x	Reading n.f.d.
	1412		**Watching/listening to television and video**
		14121	Watching/listening to television
		14122	Watching/listening to video programmes
	1413		**Listening to radio and audio devices**
		14131	Listening to radio programmes
		14132	Listening to other audio media
		1413x	Listening to radio and audio devices n.f.d.
	1414		**Using computer technology**
		14141	Using computer technology for reading
		14142	Using computer technology for video/audio
		14143	Surfing the Internet; downloading, uploading
		1414x	Using computer technology n.f.d.
142			**Related activities: visiting library**
	1420		**Visiting library**
		14200	Visiting library
143			**Travel related to mass media**
	1430		**Travel related to mass media**
		14300	Travel related to mass media
149			**Mass media n.e.c.**
	1490		**Mass media n.e.c.**
		14900	Mass media n.e.c.

15   Personal care and maintenance

151   **Core activities: time spent in personal care and maintenance**

    1511   **Sleep and related activities**

        15111   Night sleep/essential sleep

        15112   Incidental sleep/naps

        15113   Sleeplessness

        1511x   Sleep and related activities n.f.d.

    1512   **Eating and drinking**

        15121   Eating meals/snack

        15122   Drinking other than with meal or snack

        1512x   Eating and drinking n.f.d.

    1513   **Personal hygiene and care**

        15131   Personal hygiene and care

        15132   Health/medical care to oneself

    1514   **Receiving personal and health/medical care from others**

        15141   Receiving personal care from others

        15142   Receiving health/medical care from others

    1515   **Religious activities**

        15151   Private prayer, meditation, and other informal spiritual activities

        15152   Participating in religious activities (formal practice of religion)

    1516   **Activities associated with resting, relaxing**

        15161   Doing nothing; resting, relaxing

        15162   Smoking

        15163   Reflecting/meditating, thinking, planning

152   **Travel related to personal care and maintenance activities**

    1520   **Travel related to personal care and maintenance activities**

        15200   Travel related to personal care and maintenance activities

159   **Personal care and maintenance activities n.e.c.**

    1590   **Personal care and maintenance activities n.e.c.**

        15900   Personal care and maintenance activities n.e.c.

ANNEX 21. TRIAL INTERNATIONAL CLASSIFICATION OF ACTIVITIES FOR TIME-USE STATISTICS (ICATUS) *

01 Work for corporations/quasi corporations, non-profit institutions and government (formal sector work) [a]

Includes:

- All activities performed in relation to employment in corporations/quasi-corporations, non-profit institutions, and government
- Both paid and unpaid employment irrespective of the industrial sector of the activity and status in employment
- Work performed under apprenticeship, internship and on-the-job training programmes
- Short breaks during working hours and waiting due to delays at work
- Participation in training and studies on official time
- Activities that are not directly related to one's job but are typically performed while at the workplace or within the block of time that constitutes one's usual time in the workplace. These include idle time while waiting to begin work and shortly after work and lunch break or similar long breaks from work.
- Activities related to seeking employment or the setting up of a business
- Travel to and from the workplace

Note: The term "formal sector" shall refer to all institutional sectors other than the household sector.

011 Core activities: working in "formal sector" employment

0111 Working time in "formal sector" employment

Includes:

- Work activities as defined by the job. Working hours include usual hours (as prescribed by contract for employees or usual practice/schedule by self-employed), overtime hours (hours beyond the usual hours as prescribed by contract or usual work schedule) and extra hours (hours considered by person as neither usual nor overtime; for example, taking work home)

---

* 8 August 2003. This version of the ICATUS is available as a database on the following web site: http://unstats.un.org/unsd/cr/registry/regcst.asp?Cl=231&Lg=1

[a] The structure of the ICATUS categorizes SNA-work activities engaged in by individuals into two major groups in relation to the *institutional unit* that produces the output; activities performed by individuals as household members that input into household production, and activities performed by individuals that input into production of units belonging to sectors other than the household sector. For this purpose, institutional units are defined and classified following the 1993 SNA, as follows: An *institutional unit* is "an economic entity that is capable, in its own right, of owning assets, incurring liabilities and engaging in economic activities and in transactions with other entities." There are two main types of institutional units, namely: (a) persons or group of persons in the form of households and (b) legal or social entities whose existence is recognized by law or society independently of the persons, or other identities, that may own or control them." These units are classified into: 1. Corporations and quasi-corporations including cooperatives and limited liability partnerships; 2. Government units, national or local; 3. Households; and 4. Non-profit institutions (NPIs). Similar institutional units are grouped into five mutually exclusive institutional sectors: 1. Non-financial corporations sector, including NPIs; 2. Financial corporations sector, including NPIs; 3. General government sector, including NPIs; 4. Non-profit institutions serving households (NPISH) sector; and 5. Household sector.

– Short breaks and interruptions from work such as: coffee break; waiting due to delays in work
– Participation in training and studies on official/paid time

01111   **Working time in main job**

011110   Working time in main job

01112   **Working time in other jobs**

011120   Working time in other jobs

01113   **Working time as apprentice, intern and related positions**

011130   Working time as apprentice, intern and related positions

01114   **Short breaks and interruptions from work**

011140   Short breaks and interruptions from work

01115   **Training and studies in relation to work in the "formal sector"**

011150   Training and studies in relation to work in the "formal sector"
Includes:
– Attendance in short-term courses such as language courses, applications software courses etc., seminars on time management, employment benefits, technical/business conferences
– Attendance in part-time undergraduate/graduate courses
– For employees, attendance must be sanctioned by employer; that is to say, attendance is considered part of working time or official time. Employer may or may not cover actual cost of training or studies. Attendance may be during usual working hours or outside the usual working hours
– For self-employed, training and studies must be directly related to one's job
Examples: Attending in-house training; attending training courses, seminars, conferences on official time and studies on official time; attending classes part-time on official time

0111x   **Working time in "formal sector" employment n.f.d.**

0112   **Other breaks**
Note: These activities are generally applicable only to persons whose jobs have fixed working time schedules (for example, "8-5" jobs), have prescribed lunch break hours etc. May not be applicable for workers with more flexible working schedules such as self-employed or home-based workers.
Application: How to classify activities that are performed during the break such as eating lunch, talking, smoking etc. When simultaneous activities are recorded, each activity is to be recorded. If activities are prioritised as main, secondary etc., the specific activity being performed during the break is to be treated as the primary activity and codes 01121 or 01122 as referring to secondary activities. If simultaneous activities are not recorded, prioritization rule needs to be defined.
Exclusion: Business meetings are classified under the appropriate classes 01111-01113.

		01121	**Idle time before/after work**
		011210	Idle time before/after work
		01122	**Lunch break from work**
		011220	Lunch break from work

012   **Related activities: looking for work/setting up business in the "formal sector"**

     0120   **Looking for work/setting up business in the "formal sector"**

       01201   **Looking for work in the "formal sector"**

       012010   Looking for work in the "formal sector"
Includes:
– Preparing resumes
– Reading and replying to employment opportunities (writing, calling, mailing, sending online or by e-mail)
– Visiting labour office, employment agency, prospective employer
– Filing and fulfilling application requirements
– Being interviewed

       01202   **Looking for/setting up business in the "formal sector"**

       012020   Looking for/setting up business in the "formal sector"
Includes:
– Fulfilling legal and administrative requirements
– Applying for financing, credit
– Looking for offices, business place
– Conducting feasibility studies; "scanning" the environment

013   **Travel related to work in the "formal sector"**

     0130   **Travel related to work in the "formal sector"**

       01300   **Travel related to work in the "formal sector"**

       013000   Travel related to work in the "formal sector"
Includes:
– Travel to and from the workplace
– Travel in relation to activities in this major division
Exclusion: When travelling is intrinsic to the job (for example, driver, pilot, airline stewardess, garbage collector, sailor etc.), the activity is classified under the appropriate classes 01111-01113.

019   **Work in the "formal sector" n.e.c.**

     0190   **Work in the "formal sector" n.e.c.**

       01900   **Work in the "formal sector" n.e.c.**

       019000   Work in the "formal sector" n.e.c.

02 Work for household in primary production activities

Includes:
- All activities performed in relation to the primary production of goods by households whether for market or for own final use. A person's activity is classified as primary production of goods if it is performed in relation to the economic activities of agriculture, hunting, forestry, fishing, mining or quarrying
- Activities performed in relation to collecting, distributing and storing of water
- Participation in meetings/training and studies directly related to one's work in primary production activities
- Activities performed in relation to acquiring inputs/supplies for work and disposing of outputs
- Activities related to seeking employment and the setting up of a business
- Travel to and from the workplace

Note: In these divisions of activities it is assumed that working time arrangements are generally more informal or flexible compared to those in the formal sector. Thus, this major division does not include specific divisions for short breaks and for lunch breaks. Activities associated with such breaks from work are classified in the corresponding class; for example, eating snack/meals is classified under 15121- Eating meals/snack.

021   Core activities: working time in primary production activities

0211   Working time in primary production activities

02111   Growing of crops and trees; kitchen gardening
Includes: Growing of cereal and other crops, vegetables, fruit, nuts, spice crops, flowers and other horticultural specialties etc. (including kitchen or backyard gardening); processing for sale/storage/use (ISIC 011, 014 - agriculture services only)
Note: Growing of mushrooms and berries are included in this class as in ISIC 011

021111   Land preparation
Includes: Ploughing, use of kodale, harrowing, beating clods, slash and burn

021112   Sowing and planting operations
Includes: Seedbed preparation, sowing, transplanting

021113   Collecting and preparing organic fertilizer, carrying and spreading organic/chemical fertilizer

021114   Field/garden upkeep
Includes: Weeding, watering, trimming

021115   Harvesting
Includes: Bundling, threshing and cleaning of grain, drying crop residue

021116   Post harvest activities
Includes: Drying, seed selection, bagging and storage

021117   Other agricultural service activities
Includes: Routine repair of irrigation channels, guarding/protection of harvest, maintenance and routine repair of tools and equipment

021119   Other specified activities related to growing of crops and trees

02111x Growing of crops and trees; kitchen gardening n.f.d.

02112 Farming of animals; production of animal products; animal husbandry services
Includes:
– Farming/raising of domestic and semi-domesticated animals
– Production of raw milk and milk products on the farm
– Shearing; production of fur skins, reptile and bird skins from ranching
– Production of live animal products such as eggs, honey
– Operating poultry hatcheries
– (ISIC 011, 014- animal husbandry services only)

021121 Fodder collection; preparation of feed; feeding, watering; grazing

021122 Grooming, shoeing, cleaning; veterinary care

021123 Washing shed, coop cleaning

021124 Work related to breeding; hatching

021125 Milking and processing of raw milk

021126 Collecting, storing, grading of eggs

021127 Shearing, producing hides and skins from ranching

021128 Dung-gathering and making dung cakes

021129 Other specified activities related to animal farming, production of animal products, animal husbandry services

02112x Farming of animals; production of animal products; animal husbandry services n.f.d.

02113 Hunting, trapping and production of animal skins
Includes: Hunting and trapping animals to obtain meat, hair, skin or other products (ISIC 015, including non-commercial)

021131 Hunting and trapping wild animals
Includes: Digging holes, setting traps, keeping watch etc.

021132 Hunting birds

021133 Production of fur skins, reptile or bird skins from hunting and trapping

021139 Other specified activities related to hunting and production of animal skins

02113x Hunting, trapping and production of animal skins n.f.d.

02114 Gathering of wild products, woodcutting, gathering firewood and other forestry activities
Includes: Gathering fruit, wild fruits, medicinal and other plants; gathering minor forest produce, leaves, bamboo etc., fuel/fuel wood/twigs, raw material for crafts (ISIC 020)
Note: Picking mushrooms and berries are included in this class although they are excluded from ISIC 020

021141 Gathering medicinal and other plants for craft production or fuel
Includes: Cutting peat, hemp, betel nuts, bamboo, leaves etc.

021142 Gathering wild fruits, berries or other uncultivated crops, other edible food

021143	Woodcutting and gathering firewood
	Includes: Locating trees to be felled, picking dead or fallen branches etc.
021144	Reforestation, growing forest trees, replanting
021149	Other specified activities related to hunting, forestry, and gathering of wild products
02114x	Gathering of wild products, woodcutting, gathering firewood and other forestry activities n.f.d.

02115 **Fishing and fish/aquatic farming**
Includes:
- Catching fish and other forms of aquatic life and products and fish farming (ISIC 050 including non-commercial)
- Repair, care and maintenance of fishing boats, equipment, tools, fishnets. Includes making of nets and tools for own use.

021151	Catching fish and gathering other forms of aquatic life
021152	Gathering marine materials such as natural pearls, sponges, corals, algae, seashells
021153	Fish/aquatic farming: Breeding, rearing
021154	Fish/aquatic farming: Cleaning beds, feeding
021155	Repair, care and maintenance of fishing boats and equipment, tools, fishnets
021159	Other specified activities related to fishing, fish/aquatic farming
02115x	Fishing and fish/aquatic farming n.f.d.

02116 **Mining and quarrying**
Includes:
- Mining/extraction of salt; digging, quarrying of stone, slabs; breaking of stones for construction of building road, bridges etc.; digging out clay, gravel and sand; gold panning etc. (ISIC 1320, 1410, 1422)
- Transporting; storing and stocking

021161	Mining/extraction of salt
021162	Drilling well, boring holes etc.
021163	Quarrying of stone slabs
021164	Crushing and breaking of stones
021165	Digging out clay, gravel and sand
021166	Gold panning, mining gems etc.
	Note: Refers to low-technology mining.
021167	Transporting, storing and stocking
021169	Other specified mining and quarrying activities
02116x	Mining and quarrying n.f.d.

02117 **Collecting water**

021170	Collecting water
	Includes: Activities related to collecting, storing and distributing water

02118 **Training and studies in relation to work in primary production activities of households**

021180 Training and studies in relation to work in primary production activities of households
Includes: Availing of government training/extension services; attending business meetings of cooperatives and self-help associations; attending seminars on increasing productivity, marketing, technology and techniques etc.

0211x **Working time in primary production activities n.f.d.**

0212 **Acquiring inputs/supplies and disposing of outputs used for primary production activities of households**

02121 **Purchasing/acquiring inputs/supplies used for primary production activities of households**

021210 Purchasing/acquiring inputs/supplies used for primary production activities of households

02122 **Selling/disposing of outputs of primary production activities of households**

021220 Selling/disposing of outputs of primary production activities of households
Includes: Selling fruits, vegetables, flowers, fish etc. produced for leisure or pastime or in connection with a hobby, at garage or yard sale

022 **Related activities: looking for work/setting up business in primary production activities in household enterprise**

0220 **Looking for work/setting up business in primary production activities in household enterprise**

02201 **Looking for work in primary production activities in household enterprise**

022010 Looking for work in primary production activities in household enterprise

02202 **Looking for/setting up business in primary production activities in household enterprise**

022020 Looking for/setting up business in primary production activities in household enterprise

023 **Travel related to primary production activities of households**

0230 **Travel related to primary production activities of households**

02300 **Travel related to primary production activities of households**

023000 Travel related to primary production activities of households
Includes:
– Travel to and from the workplace
– Travel in relation to conduct of activities in this major division
Exclusions: When travelling is intrinsic to the job (for example, driver), the activity is classified under the appropriate classes 02111-02117. Travel in relation to collecting water is classified under 02117- Collecting water.

029			Work for households in primary production activities n.e.c.
	0290		Work for households in primary production activities n.e.c.
		02900	Work for households in primary production activities n.e.c.
		029000	Work for households in primary production activities n.e.c.

03 Work for household in non-primary production activities

Includes:
- All activities performed in relation to production of non-primary goods by household enterprises whether for market or for own final use. A person's activity is classified as production of non-primary goods if it is performed in relation to the manufacturing activities covered in ISIC divisions 15 to 37.
- Activities performed in relation to acquiring inputs/supplies for work and disposing of outputs.
- Participation in meetings/training and studies directly related to one's work in non-primary production activities.
- Activities related to seeking employment or the setting up of a business
- Travel to and from the workplace

Note: In these divisions of activities it is assumed that working time arrangements are generally more informal or flexible compared to those in the formal sector. Thus, this major division does not include specific divisions for short breaks and for lunch breaks. Activities associated with such breaks from work are classified in the corresponding class; for example, eating snack/meals is classified under 15121- Eating meals/snack.

031			Core activities: working time in non-primary production activities
	0311		Working time in non-primary production activities

03111 Processing of food products
Includes: Activities performed in relation to economic activities described under ISIC 151, 152, 153 such as slaughtering, preserving, curing, salting

031111 Production, processing and preserving of meat and meat products
Includes: Slaughtering, dressing, curing, smoking, drying, salting storing etc. of meat

031112 Making dairy products
Includes: Milk processing, production of butter, ghee, cheese, curd, whey, cream etc. Production of raw milk is classified under 021125- Milking and processing of raw milk

031113 Processing and preserving of fish and fish products
Includes: Drying, smoking, salting, immersing in brine etc.; production of fish meal

031114 Processing and preserving of fruits and vegetables
Includes: Pickling, salting, drying, roasting, grinding, oil pressing/production, jam- and jelly-making; canning and bottling and all activities in connection with them, for example, cleaning berries, boiling of jam or juice

031115 Processing grains
Includes:
Husking, drying, threshing grains, winnowing

Making of flour, grain mill products, starches and starch products, and prepared animal feeds

031119   Other specified activities related to processing of food products

03111x   Processing of food products n.f.d.

03112   **Making of other food products and beverages**
Includes: All activities performed in relation to economic activities under ISIC 154 and 155 such as brewing, fermenting, baking, confectionery-making

031121   Beer-brewing and making of other beverages, wines or spirits

031122   Baking bread, cakes, rice cakes, pastries, pies, tarts, biscuits

031123   Making noodles, pasta and similar products

031124   Making candy, boiled sweets, caramel, chocolate, and other sugar confectionery products

031125   Roasting seeds, nuts

031126   Roasting, grinding coffee beans

031129   Other specified activities related to making of other food products and beverages

03112x   Making of other food products and beverages n.f.d.

03113   **Making textiles, wearing apparel, leather and associated products**
Includes: All activities performed in relation to economic activities under ISIC 17, 18 and 19 such as weaving, spinning, sewing, leather work

031131   Spinning, weaving, finishing of textiles

031132   Producing articles from textile except apparel
Includes: Making blankets, rugs, pillows, rags/dust cloths, making carpets or mats by weaving, tufting, braiding etc., knitting or crocheting articles; embroidery and needlework

031133   Making wearing apparel

031134   Curing of skins and production of leather, tanning and dressing of leather

031135   Making shoes, footwear, handbags, luggage

031139   Other specified activities related to making textiles, wearing apparel, leather and associated products

03113x   Making textiles, wearing apparel, leather and associated products n.f.d.

03114   **Craft-making using all types of materials**
Includes: All activities performed in relation to economic activities under relevant classes of ISIC 20, 21, 242, 26, 289, 36 such as treating wood, carving wood, weaving baskets, welding, making bricks, tool-making

031141   Making wood products including furniture, fixtures or furnishings, statuettes and other ornaments
Includes: Cutting, carving, sanding, varnishing, painting, assembling

031142   Making baskets, wickerwork and other similar products
Includes: Weaving, varnishing etc.

031143	Fabricating utensils, cutlery, hand tools and other metal products
031144	Metal working *Includes*: Making window grills, metal gates, vehicle body
031145	Making pottery, ovens and cooking stoves, ornaments etc. from clay, plaster or cement
031146	Making paper and paper products; paper crafts
031147	Making soap, perfume, candles etc.
031149	Other specified activities related to craft-making
03114x	Craft-making using all types of materials n.f.d.
03115	**Tobacco preparing and curing**
031150	Tobacco preparing and curing
03116	**Making bricks, concrete slabs, hollow blocks, tiles etc.**
031160	Making bricks, concrete slabs, hollow blocks, tiles etc.
03117	**Making herbal and medicinal preparations**
031170	Making herbal and medicinal preparations
03118	**Training and studies in relation to work in non-primary production activities of households**
031180	Training and studies in relation to work in non primary production activities of households *Includes*: Availing of government training/extension services; attending business meetings of cooperatives and self-help associations; attending seminars on increasing productivity, marketing, technology and techniques etc.
0311x	**Working time in non-primary production activities n.f.d.**
0312	**Acquiring inputs/supplies and disposing of outputs used for non-primary production activities households**
03121	**Purchasing/acquiring inputs/supplies used for non primary production activities for households**
031210	Purchasing/acquiring inputs/supplies used for non primary production activities for households
03122	**Selling/disposing of outputs of non-primary production activities of households**
031220	Selling/disposing of outputs of non-primary production activities of households *Includes*: Selling handicrafts, food products etc. produced for leisure or pastime or in connection with a hobby, at garage or yard sale
032	**Related activities: looking for work/setting up business in non-primary production activities in household enterprise**
0320	**Looking for work/setting up business in non-primary production activities in household enterprise**
03201	**Looking for work in non-primary production activities in household enterprise**

		032010	Looking for work in non-primary production activities in household enterprise
		03202	**Looking for/setting up business in non-primary production activities in household enterprise**
		032020	Looking for/setting up business in non-primary production activities in household enterprise
033			**Travel related to non-primary production of household**
	0330		**Travel related to non-primary production of household**
		03300	**Travel related to non-primary production of household**

033000   Travel related to non-primary production of household
Includes:
– Travel to and from the workplace
– Travel in relation to activities in divisions in this major division
Exclusions: When travelling is intrinsic to the job (for example, driver), the activity is classified under the appropriate classes 03111-03117.

039			**Work for household in non-primary production activities n.e.c.**
	0390		**Work for household in non-primary production activities n.e.c.**
		03900	**Work for household in non-primary production activities n.e.c.**
		039000	Work for household in non-primary production activities n.e.c.

04   Work for household in construction activities

Includes:
– All activities performed in relation to construction activities by household enterprises either for income or for own capital formation
– Activities performed in relation to acquiring inputs/supplies for construction work
– Participation in meetings/training and studies directly related to one's work in construction activities
– Activities related to seeking employment or the setting up of a business are included in this major division
– Travel to and from the workplace

Note: In these divisions of activities it is assumed that working time arrangements are generally more informal or flexible compared to those in the formal sector. Thus, this major division does not include specific divisions for short breaks and for lunch breaks. Activities associated with such breaks from work are classified in the corresponding class; for example, eating snack/meals is classified under 15121- Eating meals/snack.

Exclusions: Minor repairs done on own dwelling, farm sheds, fences etc. is not considered as capital formation and is classified under 06113 - Do-it-yourself decoration, maintenance and small repairs.

041			**Core activities: working time in construction activities**
	0411		**Working time in construction activities**

                     Includes: Laying bricks, plastering, glazing, thatching, cutting glass, plumbing, painting, wallpapering, carpentry, tiling, electric wiring, floor sanding, installing carpets

		04111	**Construction and repair for own capital formation**

041111	Building of own house
041112	Major home improvements and repairs *Includes*: Additions to, remodelling and major repairs done to the house, garage, roof
041113	Building and repair of animal and poultry sheds/shelter, business place, field walls/fences, storage facilities for farm produce, irrigation
041119	Other specified activities related to construction and repair for own capital formation
04111x	Construction and repair for own capital formation n.f.d.
04112	**Construction and repair of buildings, roads, dams and other structures**
041120	Construction and repair of buildings, roads, dams and other structures *Includes*: Preparing building site; demolition or wrecking of buildings and other structures; building of complete constructions, installation and completion
04113	**Community-organized construction and major repairs of roads, buildings, bridges, dams etc.**
041130	Community organized construction and major repairs of roads, buildings, bridges, dams etc.
04114	**Training and studies in relation to work in construction activities in household enterprise**
041140	Training and studies in relation to work in construction activities in household enterprise *Includes*: Availing of government training/extension services; attending business meetings of cooperatives and self-help associations; attending seminars on increasing productivity, marketing, technology and techniques etc.
0411x	**Working time in construction activities n.f.d.**
0412	**Acquiring inputs/supplies for construction activities for household production**
04120	**Purchasing/acquiring inputs/supplies for construction activities for household production**
041200	Purchasing/acquiring inputs/supplies for construction activities for household production
042	**Related activities: looking for work/setting up business in construction activities in household enterprise**
0420	**Looking for work/setting up business in construction activities in household enterprise**
04201	**Looking for work in construction activities in household enterprise**
042010	Looking for work in construction activities in household enterprise
04202	**Looking for/setting up business in construction activities as household enterprise**
042020	Looking for/setting up business in construction activities as household enterprise

043			**Travel related to construction activities of households**
	0430		**Travel related to construction activities of households**
		04300	**Travel related to construction activities of households**
		043000	Travel related to construction activities of households

Includes:
- Travel to and from the workplace
- Travel in relation to activities in divisions in this major division

*Exclusion*s: When travelling is intrinsic to the job (for example, driver), the activity is classified under 04111 and 04112.

049			**Work for household in construction activities n.e.c.**
	0490		**Work for household in construction activities n.e.c.**
		04900	**Work for household in construction activities n.e.c.**
		049000	Work for household in construction activities n.e.c.

05 Work for household providing services for income

Includes:
- All activities performed in relation to production of services by household enterprises for income
- Paid domestic work
- Activities performed in relation to acquiring inputs/supplies for work in service activities
- Participation in meetings/training and studies directly related to one's work in service activities
- Activities related to seeking employment or the setting up of a business
- Travel to and from the workplace.

Note: In these divisions of activities it is assumed that working time arrangements are generally more informal or flexible compared to those in the formal sector. Thus, this major division does not include specific divisions for short breaks and for lunch breaks. Activities associated with such breaks from work are classified in the corresponding class; for example, eating snack/meals is classified under 15121 - Eating meals/snack.

Exclusions: Services for own final use are not considered work within the SNA production boundary and are classified under major division 05 and 06. Unpaid services rendered to other households or on a voluntary basis are classified under major division 07.

051			**Core activities: working time in providing services for income**
	0511		**Food vending and trading**
		05111	**Preparing and selling food and beverage**

Includes:
- Cooking, preparing and packing food and drinks
- Selling of prepared foods and drinks for immediate consumption
- Catering and takeout activities

		051111	Preparing/packing food and beverage preparations
		051112	Selling/delivering food and beverage preparations
		051113	Putting up food stalls; cleaning and maintenance
		051119	Other specified activities related to preparing and selling food and beverage

341

05111x	Preparing and selling food and beverage n.f.d.
05112	**Petty trading, door-to-door vending, street vending, hawking**

Includes:
- Resale of new and used goods in fixed locations, open spaces, closed spaces
- Buying goods for resale

Note: Sale of own-produced goods in major divisions 02 and 03 are classified under classes 02122 and 03122, respectively.

Note: For door-to-door and street vending and hawking, travelling to the area where vending takes place is classified under division 053- Travel related to providing services for income. However, travelling while in the general area where vending and hawking take place is considered intrinsic to the activity and travel time is included in classes 051122 and 051123.

051121	Petty trading

Includes: Buying and selling at a regular venue or fixed location

051122	Door-to-door vending

Includes: Selling by going from house to house, building to building, room to room

051123	Street vending, hawking and other itinerant trading
051129	Other specified activities related to petty trading and vending activities
05112x	**Trading n.f.d.**
0512	**Providing repair, installation and maintenance services**
05121	**Fitting, installing, tool-setting, maintaining and repairing tools and machinery**
051210	Fitting, installing, tool setting, maintaining and repairing tools and machinery
05122	**Repair of vehicles**
051220	Repair of vehicles
05123	**Repair of personal goods**
051230	Repair of personal goods

Includes: Repair of clothes, shoes, bags

05124	**Repair of household goods**
051240	Repair of household goods

Includes: Repair of appliances, furniture, linen

0513	**Providing business and professional services**
05131	**Renting out rooms, sleeping space and associated work**
051310	Renting out rooms, sleeping space and associated work
05132	**Lending and collecting money; foreign exchange**
051320	Lending and collecting money; foreign exchange
05133	**Typing, word-processing, programming, encoding**
051330	Typing, word-processing, programming, encoding
05134	**Accounting, bookkeeping, legal and related services**

	051340	Accounting, bookkeeping, legal and related services
	05135	**Tutoring**
	051350	Tutoring
	05136	**Provision of medical and dental services**
	051360	Provision of medical and dental services
	05137	**Provision of nursing/therapy services**
	051370	Provision of nursing/therapy services
0514		**Providing personal care services**
	05141	**Provision of personal care services**
	051410	Provision of personal care services

051410 Provision of personal care services
Includes: Haircuts, hairdressing, cosmetic treatments, giving manicures/pedicures, massaging, prostitution

	05142	**Provision of non-professional health-care**
	051420	Provision of non-professional health-care

0515 **Transporting goods and passengers**
Includes:
– Driving motorized vehicles, hand and pedal vehicles, animal-drawn carts etc.; sailing/rowing boats, barges etc.; piloting aircraft
– Carrying and loading goods
– Maintaining and repairing vehicles, boats etc.
– Waiting for passengers, cargo

	05151	**Transporting goods**
	051510	Transporting goods
	05152	**Transporting passengers**
	051520	Transporting passengers
0516		**Paid domestic services**
	05160	**Providing paid domestic services**

051600 Providing paid domestic services
Includes:
– All work by domestic staff as main job for remuneration in cash or in kind
– All types of activities defined in major divisions 05 and 06

0517 **Meetings/training and studies**

05170 **Training and studies related to work in service activities**

051700 Training and studies related to work in service activities
Includes:
– Availing of government training/extension services
– Attending business meetings of cooperatives and self-help associations
– Attending seminars on skills upgrading, technology and techniques etc.

051x **Working time in providing services for income n.f.d.**

052			Related activities: looking for work/setting up business in service activities in household enterprise
	0520		Looking for work/setting up business in service activities in household enterprise
		05200	Looking for work in service activities in service activities in household enterprise
		052000	Looking for work in service activities in service activities in household enterprise
053			Travel related to providing services for income
	0530		Travel related to providing services for income
		05300	Travel related to providing services for income
		053000	Travel related to providing services for income

053000 Travel related to providing services for income
Includes:
– Travel to and from the workplace
– Travel in relation to activities in this major division

Exclusions: When travelling is intrinsic to the job (for example, driver), the activity is classified under the appropriate division of activities in this major division.

059			Work for household providing services for income n.e.c.
	0590		Work for household providing services for income n.e.c.
		05900	Work for household providing services for income n.e.c.
		059000	Work for household providing services for income n.e.c.

06 Providing unpaid domestic services for own final use within household

Includes:
– Preparing and serving food
– Cleaning, sweeping etc. of dwelling and surroundings
– Clothes care
– All aspects of household management
– Shopping
– Travel in relation to the activities in this major division

Note: Unpaid domestic services for own final use within the household are considered work in relation to the general production boundary (housework) but not in relation to the SNA production boundary.

Exclusion: Unpaid domestic services performed for other households is classified under major division 08.

061			Core activities: working time in providing unpaid domestic services for own final use
	0611		Unpaid domestic services
		06111	Food management
		061111	Preparing meals/snacks
		061112	Serving meals/snacks

061113   Cleaning up after food preparation/meals/snacks

061119   Other specified activities related to food management

06111x   Food management n.f.d.

06112   **Cleaning and upkeep of dwelling and surroundings**

061121   Indoor cleaning
Includes: Routine cleaning of rooms, bathrooms, kitchen etc.; sweeping, vacuuming, washing, scrubbing, making beds, tidying, picking up, dusting, washing windows, arranging the home; polishing/waxing floors and furniture; seasonal cleaning

061122   Outdoor cleaning
Includes: Routine outdoor cleaning of garage, yard, pool, frontage, pavement and lawns, outhouse etc.; raking of leaves, snow shovelling, putting on storm windows

061123   Recycling; disposal of garbage

061124   Care of outdoor garden, landscaping, trimming, grounds/yard/lawn maintenance

061125   Heating and water supply (including tending furnaces, boilers and fire places)

061126   Making various household arrangements
Includes: Making various kinds of arrangements of tasks at home, in a weekend house; putting food away for storage; arranging clothes for household members' immediate use; collecting mail from mailbox; hanging up curtains; moving to new place to live; tending indoor flowers; packing/unpacking for trip or disposal/removal or storing

061129   Other specified activities related to cleaning and upkeep of dwelling and surroundings

06112x   Cleaning and upkeep of dwelling and surroundings n.f.d.

06113   **Do-it-yourself decoration, maintenance and small repairs**

061131   Do-it-yourself improvement, maintenance and repair of dwellings
Includes: Painting, plastering, minor repairs to ceiling, floor, walls, roof; paving of driveway, carpentry work, plumbing, wiring

061132   Installation, servicing and repair of personal and household goods
Includes: Assembling of household equipment and appliances, cleaning/servicing/repairing of household appliances, furniture and other durable goods

061133   Vehicle maintenance and minor repairs
Includes: Cleaning, greasing, minor repairs of cars, motorcycles, bicycles etc.

061139   Other specified activities related to do-it-yourself decoration, maintenance and small repairs

06113x   Do-it-yourself decoration, maintenance and small repairs n.f.d.

06114   **Care of textiles and footwear**

061141   Hand-washing; loading/unloading washing machine

061142	Drying; hanging out, bringing in wash
061143	Ironing/pressing
061144	Sorting, folding, storing
061145	Mending/repairing and care of clothes; cleaning and polishing shoes
061149	Other specified care of textiles and footwear
06114x	Care of textiles and footwear n.f.d.
06115	**Household management**
061151	Paying household bills (utilities, cable television etc.)
061152	Budgeting, organizing, planning
061153	Selling, disposing of household assets
061159	Other specified household management
06115x	Household management n.f.d.
06116	**Pet care**
061161	Daily care including feeding, cleaning, grooming, walking
061162	Taking pets for veterinary care
061169	Other specified pet care
06116x	Pet care n.f.d.

0612   **Shopping**

06121   **Shopping for/purchasing of goods and related activities**

Includes:
– Purchasing consumer and capital goods
– Window-shopping
– Canvassing and comparing prices of a product
– Online shopping

Note:
– Travel to and from shops is classified under 062
– Walking around in shopping centre for the purpose of canvassing or comparing prices for a specific good/product in mind is classified under the specific groups

061211   Shopping for/purchasing of consumer goods
Includes: Shopping for/purchasing of consumer goods: food products and household supplies (groceries); takeout food; medical supplies; school supplies; gasoline; clothes

061212   Shopping for/purchasing of durable/capital goods
Includes: Cars, household appliances, articles and equipment; furniture; house

061213   Window shopping
Includes: Wandering around looking in shops, flea markets etc. not in connection with canvassing specific goods

061219   Other specified shopping for/purchasing of goods and related activities

	06121x	Shopping for/purchasing of goods and related activities n.f.d.	
	06122	**Shopping for/availing of services and related activities**	

Includes:
- Telephone calls in relation to canvassing, setting up appointments etc.
- Giving instructions to repairman, installers
- Going to place of service

Note: Availing of all types of government services are classified under 061227.

Note: Availing of personal and health/medical care services for own self is classified under 15141 or 15142.

Note: Availing of educational, training, other related services for own self is classified under appropriate major divisions of 09, 12 and 12.

Note: Travel to and from place of service is classified under 062.

Note: Waiting at place of service is classified under the appropriate division in this major division.

061221	Shopping for/availing of repair and maintenance services
061222	Shopping for/availing of administrative services

Includes: Banking, legal, renting, paying bills for services, using automated teller machine (ATM), posting letter

061223	Shopping for personal care services (not for oneself)
061224	Shopping for medical and health-care services (not for oneself)
061225	Shopping for/availing of childcare services
061226	Shopping for educational services
061227	Availing of government/public services
061229	Other specified shopping/availing of services
06122x	Shopping for/availing of services and related activities n.f.d.

061x   **Working time in providing unpaid domestic services for own final use n.f.d.**

062   **Travel related to provision of unpaid domestic services**

     0620   **Travel related to provision of unpaid domestic services**

       06200   **Travel related to provision of unpaid domestic services**

         062000   Travel related to provision of unpaid domestic services
Includes: Driving oneself or a household member to and from places

069   **Unpaid domestic services n.e.c.**

     0690   **Unpaid domestic services n.e.c.**

       06900   **Unpaid domestic services n.e.c.**

         069000   Unpaid domestic services n.e.c.
Includes: Activities of short duration that do not fit into other divisions

07 Providing unpaid caregiving services to household members

Includes:

All activities in relation to unpaid services for the care of children and adults of one's household including care provided to members of the household who are sick or disabled

Travel in relation to the activities in this major division

Note: For purposes of child-care activities, countries will have to specify an upper age limit. One criterion for selecting such a limit is a legally specified age under which a child cannot be left alone without adult supervision. If no such law exists in a country, then the age limit would be the age accepted by convention or practice when children can be left alone without constant care and supervision.

Note: Unpaid caregiving services for own household are "non-SNA" work activities.

Note: Receiving caregiving services is classified under 15141 and 15142.

Exclusion: Unpaid caregiving services performed for other households is classified under major division 08

071   **Core activities: working time providing unpaid caregiving services to household members**

0711   **Childcare**

07111   **Caring for children/physical care**

071111   General childcare

Includes: All activities related to care of very young children (for example, 0-4 years of age) or children who need constant care and supervision: carrying, feeding/nursing, cleaning, bathing, changing diapers.

Note: For care of older children, caregiving activities are classified under 0711.

071112   Putting children to bed

071113   Getting children ready for school

071114   Giving personal care to children

071115   Giving medical/health-care to children

071119   Other specified physical care of children

07111x   Caring for children/physical care n.f.d.

07112   **Teaching, training, helping children**

071121   Teaching children

071122   Reading, playing and talking with children

071123   Giving emotional support to children

071129   Other specified teaching, training, helping activities

07113   **Accompanying children to places**

Note: Travel time to and from the place of service is classified under 072-Travel related to unpaid caregiving services to household members

Note: Waiting is included in the appropriate division in this major division

071131   Accompanying children to receive personal services

071132   Accompanying children to receive medical/health services

071133   Accompanying children to school, day-care centres

		071134	Accompanying children to sports, lessons etc.
		071135	Taking children on excursions, museum visits and similar outings; coordinating or facilitating child's social or non-school activities
		071139	Accompanying children to other specified places
		07113x	Accompanying children to places n.f.d.

07114   Minding children (passive care)

071140   Minding children (passive care)
Includes:
– Caring for children without the active involvement implied in 07111-07113
– Monitoring children playing outside or sleeping, preserving a safe environment
– Being an adult presence for children to turn to in need
– Supervising games

0712   Adult care

07121   Caring for adults/physical care

071211   Giving personal care to adults

071212   Giving medical/health-care to adults

071219   Other specified physical care of adults

07121x   Caring for adults/physical care n.f.d.

07122   Caring for adults/emotional support

071220   Caring for adults/emotional support

07123   Accompanying adults to places
Note: Travel time to and from the place of service is classified under 072 - Travel related to unpaid caregiving services to household members.
Note: Waiting is included in the appropriate division in this major division.

071231   Accompanying adults to receive personal services

071232   Accompanying adults to receive medical/health services

071233   Accompanying adults for shopping

071234   Accompanying adults to social activities

071235   Accompanying adults to cultural, sports and entertainment venues

071239   Accompanying adults to other specified places

07123x   Accompanying adults to places n.f.d.

071x   Working time providing unpaid caregiving services to household members n.f.d.

072   Travel related to unpaid caregiving services to household members

0720   Travel related to unpaid caregiving services to household members

07200   Travel related to unpaid caregiving services to household members

072000   Travel related to unpaid caregiving services to household members
Includes: Driving oneself or a household member to and from places

079	Providing unpaid caregiving services to household members n.e.c.	
	0790	Providing unpaid caregiving services to household members n.e.c.
	07900	Providing unpaid caregiving services to household members n.e.c.
	079000	Providing unpaid caregiving services to household members n.e.c.

08 Providing community services and help to other households

Includes:
- Both voluntary and obligatory services for the benefit of members of the community as well as unpaid help extended to other households (such as households of relatives, friends and neighbours)
- Travel in relation to the activities in this major division

Note: Service activities in this major division are considered work in relation to the general production boundary but not in relation to the SNA production boundary.

081	**Core activities: working time providing community services and help to other households**	
	0811	**Unpaid help to other households**
		Includes: Direct unpaid help given to other households and not through an organized effort
	08111	**Household maintenance and management as help to other households**
	081111	Preparing and serving meals as help to other households
	081112	Cleaning and upkeep as help to other households
	081113	Care of textiles as help to other households
	081114	Household management as help to other households
	081115	Pet care as help to other households
	081119	Other specified help to other households
	08111x	Household maintenance and management as help to other households n.f.d.
	08112	**Shopping for/purchasing of goods and services as help to other households**
	081121	Shopping for/purchasing of goods as help
	081122	Shopping for/purchasing of services as help
	081129	Other specified shopping/purchasing as help
	08112x	Shopping for/purchasing of goods and services as help to other households n.f.d.
	08113	**Construction, renovation and repairs of dwellings and other structures as help to other households**
	081130	Construction, renovation and repairs of dwellings and other structures as help to other households
	08114	**Repairs of consumer and household goods as help to other households**
	081140	Repairs of consumer and household goods as help to other households
	08115	**Unpaid help in business/farm and employment as help to other households**

| | 081150 | Unpaid help in business/farm and employment as help to other households |

08116   **Childcare as help to other households**

081160   Childcare as help to other households

08117   **Adult care as help to other households**

081170   Adult care as help to other households

08118   **Transportation assistance to other households**

081180   Transportation assistance to other households

0812   **Community-organized services**

08121   **Community organized work: cooking for collective celebrations etc.**

081210   Community organized work: cooking for collective celebrations etc.

08122   **Work on road/building repair, clearing and preparing community land, cleaning (streets, markets etc.)**

081220   Work on road/building repair, clearing and preparing community land, cleaning (streets, markets etc.)

08123   **Organizing and work on community-based assistance to villages, other sublocations**

081230   Organizing and work on community-based assistance to villages, other sublocations

08124   **Organizing and work on community-based assistance to families and individuals**

081240   Organizing and work on community-based assistance to families and individuals

0813   **Organized unpaid volunteer services**
Includes: Unpaid (or for minor fee) volunteer work for or through organizations: professional, union, political, civic, religious, fraternal, social, cause-oriented etc.

08131   **Volunteer work for organizations (not directly for individuals)**

081310   Volunteer work for organizations (not directly for individuals)
Includes:
- Volunteering to do office/administrative work, correspondence, assistance repairs and other odd jobs for the organization
- Giving information, distributing leaflets for volunteer organizations, neighbourhood groups, school associations, professional, religious and civic organizations
- Work as committee member, fund-raising activities
- Participation in civic, professional, fraternal, political etc. organizations

Note: Attendance in meetings is classified under 082.

08132   **Volunteer work through organizations (extended directly to individuals)**

081320   Volunteer work through organizations (extended directly to individuals)
Includes:
- Care of the elderly, sick or disabled, through an organization, including transportation assistance, hospital visitation

- Teaching or supervising, tutoring, mentoring or course instruction, coaching, refereeing etc. in sports and gymnastics
- Leading youth group, for example, scout or boy/girl guide leader; working as volunteer in a childcare group, teaching or supervising children
- Leading or organizing a self-help group, support groups (Alcoholics Anonymous (AA), Acquired Immunodeficiency Syndrome (AIDS) support, abused women etc.)

Note: Attendance in meetings is classified under 082

081x   **Working time providing community services and help to other households n.f.d.**

082   **Related activities: attendance in meetings**

0820   **Attendance in meetings**

08200   **Attendance in meetings**

082000   Attendance in meetings
Includes: All kind of meetings etc. arranged by social, political, scouting, religious, fraternal and other organisations, informal clubs and groups
Exclusions: Attendance in business meetings of corporations, cooperatives, and similar groups are classified in appropriate divisions of major divisions 01-05

083   **Related activities: other community services**

0830   **Other community services**

08300   **Involvement in civic and related responsibilities**

083001   Involvement in civic and related responsibilities

083002   Attending to civic obligations
Includes: Registering to vote, voting; serving as witness; reporting crimes, social disturbances

083009   Other specified involvement in civic and related responsibilities

08300x   Involvement in civic and related responsibilities n.f.d.

084   **Travel related to community services and help to other households**

0840   **Travel related to community services and help to other households**

08400   **Travel related to community services and help to other households**

084000   Travel related to community services and help to other households
Includes: Driving oneself or non-household member to and from places

089   **Community services and help to other households n.e.c.**

0890   **Community services and help to other households n.e.c.**

08900   **Community services and help to other households n.e.c.**

089000   Community services and help to other households n.e.c.

09 Learning

Includes:

– Attendance of classes at all levels of instruction: pre-primary, primary, secondary, technical and vocational, higher education, extra or make up classes

– Literacy and other special programmes for handicapped children, adults, and other groups who have no opportunity to attend school

– Completing homework assignments, private studies, research, studying for examinations in relation to courses

– Attending short-term courses, seminars etc. in relation to one's own professional development

– Travel to and from classes and school activities

Exclusion: Training and studies in relation to a current job is classified under specific divisions in major divisions 01-05; courses related to hobbies, sports are classified under respective divisions in major divisions 12 and 13

091   Core activities: time spent in learning activities

0911   General education

Includes:

– Studying, attendance of classes, self-study in relation to distance education courses

– Non-study activities carried out in relation to co-curricular and extra-curricular programmes

– Breaks at place of education

Note: General education refers to studies at primary, secondary and tertiary education institutions as part of formal education system including general and vocational training

09111   School/university attendance

091111   Attending class/lecture including taking examinations

091112   Engaging in co-curricular and extra-curricular activities
Includes: Participation in varsity and intramural sports, activities of speech and drama clubs, glee clubs, cheering squads, school publications

091119   Other specified activities related to school/university attendance

09111x   School/university attendance n.f.d.

09112   Breaks/waiting at place of general education

091120   Breaks/waiting at place of general education
Includes: Activities performed during time between classes; for example, walking to classroom or laboratory room, returning/borrowing a book to/from the library
Exclusion: Eating meals or snacks is classified under 15121.

09113   Self-study for distance education course work (video, audio, online)

091130   Self-study for distance education course work (video, audio, online)

0912   Homework, course review, research and activities related to general education

09120   Homework, course review, research and activities related to general education

| 091200 | Homework, course review, research and activities related to general education |
| | *Includes*: |

– Doing homework, class projects
– Preparing research papers for classes including researching in library, on the Internet, word-processing
– Being tutored or assisted with courses
– Consulting teacher or course master, seeking clarification, guidance etc.
– Reviewing for class and course examinations

0913   **Additional study, non-formal education and courses during free time**

     09130   **Additional study, non-formal education and courses during free time**

     091300   Additional study, non-formal education and courses during free time
Includes:

– Attendance in retraining courses, foreign language courses, computing courses, business and secretarial courses (such as management, book-keeping, typing etc.), creative courses,
  training on small-scale business management and entrepreneurship, driving school
– Self-taught courses and other study during free time.

Exclusions:

Attendance in courses taken in relation to hobbies and recreational games, sports etc. are classified under major divisions 12 and 13

Attendance in courses taken in relation to career/professional development are classified under 0914.

0914   **Career/professional development training and studies**

     09140   **Career/professional development training and studies**

     091400   Career/professional development training and studies
Includes:

– Attendance in seminars, short-term courses, certification courses, review courses for professional/certification examinations etc.
– Taking professional/certification examinations

Exclusions:

– Studies and training at work or paid for by current employment are classified under appropriate divisions of major divisions 01-05.
– Formal education courses such as graduate education are classified under 09111 or 09113.

091x   **Learning n.f.d.**

092   **Related activities: other activities carried out in relation to learning activities**

     0920   **Other activities carried out in relation to learning activities**

     09200   **Other activities carried out in relation to learning activities**

     092000   Other activities carried out in relation to learning activities
Includes:

– Preparing for school, including packing books, lunch box
– Selecting school/university, choosing courses, enrolling, paying fees

093			Travel related to learning
	0930		Travel related to learning
		09300	Travel related to learning
		093000	Travel related to learning

Includes:
- Travel to and from learning activities, including waiting time
- Driving oneself to place of education etc.

099			Learning activities n.e.c.
	0990		Learning activities n.e.c.
		09900	Learning activities n.e.c.
		099000	Learning activities n.e.c.

10 Socializing and community participation

Includes:
- Socializing and communicating and participating in community events
- Travel in relation to socializing and community participation

101 Core activities: time spent in socializing and community participation

1011 Socializing and communication

Includes:
- Talking, gossiping generally of a personal/social nature or of unspecified content
- Performing activities/going to places or events together
- Visiting and receiving visitors
- Reading and writing mail of a personal/social nature

Exclusions: Telephone conversations and correspondence not of a personal/social nature are classified under appropriate major divisions

10111 Talking, conversing

101111	Talking/conversing face to face
101112	Talking/conversing by telephone, texting, short-wave radio etc.
101113	Cyber-chatting including instant messaging, discussion groups etc.
101119	Other specified activities related to talking/conversing
10111x	Talking, conversing n.f.d.

10112 Socializing activities

101121	Doing activities/going to places or events together
101122	Receiving visitors
101123	Visiting friends and relatives
101124	Hosting parties, receptions, similar gatherings
101125	Attending parties, receptions, similar gatherings
101126	Socializing at bars, clubs
101129	Other specified socializing activities

		10112x	Socializing n.f.d.	

10113   **Reading and writing mail**

101130   Reading and writing mail
Includes:
– Reading and writing letters, postcards
– Reading and writing e-mail

10114   **Unsocial/antisocial/negative social activities**

101140   Unsocial/antisocial/negative social activities
Includes:
– Conflict of some kind
– Quarrelling, arguing, verbal assault (both committing and receiving)
– Fighting, physical threat or assault (both committing and receiving)

1011x   **Socializing and communication n.f.d.**

1012   **Participating in community cultural/social events**

10121   **Participating in community celebrations of cultural/historic events**
Includes: Engaging in preparations for such as rehearsals and actual participation in community cultural events such as feast days of patron saints, parades commemorating historic events; community celebrations or rites related to weddings, funerals, births and other rites of passage other than the religious ceremony
Exclusion: Unpaid services in relation to these events such as cooking, constructing stage, organizing, collecting contributions, preparing costumes etc. are classified under 08121

101210   Participating in community celebrations of cultural/historic events

10122   **Participating in community rites/events (non-religious) of weddings, funerals, births and similar rites-of-passage**

101220   Participating in community rites/events (non-religious) of weddings, funerals, births, and similar rites of passage

10123   **Participating in community social functions (music, dance etc.)**

101230   Participating in community social functions (music, dance etc.)

1012x   **Community participation n.f.d.**

102   **Travel related to socializing and community participation**

1020   **Travel related to socializing and community participation**

10200   **Travel related to socializing and community participation**

102000   Travel related to socializing and community participation
Includes:
– Travel to and from socializing and community participation activities, including waiting time
– Driving oneself to place of socializing and community participation etc.

109   **Socializing and community participation n.e.c.**

1090   **Socializing and community participation n.e.c.**

10900   **Socializing and community participation n.e.c.**

109000   Socializing and community participation n.e.c.

11 Attending/visiting cultural, entertainment and sports events/venues

Includes:
– Visiting cultural events or venues, exhibitions
– Watching shows, movies
– Visiting parks, gardens, zoos
– Visiting amusement centres, fairs, festivals, circus
– Watching sports events
– Travel to and from places
Note: Buying tickets, queuing/waiting in line are classified under the specific divisions

111	**Core activities: time spent attending cultural, entertainment and sports events**	
1111	**Attendance at organized/mass cultural events**	
11111	**Visit museum, art gallery, historical/cultural park, heritage site**	
111110	Visit museum, art gallery, historical/cultural park, heritage site	
11112	**Attendance at movies/cinema**	
111120	Attendance at movies/cinema	
11113	**Attendance at theatre, opera, ballet, concerts**	
111130	Attendance at theatre, opera, ballet, concerts	
11119	**Attendance at other specified mass cultural events**	
111190	Attendance at other specified mass cultural events	
1112	**Attendance at parks/gardens, shows**	
11120	**Attendance/visit to zoo, animal park, botanic garden, amusement centre, fairs, festivals, circus, animal shows, plant shows**	
111200	Attendance/visit to zoo, animal park, botanic garden, amusement centre, fairs, festivals, circus, animal shows, plant shows	
1113	**Attendance at sports events**	
11131	**Attendance at professional sports events**	
111310	Attendance at professional sports events	
11132	**Attendance at amateur sports events**	
111320	Attendance at amateur sports events	
111x	**Attendance at cultural, entertainment and sports events n.f.d.**	
112	**Travel related to attending/visiting cultural, entertainment and sports events/venues**	
1120	**Travel related to attending/visiting cultural, entertainment and sports events/venues**	
11200	**Travel related to attending/visiting cultural, entertainment and sports events/venues**	

112000	Travel related to attending/visiting cultural, entertainment and sports events/venues
	Includes:
	– Travel to and from cultural, entertainment and sports events/venues, including waiting time
	– Driving oneself to cultural, entertainment and sports events/venues etc.

119   **Attending/visiting sports, entertainment and cultural events/venues n.e.c.**

1190	**Attending/visiting sports, entertainment and cultural events/venues n.e.c.**
11900	**Attending/visiting sports, entertainment and cultural events/venues n.e.c.**
119000	Attending/visiting sports, entertainment and cultural events/venues n.e.c.

12   Hobbies, games and other pastime activities

Includes:
– Active participation in arts, music, theatre, dance (not as a job)
– Engaging in technical hobbies such as collecting stamps, coins, trading cards; computing, programming; crafts
– Playing games
– Taking courses in relation to hobbies
– Travel to and from places

121   **Core activities: hobbies, games and other pastime activities**

1211	**Visual, literary and performing arts (as hobby) and related courses**
12111	**Visual arts**
121110	Visual arts
	Includes: Painting, photography, sculpture, pottery/ceramics, drawing, graphics
12112	**Literary arts**
121120	Literary arts
	Includes: Writing novels, poetry, personal diary/journal, other writing (not letters)
12113	**Performing arts (dance, music, theatre)**
121130	Performing arts (dance, music, theatre)
	Includes:
	– Active participation in dance and choreography
	– Playing a musical instrument (include practising, whistling), playing in a band; singing in a choir/chorus group (but not for church choir), group singing, karaoke/videoke singing
	– Acting in plays, drama (including rehearsals and actual performance)
	– Designing of props, costumes; working as stage crew
1211x	**Visual, literary and performing arts n.f.d.**
1212	**Technical hobbies and related courses**
12120	**Technical hobbies and related courses**

358

121200   Technical hobbies and related courses
Includes:
- Collecting stamps, coins, trading cards etc.
- Working on cars such as customizing, painting
- Computing, programming as a hobby
- Carpentry and woodworking as a hobby
- Crafts-making as a hobby

Exclusion: Income-generating hobbies in terms of services provided or outputs produced and sold are classified under appropriate divisions in major divisions 02-05.

1213   **Playing games and other pastimes and related courses**

12131   **Solo games**

121310   Solo games
Includes: Playing with dolls, toys, cats, dogs etc.; doing crossword puzzles, solitaire, puzzles etc.

12132   **Card games, board games**

121320   Card games, board games
Includes:
- Playing cards such as hearts, bridge etc.
- Playing board games such as dominos, chess, checkers, backgammon, Monopoly, Yahtzee, Sorry etc.

Exclusion: Betting on games is classified under 12135

12133   **Computer games (including arcade and video games)**

121330   Computer games (including arcade and video games)

12134   **Social/group games**

121340   Social/group games
Includes: Scavenger hunt, Easter egg hunt, hide-and-seek, hopscotch

12135   **Gambling**

121350   Gambling
Includes:
- Playing lotto and similar lotteries
- Off-track betting (horse racing, sports etc.)
- Playing casino games (blackjack, baccarat, roulette etc.)
- Purchasing lotto, lottery, sweepstake tickets, including waiting
- Online gambling

1213x   **Playing games and other pastimes n.f.d.**

122   **Travel related to hobbies, games and other pastimes**

1220   **Travel related to hobbies, games and other pastimes**

12200   **Travel related to hobbies, games and other pastimes**

122000   Travel related to hobbies, games and other pastimes
Includes:
- Travel to and from places, including waiting time
- Driving oneself to places

129   **Hobbies, games and other pastimes n.e.c.**

    1290   **Hobbies, games and other pastimes n.e.c.**

        12900   **Hobbies, games and other pastimes n.e.c.**

        129000   Hobbies, games and other pastimes n.e.c.

13   Indoor and outdoor sports participation and related courses

Includes:
- Active participation in indoor and outdoor sports (not as a job)
- Coaching, training
- Looking for gym, exercise programme, trainer
- Assembling and readying sports equipment at the sports centre
- Taking courses in relation to sports
- Travel to and from places

131   **Core activities: time spent participating in sports and outdoor activities**

    1311   **Participating in sports**

        13111   **Walking and hiking; jogging and running**

        131110   Walking and hiking; jogging and running

        13112   **Biking, skating, skateboarding**

        131120   Biking, skating, skateboarding

        13113   **Aerobics, yoga, weight-training and other fitness programmes**

        131130   Aerobics, yoga, weight-training and other fitness programmes
            Includes: Gymnastics, calisthenics, weights training, tae-bo

        13114   **Ball games, individual sports**

        131140   Ball games, individual sports
            Includes: Lawn tennis, table tennis, squash, racquetball, golf, bowling etc.

        13115   **Ball games, team sports**

        131150   Ball games, team sports
            Includes: Basketball, football, soccer, volleyball, hockey, rugby etc.

        13116   **Water sports**

        131160   Water sports
            Includes: Swimming, boating, surfing, kayaking, diving

        13117   **Winter/ice/snow sports**

        131170   Winter/ice/snow sports
            Includes: Skiing, ice skating, sledding

        13118   **Contact sports**

        131180   Contact sports
            Includes: Judo, tae kwon do, karate, wrestling, boxing

    1312   **Camping and other outdoor activities**

        13121   **Camping**

	131210	Camping
	13122	**Horseback-riding**
	131220	Horseback-riding
	13123	**Pleasure drives; sightseeing**
	131230	Pleasure drives; sightseeing
131x		**Indoor and outdoor sports participation n.f.d.**
132		**Travel related to indoor and outdoor sports participation and related courses**
	1320	**Travel related to indoor and outdoor sports participation and related courses**
	13200	**Travel related to indoor and outdoor sports participation and related courses**
	132000	Travel related to indoor and outdoor sports participation and related courses

Includes:
  – Travel to and from places, including waiting time
  – Driving oneself to places
Exclusion: Pleasure driving is classified under 13123

139		**Indoor and outdoor sports participation and related courses n.e.c.**
	1390	**Indoor and outdoor sports participation and related courses n.e.c.**
	13900	**Indoor and outdoor sports participation and related courses n.e.c.**
	139000	Indoor and outdoor sports participation and related courses n.e.c.

14 Mass media

Includes:
  – Reading (not strictly in relation to work, learning)
  – Watching/listening to television and video
  – Listening to radio and other audio devices
  – Use of computer technology (not strictly for work, learning, household management, shopping)
  – Going to the library (not strictly for work, learning)
  – Travel to and from places
Exclusions: Mass media use strictly in relation to work, learning, household management, shopping, is classified under the specific divisions in major divisions 01-05, 06 and 09

141		**Core activities: time spent using mass media**
	1411	**Reading**

Note: Reading using computers and related technology is classified under 14141.
Exclusion: Reading religious books in relation to practice of religion is classified under 1515

	14111	**Reading books**
	141110	Reading books
	14112	**Reading periodicals**

361

141120	Reading periodicals

141120 Reading periodicals
Includes: Reading newspapers, magazines, news magazines, newsletters

14119 **Reading other specified materials**

141190 Reading other specified materials

1411x **Reading n.f.d.**

1412 **Watching/listening to television and video**
Note: Watching/listening to television and video strictly in relation to learning and work activities is coded in major divisions 01-05 or 09.

14121 **Watching/listening to television**

141211 Watching/listening to television (regular programming)

141212 Watching/listening to television (time-shifted programming)

141219 Other specified activities related to watching/listening to television

14121x Watching/listening to television n.f.d.

14122 **Watching/listening to video programmes**
Note: Video media includes video cassette recorders (VCR), video compact disk (VCD), digital videodisc (DVD) players and devices other than the computer. Watching/listening using a computer is classified under 14142.

141221 Watching/listening to rented/purchased movies

141222 Watching/listening to rented/purchased video programmes other than movies

141229 Other specified activities related to watching/listening to video

14122x Watching/listening to video programmes n.f.d.

1413 **Listening to radio and audio devices**
Note: Listening to radio and other audio media strictly in relation to learning and work activities is coded in major divisions 01-05 or 09.

14131 **Listening to radio programmes**

141310 Listening to radio programmes

14132 **Listening to other audio media**

141320 Listening to other audio media
Includes: Listening to recorded music; listening to audio books
Note: Audio media includes CD, tape, record, MP3 players. Listening using a computer is classified under 14142.

1413x **Listening to radio and audio devices n.f.d.**

1414 **Using computer technology**
Includes: Use of computers and the Internet/Web technologies to read or access information, watch and listen to programmes, music etc.
Exclusions: Use of computer/Web technology strictly for work, learning, household management, socializing and communicating is classified under appropriate divisions in these major divisions

14141 **Using computer technology for reading**

141410 Using computer technology for reading
Includes: Reading news and regularly updated information; reading e-books, information on CD-ROM

14142	**Using computer technology for video/audio**
141420	Using computer technology for video/audio *Includes*: Watching/listening to (live) Internet radio, music, video; playing music, video files/programmes on the computer
14143	**Surfing the Internet; downloading, uploading**
141430	Surfing the Internet; downloading, uploading *Note*: If purpose of surfing is specified, code appropriately; for example, for shopping, code to 06121 or 06122; for paying household bills, code to 06115; for online course, code to 09111 or 09113 as appropriate
1414x	**Using computer technology n.f.d.**

142   **Related activities: Visiting library**

     1420   **Visiting library**

       14200   **Visiting library**

       142000   Visiting library

143   **Travel related to mass media**

     1430   **Travel related to mass media**

       14300   **Travel related to mass media**

       143000   Travel related to mass media
               Includes:
- Travel to and from places, including waiting time
- Driving oneself to places

149   **Mass media n.e.c.**

     1490   **Mass media n.e.c.**

       14900   **Mass media n.e.c.**

       149000   Mass media n.e.c.

15   Personal care and maintenance

Includes:
- Activities required by the individual in relation to biological needs: sleeping, eating, resting etc.
- Performing own personal and health-care and maintenance or receiving this type of care
- Activities in relation to spiritual/religious care
- Doing nothing, resting, relaxing
- Meditating, thinking, planning

Exclusions:
- Shopping for personal care and health-care services is classified under 06122
- Participation in volunteer work for religious organizations is classified under appropriate divisions in major division 08
- Participation in choir practices, social events of churches etc. is classified under appropriate divisions under major division 10 and 12

151   **Core activities: time spent in personal care and maintenance**

     1511   **Sleep and related activities**

15111		**Night sleep/essential sleep**
	151110	Night sleep/essential sleep

Includes: Time in bed before and after sleep (if able to specify)

Note: Refers to longest sleep for the day; may occur at night or during daytime

15112		**Incidental sleep/naps**
	151120	Incidental sleep/naps
15113		**Sleeplessness**
	151130	Sleeplessness
1511x		**Sleep and related activities n.f.d.**
1512		**Eating and drinking**
15121		**Eating meals/snack**
	151211	Eating a meal (including drinks taken with meal)
	151212	Eating a snack (including drinks taken with snack)
15122		**Drinking other than with meal or snack**
	151220	Drinking other than with meal or snack
1512x		**Eating and drinking n.f.d.**
1513		**Personal hygiene and care**
15131		**Personal hygiene and care**
	151310	Personal hygiene and care

Includes:
– Personal/private activities such as "toilet activities", washing, showering, bathing, brushing teeth
– Personal grooming such as combing hair, dressing up/changing clothes, putting on make up, shaving, trimming nails

15132		**Health/medical care to oneself**
	151320	Health/medical care to oneself

Includes:
– Monitoring blood pressure, sugar level, applying home diagnostic tests etc., administering medication, including wound treatment, insulin injections and aerosol for asthma
– Being sick in bed/prescribed bed rest, convalescence, rehabilitative rest

1514		**Receiving personal and health/medical care from others**
15141		**Receiving personal care from others**
	151410	Receiving personal care from others

Includes:
– Receiving personal care from household members
– Visits to saloon, beauty parlour, barber shop, for personal services for self such as haircut or hair styling, manicure, pedicure, massage etc.

15142		**Receiving health/medical care from others**

		151420	Receiving health/medical care from others

Includes:
– Receiving health/medical care from members of the household
– Visits to doctor, dentist, alternative care practicioner, therapist etc.

1515   **Religious activities**

    15151   **Private prayer, meditation and other informal spiritual activities**

    151510   Private prayer, meditation and other informal spiritual activities

Includes:
– Prayer and meditation at home
– Visiting church, synagogue, temple, shrine for prayer, meditation, offerings
– Consulting with religious/spiritual adviser
– Consultations with spiritualists/spiritists, psychics, astrologers, fortune-tellers etc.

    15152   **Participating in religious activities (formal practice of religion)**

    151520   Participating in religious activities (formal practice of religion)

Includes:
– Religious practice and services
– Religious practice carried out in a small informal group
– Participating in religious ceremonies, weddings, baptism, confirmation, first communion, funerals etc.

1516   **Activities associated with resting, relaxing**

    15161   **Doing nothing; resting, relaxing**

    151610   Doing nothing; resting, relaxing

    15162   **Smoking**

    151620   Smoking

    15163   **Reflecting/meditating, thinking, planning**

    151630   Reflecting/meditating, thinking, planning

152   **Travel related to personal care and maintenance activities**

    1520   **Travel related to personal care and maintenance activities**

    15200   **Travel related to personal care and maintenance activities**

    152000   Travel related to personal care and maintenance activities

Includes:
– Travel to and from places, including waiting time
– Driving oneself to places

159   **Personal care and maintenance activities n.e.c.**

    1590   **Personal care and maintenance activities n.e.c.**

      15900   **Personal care and maintenance activities n.e.c.**

      159000   Personal care and maintenance activities n.e.c.

ANNEX 22. CORRESPONDENCE TABLE RELATING THE EUROSTAT CLASSIFICATION TO THE TRIAL ICATUS [a]

Eurostat list		Trial ICATUS	
0	**PERSONAL CARE**		
000	Unspecified personal care		
01	SLEEP		
010	Unspecified sleep		
011	Sleep	15111	Night sleep/essential sleep
		15112	Incidental sleep/naps
		15113	Sleeplessness
012	Sick in bed	15132	Health/medical care to oneself
02	EATING		
020	Unspecified eating		
021	Meals, snacks and drinks	15121	Eating meals/snack
		15122	Drinking other than with meal or snack
03	OTHER PERSONAL CARE		
030	Unspecified other personal care		
031	Wash and dress	15131	Personal hygiene and care
039	Other specified personal care	15132	Health/medical care to oneself
1	**EMPLOYMENT**		
100	Unspecified employment		
11	MAIN JOB		
111	Working time in main job	01111	Work in main job
			Note: Also includes categories 02-05 if main jobs
		01115	Training and studies in relation to work
			Note: Also all corresponding division in categories 02-05
112	Coffee and other breaks in main job	01114	Short breaks and interruptions from work
12	SECOND JOB		
121	Working time in second job	01112	Work in other jobs
			Note: Also includes categories 02-05 if second job
		01115	Training and studies in relation to work
			Note: Also all corresponding divisions in categories 02-05
122	Coffee and other breaks in second job	01114	Short breaks and interruptions from work
13	ACTIVITIES RELATED TO EMPLOYMENT		
130	Unspecified activities related to employment		
131	Lunch break	01122	Lunch break from work
139	Other specified activities related to employment	01121	Idle time before/after break

[a] Activities that the two classification categorize differently appear in shaded area

Eurostat list		Trial ICATUS	
		01201	Looking for work
		01202	Looking for/setting-up business
			Note: Also all corresponding divisions in categories 02-05
2	**STUDY**		
200	Unspecified study		
210	Unspecified activities related to school or university		
211	Classes and lectures	09111	School/university attendance
		09113	Self-study for distance education courses
212	Homework	09120	Homework, course review, research related to general education
219	Other specified activities related to school or university	09112	Breaks/waiting at place of general education
		092	*Other activities carried out in relation to learning activities*
22	**FREE-TIME STUDY**		
221	Free-time study	0913	Additional study, non-formal education
		0914	Career/professional development training and studies
		1212	*Technical hobbies and related courses*
		13	*Sports-related courses*
3	**HOUSEHOLD AND FAMILY CARE**		
300	Unspecified household and family care		
31	FOOD MANAGEMENT		
310	Unspecified food management		
311	Food preparation	06111	Food management
312	*Baking*	*03112*	*Making of other food products and beverages*
313	Dishwashing	06111	Food management
314	*Preserving*	*03111*	*Processing of food products*
		03112	*Making of other food products and beverages*
319	Other specified food management	06111	Food management
32	HOUSEHOLD UPKEEP		
320	Unspecified household upkeep		
321	Cleaning dwelling	06112	Cleaning and upkeep of dwelling and surroundings
322	Cleaning yard	06112	Cleaning and upkeep of dwelling and surroundings
323	*Heating and water*	*02114*	*Gathering of wild products, woodcutting and gathering firewood and other forestry activities*
		02117	*Collecting water*
		061125	Heating and water supply
324	Various arrangements		*Note: No corresponding category in ICATUS*
329	Other specified household upkeep	069	Unpaid domestic services n.e.c.

Eurostat list		Trial ICATUS	
33	MAKING AND CARE FOR TEXTILES		
330	Unspecified making and care for textiles		
331	Laundry	06114	Care of textiles and footwear
332	Ironing	061143	Ironing/pressing
333	*Handicraft and producing textiles*	*03113*	*Making textiles, wearing apparel, leather and associated products*
339	Other specified making and care for textiles	06114	Care of textiles and footwear
34	GARDENING AND PET CARE		
340	Unspecified gardening and pet care		
341	*Gardening*	*02111*	*Growing of crops; kitchen-gardening*
342	*Tending domestic animals*	*02112*	*Farming of animals*
343	Caring for pets	06116	Pet care
344	Walking the dog	06116	Pet care
349	Other specified gardening and pet care	06116	Pet care
35	CONSTRUCTION AND REPAIRS		
350	Unspecified construction and repairs		
351	House construction and renovation	04111	Construction and repair for own capital formation
352	Repairs of dwelling	061131	Do-it-yourself improvement, maintenance and repair of dwellings
353	Making, repairing and maintaining equipment	061132	Installation, servicing and repair of personal and household goods
354	Vehicle maintenance	061133	Vehicle maintenance and minor repairs
359	Other specified construction and repairs	061139	Other specified activities related to do-it-yourself decoration, maintenance and small repairs
36	SHOPPING AND SERVICES		
360	Unspecified shopping and services		
361	Shopping	06121	Shopping for/purchasing of goods
362	Commercial and administrative services	06122	Shopping for/availing of services
363	*Personal services*	*15141*	*Receiving personal care*
		15142	*Receiving health/medical care*
369	Other specified shopping and services	06121	Shopping for/purchasing of goods
		06122	Shopping for/availing of services
37	HOUSEHOLD MANAGEMENT		
371	Household management	06115	Household management
38	CHILDCARE		
380	Unspecified childcare		
381	Physical care and supervision	07111	Caring for children: physical care
382	Teaching the child	07112	Teaching, training, helping children
383	Reading, playing and talking with child	071122	Reading, playing and talking with children
384	Accompanying child	07113	Accompanying children to places
		07114	Minding children (passive care)
389	Other specified childcare	079	Providing unpaid care-giving services to household members

Eurostat list		Trial ICATUS	
39	HELP TO AN ADULT FAMILY MEMBER		
391	Help to an adult family member	07121	Care for adults: physical care
		07122	Care for adults: emotional support
		07123	Accompanying adults to places
4	**VOLUNTEER WORK AND MEETINGS**		
400	Unspecified volunteer work and meetings		
41	ORGANIZATIONAL WORK		
410	Unspecified organizational work		
411	Work for an organization	08131	Volunteer work for organizations
412	Volunteer work through an organization	08132	Volunteer work through organizations
419	*Other specified organizational work*	*08121*	*Community-organized work: cooking for collective celebrations etc*
		08122	*Work on road/building repair, clearing and preparing community land, cleaning (streets, markets etc.)*
		08123	*Organising and work on community-based assistance to villages, other sublocations*
		08124	*Organising and work on community-based assistance to families and individuals*
42	INFORMAL HELP TO OTHER HOUSEHOLDS		
420	Unspecified informal help		
421	Food management as help	08111	Household maintenance and management as help to other households
422	Household upkeep as help	08111	Household maintenance and management as help to other households
423	Gardening and pet care as help	08111	Household maintenance and management as help to other households
424	Construction and repairs as help	08113	Construction, renovation and repairs of dwellings and other structures as help to other households
		08114	Repairs of consumer and household goods as help to other households
425	Shopping and services as help	08112	Shopping for/purchasing of goods and services as help to other households
426	Help in employment and farming	08115	Unpaid help in business/farm and employment as help to other households
427	Childcare as help	08116	Childcare as help to other households
428	Help to an adult of another household	08117	Adult care as help to other households
429	Other specified informal help	089	Community services and help to other households n.e.c.
43	PARTICIPATORY ACTIVITIES		
430	Unspecified participatory activities		
431	Meetings	082	Attendance in meetings

369

Eurostat list		Trial ICATUS	
432	*Religious activities*	*15151*	*Private prayer, meditation, and other informal spiritual activities*
		15152	*Participating in religious activities*
439	Other specified participatory activities	08300	Involvement in civic and related responsibilities
		089	Community services and help to other households n.e.c.
5	**SOCIAL LIFE AND ENTERTAINMENT**		
500	Unspecified social life and entertainment		
51	SOCIAL LIFE		
510	Unspecified social life		
511	Socialising with family	10112	Socializing activities
512	Visiting and receiving visitors	10112	Socializing activities
513	Feasts		
514	Telephone conversation	10111	Talking, conversing
519	Other specified social life	*10114*	*Unsocial/antisocial/negative social activities*
		109	Socializing and community participation n.e.c.
52	ENTERTAINMENT AND CULTURE		
520	Unspecified entertainment and culture		
521	Cinema	11112	Attendance at movies/cinema
522	Theatre and concerts	11113	Attendance at theatre, opera, ballet, concerts
		11113	Attendance at theatre, opera, ballet, concerts
523	Art exhibitions and museums	11111	Visit museum, art gallery, historical/cultural park, heritage site
524	*Library*	*142*	*Visiting library*
525	Sports events	11131	Attendance at professional sports events
		11132	Attendance at amateur sports events
529	Other specified entertainment and culture	*10121*	*Participating in community celebrations of cultural/historic events*
		10122	*Participating in community rites/events (non-religious) of weddings, funerals, births and similar rites of passage*
		10123	*Participating in community social functions (music, dance etc.)*
		1112	Attendance/visit to zoo, animal park, botanic garden, amusement center, fairs, festivals, circus, animal shows, plant shows
		119	Attending/visiting sports, entertainment and cultural events/venues n.e.c
53	RESTING: TIME OUT		
531	*Resting: Time out*	*15161*	*Doing nothing; resting, relaxing*

Eurostat list		Trial ICATUS	
		15162	*Smoking*
		15163	*Reflecting/meditating, thinking, planning*
6	**SPORTS AND OUTDOOR ACTIVITIES**		
600	Unspecified sports and outdoor activities		
61	PHYSICAL EXERCISE		
610	Unspecified physical exercise		
611	Walking and hiking	13111	Walking and hiking; jogging and running
612	Jogging and running	13111	Walking and hiking; jogging and running
613	Biking, skiing and skating	13112	Biking, skating, skateboarding
614	Ball games	13114	Ball games, individual sports
		13115	Ball games, team sports
615	Gymnastics	13113	Aerobics, yoga, weight-training and other fitness programmes
616	Fitness	13113	Aerobics, yoga, weight-training and other fitness programmes
617	Water sports	13116	Water sports
619	Other specified physical exercise	13117	Winter/ice/snow sports
		13118	Contact sports
		1312	Camping
		13122	Horseback-riding
		139	Indoor and outdoor sports participation and related courses n.e.c.
62	PRODUCTIVE EXERCISE		
620	Unspecified productive exercise		
621	*Hunting and fishing*	*02113*	*Hunting, trapping and production of animal skins*
		02115	*Fishing and fish/aquatic farming*
622	*Picking berries, mushrooms and herbs*	*02114*	*Gathering of wild products, woodcutting and gathering firewood and other forestry activities*
629	Other specified productive exercise		*Note: No corresponding category in ICATUS*
63	SPORTS RELATED ACTIVITIES		
631	Sports related activities	139	Indoor and outdoor sports participation and related courses n.e.c.
7	**HOBBIES AND GAMES**		
700	Unspecified hobbies and games		
71	ARTS		
710	Unspecified arts		
711	Visual arts	12111	Visual arts
712	Performing arts	12113	Performing arts
713	Literary arts	12112	Literary arts
719	Other specified arts	129	Hobbies, games and other pastimes n.e.c.
72	HOBBIES		
720	Unspecified hobbies		
721	Collecting	1212	Technical hobbies and related courses
722	Computing – programming	1212	Technical hobbies and related courses

371

Eurostat list		Trial ICATUS	
723	*Information by computing*	*14141*	*Using computer technology for reading*
		14142	*Using computer technology for video/audio*
724	*Communication by computing*	*10113*	*Reading and writing mail*
725	Other computing		
726	*Correspondence*	*10113*	*Reading and writing mail*
729	Other specified hobbies	129	Hobbies, games and other pastimes n.e.c.
73	GAMES		
730	Unspecified games		
731	Solo games and play	12131	Solo games
732	Parlour games and play	12132	Card games, board games
		12134	Social/group games
733	Computer games	12133	Computer games (including arcade and video games)
734	Gambling	12135	Gambling
739	Other specified games	129	Hobbies, games and other pastimes n.e.c.
8	**MASS MEDIA**		
800	Unspecified mass media		
81	READING		
810	Unspecified reading		
811	Reading periodicals	14112	Reading periodicals
812	Reading books	14111	Reading books
819	Other specified reading	14119	Reading other specified materials
82	TV AND VIDEO		
821	Watching TV	14121	Watching/listening to television
822	Watching video	14122	Watching/listening to video programmes
83	RADIO AND MUSIC		
830	Unspecified listening to radio and music		
831	Listening to radio	14131	Listening to radio programmes
832	Listening to recordings	14132	Listening to other audio media
9	**TRAVEL AND UNSPECIFIED TIME USE**		*Note*: No corresponding main category. Included as division within each main category
90	TRAVEL BY PURPOSE		
900	Unspecified purpose		
901	Travel related to personal care	152	Travel related to personal care and maintenance activities
911	Travel as part of/during main job	013	Travel related to work in the formal sector *Note: Also include corresponding divisions in categories 02-05*
912	Travel as part of/during second job	013	Travel related to work in the formal sector *Note: Also include corresponding divisions in categories 02-05*
913	Travel to/from work	013	Travel related to work in the formal sector *Note: Also include corresponding divisions in categories 02-05*

Eurostat list		Trial ICATUS	
921	Travel to/from school or university	093	Travel related to learning
922	Travel related to free time study	122	Travel related to hobbies, games and other pastimes and related courses
		132	Travel related to indoor and outdoor sports participation and related courses
931	Travel related to household care	062	Travel related to provision of unpaid domestic services
936	Travel related to shopping and services	062	Travel related to provision of unpaid domestic services
938	Transporting a child	072	Travel related to unpaid caregiving services to household members
939	Transporting an adult family member	072	Travel related to unpaid caregiving services to household members
941	Travel related to organisational work	084	Travel related to community services and help to other households
942	Travel related to informal help	084	Travel related to community services and help to other households
		08118	Transportation assistance to other households
943	Travel related to participatory activities	084	Travel related to community services and help to other households
951	Travel related to social life	102	Travel related to socializing and community participation
952	Travel related to entertainment and culture	112	Travel related to attending/visiting cultural, entertainment and sports events/venues
961	Travel related to sports and outdoor activities	132	Travel related to indoor and outdoor sports participation and related courses
971	Travel related to hobbies	122	Travel related to hobbies, games and other pastimes and related courses
		143	Travel related to use of mass media
981	Travel related to changing locality		*Note: Included in all travel related to categories 10-13*
982	*Driving for pleasure*	*13123*	*Pleasure drives*
995	Filling in the time-use diary		
999	Unspecified time use		

GLOSSARY

Account A tool which that records, for a given aspect of economic life, the uses and resources or the changes in assets and liabilities and/or the stock of assets and liabilities existing at a certain time.

Activity Human behaviour in terms of what is being done and when, during a specified period of time.

Activity sequence The relationship of an activity to the activity that precedes it.

Episode One occurrence of an activity.

Full time diary A diary in which the respondent reports each activity successively from the time of waking up, including the time an activity began and ended through the 24-hours of the day.

Goods Physical objects for which a demand exists, over which ownership rights can be established and whose ownership can be transferred from one institutional unit to another by engaging in transactions on markets.

Gross domestic product (GDP) The total unduplicated output of economic goods and services produced within a country as measured in monetary terms according to the System of National Accounts (SNA). GDP as defined in the 1968 SNA includes subsistence production produced by households for their own use, valued at current local prices for comparable commodities.

Household A small group of persons who share the same living accommodation, who pool some, or all, of their income and wealth and who consume certain types of goods and services collectively, mainly housing and food.

Household production As defined in the SNA1993, production activities engaged in by members of household unincorporated market enterprises and household unincorporated enterprises producing for own final use. Informal sector enterprises are part of household unincorporated market enterprises. Household members engaged in production for own final use "work" in household enterprises.

Income The maximum amount that a household, or other unit, can consume without reducing its real net worth.

Informal sector Regarded as a group of production units that, according to the definitions and classifications provided in the System of National Accounts (Rev.4), form part of the household sector as household enterprises or, equivalently, unincorporated enterprises owned by households. The informal sector is defined irrespective of the kind of workplace where the productive activities are carried out, the extent of fixed capital assets used, the duration of the operation of the enterprise (perennial, seasonal or casual), and its operation as a main or secondary activity of the owner.

Light time diary Diary in which the respondent reports the time at which each activity occurs. The 24-hours of the day are accounted for in terms of a pre-identified comprehensive list of activity categories.

Market producer A producer who sells most or all of his or her output at prices that are economically significant.

Non-market producer A producer who provides most of his or her output to others free or at prices that are not economically significant.

Non-profit institutions (NPIs) Legal or social entities created for the purpose of producing goods and services whose status does not permit them to be a source of income, profit or other financial gain for the units that establish, control or finance them.

Non-profit institutions serving households (NPISHs) NPIs that are not financed and controlled by government and that provide goods or services to households free or at prices that are not economically significant.

Output Those goods or services that are produced within an establishment that become available for use outside that establishment.

Primary activity The activity whose value added exceeds that of any other activity carried out within the same unit (the output of the principal activity must consist of goods or services that are capable of being delivered to other units even though they may be used for own consumption or own capital formation).

Production A physical process, carried out under the responsibility, control and management of an institutional unit, in which labour and assets are used to transform inputs of goods and services into outputs of other goods and services.

Production boundary	All production actually destined for the market, whether for sale or barter, all goods or services provided free to individual households or collectively to the community by government units or NPISHs, all goods produced for own use, own-account production of housing services and services produced by employing paid domestic staff.
Satellite accounts	Accounts that provide a framework within which to accommodate elements that are included in the central accounts, explicitly or implicitly, plus complementary elements (either monetary or in physical quantities), and possibly alternative concepts and presentations.
Secondary activity	An activity carried out within a single producer unit in addition to the principal activity and whose output, like that of the principal activity, must be suitable for delivery outside the producer unit.
Self-reporting time diary	A time diary designed to allow the respondent to report his or her own time use by recalling activities carried out.
Simultaneous activities	Two or more parallel activities engaged in by a person over an interval of time.
Stylized analogue	A version of a diary in which the respondent is asked to recall the amount of time he or she allocated to specified activities over a specified period such as a day, week or year.
Time diary	A diary that enables the respondent to report all activities undertaken over a prescribed period of time.
Time-use statistics	Quantitative summaries of how people spend or allocate their time over a given period of time.
Twenty-four-hour time diary	Facilitates the chronological and exhaustive recording of all activities of a respondent over 24 hours.
Unemployed person	According to a recommendation adopted by the International Conference of Labour Statisticians in 1982, all persons who during the reference period were: (a) "without work", that is to say, were not in paid employment or self-employment as specified by the international definition of employment; (b) "currently available for work", that is to say, were available for paid employment or self-employment during the reference period; or (c) "seeking work", that is to say, had taken specific steps in a specified recent period to seek paid employment or self-employment.

Volunteer work	Generally refers to unpaid work activities which can be SNA or non-SNA production as well as market or non-market. All volunteer work producing goods (including community-organized major construction such as of roads, dams, wells etc.) constitutes SNA production. Instances of unpaid volunteer work in non-household institutions producing services with employed workers constitute SNA production activities. Unpaid volunteer services to other households, the community (except organized major construction such as of roads, dams, wells), neighbourhood associations or other informal associations, are non-SNA production activities.
Wages	Compensation of employees as the sum of wages payable in cash and in kind. Wages in cash consist of wages payable at regular weekly, monthly or other intervals, including payments by results and piecework payments, plus allowances such as those for working overtime, plus amounts paid to employees away from work for on holiday; plus ad hoc bonuses and similar payments, and commissions, gratuities and tips received by employees. Wages in kind consist of remuneration in the form of goods and/or services that are not necessary for work and can be used by employees in their own time, and at their own discretion, for the satisfaction of their own needs or wants or those of other members of their households.

REFERENCES

Acharya, M. (1982). Time use data and the living standards measurement study. Living Standards Measurement Study (LSMS) Working Paper, No. 18. Washington, D.C.: World Bank.

Al-Asi, S. (2000). Time use survey: a Palestinian example. Paper presented at the United Nations Expert Group Meeting on Methods of Conducting Time-use Surveys, 23-27 October 2000, New York

Allardt, E. (1975). *Having, Loving and Being: Social Welfare in the Nordic Countries.* Lund, Sweden: Argos.

Anderson, N. (1961). *Work and Leisure.* New York: Free Press of Glencoe.

Arboleda, H. (2001). Time-use data and valuation of unpaid work. Unpublished document.

Ås, D. (1978). Studies of Time Use: Problems and Prospects. *Acta Sociologica*, vol. 15, No. 2, pp. 125-141.

Asia Society, The (1978). Report of the workshop on time-use data: policy uses and methods of collection. Asian Development Seminars Program of the Asia Society.

Australian Bureau of Statistics. (1992). *Time Use Survey, Australia: User's Guide.* Canberra, Australia.

_____ (1996a). 1997 Time Use Survey. Household Form. Unpublished document. Canberra, Australia.

_____ (1996b). 1997 Time Use Survey. Individual Questionnaire. Unpublished document. Canberra, Australia.

_____ (1996c). 1997 Time Use Survey. Time Use Diary. Unpublished document. Canberra, Australia.

_____ (1997a). 1997 Time use survey diary coding rules. Unpublished document. Canberra, Australia.

_____ (1997b). *How Australian Use their Time.* Canberra, Australia.

_____ (1997c). Quality control procedures for processing the 1997 Australia Time Use Survey. Unpublished document. Canberra, Australia.

Bailar, B.A., L. Bailey and C. Corby (1978). A comparison of some adjustment and weighting procedures for survey data. In *Survey Sampling and Measurement*, N.K. Namboodiri, ed. New York: Academic Press.

Bittman, M. (2000). Issues in the design of time-use surveys for collecting data on paid and unpaid work. Paper presented at the United Nations Expert Group Meeting on Methods of Conducting Time-use Surveys, 23-27 October 2000, New York, 17 October 2000 ESA/STAT/AC.79/6.

Blanke, K. M. (1993). The with whom coding. Paper presented at the International Association for Time Use Research Conference, Amsterdam, Netherlands.

Brick, J.M., and G. Kalton (1996). Handling missing data in survey research. *Statistical Methods in Medical Research*, vol. 5, pp. 215-238.

Brogan, D.J. (1998). Pitfalls of using standard statistical software packages for sample survey data. In *Encyclopedia of Biostatistics*, P. Armitage and T. Colton, eds., New York: John Wiley.

Central Statistical Organisation, Ministry of Statistics and Programme Implementation, Government of India. (2000). *Report of the Time Use Survey*. New Delhi.

Chapin, F. S. (1974). *Human Activity Patterns in the City: Things People Do in Time and in Space*. New York: John Wiley and Sons.

Chapman, D.W., L. Bailey and D. Kasprzyk (1986). Nonresponse adjustment procedures at the United States Bureau of the Census. *Survey Methodology*, vol. 12, pp. 161-180.

Colledge, M., and E. Boyko (2000). Collection and classification of statistical metadata: the real world of implementation. Proceedings of the Second International Conference on Establishment Surveys, New York.

Commission of the European Communities, International Monetary Fund, Organisation for Economic Co-operation and Development, United Nations and World Bank (1993). *System of National Accounts 1993*. Sales No. E.94.XVII.4.

Conference of European Statisticians (2001). *Report of the March 2001 Work Session on Statistical Data Confidentiality*. Conference of European Statisticians, Forty-ninth Plenary Session. June 2001. Geneva. CES/2001/31.

Deville, J.-C., and C.-E. Särndal (1992). Calibration estimators in survey sampling. *Journal of the American Statistical Association*, vol. 87, pp. 376-382.

Djerf, K. (1997). Effects of post-stratification on the estimates of the Finnish labour force survey. *Journal of Official Statistics*, vol. 13, pp. 29-39.

Direction de la Statistique (1999). *Condition socio-economique de la femme au Maroc. Enquête nationale sur le budget temps des femmes 1997/98. Rapport de Synthèse*, vol. 1. Rabat.

_____ (1999). *Les emplois du temps de la femme au Maroc. Enquête nationale sur le budget temps des femmes 1997/98. Rapport de Synthèse*, vol. 2. Rabat.

Dow, G. K., and F. T. Juster (1985). Goods, time, and well-being: the joint dependence problem. *Time, Goods, and Well-Being*, F. T. Juster and F. P. Stafford, eds. Ann Arbor, Michigan : Institute for Social Research, University of Michigan.

Drago, R., and others (1999). New estimates of working time for teachers, available from http://www.bls.gov/opub/mlr/1999/04/art4full.pdf (accessed 15 March 2004).

Elliot, D. (1991). *Weighting for Nonresponse: A Survey Researcher's Guide*. London: Office of Population Censuses and Surveys.

_____, A. S. Harvey, and D. Procos (1976). An overview of the Halifax time-budget study. *Society and Leisure*, vol. 3, pp. 145-159.

Eurostat (1999). *Proposal for a Satellite Account for Household Production*. Luxembourg : Eurostat.

_____ (2000a). *Guidelines on Harmonised European Time Use Surveys*. Luxembourg: Eurostat.

_____ (2000b). Methodological guidelines on harmonised European time-use surveys: with reference to experiences of the European time use pilot surveys. Paper presented at the Expert Group Meeting on Methods for Conducting Time-Use Surveys. 23-27 October 2000. New York. ESA/STAT/AC.79/15.

Federal Statistical Office of Germany (1995). *Die Zeitverwendung der Bev`lkerung: Methode und erste Ergebnisse der Zeitbudgeterhebung 1991/92* (The time use of the population: Method and first results of the time budget collection 1991/92). Wiesbaden, Germany.

Fellegi, I. P., and D. Holt (1976). A systematic approach to automatic edit and

379

imputation. *Journal of the American Statistical Association*, vol. 71, No. 353 (March). pp. 17-35. As cited in Statistics Canada. (1998b) pp. 35-36

Fleming, R., and A. Spellerberg (1999). *Using time use data: A history of time use surveys and uses of time use data.* Auckland: Statistics New Zealand.

Floro, M. (1995). Economic restructuring, gender and the allocation of time. *World Development*, vol. 23, pp. 1913-1929

Fuller, W.A. (1991). Regression estimation in the presence of measurement error. In *Measurement Errors in Surveys*, P.P. Biemer and others, eds., New York: Wiley. pp. 617-635.

_____ (1995). Estimation in the presence of measurement error. *International Statistical Review*, vol. 63, pp.121-147.

Gershuny, J. (1995). Time budget research in Europe. *Statistics in Transition*, vol. 2, pp. 529-551.

_____, and others (1986). Time budgets: preliminary analysis of a national survey. *Quarterly Journal of Social Research*, vol. 2, No. 1.

Glorieux, I., and M. Elchardus (1999). What does your time mean? Some arguments for including indicators on the meaning of time use in time budget research. Paper presented at the 1999 International Association for Time Use Research (IATUR) Conference entitled "The State of the Time Use Research at the End of the Century". University of Essex, Colchester, United Kingdom, 6 - 8 October.

Granquist, L. (1984). On the role of editing. *Statistisk tidskrift*, vol. 2, pp. 105-118. As cited in Statistics Canada (1998b), pp. 35-36.

Grønmo, S. (1978). The issue of Saturday retail closing in Norway: some consumer welfare aspects. **Paper** presented at the Corporate Social Concerns and Public Policy Conference, Bergen, Norway.

Grosh, M., and P. Glewwe, eds. (2000). *Designing Household Survey Questionnaires for Developing Countries: Lessons from Fifteen Years of LSMS Experience*, Washington, D.C.: World Bank.

Haraldsen, G. (2000). A framework for data collection on time use: relating objectives, design and resources. Paper presented at the Expert Group Meeting on Methods for Conducting Time-use Surveys, 23-27 October 2000. New York. ESA/STAT/AC.79/8.

Harvey, A.S. (1982). *Role and Context: Shapers of Behaviour.* Studies in Broadcasting. Tokyo: Nippon Hoso Kyokai (NHK).

_____ (1993). Guidelines for time use data collection. *Social Indicators Research*, vol. 30, Nos.2/3, pp. 197-228.

_____ (1997). From activities to activity settings: behaviour in context. In *Activity-Based Approaches to Travel Analysis* D. Ettema and H. Timmermans, eds. New York: Pergamon Press.

_____ (1999). Time use research: the roots to the future. In *Time use: Research, Data and Policy: Contributions from the International Conference On Time Use (ICTU)*, J. Merz and M. Ehling, eds. University of Lüneburg, 22-25, April 1998. Baden-Baden, Germany: NOMOS Verlas gesellschaft, p.125, para. 1.

_____ (2000). All you need is ...: time-use research lessons from an international socio-economic perspective. Working paper. Saint Mary's University, Time Use Research Program. Halifax, Nova Scotia.

_____, and W. S. Macdonald (1976). Time diaries and time data for extension of economic accounts. *Social Indicators Research*, vol. 3, No. 1, pp. 21-35.

Harvey, A.S., and D. Olomi (1997). Economic framework for a categorization of activities. Unpublished document.

Harvey, A.S., and M. Royal (2000). Use of context in time-use research. Time Use Research Program, Saint Mary's University, Halifax, Nova Scotia. Paper presented at the Expert Group Meeting on Methods for Conducting Time-use Surveys. 23-27 October 2000. New York, ESA/STAT/AC.79/16.

Harvey, A.S., and J. Spinney (2000a). Activity and contextual codes: implications for time use coding schemes. Paper presented at the International Association for Time Use Research Conference, Belo Horizonte, Minas Gerais, Brazil.

_____ (2000b). *Life On & Off the Job: Time Use Study of Nova Scotia Teachers*, Halifax, Nova Scotia: Time Use Research Program, Saint Mary's University.

Harvey, A.S., and M. E. Taylor (1999). Activity settings and travel behaviour: a social contract perspective. *Transportation*, vol. 27, pp. 53-73.

_____ (2000). Time use. In *Designing Household Survey Questionnaires for Developing Countries: Lessons from Fifteen Years of LSMS Experience*, M. Grosh and P. Glewwe, eds. Washington, D.C.: World Bank, chap. 22.

Harvey, A.S., and C. Wilson (1998). Evolution of daily activity patterns: a study of the Halifax Panel Survey. Paper presented at the International Time Use Research Association Conference, in connection with the International Sociological Congress, Montreal, Quebec.

Hirway, I. (1999). *Estimating Work Force using Time Use Statistics in India and its Implications for Employment Policies*. Proceedings of the International Seminar on Time Use Studies. Ahmedabad, India.

Hofferth, S. (2000). Family reading to young children: social desirability and biases in reporting. Paper presented at the Workshop on Time-Use Measurement and Research, 27-28, May 1999, Washington, D.C. In *Time-use Measurement and Research: Report of a Workshop*, M. Ver Ploeg and others, eds. (2000). Washington, D.C.: National Academy Press.

Hoffmann, E. (1990). *Surveys of Economically Active Population, Employment, Unemployment and Underemployment: An ILO Manual on Concepts and Methods*. Geneva.

_____ (1995). What kind of work do you do? Working Paper, No. 95-1. International Labour Office. Geneva.

_____ (1997). Capturing 'industry' in population censuses and surveys: reflections on some methodological issues. Paper presented at the Third Meeting of the Expert Group on International Economic and Social Classifications, 1-3 December, New York.

_____ (2001). Coding occupation and industry in a population census. Working Paper, No. 2001-2 (International Labour Office, Bureau of Statistics). Geneva.

_____, and A. Mata Greenwood (2000). Statistics on working time arrangements: issues and the role of time-use surveys. Paper presented at the Expert Group Meeting on Methods for Conducting Time-use Surveys. 23-

27 October 2000, New York. ESA/STAT/AC.79/11.

Holz, E. (1999). Time use and microdata access: scientific and public use files-problems and international solutions. In *Time use Research, Data and Policy: Contributions from the International Conference on Time Use (ICTU)*, J. Merz and M. Ehling, eds. University of Lüneburg, 22-25, April 1998. Baden-Baden, Germany: NOMOS Verlas gesellschaft.

Horrigan, A. C., and others (1999). A Report on the feasibility of conducting a time-use survey. Paper presented at the Workshop on Measurement of and Research on Time Use, 27-28, May, National Academy of Sciences, Washington, D.C.

Hungarian Central Statistical Office (2000). *Time Use, 1986-1999, Autumn*. Budapest: Hungarian Central Statistical Office.

Ilahi, N. (2000). The intra-household allocation of time and tasks: what have we learned from the empirical literature? *Policy Research Report on Gender and Development*. WP Series, No. 13. Washington, D.C.: World Bank.

International Research and Training Institute for the Advancement of Women (INSTRAW) (1995). *Measurement and Valuation of Unpaid Contribution: Accounting Through Time and Output*. Santo Domingo.

Juster, F. T. (1985). The validity and quality of time-use estimates obtained from recall diaries. In *Time, Goods and Well-Being*, F. T. Juster and F. P. Stafford, eds. Ann Arbor, Michigan: Institute for Social Research, Survey Research Center, University of Michigan.

_____ (2000). Time use data: analytic framework, descriptive finding, and measurement issues. Paper presented at the Workshop on Time-Use Measurement and Research, May 27-28, 1999, Washington, D.C. In *Time-use measurement and research: Report of a workshop*, M. Ver Ploeg and others, eds. Washington, D.C.: National Academy Press.

Kalton, G. (1979). Ultimate cluster sampling. *Journal of the Royal Statistical Society*, Series A, vol. 142, pp. 210-222.

_____ (1983). *Compensating for Missing Survey Data*. Ann Arbor, Michigan: Institute for Social Research, University of Michigan.

_____ (1985). Sample design issues in time diary studies. In *Time, Goods and Well-Being*, F.T. Juster and F.P. Stafford, eds., Ann Arbor, Michigan: Institute for Social Research, University of Michigan, pp. 93-112

_____ (2000). Seminar on measuring non-sampling error in surveys. Unpublished seminar notes. United Nations Statistics Division.

_____ , and D. Kasprzyk (1986). The treatment of missing survey data. *Survey Methodology*, vol. 12, pp. 1-16.

Kinsley, B. L., and T. O'Donnell (1983). *Explorations in Time Use*, vol. 1. *Marking Time: Methodology Report of the Canadian Time Use Pilot Study*, 1981. Ottawa: Department of Communications, Employment and Immigration.

Kish, L. (1965). *Survey Sampling*. New York: Wiley.

_____ (1992). Weighting for unequal Pi. *Journal of Official Statistics*, vol. 8, pp. 183-200.

_____ (1995). Methods for design effects. *Journal of Official Statistics*, vol. 11, pp. 55-77.

_____ , R. Groves and K. Krotki (1976). Sampling errors for fertility surveys. *World Fertility Survey*

Occasional Papers, No. 17, The Hague: International Statistical Institute.

Kitterød, R.H. (2000). Does the registration of parallel activities in time use diaries affect the way people report their main activities? Paper presented at the National Conference of Sociology, Sociology in Norway: 50 Years After, 9-12 November 2000, Ulvik, Hardanger.

Lemaitre, G., and J. Dufour (1987). An integrated method for weighting persons and families. *Survey Methodology.* vol. 13, no. 2, pp 199-207. Statistics Canada.

Lepkowski, J., and J. Bowles (1996). Sampling error software for personal computers. *The Survey Statistician*, vol. 35, pp. 10-17.

Liepmann, K. (1944) *The Journey to Work.* London: Kegan Paul, Trench, Trubner and Co.

Lingsom, S. (1979). Advantages and disadvantages of alternative time diary techniques: a working paper. Statistisk Sentralbyra, Oslo.

Lohr, S.L. (1999). *Sampling: Design and Analysis.* Pacific Grove, California: Duxbury Press.

Lundström, S., and C.-E. Särndal (1999). Calibration as a standard method for treatment of nonresponse. *Journal of Official Statistics*, vol. 15, pp. 305-327.

Macro International, Inc. (1996). *Sampling Manual.* DHS-III Basic Documentation, No. 6. Calverton, Maryland.

Madow, W.G., H. Nisselson, and I. Olkin, eds. (1983). *Incomplete Data in Sample Surveys*, vols. 1-3. New York: Academic Press.

Meekers, D. (1991). The effect of imputation procedures on first birth intervals: evidence from five African fertility surveys. *Demography*, vol. 28, No. 2, pp. 249-260.

Mendez Carniado, P. (2000) *Country Report: Mexico*, Paper prepared by for the Expert Group Meeting on Conducting Time-use Surveys, 23-27 October 2000, New York.

Merton, R. K. (1967). *On Theoretical Sociology.* London: Macmillan Publishing.

Michelson, W. (1985). *From Sun to Sun: Daily Obligations and Community Structure in the Lives of Employed Women and their Families.* New Jersey: Rowman and Allanheld Publishers. Totowa.

_____(1993). *Towards Exploration of Meaning and Outcomes in Connection with Time-use Data.* Kingston, Ontario: Queen's University.

Mpetsheni, Y., and D. Budlender (2000). Country paper: South Africa Time Use Survey 2000. Paper prepared by for the Expert Group Meeting on Conducting Time-use Surveys, 23-27 October 2000, New York.

Niemi, I., S. Kiiski, and M. Liikkanen (1981). *Use of Time in Finland.* Helsinki: Central Statistical Office of Finland.

Noov, Y. (2000) *Country Report: Mongolia Time Use Survey 2000.* Paper prepared by for the Expert Group Meeting on Conducting Time-use Surveys, 23-27 October 2000, New York.

Pandey, R., and I. Hirway (2000). *Conducting the time-use survey- Indian experience.* Paper prepared by for the Expert Group Meeting on Conducting Time- use Surveys, 23-27 October 2000, New York.

Potter, F.J. (1990). A study of procedures to control extreme sampling weights. 1990 Proceedings of the Survey Research Methods Section of the American Statistical Association, pp. 225-230.

Quizon, E. K. (1978). Time allocation and home production in rural Philippine households. *The Philippine Economic Journal*. vol. 17, pp. 185-202.

Robinson, J. (1977). *How Americans Use Time: A Social-Psychological Analysis of Behavior*. New York: Praeger Publishers.

_____ (1985). The validity and reliability of diaries versus alternative time-use measures. In *Time, Goods and Well-Being*, F. T. Juster and F. P. Stafford, eds. Ann Arbor, Michigan.: Institute for Social Research, Survey Research Center, University of Michigan.

_____ (1999). The time-diary method. In *Time use Research in the Social Sciences*, W.E. Pentland and others, eds. New York: Kluwer Academic Plenum Publishers.

_____ (2000). Methodological features of the time diary method. Paper presented at the Workshop on Time-Use Measurement and Research, 27-28 May, 1999, Washington, D.C. In *Time-use measurement and research: Report of a workshop*, M. Ver Ploeg and others, eds. Washington, D.C.: National Academy Press.

Rust, K., and J.N.K. Rao (1996). Variance estimation for complex surveys using replication techniques. *Statistical Methods in Medical Research*, vol. 5, pp. 283-310.

Rydenstam, K. (2000). The "light" time diary approach. Paper prepared at the Expert Group Meeting on Methods for Conducting Time-use Surveys, 23-27 October 2000.

_____, and A. Wadeskog (1998*). Evaluation of the European Time Use Pilot Studies*. Luxembourg: Statistical Office of the European Communities, Statistics Sweden.

Scheuch, E. K. (1972). The time-budget interview. In *The Use of Time: Daily Activities of Urban and Suburban Populations in Twelve Countries*, A. Szalai, ed. The Hague: Mouton.

Schon, A. (1999). Methodological and operational dimensions on time-use Survey in the Republic of Korea. In *Proceedings of the International Seminar on Time Use Studies*. 7-10 December. New Delhi, India: Central Statistical Organisation.

_____ (2000). Country report: Republic of Korea 1999 time-use survey. Paper presented at the Paper presented at the Expert Group Meeting on Methods for Conducting Time-use Surveys, 23-27 October 2000, New York. ESA/STAT/AC.79/14.

Scott, C. (1992). Sample design. In *The Social Dimensions of Adjustment Integrated Survey*, L. Demery and C. Grootaert, eds. SDA Working Paper, No. 14. Washington, D.C.: World Bank.

Sharot, T. (1986). Weighting survey results. *Journal of the Market Research Society*, vol. 28, pp. 269-284.

Shaw, S. (1985). The meaning of leisure in everyday life. *Leisure Sciences*, vol. 7, No. 1, pp. 1-24.

Sorokin, P., and C. Q. Berger (1939). *Time Budgets of Human Behaviour*. Cambridge, Massachusetts: Harvard University Press.

Statistics Canada. (1998a). *General Social Survey, Cycle 12: Time Use (Questionnaire Package)*. Ottawa.

_____ (1998b). *Quality Guidelines*, 3rd ed. Ottawa.

_____ (1998c). *Data Quality Statements*. Ottawa.

_____ (1999a). *1998 GSS Cycle 12 User's Guide*. Ottawa.

_____ (1999b). *Overview of the Time Use of Canadians in 1998*. Ottawa.

_____ (2000a). *Incentive Effect on Response Rates for the 1997 Survey of Household Spending*. Ottawa.

_____ (2000b). Collecting time-use data including context variables and simultaneous activities at Statistics Canada. Expert Group Meeting on Methods for Time-use Surveys, 23-27 October 2000. ESA/STAT/AC.79/17.

Statistics New Zealand. (1998a). Time Use Survey 48 Hour Diary, available from http://www.stats.govt.nz/domino/ external/quest/sddquest.nsf/12df43879 eb9b25e4c256809001ee0fe/db67038b8 c4440294c2568310017d07f?OpenDoc ument (accessed 15 March 2004).

_____ (1998b). Time Use Survey (Household Questionnaire), available from http://www.stats.govt.nz/ domino/external/quest/sddquest.nsf/12 df43879eb9b25e4c256809001ee0fe/92 2fd694505f734a4c2569580009ae2e/$F ILE/HQandHF.PDF (accessed 15 March 2004).

_____ (1999). *Users' Guide*. New Zealand Time Use Survey. Auckland.

Statistics Sweden. (1971). *Lärarnas arbete: En statistisk arbetsstudie* (Teachers' work: a statistical survey on teachers' work). Stockholm.

_____ (1999). *The overall monitoring of annual national indicators survey*. Technical report from an advisory trip to Oman, January 24 to February 5, 1999. Stockholm.

Stinson, L. (1997). *Cognitive testing phase 1: The American Time-use Survey (ATUS) - Summary Questions*. Washington, D.C.: United States Government, Bureau of Labour Statistics.

Szalai, A., ed. (1972). *The Use of Time: Daily Activities of Urban and Suburban Populations in Twelve Countries*. European Coordination Centre. The Hague: Mouton.

Tremblay, V. (1986). Practical criteria for definition of weighting classes. *Survey Methodology*, vol. 12, pp. 85-97.

United Nations. (1977). *The Feasibility of Welfare-Oriented Measures to Supplement the National Accounts and Balances: A Technical Report*. Studies in Methods, No. 22, Sales No. 79.XVII.12.

_____ (1978). Progress report on the development of statistics of time-use: report of the Secretary-General. Submitted to the Statistical Commission at its twentieth session (20 February - 2 March 1979). E/CN.3/519.

_____ (1984). *Handbook of Household Surveys (Revised Edition)*. Studies in Methods, No. 31, Sales No. E.83.XVII.13.

_____ (1990). *Methods of Measuring Women's Participation and Production in the Informal Sector*. Studies in Methods, No. 46, Sales No. E.90.XVII.16.

_____ (1995). *The World's Women, 1995: Trends and Statistics*. Social Statistics and Indicators, No. 12, Sales No. E.95.XVII.2 and corrigendum.

_____ (1996). *Report of the Fourth World Conference on Women, Beijing, 4-15 September 1995*, United Nations publication, Sales No. E. 96.IV.13.

_____ (1997a). Concept paper. Presented at the Expert Group Meeting on the Trial International Classification of Activities for Time-Use Statistics, 11 November, 1997.

_____ (1997b). *Handbook for Producing National Statistical Reports on Women and Men*. Social Statistics and Indicators, No. 14, Sales No. E.97.XVII.10 and corr. 1

_____ (2000). Report of the Expert Group Meeting on Methods for Conducting Time-Use Surveys. 23-27

385

October 2000, New York. ESA/STAT/AC.79/23.

_____ (2001a). *Handbook on Population and Housing Census Editing*. Studies in Methods, No. 82. Sales No. E.00.XVII.9.

_____ (2001b). *Handbook on Census Management for Population and Housing Censuses*, Studies in Methods, No. 83/Rev.1., Sales No. E.00.XVII.15.Rev1.

_____, Economic Commission for Europe (UN-ECE) and Eurostat (2001a). Working paper, No. 3. Statistical disclosure control in practice: some examples in official statistics of Statistics Netherlands. Presented at the Joint ECE/Eurostat Work Session on Statistical Data Confidentiality, 14-16 March 2001, Skopje, the Former Yugoslav Republic of Macedonia.

_____ (2001b). Working paper, No. 13: providing greater accessibility to survey data analysis. Presented at the Joint ECE/Eurostat Work Session on Statistical Data Confidentiality, 14-16 March 2001, Skopje, the Former Yugoslav Republic of Macedonia.

_____ (2001c). Working Paper, No. 25: Statistical microdata: confidentiality protection versus freedom of information. Presented at the Joint ECE/Eurostat Work Session on Statistical Data Confidentiality, 14-16 March 2001, Skopje, the Former Yugoslav republic of Macedonia.

United Nations Children's Fund (UNICEF) (2000). *End-Decade Multiple Indicator Survey Manual*, New York: Division of Evaluation, Policy, and Planning.

United Nations Development Programme (UNDP) (1999). Project document on gender equality in the Asia-Pacific region.

United States Bureau of Labour Statistics (1997). Using a time-use approach to measure the frequency and duration of non-market work. Unpublished report.

_____ (2000a). A note on consecutive-day attempts to recontact respondents. Unpublished technical note.

_____ (2000b). A note on day-of-the-week substitution. Unpublished document.

Väisänen, P. (1998). Design effect of a household-based sample for time use variables in pilot surveys. Paper presented at the Twenty-first Conference of Nordic Statisticians, Workshop on Time-Use Surveys, Lillehammer, Norway.

_____ (1999). The estimation procedure of the Finnish Time Use Survey. Paper presented at the Time Use Survey Task Force, 2-3 December. Helsinki, Finland.

Vale, S., and M. Pellegrino (2000). The metadata problem in the Eurostat context. Working paper 1.1. Presented at Eurostat Workshop on Statistical Metadata, 2000, Luxembourg.

Verma, V. (1993). *Sampling Errors in Household Surveys*. NHSCP Technical Study INT-92-P80-15E. United Nations Statistical Division

_____ and T. Lê (1996). An analysis of sampling errors for the Demographic and Health Surveys. *International Statistical Review*, vol. 64, pp. 265-294.

Ver Ploeg, M., and others, eds. (2000). *Time-use Measurement and Research: Report of a Workshop*. Washington, D.C.: National Academy Press.

Wolter, K. (1985). *Introduction to variance estimation*. New York: Springer-Verlag.

World Bank (1996). *A Manual for Planning and Implementing the Living Standards Measurement Study Survey*. LSMS

Working Paper No. 126. Washington D. C.

World Fertility Survey. (1975). *Basic Documentation: Manual on Sample Design.* The Hague-Voorburg: International Statistical Institute.

Zuzanek, J. (1999). Experience sampling method: current and potential research applications. Paper presented at the Workshop on Measurement of and Research on Time Use, 27-28 May. Organized by the Committee on National Statistics of the United States National Academy of Sciences, Washington, D.C.

Litho in United Nations, New York
04-46994—April 2005—2,350
ISBN 92-1-161471-6

United Nations publication
Sales No. E.04.XVII.7
ST/ESA/STAT/SER.F/93